My Brother
EDDIE

To Darlene
from

Hazel

My Brother EDDIE

A Courageous Life

Hazel Higgins

Prairie Junction Press
PUEBLO, COLORADO

First printing 2005

ISBN 0-9764522-3-5   LCCN 2004195218

**ATTENTION CORPORATIONS, UNIVERSITIES, COLLEGES, AND
PROFESSIONAL ORGANIZATIONS:** Quantity discounts are available on bulk
purchases of this book for educational, gift purposes, or as premiums for increasing
magazine subscriptions or renewals. Special books or book excerpts can also be created
to fit specific needs. For information, please contact Prairie Junction Press,
P.O. Box 9281, Pueblo, CO 81008,
email: PrairieJunction@yahoo.com
www.AsEverEddie.com

DEDICATION

To our Mother,
Ethel Melinda,
whose strength and wisdom
sustained us all.

TABLE OF CONTENTS

ACKNOWLEDGMENTS

R. P. Dickey, poet, scholar, and translator, who encouraged me to finish Eddie's book. "Work like a sled dog and don't stop until you are finished! We need inspiration!"

Leona Foster, R. P. Dickey's love and companion, whose art and calligraphy enhanced his poetry.

Jim Pettijohn, probably Eddie's (and my) best friend.

Juanita "Nic" Flanigan, lifelong friend and mentor whose love and understanding has helped me along the way.

Kenny and Carol Pace, who gave Eddie both friendship and help when needed.

Bob Bernstein, who believed in me and helped me when I needed help.

Charlie and Ione Owen, for their constant caring, love, and encouragement.

Dave and Betty Batt, whose confidence in Eddie's ability to achieve the impossible helped in his transition to manhood.

John Seeley, who encouraged Eddie to take the final step into marriage and fatherhood.

Bob Hastings, Eddie's 'Cuz,' who helped him conquer the intricacies of 'big machinery.'

Marilee Swirczek, head of the Lone Mountain Writers' Group at Northern Nevada Community College for her encouragement.

Barbara Wies, co-editor and publisher of Range Magazine, for her preliminary editing and critique of My Brother Eddie.

To Eddie's children who have waited impatiently for this book to be finished.

My thanks to Deb Ellis and the staff at About Books, Inc., who made a hard job look easy.

And finally to Elizabeth (Betty Alora Thomson) Anderson and her husband, Alan Anderson for their final editing and proofing, and to Deryck Santos who came to Betty Alora's rescue when she needed computer help.

1 *On the Edge*

*A*lthough we had traveled all night and it was now almost noon, Eddie and I stood wide-awake on the brink of the Grand Canyon. We lived in the West, but this was something that defied all our conceptions of space and time. It was as if all that had gone before was spread before us. Each stratum of brightly colored stone had its own story to tell.

"What am I going to do?" my brother asked.

"Do you realize that this is the first time you have asked me a question like that since you were a little boy?" I said.

"What did I ask you then?"

"I'll never forget it Eddie. With just about the same kind of look on your face as you have right now you asked me, 'Hazie, why don't I got arms like other little boys?'"

"Yes," Eddie said, "And you told me that God hadn't given me arms but that you were sure that He would give me many other things that would be much better! I guess I wasn't three years old then, but I remember. I've remembered all my life. And I guess He has." Eddie looked out over the canyon. "But now, well, I don't know. I suppose it's just that I'm afraid to take everything He has to offer. It just doesn't seem to me that a girl as wonderful as Betty would want to marry a guy like me. That's all."

"Eddie, I don't think you're being fair to Betty. If I were in her shoes, I'm sure…" my voice trailed off into nothing. *Would I marry a man born without arms? Would I let myself in for the stares and questions that would be directed at us?*

1

Could I adjust to a private life more private and a public life more public than other people have to live? Could there be a love great enough, understanding enough?

Would I feel myself a martyr? Would I help him too much and make him feel dependent? Would I find myself making excuses for him? Would the doubts of friends and family change my mind?

Would I cringe or shrink from the intimate personal things I would have to do for him? When I saw his body naked, would I unconsciously draw away from him or want to hold him in my arms and love him, not with pity, but as a woman hungry for her husband's passionate embrace? Would I live in fear that my babies would be born without arms?

Would I let myself fall in love to the point where there would be no questions, only a one-ness that nothing could part?

Suddenly, with a perception so clear that a voice seemed to be speaking to me, I knew that I would and that I could. If I could only make Eddie understand.

Betty was beautiful, tall, and blonde, with a lovely body, deep blue eyes and an intense loyalty. She and Eddie had been going together almost a year and I had never seen Eddie so happy or relaxed around a girl.

"Hazel, she's the first girl I've ever known that I can ask to go anywhere and she isn't ashamed of me," Eddie once told me, "Usually, if I got up enough courage to ask a girl to go to a show, she would make some excuse. If she did go, she would act embarrassed when I asked her to take money out of my pocket to pay for the tickets.

"If we had anyone else with us and they wanted to go somewhere after the show for a bite to eat, my date would pipe up with, 'Oh, let's go to Jerry's Drive-In! Don't you all just love Jerry's?' They'd sort of giggle and I would shrivel up when I really wanted to shout out: 'Sure, let's go to Jerry's, so we can stay in the car and your friends won't see you're out with that Higgins' kid that was born without arms!'"

In the year Eddie and Betty had been going together, they had been everywhere and done everything. She was teaching him to dance. They had dined at the nicest restaurants and gone on long trips together. No, Betty wasn't ashamed of Eddie; if anything, she was proud of him. Her every action proved this for all the world to see. She could have gone with dozens of other fellows. I knew that she must love Eddie very much.

Eddie's voice nudged at me. "What are you so sure of?" Eddie asked with a lop-sided little grin. The wind blew a stray lock of hair back from his forehead. His intense blue eyes under the heavy, dark brows demanded an answer.

"I was just going to say that if I were in Betty's shoes and I told you that I loved you and I knew that you loved me, and still you let me go away....well, I'd be wondering what was wrong with me!" I unconsciously raised my hand and pushed the hair back from his forehead.

"I didn't tell her she had to go. I just told her that I didn't think we should get married and that maybe if she went back home for a while and went out with plenty of other guys, she would feel differently about us. That's all," Eddie stated with bravado but his voice faltered and his eyes mirrored the deep hurt inside.

"What did Betty say when you told her that?" I asked.

"Oh, she said it didn't matter to her whether we got married or not. Said she wanted to and she thought I was being silly, but that if I didn't want to marry her, she still wanted to be with me." He paused for a second, then rushed on, "Said she loved me, and that was the only thing that mattered!" Then he stuck his chin down in his coat collar and watched the toe of his shoe as he made circles in the dust.

"You do love her very much, don't you Eddie?" I put my arm around his shoulder.

"Love her? My God, how I love her. I would do anything for her. All I've done since she left is think of her, of all the fun we've had together, how she laughs, how proud she is, all the little things...you know!" Then he said, almost as if to himself, "But, I can't hurt her."

I knew. I'd known the night before when Eddie and Betty had asked me to go to the bus with them in Colorado. It was almost as if they had asked me to be with them to give them the courage to say good-bye. But it really wasn't good-bye, was it? Betty said, "You'll write, won't you Eddie?" He answered, his voice gruff, "Sure, if you'll answer?" and she said, "You know I will."

Everyone else was on the bus and the driver was impatient. Betty put her arms around Eddie and held him close. As they kissed they were unaware of the curious stares. As I watched them, I caught myself thinking, "What must it be like not to be able to put your arms around your girl?" then I realized that it wouldn't matter if your girl hugged you the way Betty was hugging Eddie.

The mules in the pack train looked like tiny specks as they picked their sure-footed way along the narrow trail carved out of the canyon wall far below, the humans so trusting as they sat astride and looked over into nothing. Just one misstep and they would be hurtled into oblivion.

I thought about Eddie, standing on the brink of the greatest decision of his life, just a tiny speck. Maybe all that happened to him before was only a training ground.

"Eddie, why are you so afraid of marriage? You have met every other obstacle. This is just another challenge! You would have Betty beside you to help. Everything will work out! I'm sure it will!"

"Maybe. Maybe it would. I don't know." Then his mood shifted. He grinned and said, "Come on, let's go back to the cabin and see if Mom and Dad are ready to eat lunch. I'm starved!"

Matching his mood, I answered, "I hope they took a nap but I doubt it. They're like little kids. I've never seen people Dad and Mom's age enjoy a trip and new places as much as they do!"

At seventy-six Dad still enjoyed riding a horse. Although he said he couldn't flip a fly right into the mouth of a trout with quite the skill he had as a young man, he always caught more than his share. Dad was bald on top with a white fringe around the edge. He'd gained weight and his cheeks were as round as a chipmunk's, but his blue eyes were still vivid and had that twinkle that made Mom back up and say, "Now Art, you quit teasing me."

Mom would always seem young. At sixty-five, she still liked to fly kites with her grandchildren and taught them to make terrific birdhouses. She could out-walk any of us, knew the names and calls of all the birds, the names of the wild flowers and exactly where to find the first Johnny-jump-ups in spring.

Now as Eddie and I walked along, enjoying the brisk coolness of the pine scented air, we saw friendly puffs of smoke curling from the chimney of our rented cabin perched on a solid point of rock jutting out over the canyon. We knew Mom hadn't been able to wait until night to build a fire in the fireplace.

"How about some lunch, aren't you and Dad hungry?" Eddie asked as we entered. Kicking off his shoes, he went over to the bed, reached up, and tickled Dad in the ribs. We laughed as Dad awoke with a snort, grabbing for his hearing aid and glasses all at once. He peered up at Eddie, trying to adjust to the bright sunlight streaming through the big picture window that took up one wall of the cabin. He didn't answer until he had adjusted his hearing aid and put on his glasses. Then, "What did you say, Son?" he asked in the loud voice of a person almost deaf.

"I said, 'how about eating?!'" Eddie spoke loudly. To Mom he said in a lower voice, "Did you and Dad get some sleep?"

"Your Dad stretched out on the bed and was snoring in no time at all. I was going to nap too, but I heard a noise on the porch and when I looked out there were two deer right at the door. I went out and they didn't even run away! In fact, they came right up to me! I touched one of them!"

We walked up the wide wooden steps to Bright Angel Lodge that wasn't far from our cabin. Inside, a mammoth fireplace rose to the heavy beamed ceiling at one side of the huge lounge. On the other side were shops that displayed all manner of curios and beautiful rings, bracelets, and necklaces hammered out of silver by the Indians. Priceless Indian rugs woven by hand from the wool of their shaggy sheep covered the floors. We pulled ourselves away reluctantly. We could come back to all these things later. For now the subdued chatter and clatter of the dining room beckoned.

We found a secluded table near the window where we could watch the canyon and where Eddie wouldn't feel so conspicuous. When we ate in public one of us always helped Eddie. He could eat with his feet or lean down and eat with his mouth, but it was easier for him and less noticeable if we cut his food and fed him. Even so, there were always a few polite stares directed his way.

A little boy about three said loud enough for everyone to hear: "Mommy! Look at that man! He doesn't have any arms." His mother, red to the roots of her hair, tried to shush him, but there was no keeping him quiet. "Mommy!" This time he did speak more quietly, but even so his words carried plainly, "Mommy, look! They have to feed him like a baby!" At this point, the father leaned down to the little boy. I don't know what he said but the boy ate the rest of his meal in silence, though he still watched Eddie intently. Eddie, always fond of children and used to their outspoken curiosity, turned to me and said, "Poor little guy, he can't help asking questions. I hope they don't give him hell."

After lunch, Eddie and I walked on ahead. "Did you tell Betty why we were taking this trip to Los Angeles?"

"Yes, I did." He hesitated as if reluctant to go on.

"What did she think about it?" I prodded.

"Well, she said she didn't think I needed artificial arms. Said I could do almost everything without them and she could help me with the few things I couldn't do for myself."

"What do you think?"

"If you want the truth, Hazel, maybe it's because I don't want to be disappointed, but somehow I feel that they won't work."

He evidently saw the disbelief on my face "As much as I would like to have artificial arms that are really useful, I don't see how they can work for me. I have no stub at all, you know."

"We can't lose hope now, Eddie."

"Well, in a few days we'll know for sure," Eddie said.

"Yes," I answered, "and in the meantime we're going to enjoy this trip, aren't we?" I hoped my own enthusiasm would carry him through the days ahead.

"We sure are! I've always wanted to see California and it's the first time Dad and Mom have been out of Colorado in forty years. It's about time they had a little fun and I'm sure not going to spoil it for them!"

During the remainder of the afternoon, my thoughts kept turning back to the time when Dad and Mom were young. Memories more vivid than the panorama that spread before me; Eddie's birth, the joy, and the inspiration he had brought to all of us; the worry, wondering when his being different was going to strike at him, the realization of how very little we could do to ease the hurt.

2 *December 3, 1926*

I was twelve when Eddie was born, old enough to understand where babies came from but young enough to have absorbed too many old wives' tales and superstitions about birth.

Our family lived at Lime, a small limestone quarry town about twelve miles south of Pueblo, Colorado. Dad worked for the mining department of the Colorado Fuel and Iron Company (CF&I), the last six years at Lime. The CF&I sent him to the DuPont Training School to learn about dynamite and he was in charge of all blasting and drilling operations at the quarry, a dangerous and demanding job.

The two hundred or so people who made up the population of the camp were of many different nationalities. Most of them had brought their old country ideas and customs right along with them.

Girls my age talked, whenever they could, about boys and all the other things that went along with that. The birth of new sister or brother was an event to be hashed over for weeks.

The morning my little brother was born, my nine-year-old sister Mickie and I were routed out of bed about five o'clock in the morning and told to go next door and ask Aunt Jody to hurry to our house. We were told to stay there and go to bed.

Too excited to go back to bed, we finally woke Evelyn, Aunt Jody's daughter. Evelyn was fifteen and her mother delivered or helped deliver almost all the new babies in camp. We listened wide-eyed as Evelyn tried to answer our questions.

By nine-thirty, when we heard the back gate slam, Evelyn had cleared away most of the mysteries surrounding having a baby. We hurried out to meet Aunt Jody, but as she rushed by me without a word, I saw she was crying. I had never seen Aunt Jody cry. Believing that my mother must surely be dead, I raced back to our house.

I ran straight to Mom's room. She looked weary, her heavy black hair disarranged on the pillow, but she had a beautiful smile on her face, and she was alive. And awake. Holding out her hand, she told me I had a baby brother and that she was fine. I asked to see the baby and she said, "Of course, ask Dr. Epler."

The "something is wrong" feeling returned as I walked into the kitchen. I looked past Dr. Epler and saw my father's face. My heart stood still. I could feel my knees start to shake as I went toward him. Dad looked up at me with a mute, blank stare, unrestrained tears streaming onto the white shirt that he had put on just for this big occasion.

I felt old as I looked at him sitting there. I wanted to comfort him. I couldn't understand why he looked as he did. He should be happy. He'd been so sure this time he'd get his boy. I went closer.

"What's the matter, Dad? Why are you crying? You've got your baby boy!"

He drew back as I reached out. "Yes, I've got my boy. I always wanted a son. Now I've got one all right, but he doesn't have any arms!" and he sobbed out loud, not covering his face. Just sitting there.

I didn't understand. I looked toward Dr. Epler, he nodded, then said, "Come over here, Hazel, and have a look at your new brother!"

Somewhat dazed by Dad's words, I went slowly towards the table. I looked into a tiny, wrinkled, snub-nosed little face but when I reached down and felt for his arms, it was true! He didn't have arms! My heart beat in fierce anger against a God who could do such a thing to a tiny baby.

I stood there, I don't know how long, my tears dripping onto empty sleeves that would never know flailing little arms or feel the soft outing-flannel nightgown Mom had so lovingly embroidered. I watched the dear little face and saw it pucker.

As the baby started to cry, Dad came over and grabbed Dr. Epler by the arm. "You can't take him to her! You should have let him die when you saw how he was! She can't stand it! She always checks to see if they're all right! I'm telling you, Doc! You can't do it!"

Dr. Epler was at a loss as to how to handle this strong, usually gentle, man who was now acting like a maniac. He motioned to me and told me to bring in Aunt Jody. I ran next door, glad of a chance to do something useful.

Aunt Jody came back with me. She seemed all right now, but different somehow. Eddie started to change everyone's life from the moment he was born.

I went outside, closing the door softly behind me; shutting the sorrow inside that small house. I sat in the swing Dad made, kicking up little puffs of dust. I knew I was scuffing my new shoes but I didn't care. Thoughts pounded inside my head. What could have caused this terrible thing to happen?

Maybe if Mom hadn't worked so hard trying to get our little ranch in shape so we could move back to it after the baby came. Maybe if we moved back to Lime sooner, so she wouldn't have had to carry water and chase the cows. Perhaps it was because of the day that little cyclone had blown the brooder house away scattering the baby chicks for a mile or so. When we had tried to gather them, many of their legs had been torn off and they were horribly mangled.

I remembered the summer I was six. We'd just bought the ranch. Mom wanted it for security in case Dad was laid off. We'd lived there when the quarry shut down and Dad was out of work. It wasn't a good ranch and there wasn't enough rainfall for it to be a good farm. Just a dry-land piece of ground. But Mom, my sister Mickie, and I loved it. We loved the squatty cedar trees on the gentle slopes of the hills, the Johnny-jump-ups and blue-bells that blanketed the valleys in the spring, and Old Baldy towering in the west with snow on his bald head all summer.

Mom and Dad had thrown up a shack good enough to live in through the summer. Mom worked harder than anyone trying to get it fixed up so we could live there all the time. But Dad didn't love it. He hated it. Dad was full of hate that summer and he was always telling Mom she was trying to make a dirt farmer out of him. She'd answer back that he was "just a Company man."

Someone dropped a stray pregnant cat on the highway. Mickie and I wanted to keep her after she had her kittens but Dad refused. He ordered Mom to drown the kittens. Mickie and I cried so hard that Mom helped us hide them in an old shed, telling us however, that when we moved back to Lime in the fall we would have to give them away.

Mickie and I were very careful. We'd wait until Dad went to the fields, then we'd go to the shed and get the tiny kittens out. Sitting there, with the sun warm on our backs, we'd play with them. One day, we were playing with the soft little kittens, making them chase our fingers, feeling their sharp claws dig into our flesh when they got too excited, watching them as they tumbled over one another in the warm dirt.

Suddenly, a shadow fell across us. We looked up. Dad stood there, a scowl blackening his face. He was a stranger, not the Dad I knew and loved. He didn't say a word, just reached down, picked up a kitten, held it by its back legs, and smashed its brains out against the side of the shed! We clutched the others to us, but he reached down, took them from our nerveless fingers and smashed them, one by one, methodically, until they were all five limp, inanimate pieces of dirty fur lying at our feet. He just looked through us, then walked away.

We didn't cry. For the moment we were too stunned. Silently we gathered the poor, broken bodies in the skirts of our dresses and started for the house. My stomach churned with hate, and I felt hard little spots dancing behind my eyes. I could hardly hold up my skirt, and I could feel the warm lumps hit my thighs as I walked.

Reaching the house, we went in and just held our skirts open so Mom could see. Mickie started to sob. Mom looked, and then knelt down. With her arms holding us tight, she brokenly tried to explain to us why Dad had done such a cruel thing. She tried to make us understand that he wasn't really killing kittens. He was just mad because it hadn't rained, because he hated farming, because the quarry had shut down and he was out of work, and because, most of all we had disobeyed him. She said it was her fault. We tried to understand, tried to forget and forgive. I never did.

Now I remembered. And I was afraid. Great fear numbed my body. What if Dad should try to harm the baby just because he didn't have arms? Dad wanted a boy for so long, and now he wasn't perfect. I'd heard him tell the doctor that he should have let the baby die!

"*Oh, God,*" I prayed, "*please don't let him hurt the poor, helpless, little baby! Don't let him hate my baby brother!*"

Then I thought of our neighbors in Lime. When a baby was born there was always a christening party with home-made wine, delicious anisette, cakes and cookies, and all kinds of good things to eat. Everyone had a good time, got a little drunk, congratulated the mother and father, and blessed the new-born babe.

Oh, dear God, I thought, how are they going to act now? How is my mother going to act? What will my Dad do? What are they going to say to people?

I finally went back into the house and discovered that I had only been gone a short time. As I opened the door, I heard Dad say, "You can't tell her! You've got to think of something!" It felt like I had never left the room.

Mom had to be told. Dr. Epler had stalled as long as he could. He was a busy doctor. Other patients needed him and he was several miles from town. The tall doctor put his hand on Dad's shoulder, saying, "Look at me, Art! Believe me when I tell you that God will help your wife. He will help you too, in your time of sorrow, if you will let Him!"

Dad threw the doctor's arms from his shoulder, and then he spit these words, "God damn God! What kind of a God is it who would let this happen?"

Dr. Epler looked at Aunt Jody, his shaggy head bowed a little, his kind eyes tired. "Perhaps you can make him realize that Mrs. Higgins must be told. Women seem to have a way of making us men understand things."

Aunt Jody took Dad aside. I never knew what they said, but I finally heard Dad say, "All right, Doctor. You tell her, I'll be in shortly."

No one noticed me as I tiptoed after Dr. Epler and Aunt Jody as they went into Mom's room. Mom was lying there with her eyes closed, but when we entered the room she opened her eyes, turned on her side toward us, and started to bring the covers down from her shoulders, preparing a place for them to put her baby. She looked up. When no one said anything, she looked first at Aunt Jody, then at me. I knew my lower lip was quivering, but I couldn't hold it still.

Mom's face turned white, and she held out her arms, "Where is my baby? Why didn't you bring him to me? He isn't dead? What's wrong with him?"

Dr. Epler sat down on the edge of the bed, taking Mom's work-worn hand in his own. "Your baby was born without arms, Ethel. I don't know why, but he doesn't have any arms. He is perfectly formed and absolutely normal in every other way, but he doesn't have arms!"

Aunt Jody moved to the far side of the bed. I had the feeling that she was going to try to keep Mom from getting up.

Mom closed her eyes, not saying anything for a few moments. Then she said, "Bring my baby to me! He needs me, poor little darling!"

Dad came into the room with Dr. Epler as he brought the baby to Mom. He sat down on the side of the bed, and watched as Mom unwrapped the blankets and slowly took off the little garments. Unheeded tears slipped silently down her cheeks. She looked at Dad and said one word, "Why?"

Dad stroked her arm gently, and then patted the baby's red, wrinkled forehead. "I don't know why, old girl. We'll just have to make the best of it. That's all. It will be sort of rough on the little feller though."

We all left the room. I could hear Dad sobbing, but I also heard Mom's voice soothing him.

"I think they will be all right," Dr. Epler said then. "I will be out first thing in the morning and I would like to bring Dr. Heller with me. This is an extraordinary thing! I would like his opinion." He then turned to Aunt Jody, "Mrs. Christie, keep a close eye on Mrs. Higgins. She is very quiet about this. One can never tell what might happen. See that someone is with her at all times."

Although Mom's heart was breaking, I knew there was never any thought of harming herself or the baby, or of placing my brother in an institution. That wasn't the stuff of which she was made, or Dad either.

If I had only remembered how Mom had always swept Dad along with her in some of her seemingly impossible schemes, I would have been saved some of the torment of that day. Dad might bellow like a bull at some of Mom's ideas, but he usually ended up by following her lead, sometimes even boasting a little when her plan turned out well.

Later, I did remember one incident at the ranch that had happened a couple of years before.

"What are you going to shoot, Art?" Mom asked, when Dad came in to get the gun. "I didn't know there was a hawk around!" She started out the door with him.

"Now you get back in the house, Ethel! Old Daisy has stepped in a prairie dog hole and broke her leg! I'm going to shoot her and put her out of her misery!" Dad tried to get Mom to stay in the house. He knew how she loved our old milk-cow.

"You just wait a minute, Art Higgins! You're not going to shoot that milk cow just because she broke her leg! Here now, let me find an old sheet and you start tearing strips off it while I get some other things."

As she talked, she handed Dad a sheet she produced out of nowhere and started gathering up scissors, safety pins, and big box of plaster of Paris. She handed stuff to Mickie and me and picked up some splint material from the woodpile.

Daisy had somehow managed to hobble under the three-sided pole barn. When she saw us coming, she didn't budge; just stood there waiting. She seemed to know we would help her. Like most dumb animals when they are badly hurt, she stood quietly, instinctively bracing herself when Mom or Dad pulled on her broken leg, sometimes looking at Mom with soft, trusting brown eyes. After much swearing on Dad's part, bracing his feet on her side, and pulling bones into what Mom thought was the right position, Dad was told, "Hold it straight now, just like I've got it, until I can get these splints in place."

Mom first wrapped strips of sheet around the leg, then splints, followed by tighter sheet strips. Then she started dipping strips into the plaster mix; winding, shaping, patting, and smoothing until Daisy had a leg that looked like a tree stump.

Mom stood up, stretched a kink out of her back, and said, "Art, do you know where that wide belt is that you brought from the quarry? That long belt that was on some kind of conveyor? We could put that under Daisy's belly and lift her up on the big beam." Mom looked up at the beam they used to hang steers and hogs when they butchered.

"Yes, I sure do. That would work! All we'd need to do is get her a couple inches off the ground until the bone knits!" Suddenly he was smiling. He went to get the belt and the come-along to hoist Daisy.

13

The broken leg did mend and Daisy lived to give us several more calves and lots of delicious milk.

So it shouldn't have surprised me when Mom said, "Bring my baby to me. Poor little darling, he needs me!" Or that Dad cursed God but went right along with Mom. Later when Mom decided that Eddie was going to be treated as much like other children as possible, Dad went along with that, too.

By the time the sun started to set in the sky that evening of Eddie's first day, I knew Mom and Dad were going to accept Eddie's handicap. They didn't understand. They wouldn't know what to say or how to act for awhile, but they did accept it.

3 Why?

efore Eddie was born, we usually had a quick supper after Dad got home on Saturday evening, then piled into the car and drove nine miles to Pueblo. Groceries were much cheaper there than at the Company Store, but for the last three Saturdays, Mom went to town early by herself. As soon as she heard the back gate slam on Friday afternoon, she'd call to Mickie and me, "All right now, you two get in here. Get out of your school clothes and help me get this work finished! I've got to go to town early in the morning!"

We'd hurry in, talking quietly to one another, wondering why Mom wouldn't let us go along. The first time we had asked to go, but Mom said, "No, you stay and help Aunt Jody take care of your baby brother. Finish the cleaning and behave yourselves."

Mickie protested to me: "I don't see why we can't go!, Aunt Jody takes care of the baby at her house and hardly lets us touch him! Besides, Mom's always cranky anymore!"

"Sure, she's cranky. She worries about the baby!" I wasn't sure why Mom was cross, but I had to tell Mickie something. I was curious, too, about why Mom went by herself and I missed her singing as she went about her chores.

One night, after Mickie and I were in bed, I heard sounds from the kitchen. I could hear Dad walking. A loose floorboard creaked under his weight. I heard him lift the lid on the old cook stove, pour coal noisily into the fire box, slam the lid back in place and with a loud, angry thump bang the coal scuttle back on the floor.

"Hell, Ethel!" His voice raised in exasperation.

"Sssh, Art, you'll wake the children." After a pause, I heard her say, "Now..." and I couldn't hear the rest, but it sounded like she was trying to talk Dad into something.

First I heard Dad's fist crash on the table hard enough to rattle the cover on the sugar bowl, then I heard him scrape his chair back from the table. I could almost see him pacing angrily back and forth as his heavy steps sounded through the small house.

"God damn it, Ethel!" his voice bellowed. I looked over at Mickie sleeping quietly beside me, feeling the cold air of the bedroom creep around me as the covers slipped off my shoulders.

"God damn it!" he said again. "Why do we have to submit to all these tests? Isn't it enough that we have a son born without arms? Do we have to drag all your family history into it! Who had buck teeth? Who had soft bones? Who had this? Who had that? I tell you, none of my family or yours ever had a damn thing wrong with them! All of them healthy as a bunch of horses, lived to be in their eighties or older unless they had an accident!"

"Art, be reasonable!" Mom's voice was high now, trying to subdue him. "Dr. Epler is only trying to find out why! I want to know why too, and then maybe I can quit blaming myself. You only have to come in tomorrow! Just this last test, then we'll know!"

I crept out of bed, trying not to hop when my feet hit the icy floor. Silently, I made my way to the closed kitchen door and stood there, feeling a tiny breath of warm air curl though the cracks around the door and disappear into the cold of the bedroom. I could hear my tiny brother breathing from his little bed, placed beside Mom and Dad's big bed, and wondered how he and Mickie could sleep so soundly through all this racket.

"Don't you see, Art?" Mom went on, her voice low, "It's only right we should know all we can as to why Eddie was born this way so we can tell the children when they grow up that it isn't our fault. It would be terrible if when they marry they wanted children and were afraid to have them!"

Dad paced the floor again. "Well, I guess you're right old girl. I'll get off work tomorrow and go in with you. Don't know what good it's going to do though."

I hurried back to bed, shivering as I got down under the heavy quilts, snuggling close to Mickie and the warm spot she made.

The following Saturday, Mom went to town by herself again. When she came back late that afternoon, I ran out to help her bring in the packages. Right away, I noticed that she was different. She was singing under her breath and she carried herself a bit straighter. She knelt down and drew Mickie and me into her arms, hugging us tight.

I couldn't sleep that night. Shamelessly, I groped my way to the closed door of the kitchen and listened.

"See Art, it wasn't so bad! At least I don't feel that it's your fault or mine, and I was worried about that. The doctor has finally convinced me that things like this can happen to anyone. There isn't a medical reason. It just happens, that's all! You heard Dr. Epler say it has nothing to do with our age, that we could have more children if we wanted to and they would be all right!"

"Well, sure I'm glad Ethel. Glad to know it's not our fault. But we're not going to have any more kids! You can damn well count on that!" Dad's voice still sounded angry, but it had lost some of its sharp edge.

I hurried back to bed, not minding the cold, happy that my Mom and Dad were happier. In the days that followed, I noticed that Dad talked more, and started teasing Mom a little the way he used to. And he was paying more attention to the baby.

Mom might have accepted God's will, but she wasn't going to leave it all to God. She was determined to give Him all the help she could to insure that Eddie grew up to be a strong, healthy boy.

Every morning before his bath, she undressed him, then holding his tiny feet, she would lift his behind off the table, flexing his back. She would lift first one leg then the other high in the air. Placing her hands under his perfect, square little shoulders, she would raise him gently, gradually, to a sitting position and then back down and over on his tummy for some more. As Eddie grew older, she devised more strenuous exercises. Eddie loved it. When Dad came home, he would give his little son a workout, too.

One balmy day in April, 1927, when Eddie was about four months old, Mickie and I were out in the yard raking leaves from under the old apple trees, spreading them over the little plot that Dad would spade up for a garden. A smell of spring rain hung in the air. Trees were bursting with buds. The grass was getting green.

Our next door neighbors, the Rennies, had a daughter a few weeks younger than Eddie. Celia Jane became a barometer for Eddie's progress. Mom asked Patsy Rennie to come to our house. "We can do our mending together. I'll put a quilt down on the grass and the kids will enjoy being out of their buggies."

"Sure, that's a good idea; I don't think they'll go very far," Patsy laughed.

Celia Jane could sit up, and Mom could see Eddie's frustration as he tried to imitate her.

When Dad came home from work, the first thing Mom said was "Art, I want you to make a play pen for those babies! Something solid with good strong sides. I think Eddie could learn to sit up if he had something to lean against."

When Celia Jane picked up a toy with her hands, Eddie did the same with his toes. Watching for any lagging on his part, we were gratified. From the first, Eddie used his feet and toes as easily as other children used their hands. But he still couldn't sit up on his own.

Many bumps and many trials later, Eddie did learn to sit up. It took some time for him to be sure of his balance, but soon he learned that he wouldn't hurt himself if he rolled over. When Celia Jane crawled, Eddie scooted. He never crawled. He just sat up straight, brought his knees up to his chest, then straightening his legs out, he scooted wherever he wanted to go. When the weather got too cold to work outside, Patsy brought her mending and sat with Mom in the warm kitchen, the kids playing on the floor.

I usually had school work to do, and I sat at the big round oak table, a little spot cleared for my books amidst the ordered mess of Dad's overalls, Eddie's pants, and the hodge-podge of old material used for patches. I bowed my head over my books and listened to the tidbits of gossip.

Pushing a wisp of bright red hair back from her face, Patsy sorted through the pile of socks she brought. "I think I'll start on the worst ones first; darning always seems easier that way," Patsy said, her head lowered as she pushed the gray darning cotton through the eye of the needle.

"It keeps me busy sewing patches on the seats of Eddie's pants, the way he scoots everywhere!" Mom carefully placed a patch just right. Then, with an expert turn of the wheel and a pressure of her foot on the treadle of the old-fashioned sewing machine, she quickly stitched and back-stitched a patch neatly in place.

"They'll both be walking soon, Ethel, then..." Patsy flushed and didn't finish what she started to say.

I bent my head over my arithmetic, but the numbers blurred. With my head still lowered, I watched Eddie and Celia Jane, as they sat on the floor playing; grunting and gurgling at each other in their own language.

Mom made both of them rag dolls with bright yellow yarn hair, big red embroidered mouths and shoe button eyes. Eddie held his doll by the hair, the yarn grasped between the toes of his right foot. He'd slide the doll in a half circle on the floor, then let go. The doll wouldn't slide very far, but Eddie would scoot over, get the doll into position with his feet, then grabbing it by the hair again, would start his game all over. Celia Jane tired of this game and crawled over to her mother's chair, pulling herself to a standing position, clutching at her mother's dress, whimpering to be picked up. Eddie looked at her for a moment, and then scooted over beside Mom's chair. His big, blue eyes questioning, he looked first at Mom, then at Celia Jane, watching this other baby who could pull herself up and stand.

Mom pushed her chair back from the sewing machine, reached down and picked up her small son, cradling him close against her for a moment. Then she searched through her scraps and found two pieces of bright print. Handing one of them to Celia Jane, then holding the other piece near Eddie's toes, she watched with a sad little smile as he clutched it, then waved it in the air.

"Well, I guess I'd better fix supper." She rose from her chair, Eddie still in her arms. "I don't know where the afternoon has gone to!"

"I'd better get home, too," Patsy suddenly seemed in a hurry as she gathered up her darning and bundled Celia Jane against the cold.

Late the next evening Dad returned from town loaded down with packages. On his last trip from the car, he came in, a little happy gleam in his eye, with an awkward, carelessly wrapped package under his arm.

"Ooh, Daddy, what's that?" Mickie squealed, sensing that the package wasn't anything Mom had sent for.

"Wait and see! I suppose the boy's asleep?" Dad asked.

"Why, of course. He's been asleep for awhile. What on earth have you got there, anyway?" Mom started to take the package from him, but Dad drew back.

"Just a minute now! It's a birthday present for the little feller!" He put the package on the floor, and slowly stripped off the heavy brown wrapping paper.

"Why, Art!" Mom said, then we were all on our knees, looking at the strange device. "Taylor Tot," was written across the front bar. I pushed it back and forth, marveling at the way the front wheels swivelled.

"I thought maybe the boy could learn to walk in this! What do you think, old girl?"

"You know, Art, I think he can!" I could tell Mom was excited. "This little back will keep him from falling out, and when he gains confidence enough to stand up, if he does start to fall, it will hold him in!"

"Oh Mom! Get him up and let's see what he does!" I couldn't wait.

"Don't be silly, he needs his rest. I can see tomorrow is going to be a big day for him!" Mom could hardly contain herself.

The next day was Sunday. As soon as Eddie was up and dressed, we all gathered around as Dad gingerly placed him in the Taylor Tot.

"Wait a minute Art! Hold him until I get a pillow to brace him!" Mom hurried back with a pillow that she stuffed between Eddie's body and the tray on the front of the walker. "Now, let him go; let's see what happens!"

Dad gently pushed the walker around the room, Eddie's feet half dragging along the floor.

"He'll have to get the feel of the floor under his feet, before he knows what to do. Maybe..." Dad held Eddie in a standing position. "Now, push real easy..." He nodded to Mom and she pushed a tiny bit as Dad held Eddie straight. Eddie stamped his feet, yelling with glee at this new game and all the attention he was getting. But the moment Dad let go he sat down and reached with his toes toward the front wheel, which seemed to fascinate him.

Dad shook his head, "Guess we'll just have to leave him alone and let him figure it out for himself. But, by God, I think this is the ticket! I think it'll do the trick!" He beamed. "I've been trying to think of something I could make myself for quite awhile now. Then yesterday, I saw this contraption in the hardware store. I just knew this was it! Paid a little more than we can afford, but what the hell!" He patted Mom's arm as they stood there and looked down at Eddie experimenting with his new toy.

By Christmas Eddie was going everywhere in his walker. By spring, he could stand up and drag the walker along with him. Then he started crawling out of it and trying the new experience of walking by himself. He soon learned to roll up in a tight ball and turn a somersault when he lost his balance and started to fall. Even so, he acquired an almost permanent bump on his forehead from some nasty spills. Undaunted, he seldom cried and as time went on, he attained such a good sense of balance that he seldom fell.

After supper one night, Mom stopped us as we started to get up from the table. "Wait, I want to talk to all of you!" she commanded as she shooed us into the bedroom. Eddie was in the living room playing with his little cars. "You know Edward has been talking quite a lot?" She looked at us and waited.

Sure, we knew. I couldn't imagine what she was making such a fuss about.

"Now, I want to tell you what happened today!" She hesitated, a worried frown on her face. "I've been talking to Edward, and not realizing what I was doing, when I held him and cuddled him, I would say, 'Poor 'bused boy.' Well today he looked up at me with that sweet smile of his, and said right back to me, 'Poor 'bused boy!' just as plain as could be."

"That's terrible," Dad said, "We can't have him saying and thinking things like that!"

"No, we can't! So mind you, from now on, none of us must ever do or say a thing to make him feel that he is abused or different from other little kids!" Mom looked at all of us. We nodded and went about our after-supper chores.

It was hard not to baby Eddie, but from then on, we didn't!

4 Birthday Two and "Santy Claws"

$\mathcal{E}$ ddie's second birthday was the third of December, 1928. It was a sort of milestone for all of us, because only a year ago, none of us believed that he would ever learn to use his feet and his strong little toes to do half the things he was now doing. I still had the feeling that one day he would come to the end of the things he could do with his feet. Eddie seemed to be the only one who didn't have any fears for the future.

He talked about his birthday all day. Mom had to scold him twice for licking part of the icing off his cake. We were all glad when Dad finally got home and we could sit down to supper.

As soon as supper was over, Mom said, "Clear the table now, so there'll be room for Eddie's birthday cake and his presents!" She went to the washstand where the birthday cake was waiting for its candles to be lit.

Eddie twisted against the dishtowel holding him in his high chair and yelled, "Birthday cake!"

Dad moved closer, his hand on guard along the side of the chair. "Take it easy, Son! You're going to tip over your high chair! Give Mommy time to bring your cake!"

Mickie and I brought Eddie's presents to the table, but his eyes were on the cake, tiny candles burning bright, casting little lights over the pink frosted surface.

Mom placed the cake in front of him, and held his feet as he started to reach toward it. "No, honey, blow the candles out first! Blow hard just like you do when you blow out Daddy's match after he lights his pipe!"

Eddie looked around, his eyes dancing with joy at all this fun. He took a deep breath, swelling his chest out as far as it would go, puckered up and with a big gust, noisily blew out both candles. Then, before Mom could stop him, he buried his mouth in the pink frosting, raised up laughing and started licking icing off his face as far as his tongue could reach.

Dad laughed. Mom smiled with a "just-look-at-him" air, let go of his feet and pushed the cake out of reach. "Here, Eddie, open your presents, while Mom cuts the cake!" I pushed the tissue-wrapped little packages in front of his toes.

Mom had made him a new rag doll from a pair of brown work socks, using the white ends on the toes and heels for the face, feet, and hands. She made a doll-size pair of pants and stitched them carefully to the cotton stuffed body, with a little checked percale shirt, the whole outfit exactly like the new suit she had made for Eddie. Mickie and I bought toy cars at the dime store, and Dad got him a little hammer and a screwdriver.

Eddie tore at the paper and squealed with delight as the tiny cars fell out on the table. Grasping one between his toes, he started rolling it over the surface of the table.

"Here, look what else you got for your birthday, Son," Dad said and pushed his package toward Eddie.

Eddie tore at the paper, and when he saw what Dad had given him, he waved the hammer in the air and yelled, "Help Daddy! Fix car!" then laid them aside and started pushing the little cars again.

I noticed that Dad didn't say anything, just sat there, a thoughtful frown on his face, looking into some distant place where none of us could go.

"All right, eat our cake now, then you can get down on the floor and play with your presents!" Mom told Eddie. "I'm going to wait until later to open what I made for him. He's so excited about those little cars he won't pay any attention to anything else!"

"He liked that screw driver and hammer, all right! Just wait, before you know it, he'll be trying to help his old man work on the car!" Dad said jokingly, pride showing through the doubt in his voice.

24

Eddie was so anxious to get down on the floor and play cars that he didn't finish his cake before he started yelling, "Down! I want down! I wanna play cars!"

We washed dishes to the sounds Eddie made holding the little cars in his toes, making big circles with them, screeching around corners, tires squealing, horns honking, yelling, "Wreck!" whenever he crashed them together.

Mom finally took the cars away to get him ready for bed. "Now Sonny, do you want to see what Mommy made you for your birthday?"

"Sure! Mommy makes me present, too!" His voice was drowsy as he leaned against Mom's knee.

"Well, here then, let me try it on you!" Mom lifted his chubby weight onto her lap, then held up the little suit she'd made for him so that he could see it.

Eddie grinned and wriggled his thanks, burying his head in Mom's bosom as she removed the rompers he was wearing and buttoned the little checked shirt around his fat body, then stood him up on her lap. "Here, put your legs in these pants," she said as she put the long blue pants on him.

"I wanna see!" Eddie said, "see in mirwar!"

"All right, Mommy'll show you!" Mom picked Eddie up and went into the bedroom.

We followed. Dad reached up to switch on the light hanging from the ceiling. Mom stood Eddie on the dresser top so he could see himself in the oval of the old-fashioned mirror.

"Pretty, Eddie's pretty!" he crowed as he turned this way and that to see his reflection, then he raised his foot and felt the material of his new pants.

"Bring his doll," Mom said to me. Mom dangled the rag doll beside Eddie. "Here's a new playmate for you. See, his little suit is just like yours!"

"Oh, Mommy! Just like mine!" Eddie said, feeling the doll with the toes of his right foot as he leaned against Mom, balancing on his left leg. Suddenly he turned to Mom and gave her a sloppy kiss, saying, "Can I sleep with dolly?"

"Sure you can. What are you going to name him?" Mom said, lifting Eddie down, and going back into the warmth of the kitchen to get him ready for bed.

"Art! Little Art! Just like Daddy!" Eddie said, looking up at Dad. Dad beamed with pleasure, reached down and tousled Eddie's hair, then sat at the table, idly picking up the little hammer and screwdriver, turning them over in his callused hands.

"Well, Son, you've had a pretty good birthday for a little shaver!" Dad said to Eddie.

"Yes, he sure has," Mom agreed. "He's so tired, he's almost asleep already!" She lifted Eddie, holding him over her shoulder, cuddling her nose down into the soft place on the back of his neck as she went into the bedroom to tuck him and his doll into bed.

Mickie and I took our books to the table and started on our school lessons. Mom sat down with her darning basket. Dad got up to put some more coal in the stove.

He replaced the lid with a bang and hung the stove hook on its nail. He stood there for a while, and then said to Mom, "I didn't want to spoil Eddie's birthday, but the quarry closed down to three days a week, starting today."

"Oh, Art." Mom put down her darning, pushed her hair away from her forehead. "For how long? Do you mean all of the quarry?"

"Yes, all of it. In fact, they're giving some of the men six month leaves-of-absence, and you know what that means. Most of them won't be back!"

"Right before Christmas, too," Mom shook her head. "Well, that means we won't be able to save any money to start building a house at the ranch. We'll do good to have enough by spring to buy seed to put in a crop." Mom's voice sounded flat and discouraged.

"Yeah, well, I don't think I'll get laid off entirely, but you never know. You never can figure out just why it happens. All this talk about the stock market, etc.," Dad said. He picked up the paper but I noticed he really wasn't reading it.

Mickie and I looked at each other over our books, our hopes of moving to the ranch dashed. We knew better than to ask any questions when Dad and Mom were so worried, but we couldn't wait to get to the privacy of our cold bedroom to talk over the news.

Undressing hurriedly, but not fast enough to keep the icy fingers of cold from clutching at us, we were chilled when we jumped in between the sheets and pulled heavy quilts up around our ears. The sheets were like thin pieces of ice and we kicked our legs back and forth and moved our arms up and down until we felt our bodies start to tingle from the exercise and the warmth flowing through us. Then we started talking quietly.

"Do you think the Company'll give all the kids in camp candy and oranges for Christmas like always?" Mickie asked me.

"Oh, sure…the Company's still got plenty of money, even if they do shut the quarry down." I thought how silly Mickie was to worry about candy and oranges when probably no one would even have enough money to buy groceries.

"Well, I'll bet Mom thinks of some way to build the house, even if the darned old quarry closes clear down," Mickie said sleepily.

"I don't know how. She'd have to sell a lot more chickens and eggs to make that much money."

"Well anyway, we'll have Christmas just the same." Mickie turned her back to me and went to sleep.

I couldn't sleep. Although Mickie and I hadn't really believed in Santa Claus for years, Dad had been official camp Santa ever since we'd moved to Lime when I was five. He would dress up in a red suit and stuff a pillow in his front. Mom helped him adjust the funny white whiskers that hid all but his twinkly blue eyes. We thought he made a wonderful Santa, and he'd practice his big "Ho! Ho! Ho!" on us, before he left with the big sack over his shoulder to go to the houses of the kids who were too small to go to school where pupils received their presents at the school Christmas party.

Dad had a regular routine. He'd knock on a door. When it was opened, he'd ask in a deep, gruff voice, "Is little Mary here? Tell her Santa Claus is here to see her!" And he'd laugh a big jolly laugh, "Ho! Ho! Ho!"

When Mary was brought to the door, he'd ask, "Tell Santa now, have you been a good girl?" Of course she'd say yes. Then Dad would say, "Well, here's a present for a good little girl from Santa. Ho! Ho! Ho!" and he'd shake his pillow of a belly and make a big to-do about handing her the red, mesh stocking with a picture of Santa pasted on its bulging surface.

The stocking was always filled with exactly the same things: hard candies, a few nuts, and a big yellow orange that the Company had provided. It was great fun, and the little kids all looked forward to Santa's visit.

I fell asleep thinking about Dad in his Santa suit.

The weeks flew by, and suddenly it was Christmas Eve. Dad went to a neighbor's house to dress in his suit so Eddie wouldn't see him and then he was knocking at our door. Mickie and I crowded close beside Mom, so we could watch the expression on Eddie's face when he saw his first Santa Claus.

Fleetingly, I remembered my dream, but this was real, and as Dad started talking, I noticed that he forgot some of his lines. "Where is Eddie? Oh, there he is! Ho! Ho! Ho! Have you been a good boy?" I held my breath as he paused, almost saying "Sonny," then he held out the mesh stocking for Mom to take, knowing Eddie couldn't hold its weight in his little toes.

Then Eddie said in a shy, small voice, "I been a good boy, Santy Claws!" and Dad didn't have to pretend the gruffness in his voice as he said, "Well, here's a present for you from Santa. HO! HO! HO!" and he turned and hurried away, with Eddie's happy "Thank you, Santy Claws," drifting after him on the cold winter air.

When Dad came in later, his eyes were red and he blew his nose loudly into his handkerchief, saying, "Sure is cold out tonight!

"Well, so Santa Claus did come to see you!" Dad said acting surprised. "What did he bring you from the North Pole?" He sat down on the floor, while Eddie dumped everything out of the stocking, showing Dad each piece of candy, his little striped candy cane, and his big yellow orange.

5 A Dream vs. Colorado Fuel & Iron

*M*om was forty-one but she acted as if life was just beginning for her. And in a way it was. Dad was fifty-three, an age when most men can sit back and think about retiring, but Mom had ideas about that, too!

"Art," she said before the last snow had melted, "let's start building a house at the ranch this spring! We can work on it evenings and weekends! For that matter, the kids and I can go up every day as soon as school's out. There's a lot of things we could get done!"

Dad kept right on reading the paper and didn't answer, which was his habit when he didn't want to start on some project Mom had in mind.

Mom looked at him, put the plate of hot biscuits on the table, and called to us, "Well, let's eat now!" but the set of her jaw was stubborn, and she glanced at Dad with an "I'll-talk-to-you-later" look in her eye.

She placed Eddie in his high chair from which the tray had been removed, and tied him in with a dish towel.

"Sit still, honey, until I wash your feet." She washed and dried them, then pushed the high chair even with the table top, moving everything out of the reach of his eager toes. Silently, she filled his plate, mashing the potatoes and carrots and shredding a small piece of beef into bite-size pieces.

Eddie was learning to feed himself. It was worth all the mess to see how each day he became more adept at holding his spoon between the toes of his right foot, and getting most of the food to his mouth.

Dad finished his supper, pushed his chair back from the table, and tousled Eddie's shock of unruly blond hair. Eddie waved his spoon in the air, spattering everything with carrots.

"Now Art, don't get him upset until he's finished his supper! Look at this mess!" Mom dabbed at a blotch of carrot on her starched dress front.

Eddie threw down his spoon and struggled against the dish towel holding him securely in the high chair. "Down! I want down!"

"All right son. Here, drink your milk, then Daddy will get you out of that chair!" Dad picked up the glass of milk, and held it to Eddie's mouth, watching his small son with a tender smile. "Down! Let me down!" Eddie said again, the moment the glass was empty.

"Get a wash rag and wash his face and feet, now that you've started all this!" Mom told Dad. Eddie struggled away from the wash rag, but Dad finished the job. Picking Eddie up, he told Mom, "Eddie and I are going to take a little walk, we won't be gone long." Dad reached up to the row of pegs behind the kitchen door, got his coat and Eddie's little jacket.

"Art, don't you get to playing cards and forget what time it is! That boy has got to get to bed soon. Besides, I want to talk to you!" She put her hands on her hips and watched as Dad walked out the door, not answering.

As soon as the door closed behind them, Mickie and I flew at Mom, both of us talking at once, "Mom, are we really going to build a house at the ranch? A real house? Can we have a room all our own?"

"We're going to build a house, all right! Let's hurry and get these dishes done then we'll get out some paper and draw up plans!" Mom said, her voice determined. We started on the dishes at once, excited at the thought of building a house that would be our very own.

For all her determination, we knew it wouldn't be easy for Mom to convince Dad. Nevertheless, as soon as Eddie had been tucked into bed, Mom tackled Dad about the house project. They forgot all about Mickie and me as they argued back and forth. As we listened, our hopes would soar one moment. only to be dashed the next. Still, Mom wouldn't give up.

"But Ethel, why not live here in the Company camp? You know I won't quit the Company, and I sure don't like the idea of driving back and forth to work!"

"It's only eight miles to the ranch, Art. That's no great distance. Besides, as long as we have our cattle and plant crops, we spend most of the summer there anyway." A note of sarcasm crept into Mom's voice. "Or I suppose you figure that shack is good enough and you don't ever intend to do any more at the ranch?" Mom waited, head to one side, her hands fidgeting with the pencil and ruler, shuffling the plans spread on the table.

"I never did want to buy that piece of God-forsaken dry land in the first place, Ethel! You know that, but you had to have it! Now, you want to build a house on it. Throw good money after bad! When you get through, the house'll be worth more than the whole damned ranch!" His chair scraped as he rose and paced angrily back and forth in the confined space of the kitchen.

"Well, if you'd listened to me fifteen years ago when we first got married, we could have bought a good ranch, but…

"That was fifteen years ago, Ethel, so don't go crying over spilt milk! Besides, what's wrong with the Colorado Fuel and Iron Company? I'd like to know where else we could live as cheap as we do in these Company houses. We have water furnished for a yard and garden, a park for the kids, a club house, dances every Saturday night, our friends!" Dad stopped in front of Mom, his face red, legs spread wide apart, for the moment looking just like our old red rooster when he was trying to show his harem of hens who was boss.

"Sure," Mom said. "The Company's fine. We've got a Company store, too! They charge three times more than any other store! You run up a bill, and at the end of the month they take it out of your paycheck and you get what's left!

"Yes we have water, enough to use on a little yard and a bit of garden because the Company owns the water rights and the good land all along Purgatory River to the south where their coal mines are, and the Arkansas and the St. Charles Rivers from above Salida and Rye clear to Pueblo. Clear to the headwaters, they own land and water rights! In Wyoming they own iron mines!

"And the Company houses…Sure they're all right, but I want something of our own! I want a house on our own ground with our own water so if the Company closes down, we won't have to move!" Mom sat there, doodling all over her house plans, making big black marks with angry, futile strokes.

Dad moved to the stove, his step heavy, lifted the coffee pot. He put the pot down quietly on the crocheted hot pad in the center of the table. Silently, he took two big white cups from the crude cupboard along the wall over the wash stand. He filled them and handed one to Mom. He sat heavily, sipping at the strong brew. Then he took his glasses off, rubbed his eyes, pulled a handkerchief out of his hip pocket, and blowing on the thick lenses of his glasses, started polishing them.

"Let me do that, Art," Mom said gently. Then, her voice sharper, "And why isn't that handkerchief in the wash?" She got up, went into the bedroom, and came back with a clean hankie. Taking Dad's glasses, she went to the washstand and poured water over them. Sitting down, she carefully cleaned the lenses, holding them up to look through them, and then polishing them once more before she handed them back to Dad.

She sat sipping her coffee, watching Dad. Silent. Waiting.

Mickie and I sat near the stove, not really hidden but out of sight. Not that it would have made any difference. Mom and Dad weren't paying a bit of attention to us. The alarm clock on its shelf loudly ticked the minutes away. I could hear the bare branches of the old apple tree brush against the roof as the wind started to blow harder. In the silence hanging over the room, I thought of the Company camp as I knew it…

Lime was a typical CF&I mining camp, but it was special to me. It was laid out above the St. Charles River valley where huge cotton-wood trees towered over paths through the underbrush made by deer, raccoons, coyote, and other wild life. There were thickets of wild plums and gnarled grapevines growing over fallen logs. A large apple orchard planted by some long gone superintendent stretched to the back part of the camp, between it and the quarry. The mule barn and blacksmith shop were at the upper end of the orchard.

Streets were laid out in a grid with a park in the middle. The American boarding house was on the orchard side of the park and the Austrian boarding house was on the other side. I asked Mom once why they had two boarding houses. It seemed to me that when people came to America from other countries, they should all be Americans.

She answered, "It should be that way, but it will probably be a long time before people realize we are all equal."

The quarry itself was awesome. It was cut out of white limestone cliffs rising from the valley floor on the north side of the St. Charles River. After the top soil and vegetation were stripped from the rock, this "overburden" was hauled to a huge arroyo that served as a dump site. Once the limestone was exposed it was Dad's job to see that the drillers drilled holes in the limestone in the proper places; he would then load them with dynamite and sometimes he let me follow along when he loaded the holes. Later he would wait until all the men were out of the quarry after work to shoot these holes, and to avoid accidents, he had to be sure that all the shots had fired. It was a dangerous and painstaking job.

It was a real thrill to watch as he pushed the plunger. Chunks of stone bigger than two or three houses would mushroom up, then settle down into piles suitable for working. There were times when the stone wasn't sufficiently broken up for loading, then he would have to set "pot-shots" to make it manageable. Dust covered everything.

During the day, the quarry was a hive of activity. Men loaded the rock onto ore cars that mules pulled along the railroad spurs. Men of almost every nationality worked at loading the cars and they were paid according to how many tons of rock they got out, making bets as to whose tally sheet would be the highest at the end of the week. There would be a Portuguese with a colorful bandanna tied around his head, looking for all the world like a pirate who jumped ship and found himself doing penance on a rock pile; and next to him an Italian, singing as he loaded his ore car.

The mule-skinners were a special breed of men. They knew just how to make a stubborn mule back up to a loaded ore car and "gee and haw" him into position. Mules pulled the heavy cars along the railroad tracks that reached out like tentacles from the main spur. From there gravity and a series of switches took them on to the crusher. Once there, each car was weighed and the tonnage entered into the time book opposite the loader's name. The mule-skinners also had to see that empty cars were always ready for the loaders. When the whistle blew at five o'clock, a mule-skinner would jump onto the back of his mule (if it could be ridden), and ride the mule to the barn.

I loved that mule barn with its cavernous maw overhead filled with sweet-smelling hay; the orderly stalls and the big pole corral where each mule skinner had to snake his mule out of the milling, kicking herd each morning. The stalls were used only when needed to take care of a sick animal, shoe them, or such.

Old Bill Willis was boss of the mule barn. With his white thatch of hair and twinkly blue eyes, he always looked as if he had just been freshly shaven, scrubbed, and buttoned into stiffly starched overalls. It was his job to see that the mules were groomed and well fed and he knew each mule by name and disposition. It was also part of his job to see that the camp was kept clean, the garbage cans emptied, the alleys raked, and the little park with its patch of green lawn mowed and watered. If he needed help, he was allowed to hire some of the older boys and they invariably treated him with respect. It was a treat to hook a ride with Bill on the wagon he drove around camp when he collected garbage. He kept the wagon so clean and shiny and was himself so immaculate that collecting the garbage took on a special dignity, which he further enhanced by telling stories of his boyhood in England, but he never talked of the time in between.

The crusher frightened me. Massive machinery ground rock in its huge jaws, sorted it into different sizes and automatically loaded it into the railroad cars waiting on the siding below. From there, it was taken to the steel mill in Pueblo where it was used in the making of steel. There was always a thunderous roar around the corrugated iron structure. Thick, lung-destroying, gray dust enveloped everything near it. Lung cancer and pneumonia plagued the miners and we were forbidden to go near the crusher, but the kids in camp played "run-sheep-run" over the rest of the quarry during the long summer evenings. On a hill near the crusher sat the post office, and the schoolhouse and teacherage sat on the opposite hill.

Our house was in about the middle of the block on Orchard Row, which backed up to the orchard. The streets on the other side of the park were named First, Second, Third, and Fourth. All the houses were the same, built of wood siding painted gray with white trim. The only thing that distinguished one from the other was what people did with their gardens, flowerbeds, and decorations.

At the end of Orchard Row sat the superintendent's white house, with a porch around two sides and spacious lawns surrounded by a white picket fence. There was a huge graveled area between it and the Club House, allowing for plenty of parking and a turn around space.

The Club House was the center of camp life. It boasted a pool table, a little kitchen, a stage, and a large dance floor. The school and community got together and put on two plays a year, making costumes and stage scenery, and providing cakes and coffee. There were box suppers too, where the ladies and young girls made elaborate boxes filled with sandwiches and dessert, and the men and boys bid on the box they "thought" belonged to their wives or sweethearts. The proceeds went for various fun things throughout the year. Sometimes women from different countries donned ethnic finery and performed their national dances. In addition, several men were good musicians and the music of two or three violins, an accordion, and the piano made a good orchestra. Every Saturday night there was a dance. I still remember the strains of "Let Me Have This Last Waltz With You" and "It's Three O'clock in the Morning" (it usually was). I can see Mom and Dad dancing, slowly, softly, his arms tight around her. When the music struck its last note, he'd give her a little kiss on the ear and she would laugh and pretend to push him away.

9 Lucy's Bread

*A*lthough the quarry was partially closed and some families had moved away, an air of busy activity enlivened the camp as days grew longer and warmer. Men spaded tiny garden plots. Women raked and furrowed the freshly turned earth, getting it ready to receive seeds carefully saved from year to year, sometimes exchanged from one family to another. A sudden April shower brought out sharp odors of earth and manure and the sweet sap-smell bursting from old cottonwood trees along the river bottom.

Mickie and I, with Eddie toddling alongside, dawdled along, delivering eggs to Mom's customers, and stopping to talk to friends. At Lucy's house, we found her with sleeves rolled up, white flour on her strong brown arms, pummeling and pulling sweet dough for her bread. She braided it into elaborate twists, and then carefully placed the twists on a long board.

Eddie watched, his eyes round with curiosity. He loved bake days. Mom let him help. After rolling up his pant legs and washing his feet, she'd lift him up onto the big round kitchen table, give him a piece of dough, some sugar and cinnamon mixed in a shaker can, and let him make cinnamon rolls. His cinnamon rolls were hard as rocks from so much pounding and kneading, and had an excess of cinnamon and sugar mixed through them, but each of us always ate one and exclaimed how good they were.

"Don't you want to go out and play?" I asked him.

"No, I wanna watch Lucy make bread!" Eddie answered, intrigued by Lucy's preparations, so different from Mom's.

"Come back in an hour and watch me bake," Lucy smiled at Eddie as she set the loaves aside to rise.

We were back in an hour. Lucy placed two long twists on the board, added three large loaves, then picked the whole thing up, balancing it on her head.

"What's Lucy doin'? She's gonna drop it!" Eddie yelled. Then he quickly moved aside as Lucy walked out the open door and down the two shallow steps toward the back of the yard where her conical brick oven waited.

"Where's Lucy gonna bake her bread?" Eddie asked.

"Come along, Eddie, I show you how we bake the bread!" Lucy laughed. She lowered the board with its precious burden to a flat shelf alongside the oven and donning an old pair of gloves, Lucy pulled a triple layer of hot bricks from the oven's square opening, and then, with a long-handled hoe she raked the hot red coals into a bucket.

"See Eddie, I built the fire inside the oven before the sun was up this morning, now the oven's hot inside, all ready for the bread. Now, I sweep it out, and put the bread in—see?" Lucy suited her actions to her words. She brushed out the hot interior of the oven with an old broom, then picked up the long board, shoved it inside, and with expert little lifts and pushes, placed each loaf and twist exactly where she wanted it. Her face red from the heat, she stood up, put her gloves on again and placed the bricks carefully back in the opening.

"There now, just leave it and by suppertime it's done!" Lucy rubbed her hands across her wide hips and stood back with the satisfaction of a job well done.

"Don't you look at it?" Mickie asked, remembering how Mom would peek into our oven.

"Don't need to, I know," Lucy answered.

"Lucy, are you going to bake the bread for May Day?" I asked.

"Sure, every year I bake the loaf for the May pole," Lucy said, her voice filled with pride.

"They've already brought the pole, I saw it in front of the store this morning," I said, thinking of the tall spruce the men brought down from the mountains.

"They were peeling all the bark off the tree," Mickie said.

"Sure, they will also smear it with black axle grease. The slicker they make it, the harder it will be to climb!" I said.

"This year all the men will try extra hard; they need the money so bad," Lucy said.

"I wish Daddy could win, so we could finish our house," Mickie said, a sad note in her voice.

"Well, he can't. He's too old to try to climb that greased pole," I said, then added, "We'd better deliver the rest of these eggs and get home, Mom's going to skin us alive if we're late."

"Come on Eddie. Let's go," Mickie called to Eddie where he was sitting on the ground, playing with Lucy's three boys.

"Tell your Mamma hello," Lucy called after us.

"I wanna see the May pole," Eddie said.

"Not now, we've got to hurry. Later, we'll go over and watch them get it ready," I told him. As we walked along, I wondered if the extra eggs Mom sold for Easter would help buy building materials for the house at the ranch. All the money Dad made now went for groceries and rent with hardly anything left over.

7 The May Pole

I always thought the May pole celebration was a sort of festivity to honor the coming of spring, but Mom said that it was started by the Indians in camp. For years now, everyone in Lime had joined in the fun. The festivities started in the morning with a baseball game. A feast at noon boasted contributions from all the women in camp. In the afternoon there were sack races, egg rolling contests, foot races, games for the kids, a chance for everyone to win some little prize. The crowning event was climbing the May pole.

Bets were high all over camp as the men wagered their hard-earned money on the man they thought could climb the greased pole and snatch the prize dangling at the top for everyone to see. Word went around that the collection taken up this year was higher than ever—a hundred dollars. Mom dressed Eddie in a new suit she had made for him, carefully tucking the sleeves into the pockets and pinning them there; she brushed back his unruly thatch of hair and called Mickie and me to, "Come on!"

Dad had gone on ahead, not wanting to miss any of the ball game, but we were content to go with Mom, listening to her gossip with neighbors, talking to our girl friends, planning the events we might enter, and wondering if we could win a prize.

After the big lunch, most of us drifted away from the park where the long tables had been set up. Mom stayed behind to help the women clean up while Eddie trotted alongside Mickie and me as we made our way toward the big square in front of the Company Store where the May pole dominated the scene.

A circle had been roped off around it. The gleaming pole reached toward the bright blue sky. Its top was crowned with a sack containing Lucy's perfect loaf of bread, a jug of old Dominic's homemade red wine, and the hundred or more dollars heavy in its own pouch—dimes, quarters, dollars, even pennies that everyone donated out of their own pockets. The sack was tied securely to the top of the pole with gaily-colored ribbons that waved in the breeze. Also fastened to the pole and floating to the ground, were streamers of crepe paper in all the colors of the rainbow. Climbing the pole would be the very last thing in the long list of contests.

As the afternoon drew to a close, I saw some of the mothers furtively spit on the corner of a wadded-up hankie, and try to wipe traces of dirt and ice cream from smudged faces. The most particular even hurried their little ones home for a quick change of clothes. Mom came to join Mickie and me, and Eddie immediately stood close to Mom, clutching a fold of her skirt's starched material between his shoulder and chin. His wide blue eyes watched with fascination. Dad appeared, reached down and brushed his hand through Eddie's hair and then sat him on his shoulders.

All at once old Sam struck up a tune that sounded like "Ring Around the Rosy," but with a foreign air. Someone took down the rope surrounding the May pole, and the kids under six surged forward, picking out their favorite colors and taking hold of the streamers. The mothers of the smaller children pushed their shy charges forward, showing them how to hold on to the crisp paper, giving them a little nudge as the music swelled and the kids started to dance around the pole. The winner would be the child who didn't tear his streamer from the pole.

"I wanna dance, too!" Eddie said from his perch on Dad's shoulders, as he caught sight of Celia Jane's red head bobbing among the others around the May pole.

"Next year, honey. You're too little, you might get hurt." Mom forced a smile.

Eddie wiggled on Dad's shoulders. "I wanna dance now! Celia Jane's dancin' and I'm big as Celia Jane!" Eddie started to whimper.

"Wait a minute, Eddie. Then you can watch the men try to climb the pole. Clear to the top, up to the sky," Dad said as Eddie squirmed.

Old Sam struck a shuddering chord and the dance was over. A big teddy bear was going to a child who was too tiny and shy to do much more than stand and clutch at his colored streamer while the rest danced around him. This was the only contest of the day where the weak won out over the strong, but my eyes were too blurred to see which little kid won. My mind was repeating Eddie's words, "I wanna dance, too!" and I wondered how long we could protect him, how long it would be before he would insist on joining in games where some of us couldn't go along.

Eddie apparently forgot his disappointment when the men started climbing the pole. He'd mimic the shouts around us as man after man, naked to the waist, gleaming with sweat and black with grease, muscles rippling and knotting with effort, tried to climb the pole. Each man got three tries. Before each try, he'd rub his hands in the dirt, smear it over his chest, and make the sign of the cross as he said a little prayer that he would win.

Some of them hardly got off the ground before sliding back, and a groan would sweep over the crowd. When young Tony Mangino finally reached the top, clinging there, waving to the crowd before tearing the sack loose and sliding to the ground with his prize, the shouts that filled the air were ones of relief as much as victory.

A street dance would come later. Laughter, music, and half-drunken shouts followed the five of us as we walked home, but somehow our feet dragged in the trampled dirt of the street and our hearts didn't join the festive mood.

8 "It Was Just Pretend"

*I*t was almost June; Dad planted crops at the ranch but there wasn't much rain. If he harvested enough to feed the cattle through the coming winter he would be doing well. Mom wanted to plant trees but realized the logic in Dad's, "No Ethel. Wait until we can move to the ranch for good. We can't come up often enough to keep trees watered. They'd only die."

So Mom tended her little garden in the back yard at Lime, raised more chickens and bought more rabbits. She increased her egg business and sold fryers and young rabbits to a restaurant in town. She saved every penny she could, vowing that by next summer we'd finish the house at the ranch and move there for good.

Eddie loved the rabbits and pestered Mickie and me to let him help us feed them. We brought the feed cans to the shed where we kept the feed and placed them in rows around the sack of rolled barley for him to fill. After many tries, he learned to dip barley from the sack using an old tin cup. He'd push his fat big toe through the handle, using the rest of his toes and the sole of his foot to balance the filled cup on its journey from the sack to the waiting cans.

With the children in camp, Eddie tried to do with his feet everything they did with their hands. He couldn't climb fences, but found ways to crawl under or go around. He carried his toys tucked under his chin, and learned to pull the wagon Dad made for him by tucking the handle under his chin and bringing his square little shoulder over to clutch it tightly. He even hit back with his feet when kids struck at him in childish play.

Eddie constantly snagged his shirts crawling under the fence to play with Celia Jane next door. Woman-like, she had to be the boss in the games they played, and usually Eddie went along with her high and mighty airs. One day, I started toward the fence to call Eddie to come help feed the rabbits. Just then, he came scooting under the fence, his face tear-streaked, angry sobs changing to hurt cries.

I picked him up and held him close. "What is it, honey? Are you hurt?" Not finding any sore spots or scratches, I asked again, "Tell me, Eddie. Please stop crying and tell me what happened! Did you and Celia Jane have a fight?"

"She hit me! I kicked her, too!" Eddie squirmed in frustration and sobbed louder.

"Why did Celia Jane hit you? What did you do to her?"

"Celia Jane was pretendin' she had a May pole and she wanted me to dance with her." Eddie put his head on my shoulder, sobbing harder.

"You'll feel better if you tell Sister what happened. Come on, now. Stop crying and tell me." But he wouldn't. Finally his sobbing stopped and he squirmed against me, wanting down. I knelt beside him, asking once more, "Won't you tell me what happened, honey?"

Eddie shook his head, then in a quiet little voice, he said, "It was just pretend…" and he walked toward the shed, where the feed cans were waiting to be filled, his chubby face thoughtful, streaks of tears tracing the dirt on his cheeks. I was sure that Celia Jane wanted Eddie to dance with her around her make-believe May pole, and when he wouldn't, with a child's thoughtless cruelty, she taunted him because he didn't have arms and couldn't hold hands.

I cleaned the rabbit pens furiously, digging at the corners with the short-handled hoe, sweeping out every little bit of manure and loose straw. As I walked to the hydrant to wash out the water cans and fill them, I wondered how I could help Eddie. It would be six months until his third birthday and already he was hiding his hurt behind a wall of silence. I filled the last water can and placed it in the pen, then walked toward the shed where Eddie would have the feed cans filled and ready for me. But the cans weren't filled—and Eddie wasn't there. Around the corner of the shed I saw Eddie sitting on a piece of a stump that Dad used for a chopping block, his head down, staring at the little circles he was making in the dust with his toes. When he saw me, he looked up, a puzzled expression on his face. He asked me a question I will remember as long as I live.

"Hazie, why don't I got arms like other little boys and girls?"

I sat down on the stump beside him and silently prayed for an answer. "Honey, God didn't give you arms like other little boys and girls," I said, finally, "but I am sure God will give you many other things that will be much better!" I didn't know what else to say. Deep down inside, I was searching for a real answer, something that would make His reason acceptable.

"Eddie, listen to me. I'm sure that each day you will find something new and wonderful to do! And remember, Honey, other little kids can't do anything with their feet or toes." Then I hugged him to me hard, and said, "Okay now, Eddie?" My answer seemed to satisfy him. He smiled up at me and went into the shed, sat down, reached for his tin cup and started filling the feed cans. As I carried the feed cans to the rabbit pens, I wondered how long it would be before Eddie questioned my explanation. But he never asked me again.

Although I knew Eddie's question would hurt her, I told Mom exactly what had happened. She stroked my hair as I sat on the floor beside her chair.

"I've been expecting Eddie to ask one of us. It just happened to be you. I don't know what else you could have told him. We all thank God for miracles, and blame Him for everything unfortunate that happens to us." She was silent. When she spoke again, it was almost as though she was talking to herself, "God did see fit to take away from Eddie. I only hope He will make it up in some way. I am sure He will and perhaps it was done for a reason."

"But what reason?" I asked angrily, wondering how Mom could put so much faith in God who let Eddie be born without arms.

"It isn't for me to question, Hazel. Only to try to understand," Mom answered. "We must make the best of what we are given. Perhaps we will all be better people because of Edward, and God knows Eddie will have to be strong! Yes, Edward will make the best of what he has been given. Let's see that we all do the same." She gave my head a little pat, rose from her chair, and with her back as straight as a ramrod, walked out into the yard.

9 Pedro and Manuel Gonzales

"Well, old girl." By the way Dad called Mom "old girl" I could tell he'd been thinking hard. "I suppose we could build a house at the ranch. But if the quarry shuts down for a few months like it's been doing for the last few years, we might find ourselves in trouble. We might not be able to finish the house, you know."

"I know, Art. But it could be a start. We've just got to build up something for Eddie! Something to leave him when we're gone!" Determination made Mom's voice strong. Then, with a contagious excitement that drew all of us to look over her shoulder, she spread the house plans on the table for Dad to look at.

Dad drew his chair closer. He looked at the plans, then taking a pencil and a clean sheet of paper, he started to do some figuring of his own. "Let's build the house of adobe, Ethel. Be the best thing. Cool in summer and easy to heat in winter. It will cost less, too. We won't need as much lumber and God knows there's plenty of adobe clay on that ranch!" Dad scratched at a little place behind his ear the way he did when he was thinking.

For once Mom didn't defend the soil on the ranch. She was too busy defending the size of the bedrooms, the kind of windows she wanted, and arguing with Dad for more closet space. "And what are these little doo-daddies and circles you've drawn out away from the house?" Dad asked, squinting at Mom's careful plans.

"Why, that's where I'm going to have flower beds and those circles are where we are going to plant trees," Mom said.

"Well, you can get those highfalutin' ideas out of your head right now, Ethel! If you think I'm going to carry water from way below the road for a bunch of posies, you're mistaken." Dad angrily started to push his chair back. He should have known that Mom couldn't think of a house without trees and flowers around it.

"Nobody's asking you to hurt yourself watering my flowers. I'll do it myself!" Mom said sharply.

"We'll help you, Mom!" Mickie and I both spoke at once, then realized our mistake when Mom noticed that we were still out of bed.

"Oh, for Heaven's sake!" Mom laughed at herself for forgetting us. Gathering up the plans and Dad's figures, she hugged us. "We'll all work together, and we'll have the prettiest flower garden anyone's ever seen."

Actually, the water problem wasn't as grim as it might have been. The year before, with help, we had dug a well in the big arroyo on the other side of the road. We hit a vein of water that would keep us supplied for years.

Even before it was warm enough to start making the adobe bricks, Dad hired Pedro Gonzales and his sixteen-year-old son, Manuel. They were Mexicans of Spanish descent and the skill of making adobe bricks had been handed down in their family for generations. They were masters of the ancient art of building a house of adobe that would stand up against the heat of our summers and the bitter cold of our winters. Several weeks before they could actually start making the bricks, Dad picked Pedro and Manuel up at their little ranchito east of Pueblo. As soon as Dad stopped at Lime, where we'd been waiting impatiently, Pedro was out of the car. With an Old World gallantry, he acknowledged Dad's introductions with a sweeping bow, his stiff black hat held across his bony chest. He in turn introduced his son. I almost found myself returning a curtsy to Manuel's bow.

At last we were all in the car, the lunch Mom packed carefully placed on the floor in back. It was Mickie's turn to ride in the middle in front, so I got in back with Pedro and Manuel. All the way to the ranch, they watched the road, mumbling softly. Pedro held onto the side of the car with one hand and both of them held their stiff black hats on their heads, even though a thin black string fastened the hats tightly under their chins. I found out later that they had never ridden in an automobile before, and the mumbling I heard was prayers for their safe arrival.

As soon as we reached the ranch, almost before we could get out of the car, Mom started telling Pedro just where she wanted the house and asking all kinds of questions about foundations and a basement. Pedro listened with his head a little to one side, his thin dark face with its enormous eyes approving or disapproving without saying a word. Manuel was a silent shadow of his father, nodding "Si" when his father looked toward him. Mom had a long pointed stick gouging out lines in the dirt.

"See, I want it right about here, away from the highway and right between these two soft little hills. That way we can look out the living room windows and see the Spanish Peaks and the Sangre de Christos to the south. Don't you think that would be nice?"

"Si, Senora. This is good adobe dirt right here. Over there," he shrugged his shoulders, "it's no good!"

Dad brought the steel ruler, a big ball of binding twine and a bundle of pegs sharpened on one end. Mom held the plans. Dad and Pedro measured, drove pegs, then stretched the twine tight, squaring the corners as they went. Mickie and I tried to keep Eddie from getting tangled up in the string, and finally took him for a walk up to the little hills where we told him he might see a bunny rabbit.

"Oh, look!" Stooping, I pushed aside the dry tufts of grass. "Johnny-jump-ups!" Mickie and Eddie squatted beside me and we examined the tiny yellow violets streaked with brown. Mom always said spring was just around the corner when you found a Johnny-jump-up.

"They're everywhere. And look, here are some Easter lilies!" Mickie flitted from one patch of flowers to another.

"Sshhh. Let's be real quiet now, maybe we'll see a bunny. See their tracks all over these little patches of snow?" I pointed to the snowy areas on the north sides of the bushes and trees, and we stalked along silently. Mickie and I grinned at each other over Eddie's head; he was watching every bush, wide-eyed with excitement, trying to imitate our exaggerated steps with his fat legs.

We were watching him, afraid he might stumble or step in a cactus, when he let out a yell of, "Rabbit! Rabbit!" and jumped up and down with joy as a small frightened cottontail streaked in front of us and disappeared under a gnarled cedar tree. Going up to the tree where the snow lay in a half-melted patch on its north side, we could see the

47

rabbit's tracks where it had kicked up furrows in its haste to find a hiding place.

Coming around the tree into the bright sunshine, we stood in silence as we looked at the country around us. Our hunk of land was located on the eastern slope of one of the plateaus that fell in big steps from the foot of the Greenhorn range of mountains, visible to the south and west. Behind, about three miles to the west, the plateau ended in a sheer drop of jumbled limestone ramparts hundreds of feet to the floor of the valley below. The St. Charles River was a crooked silver ribbon, the same stream that went by the camp at Lime and finally joined the Arkansas River below Pueblo.

Along this fertile valley, too, was one of the ranches the Company owned and one of the dams where water was diverted to the big reservoirs near town that supplied water for the steel mill. Pike's Peak towered in the northwest with an ice cap on its head all summer. To the south, the Spanish Peaks were etched sharply against the blue sky. In the far distance, in almost all directions except east, the Sangre de Christos stretched, their lowest peaks higher than those of any of the other mountain ranges.

We started back to where the house would be. I tried to imagine what it would look like. I wondered how long it would be before we could move in and live at the ranch all the time.

By the first of May, the frost was out of the ground. Dad and Mom, with the dubious assistance of Mickie and me, laid the foundations, careful that they were deep and wide enough to carry the weight of the heavy adobe walls. Pedro and Manuel moved into the little shack on the ranch where they would live until their part of house building was finished.

Pedro was ready to start making the bricks. The spot he chose for their adobe hole proved to be just right. When they started mixing, adding the precise amounts of water and just enough straw as a binder to hold the bricks together, the clay-like soil mixed to a clingy, sticky consistency that turned out perfect bricks. Pedro alone knew the right proportions of earth, straw, and water. He believed the only way to mix the ingredients correctly was to stomp around in the mixture with bare feet.

I'll never forget the look on his face when he figured he had a batch of mud just right! Suddenly Pedro would become a madman, yelling at Manuel in Spanish. Manuel would bring the waiting forms, made of lumber in pairs and sized so that the finished bricks would be six inches thick, twelve inches long, and eight inches wide. Manuel would fill each form exactly. Pedro would tamp the mud into each corner and get all the air bubbles out. After they were all filled, Pedro would check them again, adding a little mud here or there, leveling each brick by scraping a straight board across the top of the form.

Mother Nature took care of the drying process. When the bricks were ready, they were placed on their sides, one against the other, leaning slightly so the air could circulate around them. Cured by the sun and wind, they were almost as tough and hard as bricks that had been fired in an oven.

By this time Eddie was quite sure of himself, and except for an occasional tumble, could pretty well walk and run anywhere he wanted. His greatest joy was to get down in the hole and help make "mud pies." Mickie and I decided that the only way to keep track of him and keep him from upsetting and drowning in the oozy stuff was for us to get down in the hole, too. So we did. We tore the bottoms off our old jeans, making shorts of them, and stomped adobe.

Also, when Eddie was down in the hole stomping around with Pedro and Manuel, we didn't have to worry about him stepping on a rattlesnake. The hole was about the only place we hadn't found them.

By evening we were a merry, muddy mess. Mom would come out with a big scrub brush and a bar of not-so-soft soap and march us down to the well below the road. We'd take turns scrubbing each other, then one of us would push up and down on the old fashioned pump handle, and cold water from the well would stream over our sun-baked bodies. Within a few weeks, the only difference between our coloring and that of the Mexican brick-makers was our sun-bleached blonde hair.

While Pedro and Manuel were making bricks, Dad and Mom were racing against time to get the floor joists bolted onto the foundations and the door and window frames made. In an adobe house, the frames are put in as the bricks are laid. You don't have a framework you can move if you change your mind.

By the time we were ready to return to Lime, Mom and Dad were worn out. Mom was up at dawn doing her housework, getting breakfast, fixing food to take with us for supper, and sorting eggs to deliver to her egg customers, so that we could meet Dad at the quarry at quitting time and go on to the ranch. Mickie and I helped all we could, but Mom was the hub around which the whole family revolved.

"Art, as soon as school is out, can you get Tony Mangino to help? He has a car. That way, the kids and I could go to the ranch in the morning and you and Tony could come up as soon as you get off work."

"I'll talk to him," Dad said. "He's a good carpenter, too. He could go ahead with the house when I have to stop and get some crops in."

"Maybe Tony would witch a well close to the house for us, too," Mom said. "He's witched a lot of wells around here, and none of them have ever gone dry." (Editor's note: "Water witching" is often, and successfully, practiced in this part of the country. Some individuals have the ability, while slowly walking across the bare land with a Y shaped piece of willow branch upturned in their hands to "feel the pull" of underground water. This editor's grandfather successfully "witched" over 30 such wells in Pueblo County in the late 1800's.)

"We'll have to get along with the well we've got for the rest of the year, Ethel. But, next spring, I suppose that's about the first thing we'd better do!" Dad brought the old car to a stop in front of the house, and we were home, but already the house at Lime seemed temporary.

10 *Depression and New Baby On The Way*

*T*he Stock Market crashed. It was October,1929. Banks were closing. There was the smell of fear in the air. Everyone wondered how long it would be before the steel mill in Pueblo shut down.

Dad was working at the CF&I's limestone quarry on Monarch Pass near Salida, Colorado, but wrote that he thought the quarry there would shut down before long as they were stockpiling ore both in Pueblo and at Monarch.

He was right. Just before Christmas he was sent home. Although the Company did keep him on for various jobs that needed to be done in Lime and at other quarries around Colorado and Wyoming, he knew that when these things were completed, he'd be out of a job, too.

One night not long before Christmas, Dad and Mom were sitting at the old, round oak table in the kitchen, talking. "Ethel, I want you to stop worrying. This baby is going to be fine. So we didn't want another child... well, we're going to have one, so we'll do our best."

"I can't help it. I've tried. I was even afraid to tell you!"

"You just stop it, now. Look at Eddie...would you ever have believed he could do all the things he is doing?" Dad got up and pulled Mom to her feet, hugging her and patting her back. Just then she looked over his shoulder and saw Mickie and me behind the stove, listening.

"You two... what am I going to do with you?" She hesitated, then, "Since you heard—you are going to have a brother or sister. It will be due the first part of June."

"We'll help you Mom. We'll do everything we can." Dad and Mom held us tight.

"Can we tell Eddie?"

"Let's wait a while to tell Eddie. He's going to be so excited he'll want to tell everyone he sees. Let's wait until about February. Maybe Valentine's Day. How does that sound?"

"Great," we both said at once.

Christmas was happy for Eddie and the smaller children still in camp. Dad was Santa Claus, as always. When he came to our house, Mom put Eddie in his arms and Dad asked the solemn-faced little boy, "Have you been a good boy, Sonny?"

"I be a good boy, Santy Claws. I be a real good boy." Eddie squirmed and tried to see what Santa was going to give him for Christmas.

Giving Eddie a hug, Santa handed him back to Mom and gave Eddie a big red stocking with hard candy and a big yellow orange in it.

"Thank you, Santy Claws. Merry Christmas."

Dad at his new forge at the Ranch.

Dad spent as much time as he could working at the ranch. Tim Quinn, the mine superintendent, was still living at camp, waiting for his next job assignment. He told Dad to take all the dynamite boxes and any other lumber and things he could use. Frank and Tony were still there and helped Dad until they could decide what they were going to do.

Dad built a large garage with a storage room and a place to put his forge from the blacksmith shop. He used extra heavy timber for the ridge pole and other roof framing so he could install a come-along that would be needed when he pulled engines or other heavy work. Eddie was with him constantly and learned some very colorful language until Mom put a stop to it.

Mom and Dad were worried about the new baby, but they tried not to let anyone know. Mom complained that Dad wouldn't let her do anything, but all Dad would say was, "It's not for me I'm asking, Ethel. It's for the baby. It won't be long now…just be patient."

Once Eddie knew he was going to have a new brother or sister, he talked about it constantly. "My baby sister will have arms and hands. I will take care of her." It was always a baby sister he talked about.

The big day finally arrived. Aunt Jody sent for Dad at the quarry. Dr. Epler was called. I straightened the already clean house, gathered bouquets of flowers and put them in vases, and helped boil water. I felt utterly useless. It didn't help that I couldn't believe "God's will" excused everything from babies being born without arms to crop failures and Stock Market crashes. I needed someone to blame all these things on and it wasn't God. I kept my thoughts to myself.

After what seemed like forever, I heard the cry of a baby. In just minutes, Aunt Jody came out of the bedroom with a squalling, reddish, messiest bundle of humanity I'd ever seen. It had arms, legs, and all the standard equipment of a baby girl. I stood helplessly by while Dr. Epler tied the cord and put drops in her eyes.

"Here, Art." He handed the baby to Dad, mess and all. "You've got a fine baby girl. Take her in and show her to Ethel, then we'll clean her up for company."

Dad didn't say a word, just held out his arms for the baby and went into the bedroom. I watched as Dad handed the baby to Mom, saying, "She's a beauty! She's a beauty!" Mom held her as tears streamed down her face. Then with a big smile, she reached up and hugged Dad.

"Let's call her Shirley Jo after Aunt Jody. Does that sound right to you, Art?" Dad nodded, and patted Mom's arm. Somehow it wasn't long before we were calling her "Jody" and the nickname stuck.

Dad sent me to get Eddie and Mickie. Aunt Jody cleaned the baby and put her in her bassinet. The moment Eddie saw her he started yelling, "I want to hold her, put her in my lap!" And he sat down in his rocking chair, holding out his fat little legs.

Aunt Jody didn't think he should hold her, but Dad said to let him, so Eddie was the first to hold the new baby. When he saw the tiny hands, he almost dumped the baby on the floor in his haste to tell Mom, "This baby has hands, and arms!" He climbed up on the bed and fairly shouted in her ear, "Mommy, listen to me. Mommy, God gave baby sister arms and hands!"

Mom held him close and answered, "Yes, Sonny. Isn't it wonderful little sister has hands and arms? She can help you now, can't she?"

"No, Mommy. I gonna help her. She's too little to help me."

So it was. For days, he met everyone at the door, and told them, "Come in and see my baby sister. She can't walk, but I can hold her."

Eddie sat in his little rocking chair. We would place Jody in his lap. He would manage to get one chubby leg up over her and would rock back and forth singing in his high treble. And he would talk to her in the best baby-to-baby talk we ever heard.

Four days after Jody was born, Lime shut down. It was almost as if the Company had anticipated the market crash and bank failures. Men who were laid off were told that when the quarry reopened, they would be expected to take a physical exam. This caused such hard feelings that Dad thought it would be hard to keep the men from rioting. They all knew that most of the older men would not be hired back and that many would lose their pensions. The Company assured Dad that he would be kept on, perhaps for a while, just a few days a month. At least he wouldn't lose his pension. Also, they assured him that the Monarch quarry would be opening again.

The Company store was boarded up, the doors to the Club House locked, and everyone given notice to move out. Rent was reduced for the few who wanted to stay on. Although the Company didn't shut off the water supply, they didn't furnish electricity and there was no one to haul trash or keep the alleys clean. As more people left, Lime became a deserted, dismal place. The orchard that had been our favorite place to play became a weed-shrouded, snake-infested jungle. The park, once the pride of the camp, had nothing left but the trees to speak of its former beauty. Without water, the grass died and weeds started to take over.

We stayed at Lime that summer because the house at the ranch wasn't finished, but we planned to move in by fall.

11 Bums and A Hero Named Jeff

*M*ickie and I were supposed to be doing the breakfast dishes, but we were sitting around the messy breakfast table drinking a last cup of coffee before getting started.

There was a knock on the door, and I yelled, "Come in." There wasn't an answer, so I thought it was our uncle who was always playing jokes. When the knock came again, we just sat still, and yelled, "Come in, what are you waiting for?"

The door slowly opened and the biggest, tallest, dirtiest bum I had ever seen walked slowly into the room. We were speechless, and scared to death. He came over to us slowly and as we shrunk into our chairs, he said, "I just wanted to know if I could trade this little can opener for a bite of breakfast?"

I finally found a weak voice, and said I would get Mom. Mickie and I both ran all the way to the well, leaving Eddie and Jody there, not thinking until Mom asked us, that the big bum could have cut their throats while we were gone. I didn't like to mention it, but I felt like saying he could have cut all our throats. We couldn't have stopped him.

When we got back, he was standing where we had left him, but talking to Eddie as if they had a lot in common. Mom listened to his story, fried him some eggs, made him pancakes from the batter left from breakfast, and gladly took the can opener. There were lots of bums on the roads those days, but Mom never refused anyone anything to eat.

Sometimes they chopped wood, sometimes they carried water. She fed them and they went on their way. They never bothered us, and never stole anything. Mom said they had a mark on our house and knew we would feed them so they were kind to us. However, she did warn Mickie and I never to open the door again if we were alone.

If the milk cows weren't too far away, Eddie liked to help drive them in to be milked in the late afternoon. One afternoon, Eddie and I started after them. Our old dog, Jeff, followed behind, stopping every now and then to sniff at prairie dog holes. We had just started through a low place where weeds all but obscured the path, when Jeff suddenly went around us and walked on ahead, thrusting his body through the weeds. Although I called to him, he stayed in front of us, walking cockily along. We were just coming to a place where the path started to widen out again, when all of a sudden, Jeff jumped into the air, yelped, then dove into the weeds. He came out with a huge rattlesnake clutched in his mouth, shaking it and shaking it until he was satisfied that the snake was dead, then he laid it down at my feet. Eddie had been walking behind me, but I lifted him in my arms as he started to cry.

Jeff was acting very odd, and I knew he had been bitten. "We'd better take Jeff home, then come back after the cows," I told Eddie. "I think the rattlesnake bit him."

Eddie was scared. "Do you think Jeff will die? He will, won't he?"

I tried to tell Eddie that Jeff wouldn't die, but we were all afraid of rattlers. We had told Eddie many times to be careful because they would kill you if they bit, so he wasn't to be consoled. He sobbed all the way home.

Dad found where the fangs had sunk deep into Jeff's jaw. Taking out his razor-sharp pocket knife, he cut into the place where the snake had left its poison, and although it bled freely, there wasn't much hope.

Mom insisted on putting a poultice on the jaw, but before night fell, the poor dog's head swelled to twice its size. Jeff lay in the shade for three days. He wouldn't touch food or water and just gazed at us when we knelt to pet him. He had a heavy, glazed look in his eyes and didn't wag his tail. Eddie was with him constantly. On the third day, Jeff lapped at the water Eddie pushed in front of his nose. Eddie came running into the house, crying, "Mom, make Jeff something to eat! He drank some water; he's going to get well!"

Mom fixed up some tasty scraps. With the pan tucked under his chin, Eddie ran to the sick dog. We all watched as Jeff tried to stand, but his wobbly legs wouldn't hold him and he slid to the ground. His jaw was still swollen badly. He looked awkward and heavy as he tried to eat. He did manage to eat part of his food. Then he slept.

When he woke, he wagged his tail, ate some more and drank a big pan full of water. We knew he was going to recover. Eddie was sure old Jeff had saved our lives and told everyone, "Jeff knew that mean old rattlesnake was hiding in those weeds. He knew that snake would bite us; that's why he went on ahead and wouldn't come back when Hazie called him. He saved our lives. That's what Jeff did!"

12 *"Man of the Family"*

*W*hen at the ranch, Eddie and old Jeff waited for the mailman every morning. The mailman tucked the letters under Eddie's chin, and gave old Jeff the paper to carry to the house. Eddie hurried to the house as fast as his fat little legs would carry him, asked Mom who the letters were from, then got permission to open them. He sat down, tore off the ends of the envelope, then tucked the letter under his chin and took it to the owner to be read.

There was a letter to Dad from the Company one morning, and after Eddie had opened it, he hurried to the shed where Dad was mixing chicken feed. "Dad, here's a letter for you. Hurry and read it and tell me what it says so I can tell Mommy.

"Well, Son, it looks as if you are going to have to be the man of the family from now on. I've got to go back to work for the Company, away up in the mountains."

"What do you mean, Dad, I got to be the man of the fam-

The "Man of the Family" with Checkers-the-Cat and Juno-the-Dog

58

ily?" Eddie stood in the doorway of the old shed, looking up at Dad, a puzzled little frown on his face.

"Just what I said, Son. You are going to have to help your mother with the ranch while I go away to work, and make some money to take care of all of us."

"I can do it. I can run this old ranch. Boy, wait 'til I tell Mom!"

Dad watched with a sad little smile as Eddie ran to the house to tell Mom the good news. In a few moments he was back, saying, "You better come quick to the house, Dad. Mom doesn't believe me what I told her."

Dad patted Eddie's head. "All right, Son, come on, we'll explain to your mother what this is all about."

Mom didn't want Dad to go, but the need for money won out. As Mom started to gather up Dad's belongings and pack them, Eddie told her, "I'll take care of you, Mommy. Dad said I could and I can."

Mom absent-mindedly wiped a tear on the corner of her apron, then lifted the small boy into her arms, and hugged him tight. "You'll always stay with your Mommy and take care of her, won't you, Son?"

"Yes, Mommy. I'll take care of you. I'll take care of Jody, and Hazie, and Mickie and all the rabbits and chickens. I'll even take care of those darned old pigs." He wiggled to get down, and Mom gave him a little pat on the bottom as he ran off to help Dad get all his last minute packing done.

The next morning we all piled in the old car to take Dad into town to catch the train to Salida. He would have to catch a ride from there with men who worked at the Monarch quarry. Dad was loaded down with a side of bacon, a couple dozen eggs, and all the other things Mom was sure he couldn't do without. She included a jar of horrible-smelling ointment to rub on his chest and a piece of a wool flannel petticoat to tie around his neck, should he happen to catch cold in that high altitude.

Waiting for the train, parting hugs and kisses, yelling all kinds of advice, and then watching the train as it pulled out of sight left me with a sob-stuck-in-my-throat sort of feeling. It was almost good to hear Mom say, "All right now, let's get home and get to work. We didn't do all our chores before we left this morning, and from now on, we are going to have to do Dad's work, too."

Eddie straightened his shoulders and said, "Yeah, you guys, come on. We got plenty of work to do." And he marched straight to the car, opened the door with his chin, and was sitting next to the driver's seat by the time the rest of us got there.

Eddie waited even more attentively for the mailman after Dad left. Dad addressed all our letters to "Edward Higgins," so Eddie didn't have to ask permission to open them. Dad wrote that he found a cabin that could be filed on, which he had done, and moved in. Although we all wanted to go see him, Mom was afraid the old car wouldn't make it, so we had to content ourselves with letters. Mom showed Eddie how to print his name, and it wasn't long before he could hold the pencil between his toes and sign his name.

Mom was confident she could handle the team and raise good crops, surely enough to feed the stock through the winter. She had a big garden, too, and at the ranch, Eddie was at Mom's heels constantly, watching her harness the plodding work horses, telling her how Dad did things, getting in the way and helping all at the same time. He went with us to pump the endless barrels of water it took for all the stock, and even took turns with us at pumping when we would let him. He had a box that he pushed up under the pump handle. Getting on the box, he would grasp the pump handle under his chin, and by raising and lowering his body, he could pump water.

It was impossible to keep shoes on Eddie. He slipped in and out of them, left them laying where he took them off and forgot all about them. He used his toes constantly and the soles of his feet were as tough as leather. Even so, Mom wouldn't let him go to the field with her when she cultivated. She was afraid he might step on a snake or get burrs in his feet. She was a little afraid of the horses, too. If they took a notion to run away, he might get in their path and be killed. So Eddie played with Jody, took care of the rabbits, and went with me when I had to go below the road to hoe the garden. I kept the weeds out of the garden patch, and he loved to pull the weeds that were too close to the plants for me to get with the hoe. He helped me keep the vegetables picked and pulled, and helped string beans and shell peas until the novelty wore off.

13 Prohibition

*P*rohibition even reached to Eddie.

Mom stuffed another clove of garlic under the fat of a big venison roast she was getting ready to marinate before baking the next day. She'd already rubbed it with spices. She called to Dad, "Art, bring me a bottle of beer, I need some of it to pour into the pan for the meat."

"We're about out of brew, but that new batch will be ready to bottle in the morning." Dad opened the bottle and handed it to Mom.

"I don't think we should make any more beer, Art. I'm afraid someone will turn us in."

"Now, quit that worrying. The Feds aren't going to come after small fry like us. Why should they arrest us when they are looking for whoever murdered the Passaranti boys and at least ten other killings they are trying to do something about?"

"I suppose so. Pueblo is getting to be worse than Chicago. Seems like there isn't a week goes by that they don't find a body. It's just terrible about the Passaranti boys. Why, I remember when Hazel and Barlo were in the same grade, he was older but they were still in the same grade." Mom stopped for a minute, thinking. "He had to work on the farm and couldn't go to school steady, like most kids."

"I remember Barlo." Dad shook his head. "They found him in a ditch not two miles from their farm, riddled with machine gun bullets. Hadn't even tried to hide him. Or bury him. It killed the old man. He died two days later."

"And Mrs. Passaranti," Mom hesitated. "Hazel and I saw her in town last Saturday and she didn't recognize me. Her daughter was leading her around and had to tell her who we were."

"I heard they were trying to sell their farm, but haven't had any luck. Probably everyone is afraid to buy it." Dad settled back in his chair.

Mom still worried, said, "Someone stopped by the other day and said the country dances had to close. Gangs from town started coming out and just took over. It's a pity when decent people can't even do a little square dancing when they've a mind to."

Moving his chair a little closer to the table, Dad filled his pipe and started puffing. Between puffs, he said, "Well, I've got this last batch of brew behind the stove, and when it's bottled that's the last I'm going to make. We'll just use it ourselves. I'm not half as scared of the law as I am of some gang that might decide that the nickels and dimes we'd make might belong to them. I don't want anyone coming around here with a shotgun. I might be forced to do a little shooting myself."

We hadn't heard Eddie come into the room, but there he was, eyes as big as saucers. "Dad, you mean we can't help you make beer anymore? You mean I can't put the caps on the bottles?"

Dad slapped his leg, and roared with laughter, "Now Sonny, of course you can help me bottle the beer. It's almost ready, too. Will be by tomorrow, and you and Mickie can help, just like you always do. That wasn't what I was talking about."

Eddie ran to tell Mickie.

"Isn't that just like a child?" Mom said. "You think they've heard all the things you don't want them to hear, and that they will be scared to death, and all they are worried about is getting to put the caps on beer bottles."

The next morning, as soon as he had taken care of the rabbits, Eddie got out the bottle capper and told Mickie to bring the empty bottles for Mom to wash and sterilize. Then he started pestering Dad to get the beer ready.

When they had the whole system set up, Eddie sat down cross-legged on the floor, the bottle capper planted firmly between his feet. Mickie stood ready to hand Dad an empty bottle. When Dad filled it from the siphon hose out of the huge crock, he placed it on the capper and held it firmly. Eddie placed the cap on the bottle with the toes of his left foot, grasped the handle of the capper between the toes of his right foot, brought the handle down strongly, and the cap was on. Good and tight, too. Mickie took the full bottle, placed it with the others, and hurried over with another empty. This was all great fun, accompanied with laughing and joking.

Dad didn't sell any of the beer. He just saved it for company or to share with Frank and Tony when they helped at the ranch.

14 Cab Arthur and Ray Shirley and Eddie and Thumper

*W*e finally moved to the ranch. With Dad at Monarch it seemed very different, somehow, not to be able to say, "Well, wait until Dad comes home and he will decide what to do." Now any decisions to be made were made by Mom.

During the time he had been off work, Dad built new rabbit pens at the ranch along the south side of the garage, making an overhang to shield them. There was a shed for the feed and extra feed and water cans for Eddie. Dad made the catches on the doors so Eddie could open and shut them easily. The height was just right for a little kid going on five.

Mom hadn't bought pigs this year, saying, "I think I'll wait until we get really settled and maybe get a well drilled so we won't have to haul water or go below the road to feed them." Everyone agreed. None of us really liked the pigs and we sure didn't like to pump any more water than necessary to fill the cistern Dad dug.

I was staying with a family in town for school, only getting home on weekends to help with the work. Time went by fast. At Christmas Eddie was five years old; we had a new year starting, and money was so scarce we didn't mention it unless it was absolutely necessary. Mom was a talented seamstress and she cut up some of her lovely long dresses to make dresses for Mickie and me.

Cab Arthur and Ray Shirley, the highway department men responsible for the stretch of highway from Pueblo to Graneros, were a Godsend that winter. They stopped to have their lunch in the warmth of our kitchen and Mom always put a fresh pot of coffee on for them.

Cab emanated strength from the top of his thatch of reddish, un-ruly hair to the toes of his heavy boots. He had piercing, honest blue eyes, and a square jaw that said "no nonsense."

Ray was his opposite in many ways; studious, slim, soft-spoken, and wispy-looking beside Cab. But he could out-work and out-think fel-lows twice his size and estimate jobs in his head faster than most men could with their slide rules.

We had some bad snowstorms that winter, but the road into our house was always plowed out. Many times travelers who were stranded were brought to our house. We put them up until they could go on their way. One Saturday morning in February, Mom picked me up in town. "Get your things together; we've got to hurry and do what I have to do and get back to the ranch!"

By ten o'clock we were on our way home, but already the wind had come up and snow was starting to blow. It was like some heavenly be-ing was dumping giant buckets of snow and ice on our planet.

When we got home, Eddie very solemnly said, "I helped Mickie, Mom, and we got the rabbits extra feed and water and the chickens are all in their house. Mickie brought in extra coal, too." And then he added, "It looks like it's going to be a helluva storm!"

Mom just hugged him. "It sure does, Sonny. I have an idea there are going to be a lot of people staying with us tonight." Cab and Ray stopped by and left a big bag of groceries. "We have a hunch you're going to need some extra coffee and bread," Ray said. "Just say this is a gift from the Department of Highways." He laughed, but was serious under the banter.

By three o'clock in the morning we had thirty weary, frightened, snowbound travelers. We made beds on the floor for the little kids. Grown-ups were standing, sitting, or lying wherever they could find a space. Eddie had long wearied of trying to be the good host and finally let Mom put him to bed.

Six o'clock came and the snow and wind hadn't let up. It sounded like all "The Banshees of Hell" were outside the house trying to tear it down and blow it away. Already drifts as high as the eaves had blown against the house, while in places the ground was bare and frozen.

Cab and Ray came in dead on their feet. They hadn't been to bed in twenty-four hours and they might have another twenty-four to go.

Cab said a dozen volunteers besides their own men had been called in for the emergency. Roads were closed from Wyoming to New Mexico, and no end to the storm in sight.

"Ray" Mom said, "if you will do something for me, I'm sure I will have enough to feed all these people. The extra food you brought has been a great help."

"What can I do, Ethel? Do you need more coal brought in?"

"Yes, more coal please, just pile it outside the back door. And take that wire catcher hanging beside the door. Catch me six of the biggest hens. Just bring them down. I can kill them here in the kitchen." As usual, if we needed extra food, Mom said, "Go catch a chicken." She usually had all kinds of canned goods and a ham or two somewhere.

As Ray went out, she rolled up her sleeves, put a big skillet of ham on to fry and started making a huge bowl of biscuit dough. The stranded travelers were going to be treated to Mom's delicious biscuits, ham and gravy.

I could see Cab's weary face relax a bit as Mom poured him another cup of coffee. "Just hang in there," she said. "It won't take long for this food to be ready. Why don't you just close your eyes for a minute and get a little rest?"

"Good idea," Cab said, and he was asleep with his head on the table in nothing flat.

There were other storms that winter, but that was the worst. It took a week to get all the cars pulled out of ditches and for everything to get back to some sense of normal. Mom started talking about building a cellar to store her canned goods and root vegetables in. She was talking about it at lunchtime one day when Cab and Ray were there.

"What kind of cellar do you need, Ethel?" Cab asked.

"Oh, something about twelve by fifteen, and about eight foot high, so I can put in shelves for my canned goods, hooks for the cured hams and bacon, some bins I can fill with sand for carrots, potatoes, squash, and such. You know, just a regular old root cellar."

"My mother had a root cellar on our farm in Kansas. Of course, it also served as a place to get away from the tornadoes." Cab sounded nostalgic. "You know, we're going to be reworking that bridge over the Muddy starting next week. What do you think, Ray? Could we bring the backhoe out here Sunday, dig the hole, and then take it on up to the site? Then when we pull those timbers, we could bring them down here and put them in place for the roof timbers of this root cellar."

"I don't know why not," Ray said. "Should work out just about right. We'll measure those timbers today while we're up there, then we'll know how big we can make the hole. You wouldn't care if it was a little bigger, would you Ethel?" Ray asked.

"Why no, of course not! It sounds like a gift from Heaven."

Mom got her cellar, not only dug, but with heavy timbers placed where they should be for the roof supports and a sheathing of corrugated iron that Cab and Ray found somewhere. They took their backhoe and placed a couple of feet of dirt on top of it all.

I told Mom it was more like an underground fortress than a root cellar and she just chuckled. "They are so used to building bridges that they do everything extra strong. Wait until your Dad sees this!" She laughed some more.

Yep, I thought, Dad will think, *Hey, that's the first thing dug around here that I haven't been on the other end of the shovel.*

Spring was in the air, bluebirds were flitting everywhere, and there were tiny patches of green showing through the soil. Mom came in one day with six newborn rabbits in her apron. They were all dead. "I don't know what happened," she said. "Old Sue wasn't supposed to have her babies for at least two weeks. I always watch her because she won't take care of them when they first come and usually has them outside the nest. What do you think could have happened?'"

"Gee, I don't know Mom. You've been keeping charts on all the does, haven't you?"

We looked at the chart, and sure enough, Sue wasn't supposed to have her little ones for at least two weeks. Mom was the only one who ever put the bucks in with the does, so there couldn't be a mistake, but something was odd. Mom dismissed it as an unfortunate accident. The babies had been born prematurely.

Not long after, Mom came to me and said, "Come with me, if you want to see something. Be very quiet."

Tiptoeing, I followed Mom to where the rabbit pens stretched in a long line along the side of the garage. Shushing me, she stopped before we reached the corner. We slowly peeked around the corner. Eddie held Thumper, his young Flemish giant buck, carefully by the loose skin behind his neck. With his other foot, Eddie reached up and unfastened the latch on the door to a doe's pen. As soon as the door was unfastened he put Thumper in with the doe. Then he stood back to watch the fun. Thumper, being young and full of life, did all that was expected of him. When he let out his little squeal and fell back on the floor of the pen, Eddie jumped up and down and laughed. He then opened the door, caught Thumper by the back of the neck again and went on to the next pen. The same thing happened again.

I started forward, but Mom grabbed my arm and motioned toward the house. "But Mom!"

"Yes, I know. But what are we going to tell him? I don't know what to do. He'll kill that buck, and it's no wonder my charts have been all mixed up and not working as they should."

We were both laughing so hard tears were running down our faces, but we knew something had to be done. Finally Eddie came to the house, a big grin on his face.

Mom said, "What have you been doing, Son?"

"Oh, I've been letting Thumper play with the other rabbits. He gets lonesome penned up by himself all the time."

"Honey, Thumper isn't playing. When you put him in with the Mamma rabbits that is how little baby rabbits are made." Mom was floundering.

"Is that why all the rabbits have their own little houses, Mom?"

"Yes, that is why. And that is why I have all these charts telling me all about each rabbit." Mom reached for the rabbit charts. "See, I write down here exactly when I put Daddy rabbit in the house with Mommy rabbit. Then I know when they are going to have their babies. That way I can watch them and see that they don't get out of the nest and die." She leaned over the charts and Eddie was intently studying them too.

"Is that why Sue's bunnies died, Mommy?"

"Yes, Sonny. You see, I didn't know, and I couldn't help her."

"Mommy, will all the mamma rabbits have babies where I let Thumper play today?" Eddie was very serious.

"Yes, I imagine they will. I'll tell you what Son, let's go out to the pens and you tell me just which pens you put Thumper in and I will mark it down. From now on you can help me keep track of when the little rabbits are supposed to come. Then after this, we'll both put Thumper in the pens and you can help me with the charts." Mom laughed and Eddie was happy.

I don't know what else she told him, but it wasn't long after that Eddie asked, very seriously, "Mommy, do dogs have to get married to have puppies?"

15 Charlie and Ione Owen and Eddie Starts School

*O*ne lovely Indian summer day, Mom and I were getting the bins ready for the vegetables that would be stored in the root cellar.

A shiny Cadillac pulled to a stop in the yard. A heavy-set, well-dressed man got out. "Do you own that land below the highway with that well and stock tank?"

"Why, yes, we do," Mom said. "How can I help you?"

"I'm Charlie Owen, Owen's Construction Company. We build roads, among other things. Let me introduce my wife, Ione. She's the other half of the team. She keeps the books and keeps the crew straight when I have to be away." He held out his hand to Ione. The woman who got out of the car had short, dark blonde hair with streaks of gray. She had an indefinable beauty.

Mom introduced herself and added, "Please call me Ethel. This is my oldest daughter, Hazel."

"We are going to build a stretch of road through here," Charlie said, "from Pueblo to the Hatchet Ranch, about twenty miles. We are looking for a good source of water and a place to put our construction camp. Is that a good well down there?"

"Yes, it never goes dry. My husband dug it in the bottom of the arroyo, cased it with three-foot corrugated casing, then off-set the pump at the side of the arroyo. The top of the well is cement over a very heavy steel plate so when we get floods, the well won't wash out. However, we have to pump it by hand, we don't have electricity here."

"That's no problem. We have our own generators and other equipment," he said. "We would want room to set up our cook shack, tool shed, bunk house, and room to park our equipment. Also our own house trailer because when we get started, we live on the job. Ione would be here all the time."

"I would like to talk to my husband," Mom said, "but he is working at the quarry at Monarch, so I will make the decision."

Charlie looked over the site, and then we all sat around the old oak table in the kitchen.

"We could pay you five hundred dollars a month for the time we would need the space. I will pay you two cents a gallon for the water we use, metered at the well head. When we are finished, if you can use them, we can leave and place wherever you want, the cook shack, the bunk house, and any other buildings we don't want to haul. What do you think, Ethel?"

I could tell Mom was flabbergasted, but she didn't show it. Her poker face was about as good as Dad's when he had a good hand. "You know Charlie, I think that is more than fair. You've got a deal." They shook hands.

Just then Eddie came into the room, sleepy-eyed from his nap. He looked from Charlie to Ione as he went over to Mom.

Charlie had started to say something but stopped in mid-sentence. They were both staring, not rudely, just dumbfounded.

Ione coaxed Eddie over and he sat on her lap. I noticed tears were streaming down her face as she said, "Babe and I," (I realized Babe was her pet name for Charlie), "we never could have children. You are truly blessed. I'm sure God gave you Eddie to take special care of."

Mom answered simply, "That's the way we feel," and so started a long friendship with two of the most wonderful people we would ever know. Eddie adored them and they loved him in return.

The Owens moved in buildings, equipment, and their house trailer. They brought along some of their own crew and, when necessary, hired men out of Pueblo. It was a very dusty, noisy work site.

Eddie was anxious to start to school but Mom couldn't bear to think of him going all by himself. None-the-less, she talked to the superintendent of schools and received permission for Eddie to go. Also the school's "bus driver," Mrs. Graham, told Mom she would keep an eye on Eddie. The school "bus" was Mrs. Graham's private car. There were only four children to ride the "bus" and only eighteen students in the entire eight classes. Eddie knew all of them, but Mom still worried about how he would get along.

Ione worried too. One day she came back from Pueblo loaded down with packages. "Ethel, come see what I got for Eddie. I hope you won't mind, but I just couldn't resist buying him some clothes for school. What do you think? Will he like them?"

When Ione and Mom showed Eddie his new clothes, he tried them all on. He strutted about the house like a little peacock and Ione laughed until the tears ran down her face. Eddie loved all this attention. He told us all about how he would be going to school next week; how he could already write his name, and told Ione that he wouldn't get his new clothes dirty.

The first day of school came too fast for everyone but Eddie. Mom packed lunch in his little tin lunch pail, and put his brand new tablet with the picture of an Indian chief on the front in his canvas satchel. It had long straps so he could carry it over his shoulder. She had talked to Mrs. Burke, who lived on a nearby ranch, and made arrangements for her son, Karl, to help Ed with his personal needs, like using the bathroom.

We all waited for Mrs. Graham's car. When Eddie was safely inside and beaming out the window at us, we watched until it was out of sight. I turned to Mom and put my arm around her shoulder.

With tears running down her cheeks, she said, "If I could just keep him little. If he could just stay a little boy so I could be with him always. I don't know how I can stand to have him away from me and depending on someone else."

I hugged her tight. "Mom, he's got to grow up. If he takes everything in life the way he has so far, you won't have to worry about him. Just don't let him know that you worry. That will help more than anything."

"Oh, I wouldn't let him know. But, I just can't help it. This is the start of his having to do things by himself. It's going to be so hard for him."

We didn't get much done that day. Ione came up about the time Eddie was due home. We were all there to meet him. He got out, made sure that he had all his school things, and with his cocky little walk and talking a mile a minute, soon put to rest our fears that he might have had a bad day. He told us he could write his name "as good as anybody!" and that he loved his teacher. Thank God!

Mom made a special trip to see his teacher the next morning. Miss Allen told her Eddie had done exceptionally well and had a good start on most of the kids as far as writing his letters and numbers. She said too, that with his sunny disposition, she was sure that he was going to be a joy to have as a pupil. Mom couldn't wait to write Dad all about it and I was proud as I could be also.

Ione and Charlie brought little things for Eddie to put in his lunch pail and some evenings they would stop by and we would all play cards together. Some of the road crew would also come up once in a while just to talk or play cards.

Mickie had met a boy, Wilson Carroll, whose family had a big ranch in the mountains above Beulah. He was out of school, but ran around with the ranch kids. On some weekends, Wilson would stay with us, helping Mom, and carrying Eddie around on his shoulders. Best of all were the nights we stayed home, inviting some of the neighbors over, popping a big bowl of popcorn and making our own music. Wilson would get out his saxophone while Mickie and I took turns on the piano and everyone sang. When Wilson hit a high note on the sax, old Jeff would lift up his head and howl, and Eddie would say, "Old Jeff can sing just as good as anyone."

One day Eddie asked Mom if he could go below the road to visit with Ione. Mom told him "No" but he started out by himself anyway. He reckoned without Jody. Although she was only two, she had a mind of her own. She toddled along behind Eddie and although he told her to go home, she followed right along. He went on through the barbed wire fence, but when Jody tried to follow she got caught on the sharp little barbs. The more she tried to get out and the more Eddie tried to help her, the more she became tangled. Her dress skirt was wound tightly around the wire. Finally, Eddie had to go get Mom.

Mom knew something was wrong when she saw the sheepish look on his face and she could tell he was about to cry. "Mom, you've got to get Sissy loose from the wire. She's crying!"

Mom got Jody untangled, and when she got Eddie and Jody safely to the house, they both got a good spanking.

Dad came home a week before Christmas and said he didn't know when he would be going back. The CF&I was going to file for bankruptcy and none of the men had any assurance as to when they would be hired back—if ever. Dad blamed everyone and everything for the condition the country was in. The farmers didn't have a market for their crops, and it was so dry that many of them couldn't raise anything anyway. It really didn't matter because what they did raise was taken over by the government and stored. Farmers were being told what they could plant and how many head of livestock they could have. More and more banks were closing.

Dad in his dry way, said, "Well old girl, it looks like we're in for one helluva ride!"

We were more fortunate than most. We had food and if necessary, we could sell off cows and chickens, keeping just a few.

Charlie and Ione Owens had been a Godsend. It would be almost another year before the highway was finished and the money from that was more than Dad made working. We were blessed.

That Christmas was the best we had ever had. We were all in good health. Eddie was doing great in school. He had started to call Dad "Art" and when we asked him why, he said, "Well, Art's a man, and he says I'm a man 'cause I help run this ranch while he's gone, so he calls me Eddie and I call him Art." So Art it was.

Charlie and Ione and four of their crew celebrated with us, as did many old friends who just dropped by. Granddad and Uncle Ray came down bringing a beautiful venison roast. Mom baked pumpkin and mincemeat pies and Ione baked a beautiful fruit cake laced with brandy.

Ione and Charlie were more than generous with gifts for everyone. Ione was a great piano player and we ended up by singing all the old Christmas carols way into the night.

"Peace on Earth …Good Will to Men…"

16 I Graduate From High School and On To Beauty School

*E*ddie was Dad's shadow that winter of 1932. If Dad worked on the car or any other piece of machinery, Eddie was beside him, bundled up in a worn-out, made-over coat, slipping his feet in and out of his loafers to hand Dad a bolt or a nut, or give him the hammer or screwdriver. Eddie seemed to know exactly which bolt went where and the reason for it. He learned to swear like a trooper and although Dad never swore in the house or around a woman, he evidently did plenty of it when working outside.

One day Eddie spilled some water on the floor. He went to get a rag to wipe it up, "god-damning" as he went. Mom listened for a minute, then said, "Sonny, after this when you do something and it makes you mad, say…" she thought about a minute, then, "Say, AXLE!"

Eddie thought for a moment, then answered, "That isn't mad enough, Mom."

"Well then, let me put it this way, Son. You're not to swear in the house or around anyone but your Dad. Do you understand me?"

"Yes Mommy. I understand." That was the end of his swearing around any of us.

Mom worked tirelessly to keep everything together. Most of the extra money from the construction company was put away for a rainy day. Dad wasn't working and didn't know when he would be called back. Banks were closing, mortgages being foreclosed.

Mom got so she didn't like to go to town to sell her eggs and pick up what groceries we had to have. Friends she met often had grim tales of losing a farm or having to sell their cattle just to get by. The sun was a

76

ball of baleful yellow in the sky and everything was bone dry. Dust storms bad enough to sandblast the paint off a car were more frequent. A sense of doom permeated everything.

The highway was taking shape. New roads were going everywhere—to the cook shack, to the Owens' trailer, the well, the bunk house, to where all the equipment was parked at night.

Our house sort of sat aloof in its own small way. With woodwork still unpainted, the outside walls the gray color of adobe, the shingles on the roof stained but not colored, it gave the appearance of all-the-sameness. Mom had planted a little silver poplar at the back of the house and Dad planted four elm trees in the front. He named them after his four children and ironically, although I was the oldest and tall and skinny, it was the short, fat tree he named after me. All these tiny sprigs were growing, but they were as dust-enveloped as everything else.

Roosevelt ran for president and promised everything. Dad said he would probably get elected but didn't see how he could work miracles. Mom said it would take God to stop the drought and bring rain and she didn't think we could count on that.

Dad kept busy building Mom a slat-house to dry vegetables in the next season. He also built a smokehouse. Mom bought two pigs to supply meat for the table.

Mom worried about the drought. Even if there was money to buy feed, you couldn't buy it if it wasn't available, or if it cost more than keeping the cattle was worth. One day she said, "You know, Old Gus has been pestering me to buy that Guernsey milk cow. But I just can't part with her."

I couldn't imagine Mom selling Bluebell, although a more worthless cow you've never seen. Mom spoiled her so rotten, and she wouldn't let her milk down for anyone else. Mom fed her bran when she milked to keep Bluebell from kicking the stool out from under her. She was just plain mean, but she had beautiful calves.

Eddie piped up, "You know what Dad told me? He said next time Old Gus came around, he was going to give him that gawl-danged cow. That's what he said." He added the last as he saw Mom start to bristle.

"Well, he'd better not sell Bluebell or any other cow on this place without asking me. He just better hadn't!"

"Now Mom. He was only talking," I said. "You know Dad wouldn't sell one of your cows without asking."

"Hazel, you know as well as I do that your Dad hates this dry land farm. Oh, he's worked hard at it, but that doesn't mean he likes it. Before we got this place and he and your Uncle Ray could figure on the quarry shutting down during the summer for a while, it was different. They had that big combine and would go out and thresh wheat. They made good money. When the price of wheat went way down they couldn't make payments on the combine and they lost it. That took the heart out of both of them for farming."

"Well Mom, you'll have to admit that from a farming standpoint, this is a sorry place. If we have rain, it's all right for a few head, but if we don't, and can't raise feed, it's no good." I loved having a place of our own, but I wasn't kidding myself that this ranch would ever make any money.

"Well, we're not going to get any more dry weather. There's no use asking for trouble before it happens."

That was her way of putting out of her mind something she didn't want to think about. For the time being, her answer had to be sufficient.

One day Ione was visiting. "Ethel, how do you keep your hair looking so good?" she asked Mom as she pushed an unruly lock from her face.

"Hazel does my hair for me. She has a real knack." Mom was proud of the way I experimented with different styles on her.

"How about doing mine?" Ione asked. "I hate taking the time to go into town once a week and I would be glad to pay you what I pay the beauty salon there."

"Why sure, I'll be glad to do it if you think I can. I can do your manicure, too."

Not long after this, I was just finishing combing Ione's hair, when she turned to me. "Hazel, what do you plan to do when you graduate from high school?"

"I don't really know. I wanted to go to college, but I know that is an impossibility. I'm going to get a summer job, and try to decide what to do."

"Have you ever thought about going to cosmetology college? I think you would be very good at it, and it is one of the few things a woman can get into without a lot of education and make good money."

"I've sort of thought of it, but it takes quite a bit for tuition and books, and I just don't have it." The last year all I had thought about was how would I be able to make enough money to live on and help out at home.

"Charlie and I know Bob and Bonnie Chesney, who own Bonnie's Beauty College in Denver. They have the best school in the state. I took the liberty of talking to Bonnie the last time I was in Denver and this is what we could do. We would be glad to pay for your tuition, books, and uniforms, and see that you have spending money. We have friends where you can stay and work for your room and board. Would you mind working for your room and board?" Her words were almost tumbling over one another.

"Gosh, no." I didn't know what to say. "I would be thrilled to death to be able to go to beauty school. I just never thought it could be possible!" I was almost stuttering with excitement.

"Well then. We'll get it all arranged. You can start this fall. It's an eight month course, so you will graduate next spring." Ione was beaming, and I could feel a tear slide down beside my nose.

"How am I ever going to pay you back? Just tell me. I'll do anything!" I threw my arms around Ione and hugged her tight.

She hugged back, "Just be the best hairdresser ever to graduate from Bonnie's. That is all the thanks Babe and I will ever expect. And, we know you will always take care of Eddie."

I hadn't planned to go to high school graduation. I didn't want to ask Mom for the money to buy a dress that I probably wouldn't wear again, so I just put it out of my mind.

When Mom picked me up the weekend before graduation, Eddie sat beside her with a big grin on his face. "Come on Hazie." He kept pestering me to hurry. "We're goin' to go shopping. We're goin' to pick out your graduation dress and I get to help!" He was so excited he couldn't keep still.

"Mom, I wasn't planning on going to graduation. I don't have to go to get my diploma." I knew she was saving every penny she could.

"Don't worry. She's gonna spend some of the money, Dad told her to." Leave it to Eddie to know everything, I thought.

We spent the whole afternoon looking at things we knew we couldn't afford and talking Eddie out of wanting to buy everything he saw. Our final choice was a lovely white crepe dress, with a slightly full skirt that made me look like I had curves I didn't have. Eddie had to feel the material and then he wanted Mom to buy me new shoes.

Eddie couldn't wait until we got home and he practically ordered me to try everything on for all the family. He was just as proud as I was. When I looked out from the stage at graduation and saw them all sitting there, it made me appreciate how hard my family had all worked to get me to this point in my life. I determined it would not be in vain.

Charlie Owen often stopped by to ask if Eddie could go with him on the job. Of course, Mom would say yes. One day Mom called to me, "I don't believe what I'm seeing. Charlie is letting Eddie steer his car. Come look!" I looked and sure enough, Ed was sitting on Charlie's lap, with both feet grasping the steering wheel.

When they came back at lunchtime, Eddie couldn't wait to tell us how he had driven all over the job all by himself. Mom just smiled and gave Charlie a big wink.

It wasn't long before Charlie was taking Eddie with him everywhere, showing him how the huge machinery worked, letting him help to shift gears, and telling him the why of it all.

17 *Eddie Flies a Plane*

*W*hen Ione suggested that Mom, Eddie, Jody and I come to Denver with her to get me started in beauty college, I knew summer was over.

Mom asked Ione, "Do you think we could be back by seven? I have some chores to do that I can't trust anyone else with." She didn't want to admit she was the only one who could milk Bluebell.

I packed what I thought I would need, and we set off early the next morning. Mickie talked Mom into letting her stay with Helen, her girlfriend in Pueblo, saying she didn't want to go to Denver.

It didn't take long to get there in Ione's Cadillac. She was a fast driver. As she said, on the kind of jobs Charlie did, you didn't waste time getting from one place to another. He flew his own plane from one job site to another much of the time.

Their home was on Monaco Drive in Denver. I had expected a nice home, but this spacious, spread-out brick rancho was sumptuous. The sunken living room had a fireplace along one wall. Ione told us the stone had come from the family ranch in Wyoming. When Mom saw the kitchen, I could imagine her thinking "Oh, what I would give to have a kitchen like this!'

Everything was furnished beautifully and in apple-pie order. I knew Ione must have help, but I didn't realize at the time that she had a full-time housekeeper.

Ione showed me to a bedroom and told me that this would be my room until I got settled in at the Bonner's, where I'd board. Then she said, "Charlie will be home in a little bit for lunch, then I have a surprise for you."

Eddie spoke up, "What kind of surprise?"

"Oh, I can't tell you, that would spoil it. You'll just have to wait." She smiled at us as if we were fellow conspirators.

Eddie fidgeted until Charlie came home, but Charlie wouldn't tell him either. He just said, "After lunch, you can come with me while the ladies go over to Bonner's." Eddie had to be satisfied for the moment. I was curious, too, but I didn't ask.

After lunch, Mom and I got in the car with Ione to go meet the Bonners. It seemed like a long way to the suburb of Englewood. Ione showed me where I would catch the streetcar to go to beauty school in downtown Denver.

We stopped in front of a red brick bungalow. Paint peeled on the white trim. The porch swing hung from one corner on a chain, the chain on the other side missing altogether. And the yard, I didn't dare look at Mom, knowing how she felt about yards.

Ione knocked. The door opened wide and Grace Bonner said, "Come in, don't mind the house. Dave's home this weekend, and when he's home I don't do a thing." Grace was so beautiful that I almost stared. She had black, curly hair, gray eyes, and the whitest skin I'd ever seen. Mom's skin must have looked like that when she was young, I thought.

Dave ambled in, about six foot three or four, sort of awkward and handsome in his own way. Dark hair and sooty brown eyes, but the first thing you noticed was his smile. It started with a crinkle at the corner of his eyes and his whole face lit up. By now, everyone had been introduced and I was standing there tongue-tied. Grace said, "Come on back, I'll show you your room. It's not very big, but you'll have the run of the house, so I hope it won't be too bad."

The room was great with a single bed, old dresser with a mirror, and an old fashioned library table and chair. I was thrilled with it and told Grace so. It would be great to have a room of my own. It would be nice to be treated as one of the family. So often, during high school, when I had worked for my room and board, this wasn't so. It was "eat in the kitchen, don't use the front door, are you sure you dusted all the book-shelves…?"

Mom liked Dave and Grace and I knew she was happy about the kind of home I would have. Their little boy, Dave, Jr., got up from his nap and we took to one another immediately. He was a small edition of Dave with Grace's gray eyes.

We said good-bye until I could get everything together and went back to Ione's house. Before long, Eddie and Charlie came back. I could see that Eddie was bursting with excitement.

Hopping from one foot to the other and looking up at Charlie, he said, "Please, can I tell them now?"

"Yes, go ahead. I can see you can't wait another minute."

"We went up in Charlie's airplane!" I heard a gasp from Mom. "And he let me drive it! We flew over the mountains and the tall buildings and scared a jackrabbit off the runway!" Eddie was talking a mile a minute.

Mom couldn't keep still, "What do you mean? You scared a rabbit off the runway?" She looked at Charlie.

Charlie explained, "I keep my plane at a small airport out east. It is more convenient for me because I can come and go more easily. The fellow who owns the airport is also my pilot when I have to go on long trips. He flies me in and I stay while he comes on back. You would have been very proud of Eddie. He flew that plane like a pro." (Eddie was five and a half years old at the time.)

Mom just answered, "I don't know what I'm going to do with you two."

Charlie took Mom, Eddie, and Jody back to the ranch. I stayed in Denver with Ione. That night, when I finally got to bed, I lay awake. I just hoped that I wouldn't disappoint everyone who had done all these wonderful things for me.

18 *Dad Sells Bluebell*

I hadn't been in Denver much more than a week when I got a letter from Eddie. It was addressed in his best printing with a return address in the upper left hand corner. He said that Dad sold Bluebell to Old Gus and that Mom was mad. *Madder than a hornet*, he wrote. I had to laugh because I knew Mom had to help him write his letter. He ended it with lots of XXX's and 000's for kisses and hugs and wrote his name.

Mom's letter covered two pages. Dad had sold her cow. Mom knew he had mis-represented Bluebell because Old Gus paid thirty dollars, which was top price. Mom feared that Old Gus would come knocking on the door and demand his money back.

Mom wrote that Owen's Construction was leveling places to set the buildings they were going to leave when their job was finished. Mom thought they'd be around until around Christmas time.

It was so good to hear from home. I didn't realize how very home-sick I had been but after a second reading and a good cry, I felt better.

Ione picked me up at Bonner's the day before Thanksgiving. When we arrived at the ranch, Eddie ran out before the car stopped. I grabbed him, gave him a big hug and then it was Ione's turn. Jody had grown. She waited her turn. When Mom folded me in her arms, I felt I was truly home.

After a while, Ione went on down to her trailer and Mom and I sat down with Dad at the old oak table and caught up on everything.

Ed and Jody were playing school; something they did constantly, Mom told me.

"Where's Mickie?" I asked.

"Oh, she's staying with Helen tonight. I guess a bunch of them are going to a school party. Wilson will bring her out about noon tomorrow." Mom got up and went to the stove and stirred a pot of stew she was fixing for supper.

Eddie came in with a sheaf of papers tucked under his chin. He spread them out on the table. Jody was right beside him, trying to help. "How are you getting along, Eddie? Do you like school?" I asked as I looked through all his work.

"Sure. It's lots of fun. We color and do hard arithmetic and write. And see, look at this..." He held a paper out to me, after deftly sorting through the stack with his toes. "This is a shadow." And he read slowly, but carefully:

> "I have a little shadow,
> That goes in and out with me,
> And what can be the use of him,
> Is more than I can see.
> He is very, very like me,
> From his heels up to his head,
> And I see him jump before me,
> When I jump into my bed."

After catching his breath, he continued, "Then we pretend to draw our shadow after we get through making the words on the paper."

"Oh, that must be fun! Which do you like to do better, to make the letters for the words, or to draw your shadow?" I asked.

"Well," Eddie hesitated as if he were bothered about something, "I'd rather make the letters because ...well, because the other kids always draw their shadows with mostly their arms stuck out, and I can't draw one like that. I can just draw a little shadow."

"You can draw your foots stuck out," Jody told him.

"Eddie, you know the shadow you draw is just your outside you, don't you?" I asked.

"Yes, I know that. But that's what you see, isn't it?" Those wide blue eyes looked up at me with doubt mirrored in their depths.

"We all have an inside us that is much different from our outside us," I said. "Take old Jeff, for instance. He's old and he really isn't a pretty dog. In fact, as dogs go, he's downright ugly. But we think he's beautiful! It's the same way with people!"

"Old Jeff is too beautiful! He's the most beautifulest dog there is!" Eddie was insistent.

"That's what I mean. If you were going to draw old Jeff's shadow you would give him the most beautiful shadow you could draw, because that is what you know about him and what you see. On the other hand, take the Devil. Why do you think you always see pictures of him with horns and a long, forked tail, and a horrible face? That's because we know that inside, he's mean and wicked. Right? That's the shadow he would make. We know he is evil."

"Is that why we always see pictures of God with a beautiful face, beautiful robes and colors, and a rainbow around his head?" Eddie asked.

"Of course, because that is the shadow he makes. We know He is good; and though we've never seen Him, if we drew His shadow, we'd draw Him a beautiful shadow, wouldn't we?"

"I'm gonna be real good, Hazie, so Eddie can draw me a bootiful shadow!" Jody was already getting out the brightest crayons she could find. At almost three, she was learning fast from Eddie.

"But Hazie," Eddie still wasn't satisfied, "if I don't have arms, I can't draw my shadow with arms, can I?"

"No, I guess you couldn't do that. But I think you could draw your shadow a little taller, and maybe brighter, because on the inside you are bright and shiny! You are going to do so many wonderful things, and be so happy about them because you can do them, that the 'inside you' will shine right through. So, the shadow you make will be big and bright and shiny, too!"

"Well, I guess now I can draw just as good a shadow as anyone!"

"Sure you can. So get out your crayons and get to work." I left them sitting there, crayons strewn over the floor, as they attempted to put my words into color.

Thanksgiving of 1932 wasn't very happy for any of us. Mom didn't laugh as she usually did and Dad just clammed up. All Eddie and Jody knew was that Mickie and Wilson were married and had gone to live at the Silver Circle Ranch in the mountains. Mom told them that we would come visit.

Sometime in the past Mom had met Wilson's mother, Annie Carroll, a mean, cantankerous soul, without a good word to say for anyone. Everyone said she was "meaner than mean." Mom worried that she wouldn't be good to Mickie, but I had a hunch that Mickie would give her mother-in-law a run for her money.

Mickie and Wilson stopped by at Christmas. Mickie told Ed and Jody that they would have a little niece or nephew in May. They were thrilled and couldn't stop asking questions. Mickie seemed more like her old self and talked about how she rode after the cattle with Grandpa Carroll. Neither Mickie nor Wilson mentioned Annie Carroll.

Charlie and Ione came by the house. "Ethel, why don't we stake out just where you want those buildings set?" Charlie asked, "And I'll have the men get that done."

"I just can't believe you're going to leave them," Mom said. "It will sure be a help to me this winter to be able to get the stock in when I have to." She hurried to get her sun bonnet and called to Eddie, "Son, do you want to come with us?"

"Sure Mom, and I'll tell Charlie where we're going to fix your chicken house." He sort of snuggled up to Charlie as they walked ahead up the hill. It didn't take long for them to decide where everything should go and set stakes for the corners.

"I'll get my man up here to level this properly. Have Art put in cement pylons. He'll know what I mean. There's no use putting in foundations when you're sitting on solid rock and when we grade it down, that's what we're going to have." By now, Charlie was used to the layers of limestone that underlay so much of the ground in this area.

When Dad got home Mom told him about the pylons and Dad said he would get them done right away. Then he surprised all of us, "You know, I've been thinking. Now would be a good time to drill a well up there on top of the hill. I could put in a big water tank so it wouldn't require a lot of pumping and let it gravity flow to everything below it. Charlie said he would leave the generator and that would take care of power until we get Rural Electrification out here. That's probably going to be a few more years. What do you think, Ethel?"

"How much would it cost, Art?"

"Charlie knows a driller with a rig that will handle a deep well. He's going to be drilling holes for Charlie on that Trinidad job. Charlie says I can help this driller and he can stop by on his way to the Trinidad job for the few days it will take."

"I'll bet Charlie finagled a price out of him." Mom couldn't keep the excitement out of her voice. "But sure, if you think we can handle it, let's do it!" She picked Eddie up and gave him a big swing.

Charlie bid on the Trinidad job and got it. Then he got a job in Laramie, Wyoming, that he hadn't counted on. Ione was taking care of setting up camp in Trinidad and Charlie was flying back and forth between jobs. Eddie was broken-hearted that they were going to leave the ranch. Ione told him that Trinidad was only eighty miles away and that she would take him with her to the job whenever she could.

When Charlie needed a dynamite man, Dad had part-time work. This helped our finances and also helped to pay for the well and the tank without dipping too heavily into savings.

Eddie spent every minute he could watching them drill the well. The driller, Ned Haines, was a bluff, hearty older man with a curly mustache and twinkly blue eyes. Eddie especially liked it when he would stop operations long enough to drop a bucket down into the hole and bring up sediments, that he would then analyze.

"What does it look like now, Mr. Haines?" Eddie would ask, trying hard not to get in the way as he watched Ned pour the contents of the long bucket onto the ground.

"Well, Eddie, we're going through some heavy black shale and we're right at six hundred feet. We ought to hit the second Dakotas any minute now. And when we hit those 'red beds' we ought to hit a good stream of water." On the way down, they had hit two good streams of water, but Haines was sure if they went deeper they might hit artesian water.

The day they hit the "red beds," Eddie ran yelling to Mom, "Come quick. We're going to hit a gusher!" Wherever he had heard that expression, no one knew. But although they didn't hit a gusher, they did hit a stream of water that came within a few feet of the top of the well.

Another thing, which even baffled Ned Haines, was that enough gas came from the well that if you lit a match it would burn in a solid fan of flame for almost ten minutes. Ned told Dad that he should think of some way to capture it so it could be used but, over time, the gas output dwindled until there wasn't enough to bother with.

Charlie had one of his backhoe men dig a hole for the water tank and left it for Dad to cement in when he had the time. The well on top of the hill was finally a reality.

19 *Bluebell Comes Home*

*C*harlie and Ione were on their way to the job in Trinidad. They gave me a ride home to spend a couple of days with my family.

It was a January weekend. Eddie was helping Dad cement the water tank. It wasn't cold enough to keep them from their underground plaster job and Dad wanted to get it finished.

Mom stuck her head over the edge of the cistern. "Art, get out of there and come down to the house!" The tone of her voice had a no-nonsense sound to it and Dad clambered up the ladder, helping Eddie, who was right behind him.

"Ol' Gus is back with that Bluebell cow and he says you've got to take her back. If you don't, he's going to report to the Cattlemen's Association that you pulled a raw deal on him!" Mom was worried. Maybe she should have spoken up after all when Dad told Ol' Gus that Bluebell was a good milk cow. Mom knew she was the sorriest cow in the whole herd, but even so, she loved her. It would serve Ol' Gus right to get the worst of a deal for a change. He'd skinned Mom and Dad plenty of times.

"He can't make me take that half-breed critter back, Ethel! Why, he'd want his thirty dollars back, and it took the last cent of it to pay the taxes on this gawl-danged dry land farm.

"It isn't that I care what Gus says to the Cattlemen's Association. Everyone around here knows we're honest and just trying to get a start. It's just his gawl-darned attitude. He sure doesn't mind digging a man when he's down and out. By God, what I've made, I've made fair and square. I'm sure not planning to build up a herd on other people's troubles!"

Everyone knew that Gus had made the money to pay for his new thousand-dollar bull by making sharp deals; he even bragged about it when he could get anyone to listen.

"Art, my little Art," Eddie was trying to soften Dad up by using his pet endearment, "If we get some white-faces, can we belong to the Cattle Man's 'sociation?"

Dad didn't answer Eddie's question as he exploded anew. "That danged no-good cow! You spoiled her so rotten no one could get near her, Ethel. Why she never had a decent calf in her life, but that doesn't give that crooked cow trader any call to make me take her back! It was a good deal; Ol' Gus said so himself!"

Mom didn't want Dad to know how much she would like to have Bluebell back, so she changed the subject. "He's probably mad as a hornet because he couldn't keep Bluebell out of that herd of prize-winning Herefords he sets so much store by." Mom paused to wipe her face with the hem of her apron. "You know how she is about fences. She was starting to make eyes at the bull when he bought her. He just couldn't keep her penned up until he found someone else to buy her, I'll bet."

"What do you mean when they make eyes at the bull, Art?" Eddie asked. "I didn't ever see them make eyes."

"That just means they're flirting, Son. Don't ask so many questions. I'd better get down there and see what that old son-of-a-gun is up to!" Dad frowned. His torn, worn overalls flapped around his skinny shanks as he hurried to where Ol' Gus waited beside his truck.

Mom followed. When they reached Ol' Gus' truck, she tried to honey him up with, "Looks like we might get a little moisture on our wheat, doesn't it?" She smiled and looked up at a puny cloud.

Ol' Gus wasn't smiling as he said, "You folks deliberately misrepresented that so-called milk cow you sold me. Why, she won't give her milk down lessen' she's stuffed with feed while she's bein' milked! Why, I can't sell that cow to nobody knowin' what she is!"

Mom spoke up, "Well, Gus, you expect to feed a cow you are milking, don't you?" She ignored Dad's baleful look.

"An' another thing, that cow doesn't have no teeth!" Ol' Gus was chewing his wad of tobacco so hard his jaws tied and untied with the effort. This was too much for Dad.

"By God, Gus! You're lying about that. Leastwise, how could she have bit you that day when you were feeling her teeth?"

The day Ol' Gus bought Bluebell, he stuck his hand in her mouth. Bluebell clamped down so hard, he let out a yelp. Any stockman knew you didn't feel a cow's teeth to tell her age.

"Art, Bluebell's teeth are all smoothed off," Mom said in a small voice. She fidgeted the toe of her worn, brown oxford a little deeper in the dirt of the road.

"What do you mean, 'smoothed off'?" Dad's look said 'I wish you'd keep your female trap shut!'

"Well, Art, Bluebell just naturally wore her teeth down trying to chew the short grass out of these rocks. If you'd paid any attention to her, you'd have known."

Dad knew when he was licked. "Well, Gus, this being the case, I reckon I ought to take that cow back, and I will. But, I can't give you your thirty dollars right now."

"What do you mean, you can't pay me my thirty dollars?" Gus demanded, hackles rising again.

Dad answered, "Just as I said. I can't pay it now. If you'd come day before yesterday, I had it sure as shootin' but today I haven't. I can give you my promise that I'll pay you the thirty dollars when I thresh my wheat. How would that be?"

"Well, I could take your word, Higgins, but I don't do business that way. You could just sign this note I have here; I'll have to charge you a little interest on that, too. And I'll be around when you thresh." Gus had his pad of made-up notes and a dirty stub of a pencil already out.

Dad sighed and signed while Mom and Eddie hurried up the hill to get the corral ready for Bluebell.

Dad finally came up to the corral and started throwing things around something fierce. He snorted as Eddie remarked, "Bluebell sure is glad to be back to her own little home."

"Let that be a lesson to you, Son. Don't you ever trust a woman. If your mother hadn't let me get into that deal, letting me stand there and tell Ol' Gus what a good cow that half-breed critter was, we wouldn't be in all this trouble. I hadn't better catch either one of you feeding that no-good cow any bran, either!" Dad stomped around, raising a dust cloud.

Eddie didn't say anything until Dad had started down the hill. "Boy, Art was really mad, wasn't he, Mommy?" He'd seen Dad mad when he was fixing the car or working on the pump, but this was the first time he had ever seen him mad at Mom.

"Don't worry now, Sonny. We'll save a little out of the egg money to buy some bran for Bluebell. Your Dad will get over this."

20 "Sawuting" the Flag and Bluebell's Calf

*W*inter was over, Easter just a few days away. April showers hadn't done more than dampen the surface of the earth. Already the sun was parching and curling the tender shoots of grass and wheat as they tried to grow through the hard ground.

Edward "Eddie" Ernest and Shirley Jo "Jody" Higgins

I came home for a few days at Easter. Jody was just three years old, Dad was working at Monarch, and Eddie would pass into second grade as soon as school was out. He and Jody played school constantly. They had little slates and Eddie would tell Jody, "Now write on your slate just exactly like I do. Then you won't be so dumb when you go to school."

Jody would try. Once in a while she would try to hold the chalk between her fat little toes, as Eddie did, to write. Eddie would look up from his printing. "No, Jody, you've got fingers. You can't do it with your toes!"

"I wanna do like you do," she would answer, but after trying for a time, she would give up and scribble with her chalk all over the slate, instead of trying to print.

Then Eddie would really get disgusted, and say, "If you can't try, you're never gonna get to go to school!"

One day, as I started to go into the room where they were playing I heard Eddie say, "All right, say after me…'I pledge allegiance to the flag'…pretend that's the flag up there." I could see that he didn't quite know how to explain to her how to salute. Jody started to repeat after him, but he stopped her, and said, "No, you're supposed to be saluting all the time you're saying it."

"But how …how do you 'sawut'?" Jody asked.

"You do it with your hand, like this." Eddie sat on the floor and put his foot to his head. Then holding his foot across his forehead, he re-cited the pledge. Jody looked at him, very puzzled.

"Yeah, but how do I do it?" she asked.

"Oh Jody," he said in a disgusted tone of voice. "I showed you, and I showed you. Here …now you stand up straight and I'll just put your hand where it's supposed to be!" He got her to stand up straight near a chair, then crawling up on the chair, he stood up, braced himself against the back of the chair and the wall, then taking her little hand in his toes, he lifted it to her forehead. After much straightening of fingers and tucking of the thumb under the palm, he was satisfied.

"Now, don't move your hand, and go look in the mirror." He jumped off the chair and followed her to the bedroom, and stood behind her. "Stand up real straight, keep your hand just like I put it and say after me…"

I followed, tip-toeing softly. I could see them in front of the low dresser. They stood solemnly and very straight. I would have given anything to get a picture of them at that moment. When she had recited after him, word for word, with only a few mistakes, she turned to him, "Eddie, how do *you* 'sawut' at school?"

"Why, I just stand up real straight," his voice had been faltering when he started to explain, and his eyes were downcast, but now he raised his head and his eyes brightened, as his voice became strong and sure. "I stand up real straight and I say it real loud, and I pretend I've got arms and hands and I salute the flag. Just like anyone else."

"That's as gooder as anything!" Jody caroled. "Wait, just wait until I show Mommy how I can 'sawut' the flag of 'Merica!"

There was only one thing they disagreed on. Eddie wouldn't let Jody play with the typewriter Charlie and Ione gave him. Neither could he understand why his teacher wouldn't let him do his lessons on it. He used it at home and could write fairly well with it. During the winter while Charlie and Ione were away, he would come to Mom and ask, "Mom, will you write what I tell you, so I can type-write a letter to Charlie and Ione?" So Mom would write what he asked her to, then he would laboriously copy it.

However, after Dad went back to Monarch, Eddie printed his letters because he wanted Dad to see how well he was doing in school. Dad kept all his letters. The first one he received, the printing was scrawled all over a full page of paper:

> 'Dear Art. I like to go to school. I lik my techur fine. I got the gum you sent us. I wuld lik to see you, you little Art. Do you see the ring arond the moon to nite goin to snow. Good nite, a kiss love XXXX OOOOO Edward'

At four, Jody was at an age when she imitated everything everyone did. She and Eddie picked out the dresses they wanted Mom or me to wear when we went to town and sometimes made too-frank comments on how we looked.

Pushing Jody into the kitchen one day and trying to act very stern, Eddie said, "Look at her, just look at her!" He waited for our attention: "She looks just like a little hussy."

I looked and forgot to wonder where he had heard the word, "hussy," but he had used it well. Jody had gotten into "likstik" and painted on a huge mouth, used plenty of rouge, and over it all had smeared some of Mom's powder. As if this weren't enough, she had gotten into my cigarettes, that Mom didn't even know I had, and had one lit. She had on the jacket to my suit, with a belt pulled tightly around her waist, my only high heels, and was carrying her little play purse.

Sensing that we weren't nearly as mad as we could have been, she slanted her eyes, and grinned wickedly up at us. She lifted the cigarette, curled her fat little finger, took a big puff, and blew smoke into the air.

Eddie was still glowering. "Look at her, she does too look like a…"

But Mom cut him off before he said it this time. "Don't say it, Sonny. But," she had to laugh, "I have to agree with you. She does." Then to Jody, "All right, Jody. Mommy isn't mad this time, but come on and let me wash all that stuff off your face, and where did you get that cigarette?"

She glared at me. I knew that she knew, and that if she thought anyone was a hussy, it was me.

Easter was over. I went back to beauty school.

On May 15, 1933, I had a call from Mom: "Hazel, can you come home for a few days? Mickie's gone into the hospital and I would like to be with her when her baby is born."

I made arrangements, caught the bus, and was there in no time. Mom was already at the hospital and the kids had endless questions. I answered them as best I could.

The next morning Mom called from the hospital. Mickie had a beautiful baby boy named William Arthur Carroll, after his grandfathers.

The day before I had to go back to Denver, I was helping Dad with some pens near the lower well. He decided that eventually he would make a loading chute for the cattle near the well in the arroyo. When Mom came after him, she was upset. "I know you can't hear too well Art, but Hazel, you should have heard me calling."

"Well Ethel, what's so important you have to keep me away from my work?" Dad was a little put out. It wasn't often we got to work together and we were enjoying ourselves.

"Come on! Hurry up!" Mom hurried toward the corral. "I want you to see Bluebell! If Ol' Gus ever hears about this...!"

Dad dropped the hammer he'd been using. His face showed genuine alarm. Mom opened the gate. She pointed toward Bluebell and the tiny, wobbly-legged calf at her side, saying, "Art, did you ever see such a perfect white-face in your life?"

With his foot, Eddie petted the still wet, curly flank of the calf at Bluebell's side. The little heifer bucked away on unsteady legs and Dad laughed out loud.

"Bluebell!" The cow turned a surprised eye at being addressed by Dad. "It's going to be worth a heap more than thirty dollars just to see the look on Ol' Gus's face when he comes to collect. Why, when he sees that calf is the spittin' image of that prize-winning Hereford bull of his, Ethel, he'll pay us two hundred dollars just to get that blasted, little white-faced heifer off the Higgins' farm!"

Mom and Eddie grinned at one another. Then an incredulous smile crossed Mom's face as Dad went into the shed and brought out a bucket and spilled some bran in the feed trough for Bluebell.

"Hey Mom!" Eddie yelled. "Look, Art's feedin' bran to Bluebell!"

"Yes Son, I guess your Dad's happy now. At last he's finally got a good-looking Hereford, sired by a registered bull. Now he thinks he's going to be a cattleman." Mom smiled again. "But most of all, he's the first man in all of Pueblo County that ever got the best of Ol' Gus!"

21 *Dust Bowl and Rattlesnake*

I graduated from cosmetology school in June of 1934 and went to work for Helen Powell in Trinidad. One day Helen decided we could take a long weekend. I was home by ten Saturday evening.

"You'll have to get used to the windows being covered up," Mom said. "The dust and wind have been so bad that I try to keep everyone in the house. When we do go out, we wrap wet rags around our faces."

"I know, Mom. I was hoping it wasn't as bad here. Yesterday in Trinidad, I had to go to the bank, and it was scary. In the middle of the day the street lights were on, the cars had their lights on, and it was so gloomy. The wind on the ground was still and quiet and the dust sifted down from the heavens as if God were sitting up there with a giant sifter filled with earth, slowly shaking it on all the bewildered mortals."

"Yes, we don't have to read about the 'Dust Bowl', we're in it!" Mom answered.

Everything seemed to be against us. There hadn't been much snow during the winter and now there wasn't any rain. The wind seemed intent on moving our little bit of topsoil to some other state, then blowing theirs back to us. Smothering clouds of dust settled everywhere, making shifting dunes that reached to the top of the fence posts.

Sweeping everything in front of them, hot, dry winds, sand-blasted the paint off the cars that crawled along the highway, their lights during the day making only little, futile tunnels through the dust. The wind actually wrenched dried tufts of wheat from the fields taking the soil along with it. The soil disappeared until in some places flinty ribs of stone showed through.

The cattle grew thinner and thinner, wandering around looking for little nips of grass.

Dad and Mom went about their chores with wet kerchiefs tied around their faces, red-eyed, and worried. Mom kept wetting the sheets she had draped over the windows. She only let the kids go out to play when the wind wasn't blowing or the dirt sifting down. She was afraid they might contract the dreaded "dust pneumonia."

I didn't tell her that I had been doing work for Ed Sipes at his mortuary. Every day a family, some with all their belongings tied to their car, would come to the mortuary. Someone had died from the pneumonia, most of them old or weak, and they were looking to get them buried. They knew they had to have a death certificate, but I'm sure that a lot of bodies were sleeping their final sleep out there in the shifting dunes.

None of the bereaved families had much cash and what they had they needed to keep in order to try to get away from this area. Ed Sipes traded burials for old furniture, dishes, whatever. Most were too proud to ask him to do what had to be done for nothing, so the pile of furniture and household goods behind the mortuary grew.

I did the ladies' hair for nothing and learned to apply the makeup used by morticians to make a person look more life-like. My pay was the gratitude these poor, worn-out, worn-down humans gave me when they looked at some relative's face and said, "She looks better than she did in life," and they would then shake my hand with tears in their eyes.

When Eddie and Jody could go out of the house, they would hurry to the barn to play with Buttercup, Bluebell's little heifer. After they had chased her for a few moments, they would go to the coolest part of the barn. Rooms were marked off with a stick in the dirt. Bits of broken china were in the corner of one area for a kitchen. Everything was fine until Eddie ordered Jody to go get the broom and sweep their imaginary floors.

As she had already pretended to do the dishes and make the beds, this order to sweep the floors was too much. Jody poked around in the yard as she pretended to look for the broom, and when Eddie called, "Come on, now! Get your work done or your Mother is gonna give you a spankin'!" she ignored him.

She spied the short-handled broom Eddie used to clean out his rabbit pens. It was half under an old door lying on some small rocks in the yard. Instead of doing what she was told, Jody began to jump gleefully up and down on the door, yelling that she didn't have to mind. "It's just pretend! I don't have to sweep the floor!" She yelled as she jumped.

Eddie had to assert his authority so he rushed over, "Come on, now, Jody! You wanted to play, so do what I tell you!"

Jody kept right on with her jumps and yells, and was so excited by her own actions that she didn't notice the change in Eddie's voice when he yelled, "Jody! Get off that door! HURRY! GET OFF THAT DOOR!"

Jody didn't pay any attention. Eddie made a running lunge at her, knocked her clear off her feet and off the door, and before she had a chance to get up, he rolled her over and over, several feet from the door.

Jody got up, fighting mad and starting to cry, but stopped in mid-sob as she looked up and saw Eddie's white, frightened face and heard what he said. "Get in the house! Quick! There's a great big rattlesnake under that door! He almost got you, Sissie! He had his head up over the edge and he hit at your leg! But he missed!" He was out of breath, but he yelled for Mom.

"Mom! Mom! Come quick! Hurry!" He screamed as they ran for the back door.

Mom was greeted with such a chorus of, "Rattlesnake! Bit Jody! Door!" that the first thing she did was grab Jody up in her arms to see if she had been bitten.

When she realized that Jody was all right, she went to the shed and got the hoe. Lifting the door gingerly with the hoe, then letting the door fall to one side, she exposed Mr. Rattlesnake. There he was, "death coiled" and ready to strike! His spade-shaped head moved slowly from side to side as he surveyed his enemy. Mom didn't give him a chance. She whacked off his head with one quick blow, then dug a hole and buried it. She looped the still-writhing body over the hoe and hung the dead snake belly side up over the barbed wire fence.

"If you hang a snake with his belly up," Eddie told Jody, "it's supposed to bring rain!"

The old legend didn't work and we didn't get any rain, but Eddie did insist that Dad pinch the rattles off the snake's tail. Eddie had a pint fruit jar almost full of rattles from snakes we had killed on the ranch.

Eddie was eight and in the fourth grade. Sometimes Mom worried that she shouldn't have let him start school when he was five, but it didn't seem to bother Eddie. He got good grades in everything but deportment. Sometimes he would get a "D" in that area. Jody would tell on him, saying, "He wiggles his ears and all the kids get to laughing so hard the teacher can't shut them up."

His strong legs made him a good runner on the softball team. He was the marble shooting champ. He would get down on one leg, and holding the other leg out in front of him, he could grasp the biggest aggie between his big toe and the one next to it and really give it a send-off in the right direction. All the kids would hurry through their work so they could fly kites as a reward. He loved kites and got to be an expert at making them, raiding Mom's old clothes bag for rags to make long tails.

He was at home with the kids he had grown up with and when a new family moved into the area, it didn't take long for the stares and whispers to stop as they accepted Eddie.

Dad had a box of leather straps, buckles and sliders, and bits of old harness kept in a big box in the garage. Eddie dumped it all out, and sitting on the short stool Dad had made for him, he sorted through the pieces until he had what he needed for a special harness. With painstaking care, he measured the pieces and fit them on Old Meg, our very patient goat. When Eddie was finished, he hitched Old Meg to the wagon and talked Jody into getting in to it. He gave the goat a flip on the rear and away they went. If she didn't upset the wagon on a tree root or get tangled up in a cedar tree, it made for one heck of a ride.

Dad gave Eddie an old Ford coil. Eddie worked for days until he figured out just what made it work and how to hook it up to all kinds of things. He learned how to thread a needle and sewed buttons on his clothes. He got interested in arrowheads and with some of his schoolmates, made an arrowhead collection.

When he was trying to figure out how to lift something or make something work for him, he would try various body positions, grunting with effort, sometimes falling or having to let go. Sometimes he just couldn't make his toes obey what his mind was telling them, but he never gave up.

Eddie couldn't swim, so when the kids played hooky and went swimming in Greenhorn Creek, which ran below the school, he went wading and caught water snakes, which he flipped at the girls to make them scream.

He never got over the embarrassment of having to ask someone to take him to the bathroom, but did if it was necessary. With this too, he worked out a schedule so that it was seldom necessary for him to go while at school.

22 *Clarence Edward Carroll*

$\mathcal{M}$ ickie had her second baby, a boy named Clarence Edward Carroll after Eddie. Mom had seen Mickie a couple of times and went to the hospital when the baby was born. I hadn't seen my sister since her first baby arrived.

Mom decided that we would make the trip to Beulah. Eddie and Jody came along, but Dad stayed home. We left early in the morning. It took us about an hour and a half to make the trip.

It was almost Halloween. In the little town of Beulah, mailbox posts had been turned into scary ghosts and hobgoblins. Shocks of corn, and pumpkins with their Jack-O-Lantern faces sat on the porches, ready to greet or scare small children.

As we got closer to North Creek and the Silver Circle Ranch, the area became more mountainous with Ponderosa pines and Silver spruce scattered here and there. Mahogany brush had already turned a bright russet. On the high slopes, aspen trees were in full golden glory.

Clarence had been born on September 12th. Mom hoped that he would be born on Dad's birthday, September 3rd. I guess she hoped it would soften him up a bit.

Wilson's Dad was known to be a good rancher. His fences were mended, his fields irrigated properly and weeded. Many said he raised the best Timothy Hay in the valley.

We met Mr. Carroll as he was coming to the lower ranch driving a herd of Herefords down from the summer pasture. Mr. Carroll was tall, taller than Wilson, with sun-reddened cheeks, a thatch of brownish hair flecked with gray poking out from under his Stetson. He had a jovial way about him. His plaid flannel shirt stretched across the muscles of his back as he stepped down from his horse and strode over to the car.

He reached a hand out to Mom, "Come up to see that new boy, I'll bet." He gave us all a proud smile. "He's going to have to go some to keep up with his big brother. They're going to be a pair to draw to."

"We've wanted to come up. I don't trust this old car too well but we decided we'd just take a chance. Hazel came in last night and we wanted to get up here before the snow flies."

"Yes, so far we've been lucky. Well, go on up to the house and as soon as we get these cattle turned in, we'll be up." He mounted his horse and giving the reins a flap, started after the cattle, turning them away from the green morsels of grass they had found along the creek.

As we drove into the yard, I saw Annie Carroll come around the corner of the house. We parked in the yard and she called out, "Come on around back, we're all out there on the porch."

For a minute I didn't see Mickie, then my eyes caught a flip of white and there she was. She was hanging diapers. There were almost two full lines and these were country clothes lines, at least thirty feet long, stretched tight between two 4"x6" posts, braced solidly.

"Well, looks like you've got a job, Sis. Can I help?" She looked worn to the ground. Where was my happy-go-lucky, to hell-with-it little sister?

"Sure, you can hang out the rest of this basket while I scrub the next load and get them in the rinse water." She went over beside the irrigation ditch and before I could help, up-ended the dirty rinse water into the ditch and started pumping water into buckets to fill the tub again. No hot water here, I thought. Then I noticed the heavy iron grate over some cinder blocks with a blackened tub setting on it. My nose told me, "lye water" half filled the tub. Two babies in diapers and if the other facilities were as primitive as this, this would make an old woman out of Mickie pretty fast.

When I came back to where she was rinsing little shirts and night-gowns, I asked, "How's it going for you? Where's Wilson?"

She turned to me with the old belligerent look on her face, "Everything's fine. Can't you see? An old witch to talk to, all she does is bitch... and Wilson went to the dance at Boseker's last night and hasn't dragged in yet. And I'm here with two little babies hanging around my neck!" Her tone was bitter and defeated.

"How about Grandpa Carroll, does he help you?"

"Yeah, he does. All he can. A few times when I was able to get away, he's taken me riding to Silver Circle. It's so beautiful up there, calm and peaceful. But there's always hell to pay. Annie makes a big fight and he's miserable, so it doesn't happen often.

"Not much I can do right now, but it won't be this way forever." She had a determined look in her eye, and I knew she would think of some way to make this mess work.

"Let me know if I can help. You know I will." I gave her a hug.

Mom had been attempting a conversation with Annie. She came over now to where Mickie and I were rinsing clothes and told me. "Go talk to Annie for a bit. I want to talk to Mickie."

"How has your summer been, Annie?" I asked, and then added, "It's so much cooler here in the mountains than it is where we live."

She gave a grunt that passed as part of an answer, and then fixed her black eyes on me, "Don't try to talk your sister into leaving here with those two boys." She gave me a baleful look.

"Oh, I wouldn't do that. I'm sure you are all getting along just fine. I would like her to come and visit me though, when the boys get big enough to leave them with you for a while."

"I'm not any baby sitter. I raised my family." She drew her lips into a thin line and that was the last word she said.

Grandpa Carroll came up about then, took us into the house to see the babies, both sound asleep, and offered us a glass of water. We looked at the two tiny boys, remarked how adorable they were, and said good-bye.

Annie Carroll never said another word.

It was a very silent ride home. Eddie and Jody didn't say a word. They had been allowed a quick peek at the babies and I knew they were very sad with that inborn knowledge little kids have when they know something is wrong.

It would be two years before I'd see my sister again.

23 A New Willys and A New Gas Station

I'd come from Trinidad to spend a weekend at the ranch. "Come on Hazel," Eddie said. "I want to take you for a ride. I've really been practicing, and you'll be surprised at what I can make that car do!"

"Just throw my seat in for me, and we'll be off." He motioned to the leather-covered cushion Mom had made for him so he could see through the windshield with ease. I was tall, and at ten years old, Eddie's legs were as long as mine, so it was no problem for him to reach the brake, clutch, and gas pedals.

He got the car started. Then, with his left foot on the steering wheel and his right foot rapidly going through all the motions of feeding gas, using the clutch to shift gears, and giving it some more gas, we were off.

"How did I do, Sis?" A tremor of pride made his voice shaky.

"Better than I could, Eddie. I always have trouble keeping this old relic going and getting it through all the gears without screeching something. I think you did great!"

"Well, I have to thank Mom for letting me practice. I backed over the harrow and punctured a tire. When I got stuck and I almost backed into the well one day, she yelled and I stopped just in time." He was grinning.

"Dad turned me loose in the old corn field and told me that when I could keep the car going without stripping all the gears, I would probably be a pretty good driver.

"He said that when he came down from Monarch the next time he was going to get Mom to sell some of the cows and buy a new car. Do you think he meant it?"

Mom shed a few tears for every one of her pets, but they were sold and the money was in the bank. Dad was down from Monarch and he and Mom were ready to go to town.

"What kind of a car do you think I should buy, son?" Dad asked Eddie.

"I guess a Chevy, but you know best, Art." Eddie took it for granted that he would be allowed to go to town on this very important occasion.

When the morning school bus pulled up, he couldn't believe it when Dad said, "Well Son, have a good day at school. Your new car will be here when you get home."

That afternoon, as the school bus neared the house, Eddie was already half out of his seat. The bus driver handed Eddie's lunch pail to Mom. Eddie yelled, "See you all tomorrow!" Then he was off like a flash.

"Oh, boy! Look at that Willys! Here Mom, take my books!" as he shrugged his shoulder toward Mom. He ran toward the car, eager to inspect the green sedan, all agleam in its newness.

"Art! can I drive it?" Not waiting for an answer, he slipped his shoes off, pulled the door open and slid under the wheel. Mom came out of the house with his leather cushion, and tucked it beneath him.

Eddie exclaimed over all the modern gadgets on the dashboard. Dad got in beside him. Eddie drove up the hill toward the barn, then around the field a couple of times and finally, with a flourish, stopped at the front door and got out.

"Gosh, Art! She sure does handle nice!"

Dad lifted the hood. Eddie clambered up onto the fender and they were lost for a moment as they looked in awed silence at the engine.

"Well, Art, I'll bet we won't have any trouble starting this little sweetheart this winter." Eddie nodded as if to verify what he was predicting.

"I wanted to buy the Chevy because that is what you wanted, Son. But, this car figured a lot less and money is important." Ed nodded in agreement and they were buddies again.

Eddie finally talked Mom into turning a small building the Owens' had left behind into a filling station.

"Mom, you know you can't depend on enough rain to make crops here. Some years there is good pasture and some there is none."

She had to agree, so Dad took a couple of weeks off work to get the station in shape. It had windows across the front, a cement floor, and a cement slab about three feet out in front of the building. Dad painted it white with dark green trim.

The gas pump was impressive with its long hose and a nozzle that Eddie said he could easily handle. Seven-year-old Jody insisted on participating. Eddie promised she could open soda bottles and help keep the place in order.

A huge Coca-Cola sign covered one entire wall of the building.

"But Eddie," I asked, "You don't sell Coke, do you?"

"No, we sell Nehi. I saw that sign down the highway one day. It needed paint and didn't look like anyone was taking care of it. So I called the sign company and they told me I could have it if I hauled it off. It seems no one had paid rent on it for a long time and they didn't want it. So I got it." He sounded proud of himself for making such a good deal. "Something really funny happened one day," He chuckled. "It was a really hot day, not long after we opened. A big car drove up. A man got out, went around, and opened the back door for a very dressed-up lady. She looked me up and down like I was some kind of a worm. Then she said, "I want an ice cold Coca-Cola."

"I told her we didn't sell Coca-Cola, but we did have Nehi, and she gave me a dirty look. 'You've got a Coca-Cola sign all across the end of your building,' she said. 'You'd better take it down if you don't sell Coca-Cola!'"

"I said, 'Lady, if I took that sign down the whole building would fall down!' It was worth it just to see the look on her face as she about tripped over herself getting back to the car." Eddie bent over laughing.

"It really wouldn't fall down, would it?" I asked.

"Yep, it sure would. That sign is that wall of the building."

From the start, the station was a small success. It was about sixteen miles from Pueblo at the end of a long climb. People who formerly had stopped for water for their over-heated engines now stopped for gas and other things, just as Eddie had predicted.

Eddie and Jody took care of the station all that summer of 1937. Eddie could take the cap off a gas tank, then getting his shoulder under the long hose, he would disengage it, put the nozzle in the tank and press on the lever that released the gas. Jody handled the oil cans because they were awkward for Eddie to carry. One of the first things they wanted to add to their supplies was an oil can opener with a spout.

Cab Arthur and Ray Shirley, the highway maintenance men, were a great help to Eddie. They brought twenty-pound cakes of ice every other day to put in the old-fashioned cooler to keep the pop cool. Sometimes they would bring a traveler who had run out of gas so Eddie could loan them a can with enough gas to get to a filling station.

Eddie could open the pop bottles and hand them to his customers. He could make change quickly and accurately. When he and Jody weren't waiting on customers, they kept their books and cleaned the station.

Eddie used his skill with tools to make shelves. He and Mom made a counter and some higher shelves. Eddie and Jody decided to put in a stock of candy and gum, promising each other that they wouldn't eat all their profits. The station didn't make a lot of money but it made enough to help, and Eddie was proud of it.

One day a car drove up and a tall, skinny fellow got out.

"I'm Ed Orazem, reporter for The Chieftain Star Journal newspaper. I've heard a lot about you and your little business here. I would like to do a write-up for the Sunday paper. Would you be interested?"

"Why sure. I guess so. I'd have to talk it over with my Mom." Eddie looked at Orazem and with a shy smile said, "Come on into the house, we'll talk with Mom."

It was arranged that Orazem would bring a photographer in the middle of the week to take pictures of Eddie and Jody tending to business and Eddie driving the car.

The year before, Eddie, who wrote by putting his tablet on the floor under his desk and holding a pencil with his foot, had won a national penmanship award. It got a write-up in "Ripley's Believe It Or Not," but this was different. It was more personal and he felt as though Ed Orazem was his friend. Orazem brought his photographer out and they spent almost half a day taking pictures and talking.

On Sunday, Eddie, Mom, and Jody went to town early and bought the paper. They purchased a copy to send to Dad at Monarch. They couldn't wait to get home, so they stopped alongside the highway to read it. Ed and Jody were thrilled to see themselves in print, and Mom said that Orazem had done a fine job.

The headline read, "Boy Without Arms Goes Into Business," then the pictures: Eddie and Jody standing in front of the station, Eddie handing a bottle of soda to an imaginary customer, Eddie driving the photographer's car and last, Eddie holding one of his pet rabbits on his lap.

I liked all of it but the last paragraph.

"Edward does not rue the fact that he was born without arms, accepting his plight philosophically. And thus far, he has not missed his arms any more than you and I have missed our wings. What he wants to do, he does with his feet."

Of course he missed having arms. He desperately wanted to be like other boys and girls. The fact that he did his best, kept up a good front, and had such a great disposition was due to many things. Mom and Dad refused from the start to spoil him and treat him differently. They didn't let him feel that he had to be protected. Too, as he grew up, he naturally did with his feet what most children did with their hands. What he couldn't do, he taught himself to do or found a way to compensate.

He had been lucky, starting school in a one-room school with children he knew. The fact that there was always so much to do around the ranch with Dad away most of the time hurried Eddie's responsibility beyond his years. Learning to drive at only 10 years old set him apart from his little circle of friends and gave him a feeling of importance. I just hoped the good start he had would sustain him through all of the things to come.

24 Christmas 1937 and A New Baby

I left my beauty shop in Trinidad in the good hands of my operators and went to spend three weeks at the ranch. I'd missed Eddie's eleventh birthday and wanted to make it up to him, plus get to be with everyone for Christmas.

I drove into the yard two days before Christmas. Eddie rushed out of the house with Jody, Bill, and Bud on his heels. Bill was four, a wiry little kid with dark hair and gray eyes. Bud, three, was a blond replica of his mother, Mickie. I hadn't seen them since the disastrous visit when Bud was only two weeks old.

Eddie hurried to the house, talking as we went, "Bill and Bud have been helping Sis and me make decorations for the tree, hurry, come and see!" The little boys hung back, shy as little kids can be with strangers.

Mom gave me a big hug. Mickie was right behind her. We all talked at once, trying to catch up.

The boys were standing by a big box in the corner, eyes bright with excitement. "Look, Hazie," Eddie said. He reached in the box and started pulling out chains made of colored paper. Next came chains of cranberries and popcorn. By now, Bill and Bud were showing me what they made and they were all bragging at once. How wonderful it was to have so much happiness over simple Christmas decorations and the joy of making them.

"Your Dad will be coming in on the train about ten in the morning," Mom said. "We'll meet him and get any last things in town. When he gets out here, he can take the kids and go cut the Christmas tree." It would be a first for Bud and Bill but the rest of us loved the ritual of finding the perfect tree.

That night, Mickie excused herself early, saying she was tired.

Mom and I sat near the old heating stove, planning what we had to do for the holiday. "Once the tree is set up, it won't take long for the kids and Art to get it decorated. He will have to be sure the candle holders are just right. And let's see…" Mom's voice trailed off as she thought of everything that had to be done.

"What do you want to cook, Mom? I can get that done."

"Yes, that would be great. We'll make a list. I think Mickie will go in to the hospital sometime tomorrow. She's ready, I can tell."

Dad arrived looking just great for a sixty-one-year-old. He was a few pounds heavier, but just as tough as ever. As soon as he finished a late breakfast, he and all the kids piled into the car. Eddie drove as they headed for the cedar and pine-covered hills behind the ranch. By mid-afternoon the tree was up, decorated by many small hands and Dad had already supervised the fudge making.

One of Mom's big turkey gobblers was ready for the oven, stuffed with her special dressing. Baked ham, mince meat and pumpkin pies were cooling on the table. Somehow, Mom found time to make her special divinity and penuche candy, saying, "Christmas wouldn't be Christmas without it."

Mickie washed all the kids' hair and I offered to do hers, knowing she must be tired, but she said she wanted to do it herself.

"When are you going to have this baby?" I asked.

"You know what? I'm going to give you all a present, a Christmas baby!" She laughed a wry, little laugh.

And she did. Mom and Dad took her to the hospital before midnight and they made it just in time. Not long after midnight, Mickie had the first baby born that Christmas Day in Pueblo.

Dad came back early in the morning. When he went to bring Mom home, he took the kids so they could look at the new baby.

Dyanna Sue Carroll

"She's got black hair and she's tiny. Mom named her Dyanna Sue Carroll," Eddie joked, "They should have named her Christmas Carroll."

"How come Mickie let Mom name the baby?" I asked Eddie.

Eddie answered with a little laugh. "Mickie told Mom that as long as she would be taking care of the baby for a while, she'd just as well name her." I didn't think this was very funny.

25 A New Menace

As Mom was getting Eddie ready for bed a couple of nights later, she called me into the bedroom and took off his shirt. "What do you think? Look at the way Eddie's back is growing. It has a curve sideways and you can see a curve going out." Mom tenderly stroked his back.

"I don't know, Mom. Eddie, does your back hurt?"

"Well, sometimes. When I study a lot or write a lot, or maybe, when I'm trying to work on something." He didn't say any more.

Most of the time he is stooping over, I thought. "Can you sit up any straighter when you are doing these things?" I asked.

"Not really, Hazie." He squirmed. "I would almost have to stop doing anything. You see, I naturally stoop over; I have to, to see what I'm doing."

"I think we should see Dr. Norman," Mom said. "I've been told he is the best bone doctor in Pueblo. What do you think, Son?"

"Well, I don't want to go to the doctor, but I will if you want me to. Please get me ready for bed, Mom. I'm sleepy."

He didn't appear sleepy. I couldn't help but think that he wanted to be alone with this unknown menace.

Later that night, Mom and I sat up talking. I tried to reassure her that Dr. Norman would have some answers, but her fears were too real.

"My God! No Arms! Isn't it enough for him to bear without this? And now his back is growing crooked!"

"Mom, there will be something to help. There's just got to be! I'm sure Dr. Norman will know what to do."

❖ ❖ ❖

After a thorough examination, Dr. Norman didn't mince any words. "Eddie, you have a definite curvature of the spine developing. It is called 'scoliosis' and the very fact that you use your feet so much is making it worse. If you could, for the rest of the school year, try not to use your feet so much and try hard to sit very straight. It might help."

"And if he isn't able to do that," Mom said, "What then? Is there anything to stop the curvature?"

Dr. Norman hesitated. Finally he said, "If that doesn't help, when school is out, I would like him to come in to the hospital and be put in a cast. That might arrest this spinal curvature.

"If it doesn't, I would like to have my brace maker, Bruce Johnson, work with me to devise a brace that you can wear, Eddie." Somehow I felt he didn't know exactly what to do.

"What do you say, Son?" Mom asked Eddie.

"I don't know. It is going to be awful hard to try not to stoop over. But I can give it a try." Eddie didn't sound too enthused.

"That's all I ask, Eddie. Just give it a try. We'll find something that will work for you." We made an appointment for three weeks down the road.

Mom kept me posted on Eddie's progress. It was almost impossible to keep Eddie from stooping over with all the things he wanted to do. By spring, the curvature was more pronounced, and Eddie agreed to the cast.

Visits to Eddie in the hospital were heartbreaking. His cast started at his hips and reached to his neck. Eddie didn't complain. He kept all the kids on the ward laughing. He would wiggle his ears, tell stories about the ranch and his pet rabbits, and how he drove the car.

When we'd visit him he always seemed cheerful, but we could see how he hated the inactivity. The boredom of being cooped up indoors and encased to the point where he could barely move was mirrored in his eyes when he talked about the ranch. He was sure we weren't giving his rabbits enough to eat, and asked constantly about how the car was working, and how Mom was getting along without him.

When Mom and I went to tell Eddie he could come home, he told us, "It's a good thing they're letting me out. I'm not going to stay in this bed in this cast another day!"

"Why, Son," Mom said, "Of course you will, if that is what the doctor says to do."

"Mom, I talked to the doctor today, myself. He said the only way this could help would be for me to stop using my feet. Well, I'm not going to quit using my feet!"

"Now, Son, just hold your horses. I'll go right now and talk to Dr. Norman. Don't you think you could quit doing some of the harder things, if it would mean that your back would be straight?"

"No, Mom!" Eddie answered in a sure voice, "I would rather die than just sit around. I'd rather have a crooked back than stop doing all the things I want to do!"

"All right, Son. I just want you to be sure." Mom left to see Dr. Norman.

After a while they came back together.

"You have to know, Eddie," Dr. Norman said, "With this condition, your back will grow more crooked over time."

"I realize that, Dr. Norman. But like I told my mother, I can't and I won't stop using my feet."

"Let me talk to Bruce Johnson and see if we can't devise a brace that will help. Would you be willing to be put back in a cast again so we could do the necessary measurements?"

"Yes, I could do that," Ed answered.

There was another story about Eddie and his cast in the local newspaper and when Mom read it to him, all the kids on the ward wanted a copy to put in their scrapbooks. It called Eddie "one of God's challenges to discontented, whining humanity."

When Eddie entered the hospital again, the kids who were still there welcomed him back. There was even another little article in the newspaper.

Eddie's brace was an elaborate affair made of steel covered with leather. It had solid pieces that fit over his shoulders and around his neck. Another piece encased his body above his hips, with vertical panels joining these with the top pieces. These left the middle of the back open, encased his sides, and met in the front. The front area laced, so it could be fastened as tightly as possible and still leave room for movement.

Almost from the first, Mom insisted that she would never have designed a brace like this one. She maintained that it allowed the curvature to push through the opening in the back. At night when she removed Eddie's brace, she massaged his back. She rubbed ointment on the places on his hips and shoulders where the leather-encased steel had worn sores on his tender flesh.

The brace was changed at frequent intervals but probably no one, the doctor included, realized how fast Eddie was growing. His legs grew longer and the brace cramped his upper body. His back grew through the opening in the brace, as Mom feared.

Mom wrote to Dad and me asking us to come to the ranch. She wanted us to go with her to see Dr. Norman.

The night before, we all sat around the old oak table. Mom turned to Eddie. "Eddie, I want you to tell your Dad and Hazel what you told me. It's important that we know how you feel about wearing this brace. When we see Dr. Norman tomorrow, we've got to know what we're going to tell him."

"I don't think it is helping a bit. I can't see what is happening but I can feel how crooked my back is growing." Eddie fidgeted but didn't back down.

"Does your back still hurt, Son?" Dad asked.

"Yes, and I think the brace makes it worse. There is just no way for it to fit and be comfortable. And I don't think they can do anything else with it." Eddie sounded sure of what he was saying.

"Well, we'll see what Dr. Norman says tomorrow." Dad got up and walked out into the yard. Mom followed him.

Eddie gave me a crooked smile. "I wish the brace helped, Hazie. Mom feels so bad that it didn't, but I don't think it is anyone's fault. It was just meant to be."

The day of our appointment was cold and blustery. We could feel another storm on the way. We left early to get all the shopping done before we had to see Dr. Norman.

Finally the nurse called us in, the rustle of her starched uniform preceding us into the consultation room. We could smell the heat from a saw as it zipped through someone's plaster cast, and heard the sudden quiet when it stopped.

Mom removed Ed's coat and shirt, but left his brace on. Dr. Norman came in, cheerful, with nice little murmurs about the weather and the impending storm while he felt around the brace, fingers under it, lifting, checking to see if it was laced tightly. He touched the curvature that came up out of the open space in the brace, never quite looking at Mom or Eddie directly.

Mom couldn't stand this any longer. "Well, what do you think Dr. Norman? Doesn't it look to you like Eddie's spine is growing in the wrong direction? It seems more curved than ever to me." She looked directly into Dr. Norman's eyes as she waited for his answer.

Finally he said, "I would like to call in Bruce Johnson. He made the brace to my specifications. I would like him to look at Eddie's back and perhaps we can modify the brace enough to correct," he hesitated, "the way Eddie's back seems to be growing."

"Do you want him to continue wearing the brace?" Mom asked.

"Oh yes," Dr. Norman sounded sure of himself. "I believe he must wear a brace. We may have to modify this one."

Mom sighed.

"And I'd like to get some x-rays taken before you leave today. My nurse will be right in and we'll get that done."

We agreed to return the next morning and Dr. Norman gave the impression that everything would turn out alright.

We did the last of our shopping and headed home. There wasn't much conversation.

At ten the next morning, Mom, Dad, Eddie, and I waited for Dr. Norman and Bruce Johnson. Dad had to go back to Monarch on Monday and I had to go back to Trinidad. We wanted an answer.

It didn't take Bruce Johnson long. "I don't think we can make a brace that will stop this growth. It has a good start and in my experience, if you try to stop it from going one way, it just finds a different path. Wouldn't you agree, Dr. Norman?"

"In this case, I'm afraid I will have to agree. If Eddie could quit using his feet and stooping over…but I'm afraid even that won't help." He was looking at Eddie as he spoke.

"You're right about that, doctor," Eddie told him. "I can't quit using my feet, so I guess I'll just have to live with a crooked back. At least I won't be some kind of a vegetable." He laughed. There was a note of relief in his voice.

Dad held out his hand to Dr. Norman. "I'm sorry it didn't work for you or for Eddie, doctor, but, I know you tried."

"If there's anything I can do," Dr. Norman said, "I will try my best to help Eddie in the future. He's way ahead of us as to how he is going to meet his life."

I knew Eddie was happy that he didn't have to wear his brace, and that should have made us all feel better.

26 *Old Jeff is Killed*

fter New Year's 1938, I made the most of the time I could spend at the ranch. Mom and I worried about Eddie's back growing crooked. However, he tried hard not to bend so much. Mom decided to cut down on a number of things that made extra work for him.

"Mom, I will sell some of my rabbits if you will sell most of the chickens." He tried to keep his tone light.

Mom made extra money each week from sales of chickens and rabbits, along with several dozen eggs to a small grocery store and her regular customers.

"Well, I could sell all but about two dozen of my best laying hens," Mom agreed. "The chickens we plan to butcher can go. I don't want you plucking another chicken!"

It had been their routine each week on Friday afternoon to get the chickens and rabbits ready for market. Eddie plucked the chickens after they had been killed and scalded. He devised a thin rope line stretched tight from the stove to the table. Mom hung the chickens by their feet on this line at the right height for him to sit on his stool, reach out, and pull out the feathers with his toes. He was very good at this job; nevertheless, he was sitting and stooping.

Mom butchered the rabbits and prepared them. Eddie would have no part of that. But he still fed, watered, and cleaned the pens of forty rabbits. He would sell all but about ten, keeping his beloved Thumper and Brownie.

"Mom, I think we should close the station, too. Just keep it open on weekends. During the winter we don't sell that much. And Mom, you've got plenty of other work to do."

"You know, I've been thinking of that," Mom said. "If someone really needs something, they can come to the house and I'll get it for them."

She turned to me. "Just like now Hazel, I don't like the idea of Jody being at the station by herself. She likes to do it, makes her feel all grown up, but she still can't really wait on anyone but soda customers. She's only eight. Anything could happen."

At that moment, Jody came running to the house, crying and sobbing. "Poor Jeff! Poor Old Jeff!" She saw Mom, turned and ran back to the station, threw open the door and ran on through to the highway. We were all on her heels.

At the highway, we stopped in our tracks. There in the road, crushed and broken, lay our dog, Jeff. Heavy as he was, Mom gathered his body in her arms and started toward the house. We could see the glazed look in his eyes and knew he couldn't possibly live through this. None of us could stop our tears.

"A car hit him, Mommy!" Jody sobbed, "They didn't even stop— they didn't even care!"

Mom sat down on the step. She held Old Jeff, sort of rocking back and forth, tears streaming down her face. Eddie, Jody, and I sat down beside her, all of us running our fingers over Jeff's rough, wiry coat. Eddie found the velvety spot beneath his ear and stroked him gently with his toes.

A tremor shook the dog and Old Jeff somehow managed a last imploring gaze toward Eddie as if to ask forgiveness for being run over by a car. "He's gone, Mom," Eddie whispered.

"Bring Jeff's old rug for me to put him on, Jody," Mom said, and Jody ran to do as she was told.

"We'll bury him on the hill, won't we Mom?" Eddie asked.

"Yes, Son." Jody returned and was hugging Old Jeff's head to her heart, "Leave him be Jody. He's all right now. His soul has gone to dog Heaven and he's happy."

"But Mommy, I don't want to bury Old Jeff. We just can't!" Jody kept crying as if her heart would break.

I held Jody close. "Listen to Mom, Jody. You know we must bury old Jeff in the little graveyard where all our pets are buried. Come on now and help us decide where."

We stopped by the shed for a shovel then trudged up the hill toward the little cemetery. Minnie, the goldfish; Mouser, the old mamma cat; Dickie, the canary bird; Chicken Little, our old hen that followed us wherever we went; even baby birds that had fallen out of the nest were given names on their own little crosses and laid to rest.

We had to push our way into the miniature burying ground surrounded on all sides by a rough circle of cedar trees. Here, crosses of varying sizes, the names faded by snow and rain, marked the graves.

"How about right here, Mom? Where the sun can shine down and keep him warm?" Eddie asked in a gruff voice as he marked out a long rectangle in the dirt with his toe.

"Is that spot all right with everyone?" Mom glanced about for our nods and started to dig. Taking turns, we finally had a deep hole squared off and lined with cedar boughs.

Mom and I walked back to the house and Mom wrapped Jeff in his old rug. Then we put him in Eddie's wagon and slowly took him to his grave. Mom and I lifted him out of the wagon and laid him softly into the cedar boughs.

We stood in a small circle and held hands as Mom said a prayer. Then she started to sing "Safe in the Arms of Jesus" and all of us chimed in. As soon as the song was over, Mom shoveled soil into the grave until it was mounded evenly.

"Mom," Jody asked, "Jeff never was bad. He won't go to Hell, will he?"

"Of course not, Sister," Eddie responded. "His spirit is in dog Heaven, like Mom told you. And remember, although you won't see him anymore, he will be at your side protecting you all the time."

"Will he, Mommy? Like the good spirits you tell us about in the wind and the rain?"

"Yes dear, and when you start across the highway without looking, and something makes you stop and think, that will be Old Jeff taking care of you!"

Mom and I walked back to the house, leaving Eddie, Jody, Bill, and Bud to haul flat white rocks to cover the grave.

Mom said, "I'm going to post some cards on the bulletin boards at the grocery store and feed store and see if I can't find another good dog. I won't feel right until I have a good watch dog."

Dad had to go back to Monarch in a couple of days but he wanted to see his old friends, Frank and Tony, before he left. Mom went with him. They were gone most of the day.

Eddie had just gotten home from school when he called to me, "Hey, look! I think Dad bought that old truck from Tony."

Sure enough, Dad was driving the truck and Mom followed in the car. "Well, Eddie," I said, "That will give you a truck to haul stuff in and save wear and tear on the car. I hope it doesn't give you any trouble."

"I don't think it will. It's old, but Dad always says Tony treats it like a baby."

As Dad got out, Eddie walked over and gave the truck a kick on the front tire. "She looks like a pretty good old truck, Art. How does she handle?"

"Just fine, Son. I thought you and Mom needed a truck around here. And it won't be any trouble for you to drive." He put his arm around Eddie's shoulders and they gave the truck a good going over.

That evening, as we sat around the oak table after supper, Dad turned to Eddie. "Son, I finished that filter box to take the iron out of the well water. Mom doesn't like her wash to look rust-colored." He gave a little laugh. "All you have to do is get some charcoal at the feed store, fill it, and divert the water through it."

"That is great, Art. How long will it work without changing the charcoal?" Mom asked.

"Probably six months, we'll see. Save the charcoal you take out, it can be washed and used again. Just get new, though, for now."

"Do you think you will be able to get back here any time soon?" Mom asked.

"No. The company is so busy stockpiling limestone that I will be lucky to get away before Thanksgiving. My super thinks we are going to get into a war in Europe. He has relatives in France and they write that they are afraid from day to day that Hitler will march on them." Whenever Dad was worried, he spoke quietly, almost as if he were afraid of being overheard.

Eddie spoke up, "Yeah, 'Mad Dog Hitler.' We talk about him in our history class. My teacher says he is going to over-run all of Europe."

"She's probably right, Son. And the CF&I will furnish steel for shells and guns." Dad couldn't keep a worried note from creeping into his voice.

"Dad, can I come to Monarch and visit with you for a couple of weeks?" Mom looked startled. This was the first she heard that Eddie wanted to visit Dad.

"Sure, Mom can put you on the train and I will pick you up in Salida. Just let me know when. You can come to the quarry with me when you want to, or stay with the Creswell's in Salida once in a while. Helen Creswell is about your age." Dad sounded pleased.

Before we went to bed, Dad gave me a big hug and said, "Keep an eye on all of them for me. Your Mom doesn't always let me know if something is going wrong."

"Yeah, I know Dad. Sometimes I have to pry it out of her, but Eddie tells me. I can depend on him."

27 Rowser

$\mathcal{M}$om had gone to town for supplies. When she drove up in the old truck about mid-afternoon, Ed and Jody ran to see what she had brought for them.

"I've got a dog and I'm scared to death of him," Mom said. "The feed store told me that Frank Zavislan had a dog for me and I went out and picked him up. We had to tie him from all four corners of the truck bed. Eddie, come on and see if you can get him to trust you. Then maybe we can get him untied and into the house."

The dog stood in the back of the trunk, head high, not giving an inch to anyone. Maybe he was afraid and didn't want to show it. His coat was a silvery gray, shading almost to black along his back and down to his paws. Around his ears and his muzzle he was black as ink. He had black question marks above his eyes.

Mom started toward the bed of the pick-up truck, but stepped back as the dog bared his teeth, a low growl starting from deep within his chest.

"Mom, he's a police dog! Just like Rin-Tin-Tin in the movies! And look at his teeth! What's happened to them?" Eddie asked, all excited.

"Frank Zavislan told me that the dog came limping into his ranch one day, half-starved and with his teeth filed down as you see them. Can you imagine anyone being that cruel to an animal?"

I couldn't imagine her bringing this beast home. At the moment, he looked as if he would be glad to have us for his next meal.

"But Mom, if he's that mean, what are we going to do with him?" I asked.

"I don't think he is mean. I just think he needs a little love. If we can get him in the house, I think I will just let him run loose there for a few days until he's sure we won't hurt him."

"Yeah, but what if he won't come in?" Jody asked, fear in her voice.

"Maybe Eddie can coax him. Dogs seem to trust Eddie. Let's get out of sight. Eddie, see if you can make up with him. Frank called him Rowser."

"Mom, you can't do that! What if that dog should lunge at Eddie? He'd tear him to pieces!" This huge animal scared me and I didn't care who knew it.

"Wait and see. Don't worry about Eddie. He'll stay out of the way until he's sure."

I didn't know how Mom could be so certain. We couldn't believe our eyes when, after about half an hour, Eddie reached up to the tie-downs and started unfastening them. Then he commanded Rowser, "All right boy, jump out of the truck and we'll go find something to eat."

He called to Mom, "Pour some milk in a pan, prop open the door, and disappear!"

Reaching up and petting him, Eddie said, "Come on now, Rowser. Let's go get something to eat." Eddie started toward the back door with the big dog right beside him. Once in a while he would look up at Eddie for reassurance and Eddie would talk to him.

When they got to the door, Rowser hesitated, looked up at Eddie and raised the black question marks above his eyes as if asking for permission to enter.

"Come on now. Follow me and we'll get you some meat to eat." Eddie put meat scraps down beside the bowl of milk. "Come on, eat. I know you must be hungry."

Rowser gave Eddie a grateful look and ate like he had never had a square meal before. Eddie got more meat scraps and watched as he ate. When he had his fill, Eddie petted the dog and talked to him. Finding an old blanket, he put it down beside his bed. "You can sleep here, Rowser. No one is ever going to be mean to you again."

Later, Mom let him have the run of the house. We didn't try to pet him. From the start, he was Eddie's dog but he seemed to like the rest of us and would obey our commands. He brought the cattle in from the far corners of the pasture and watched the chickens. He killed snakes, brought them home, and laid them on the doorstep. Eddie taught him to open the mailbox and bring the mail to the house, which he did without tearing it. All of these things made him indispensable, besides being the best watch-dog we ever had.

Rowser loved Eddie. He slept beside Eddie's bed and if he heard a noise, he was immediately on patrol until he was satisfied there was no danger. When Mom got up in the morning, she'd peek in Eddie's room and tell Rowser, "Get Eddie up, Rowser." Rowser would pull the covers off Eddie, and give his face a big slurp. He would look up at Eddie and swishing his heavy tail from side to side in joy of a task well done.

The only time he ever threatened to hurt any of us turned out to be my own fault. A swarm of bees had made their home many years before in an old well below the road near the arroyo. The bees built their nest about two feet down from the top of the bricks used to case the well. The earth had settled and caved in outside the brick casing. You could see the top of the honeycomb where it had been exposed. The inner wall of bricks was in good shape and we had no idea how far down the combs extended.

It was our plan to dig down around the outside of the combs, expose the honey we wanted to take and then fill the earth back to its former level. We didn't want to risk standing on the ancient planks that had been placed cross-wise every few feet to the bottom of the hole. Our next concern was to figure out how to keep the bees from stinging us.

We asked Mom to start thinking of some way to keep the bees away from us. Meanwhile, we loaded the back of the truck. We figured we needed a sharp shovel, a couple of long, sharp butcher knives and two big dishpans.

"Did you figure out a way to keep us safe from the bees, Mom?" Eddie asked.

"I think so. I have these heavy old net curtains that I can wrap around you. You'll need to put these hats on first, and then I can drape over the brims and tie them down tight. Hazel, you can wear these heavy gloves and a couple of pairs of heavy socks and a couple of heavy shirts and pants. That should do it for you."

"What about Eddie? I can see that would work for all of him but his feet, Mom." He would have to be able to have his toes free.

"I think he could wear two pairs of heavy socks; I'll cut the toes out. Then we'll bring the socks up over his pant legs and I think that should do it."

When Mom finished with us, we looked like something from another world. We laughed at each other and started out.

"Did you bring the butcher knives?" Eddie asked. I brandished them in reply. Before I knew what happened, I was pinned to the wall, two huge feet planted firmly against my bosom, and a big chunk of my shoulder in Rowser's teeth.

I didn't say a word. I couldn't!

Quickly taking in the situation, Eddie said sternly, "Rowser! Get down! Let go! Sit!"

Rowser looked at Eddie as if to satisfy himself that Eddie was in no danger and then slowly loosened his teeth, and more slowly lowered himself to the ground.

There he sat and there I stood. My knees started to shake and I was glad when Eddie told him, "All right now, Rowser, it's only Hazel. She won't hurt me. Now, go lie down."

Rowser looked at Eddie and did as he was told. I guess I didn't look like anything he'd ever seen before, but he at least recognized Eddie's voice.

After that encounter, robbing the bee hive didn't seem nearly so daring. Digging the trench deep enough to expose the honeycomb turned out to be the hardest part of our adventure. Bundled up as we were, it was hotter than the Hinges of Hades and we had to stop once in a while to cool off. Bees were buzzing angrily all about us but our protection was good.

"Look at that, Eddie. Just look how beautiful and white the comb is." I muttered through my netting.

"After we take what we want, we'll let them keep what's below. There could be honey clear to the bottom of the well!" Eddie sounded excited. I know I was.

We placed our pans in the bottom of the trench. As Eddie cut out squares, I pried them loose with a big spatula and dropped them, dripping, into the pans until they were heaped high.

"Let's use these old boards to cover the trench, then we can fill in with earth. What do you think, Hazie? Then it won't be so hard to do this the next time."

I carried the tools and the heavy pans back to the truck and loaded them. The bees buzzed, so we decided to drive to the house before getting rid of our hot clothes. When we were back in our everyday clothes, we counted our few stings, and laughed with pleasure.

Jody took a piece of honeycomb and started slurping the honey out of it.

Rowser was friendly to me when we returned but he had shown, without a doubt, that he meant business. We were all a little more cautious after that.

28 A Valedictorian Who Wiggles His Ears

Not long after school started that fall of 1938, I came home to help Mom get the crops in and store vegetables for the winter. She farmed corn and milo maize with a neighbor so her share of those crops would more than feed our few cattle through the winter.

By mid-afternoon we had dug beets, carrots, onions, and turnips. She had the sandboxes ready and we buried the vegetables in the cool root cellar.

At four o'clock Eddie and Jody came home. When Mom asked about school that day, Eddie tried to shush Jody. It didn't do a bit of good.

"Eddie almost got a whipping today!" she blurted. "He was being bad!"

"All right Eddie, now tell us what happened." Mom demanded.

"I was just acting silly, Mom. It was hot and all the kids were bored and it was almost time for the bell anyway." He sort of hung his head but I could see the look he darted at Jody. She was in for it.

"So what did you do badly enough that the teacher wanted to whip you? Tell me the truth, Eddie." Mom wasn't about to let him off the hook.

"Well...I just wiggled my ears and you know I can't wiggle my ears and laugh at the same time."

Jody broke in, "Yeah, Mom. He wiggled his ears and pretty soon they were all laughing so hard they didn't pay any attention to Miss Sewall."

"Well Eddie?" Mom stood there waiting for a full explanation.

"Well, Miss Sewall couldn't make the kids be quiet. She threatened but they were laughing so hard they wouldn't listen." Eddie hesitated.

"So then what happened?" Mom asked.

"Miss Sewall told me she was going to have to give me a whipping. She told Karen to go get her a stick."

Jody piped up with, "Yeah, and Karen brought in a tree limb so big it would hardly come through the door. Miss Sewall was really mad by now." Jody couldn't keep from laughing until she got a dirty look from Eddie. "She ordered Karen to take the tree limb out and bring her a board."

Mom was getting impatient. It was a rule in our home that if you got a whipping at school you got another one when you got home.

"Well, Karen came back in with a board," Eddie said, "A one-by-two about three feet long. Miss Sewall told me to bend over the desk. Well, I did. I had made up my mind that no matter how hard she swatted me, I wasn't going to cry. So I gritted my teeth and waited."

"Did she hit you?" I asked.

"Yeah, she hit me. Hard! And the board flew to pieces and fell all over the floor. I just kept bent over the desk and then Miss Sewall said, 'Eddie, go to your seat and you will stay in at recess for the next week.'"

"I hope you learned a lesson from this, Son. You'd better be on your good behavior from now on." Mom didn't say any more.

After supper I asked Eddie, "What do you think it will be like going to a big school in Pueblo next year?"

"I don't even like to think about it. I know all the kids here so well. I've grown up with them and everyone there will be a stranger." Eddie sounded sad.

"I've been thinking that it would be a good idea for me to close my shop in Trinidad and move it to Pueblo," I told Mom. "That way, Eddie could stay with me when he starts to high school. What do you think, Mom?"

"Why, I don't know. Where would you put a shop?" I could tell she was excited.

"I think it would be great, Hazie," Eddie said. "It would sure help. Heck, you spend an awful lot of time here anyway and you could spend more time in your shop if you lived in Pueblo." He was beaming.

I wondered if I had spoken too soon. "Mom, could we go into town Monday? I have an idea. Perhaps I could get a job at the beauty salon in the department store, find out what customers are like in Pueblo, and look for a location at the same time."

"Yes, we could do that. You could stay here and drive back and forth until you make up your mind. Would you keep your shop in Trinidad for now?" she asked.

"I don't see why not. It gets along very well without me as it is, part of the time. I can close it when I'm ready."

I didn't have any trouble getting a job. I took one day a week to go to Trinidad and do the book work, pay wages and go to the bank. I missed my friends there, but being at the ranch more than made up for it.

Close to Thanksgiving Dad wrote that he would be down a few days before the holiday, and he was bringing Helen Creswell with him. Eddie had become friends with Helen when he was visiting Dad in Salida. Eddie didn't say much, but I could see he was very happy about this. He worked at getting caught up on extra schoolwork and he gave his rabbit pens an extra good cleaning.

Mom invited Mickie and Victor Barlish, her new husband, but Mickie said not to count on her.

"Do you have plans while Helen is here, Eddie?"

"I think I'll drive her all around the ranch and back on the bluffs above the river and show her where we hunt deer. I want her to see my rabbits. Maybe you or Mom could drive us over by my school. What do you think, Hazie?"

"I think that should keep you pretty busy. Four days will go very fast." I didn't want to see Dad go back to Monarch. The time would go too fast for all of us.

When we picked Dad up at the train depot, Eddie and Helen managed somehow to get around behind all of us and were saying their own 'hellos.' Mom nodded toward them and Dad grinned back.

"Looks like they'll have a good time, doesn't it, old girl?" Dad's eyes twinkled as he gave Mom a little pat. Mom just smiled back and said, "Well, come on everyone. Let's get home. We've got a lot to do."

Mom got out her linen tablecloths. I washed and ironed them, swearing at the flat irons that had to be heated on top of the stove. I'd been away from the ranch long enough to forget what a chore ironing could be, and just how heavy the old fashioned irons were.

Eddie and Helen came in flushed from the cold. "Mom, do you want Helen and me to bring up the vegetables from the cellar? And how about some apples?"

"Yes, that would be fine. And bring up a ham, too. Your Dad likes his ham and eggs for breakfast."

Thanksgiving morning was cold and clear. Cedar smoke smelled like incense in the air. Indoors, noses tickled from the aroma of roasting turkey and stuffing, apple pies with cinnamon and nutmeg, and turnips waiting to be mashed.

Mom invited our old friends from Lime: Tony and Emma, and Frank and Lucy. They brought a jug of wine and the men found a corner by the stove to have a few drinks and talk about old times and what was happening now.

When we sat down at the table, improvised from saw-horses and planks, there were ten of us. Dad sat at the head, Mom at the other end beside Dyanna Sue in her high chair. Eddie sat between Helen and me. For some time he had been using a low stool for a table. He could sit in an ordinary chair and it was easy for him to stoop over a bit and bring his fork to his mouth. One of us could cut his meat if it was tough, but usually he got along fine.

Dad looked around the table. Then, in a voice gruff with emotion, he blessed the food, our family, and our good friends. We all raised a glass of wine and drank a toast to one another.

Later, as Helen helped me clear the table, I asked if she was having a good time. "Oh yes," she answered, "I don't know when I've had so much fun. I didn't know Eddie could drive a car and do all the things he can do. He told me this summer that he could, but I guess I didn't really believe him."

"I'm glad. I hope you can come again to visit with us." I was sincere about this invitation. It would help Eddie when he went to high school next fall to know that he had a friend he could write to and visit.

Eddie celebrated his thirteenth birthday with a party for all his schoolmates at Verde School. As there were only thirty-some in the entire school, he asked all of them. With parents and all the little brothers and sisters who couldn't be left at home, it would be a very big party.

"Eddie," Mom said, "We can't have this party outdoors in the winter. So let's have it at Boseker's Hall. What do you think?"

"Yeah, Mom. Can we have it in the evening so all the parents can come too?" Eddie was already thinking up ways to entertain everyone.

"We'll get Jessie and Clint Boseker to play some music for us. We can have a couple of square dances and musical chairs. How does that sound?" Mom was almost as excited at the prospect as Eddie.

Eddie sent invitations home with all his schoolmates, and invited other people he knew. Mom baked cakes. Some of the other mothers offered to bake cakes, too. Jessie let us use her huge coffeepot. Mom made lemonade.

At the height of the party, I looked out over the crowd and smiled to myself. Little girls were standing on their Dad's toes as they were twirled around. Eddie was dancing with Jody, just as they did at home sometimes. The parents were having a great time.

The next day when we went to help Jessie and Clint Boseker clean up the big hall, Eddie said, "You were so nice to let me have my birthday party here," Eddie told Jessie. "I'll never forget what a good time we all had."

Jessie gave Eddie a big hug and planted a kiss on his cheek. "Whenever you want a party, remember to have it here."

It was a good thing Eddie had a great birthday party because Christmas that year was as bad as it could get. Three days before Christmas, Eddie and Jody became very ill with scarlet fever. Mom feared it would leave them with a hearing loss or affect their eyes, as it sometimes did.

She kept their room dark and wouldn't let anyone in to see them, fearful that the contagious fever would spread.

Charlie and Ione Owens came by bringing presents, but Eddie was too sick to even say hello. When they left they made Mom promise to let them know how the kids were.

It was the second week in January before either Eddie or Jody felt like going back to school. Eddie worried that he would be behind in his schoolwork but it didn't take him long to catch up.

He was chosen Valedictorian of his class. Although he was thrilled, he didn't want to get up and give a speech before all the people at graduation. After school, he would corner Jody and say, "All right Sis, You've got to help me. Listen and tell me how I sound."

"Eddie, I don't know when you sound good or bad. Why don't you get Hazie to listen. She'll tell you if you're doing it wrong."

So Eddie enlisted my help. He went over that speech so many times I thought he could do it in his sleep. It was worth it, though. He did a wonderful job.

Dad came home for the occasion. When the program was over, Dad put his arm around Eddie's shoulder and said with tears in his voice, "I'm proud of you, Son. You're on your way. Don't ever look back."

29 Eddie Starts High School

"What am I going to do all summer, Hazie? Dad says I can't come to Monarch because they are working overtime and Saturdays." Eddie kicked at a rock in the yard. "In Dad's last letter he said he knows the company expects war in Europe, so they are stockpiling and getting ready for it."

Just then, Cab Arthur and Ray Shirley drove the Colorado State Highway truck into the yard. They still stopped at the ranch during their lunch time whenever they could. Mom called out, "Come on in, I'll put a pot of coffee on."

As they spread their lunches out on the table, Cab said, "Ethel, could you use lumber and some windows for anything around here?"

Eddie spoke up. "Mom, if you had some material, we could put that addition across the back of the house you've been talking about."

"Why yes, I suppose we could. What are they tearing down now, Cab?" Mom knew that the Highway Department always seemed to be upgrading something, which usually meant tearing down a building or bridge.

"Some of our outdated buildings have been vacant for about five years and I guess they finally decided it would be cheaper to tear them down than to have to pay taxes on them."

"Sure, I'd love to have it. It will give Eddie something to do this summer."

The next day, Cab and Ray made the ranch their first stop. They unloaded about twenty windows and a lot of lumber. It was old and part of it was in bad shape.

Eddie watched. "Gee, Mr. Arthur, that's great! I can sand those windows and paint them and they'll look good as new."

Eddie had Mom place the windows she wanted along the side of the garage that was in the shade. He could turn the windows to get at the unsanded surfaces but he couldn't lift them. When I got home at night, I was always amazed at the progress he had made during the day. I would help him until dark then we would wash up and get some supper started.

Mom hired Ad Bray to help get the side framework up on the addition and the roof on. Before summer was over, the only things left to do were putting the roof on and laying the floor. When it was finished, we had a 12' by 30' addition. At the north end there was a bedroom and a small closet. There was space for a door that could go into a basement and Mom included a brick-lined nook for the kitchen range so we wouldn't have to worry about fire. Besides the niche for the stove, there was plenty of room for a table and chairs.

"You know, I think we could build a house all by ourselves if we had to," Eddie said with a wry smile.

Mom laughed. "Sure. All we'd need is someone to give us beat-up lumber and a bunch of windows, and trade labor for a few pigs. Then we could sure put it all together." She gave Eddie a big hug.

"I think I'll write your Dad and see if we can spend some time with him two weeks from now. Hazel, if you could arrange to take off on a Saturday, we could drive up and be there in the afternoon. That way we could have Saturday night and all day Sunday with your Dad."

Eddie and Jody started jumping up and down. Dyanna Sue grabbed Mom and asked, "Can I go, too?"

"Of course, we'll all go. I know Art will be glad to see us. It can't be any fun being away from his family for such a long time."

Eddie said, with a little grin, "I'll write Helen, too, so she will know we are coming."

I tousled his hair. "I figured you would let her know." He wrote to Helen faithfully once a week and Helen wrote back.

We got to Dad's cabin in mid-afternoon. The scent of pine trees and the peaceful murmur of a little brook that ran close to the cabin was incongruous with the noise of the quarry that carried across the steep valley. It was hard to realize that all this effort being expended was due to fear of a war in Europe. But after we talked with Dad far into the night, we hadn't any doubt that the steel being made at the CF&I plant in Pueblo was being shipped to munitions makers.

We spent the next day just catching up and being together. Dad sat on the bench in front of the cabin, Dyanna Sue on his lap and Jody at his knee. He stroked their hair and talked to Mom. I sat nearby and just listened, content that we were all together.

Charlie Creswell brought Helen up early Sunday morning and Eddie and Helen went for a walk. It was great to see Eddie happy and enjoying himself. All too soon it was time to start home. Dad promised that he would get home for Christmas "come Hell or high water." I thought it would probably be more like six-foot snow drifts.

I had been looking for an apartment within walking distance of both Centennial High School in Pueblo, and my work. I finally found a one-bedroom on Eleventh Street. Eddie was excited and scared about starting high school.

Mom came in the day before, leaving Jody and Dyanna with a neighbor. She brought vegetables, home baked bread, and all kinds of good things to eat. She was as nervous as an old hen losing her last little chick, but trying very hard not to show it. She drove Eddie to school and made sure that his leather-strapped book satchel was comfortable on his shoulder. Then, not wanting to embarrass him in front of his future classmates, we said good-bye. He had a sandwich in his book bag and said he would get a drink of water at school. I thought he didn't want to carry a drink because it would be too hard to handle.

I had taken the day off work. Mom and I spent the time talking about everything we could think of except how worried we were about Eddie's first day in high school. He told us that he didn't want us to pick him up, that he would walk home from now on.

Just when Mom began to worry that something had happened to him, a bright red convertible stopped in front of the apartment house. Eddie opened the door and waited while a neatly dressed young man,

Eddie's age or older, came around and grabbed Eddie's satchel. They walked up to the door, talking a mile a minute.

Eddie introduced us, "Mom, Hazel, this is Dale Hill. Mom, he says you took care of him when he was about two years old, at Lime. His name was Dale Duff!"

"Oh for Heaven's sakes! It can't be, but it is! I remember your Dad and Mom, and then your Dad passed away. The last I heard, Dale, you were at McClelland Orphanage. That was a long time ago."

"Yes," Dale said. "After my Dad passed away, my mother left and I was put in McClelland. I don't blame her. She had no way to take care of me. Then when I was six, John Hill came along and adopted me and here I am. When I saw Eddie at school today, I remembered some of the stories my Dad told me about Eddie and how you used to take care of me. It was almost like going back in time. I couldn't wait to talk to him!" Dale stopped, out of breath, and looked from Mom to Eddie.

"You were such a dear little boy, Dale. And it looks to me like you have grown into a fine young man. I hope you and Eddie will be good friends." Mom put an arm around Dale and gave him a hug.

"Oh, I'm sure we will. We have a few classes together so I'll see him every day." Dale turned toward the door.

"I'll see you tomorrow, Dale. Thanks for giving me a ride home." Eddie walked to the door with his new friend.

"How did it go today, Eddie?" I asked.

"Well, you know, Hazie, after I got used to all the kids staring at me and after they realized I could do just about anything they could do, it went great. I was a lot better off than one boy who couldn't use his legs and had to be helped up and down all those stairs in his wheelchair. He had a young man who evidently takes care of him all the time."

Mom asked, "Did you have any trouble about the bathroom?"

"No, Mom," Eddie answered. "I have myself pretty well trained to wait until I get home, but don't worry, if I see that I am going to have to go, I can come home at lunch time. It isn't that far."

"Yes, I've been thinking," I told Eddie, "I think it would be a good idea if we both came home for lunch."

"Sounds good to me," Eddie answered.

30 Christmas 1939

*J*t was the day before Christmas, 1939. Mom pulled Eddie's coat more snugly around his shoulders as we waited for the train to bring Dad from Salida.

Eddie looked anxiously at the leaden sky, threatening snow. A little shiver shook him. A few minutes seemed like an hour until the train chugged into the station and came to a clanging stop. There were only a few passengers. I sensed Eddie's disappointment as Dad stepped down alone. Eddie hadn't said so, but I knew he hoped Dad would bring Helen.

Dad handed his packages to me, then enveloped Eddie and Mom in a big bear hug. I gave Mom the packages and it was my turn. I snuggled closer, savoring the old familiar smell of tobacco, wool shirt, and shaving lotion.

I think I see snowflakes," Mom said. "We'd better hurry and get home!"

We talked about everything on the way to the ranch, anything to keep our minds off the huge snowflakes as they hit the windshield and slid down. We were almost home before they started sticking so bad the wipers jammed. I stopped to clean them off.

"If you can keep an eye on your side of the road, Eddie, so I won't go into the ditch, I think we'll make it." I gripped the wheel and attempted to see where the road actually went. By now the snow was coming down so fast that it seemed like someone up there was just pouring it out of buckets and the wind was getting fiercer by the moment.

"Okay Hazie, Let's go! I'll yell if I can't see." Eddie stuck his head out the window, eyes squinting against the snow. We got home just in time.

Dad feared that we would be pulled into a war in Europe. "The headlines don't tell us everything," he said. We all remembered the day when the newspapers printed, "Germany invades Poland." Public sentiment seemed to dictate, "All aid short of war."

"I know that the steel mill in Pueblo is making shell casings and bomb material," Dad said. "They send it to the east or west coast for final fabrication. And they are shipping these armaments to England and France. I don't know what they are waiting for. They'd just as well get in it and get it over with." He wouldn't say any more, only that it would probably be summer before he could get home again.

Dad had to go back to Monarch the day after Christmas. The roads were cleared just in time to take him to catch his train. We said our sad farewells and went back to the ranch.

"Eddie, you can't imagine what happened today!" I called out as I came home from work one evening. Eddie looked up from his homework.

"I've been asked if I would consider a job traveling for Roux Company."

"Isn't Roux Company the one who makes hair dyes and bleaches?" Eddie asked. By now, he was familiar with all the beauty shop jargon.

"Yes, that's the one. They are bringing out a new product, a hair styling lotion called 'Lac-O-Wave.' They are looking for a stylist to introduce it to the western states."

"Well, they couldn't find anyone better than you. Are you going to do it?" Eddie asked.

"I don't know. I want to know more about what would be expected of me. Too, I want to know how you feel about staying with Mickie for about a year." I hadn't talked to Mickie but I thought she would be glad to have Eddie stay.

"That would be okay with me," Eddie said. "Vic's learning more about welding at that new school the government set up. I think if we get in a war he will go work in the ship yards."

Mickie and Vic's apartment on Eleventh Street was even closer to school than ours. It wouldn't be a problem for Eddie to get back and forth and Mickie wasn't working.

"I think you ought to do it, Hazie. You would learn a lot and when you get back," he hesitated, "you could advertise that you had traveled for Roux as a stylist." He almost sounded excited.

"Yeah, well, I guess so." I somehow felt let down. I suppose I thought Eddie would object and make me feel indispensable. "I have to find out a lot more about it. They will have a representative here on Monday."

"What do you think Mom will say?" Eddie asked.

31 *Christmas 1940*

*N*ow it was the week before Christmas, 1940. I was back in Salt Lake City where I had started work for Roux almost a year ago. I thought how Mom acted when I told her about the opportunity. She just said, "You'll have to make up your own mind. You know we'll miss you."

And Eddie, no matter how much he told me it would be great, and how much I'd learn, I could still hear the quiver in his voice when he said goodbye. They promised they'd write and I knew they would, but when I tried to get Mom to promise me that she wouldn't move with her cattle to the remote Colvin place in the spring she just said, "We'll see." And I had to be content with that.

I was assured when I was hired that I would be back in Colorado every six months. The closest I had come was now in Salt Lake City. My schedule said my next stop was San Francisco. Again, I called my boss in New York. Again, he said, "Sorry."

Travel was becoming next to impossible ever since Hitler had bombed St. Paul's Cathedral in London on October 24, 1940. On October 29th, the first draft numbers were called. Chaos reigned. Everyone seemed to be going somewhere. People were getting their affairs in order. Young men were joining the army. Several times I had to give up my flight plans and take another plane. I couldn't even be sure of room reservations all the time.

As I sat and watched Sally Eddington, the salon manager, I was thinking, Mom's last letter had been so short and noncommittal that I worried about what she left out. Mostly she just said she hoped I would be able to get home for Christmas but would understand if I couldn't.

It was just after ten o'clock. If I could get a plane out of Salt Lake to Denver, I could catch a bus to Pueblo. With luck, I could be home that evening, sometime.

"Sally, is there any possible way I can be of help to you this week?" Sally pondered. "No, in fact you would just be in the way. We are so booked up this week before Christmas that I don't know how we're going to get through it. Why?"

"You just made up my mind! I'm going to catch the next plane to Colorado." I started putting my stuff in my brief case and gathered up my coat.

Sally came around her desk and gave me a big hug. "We'll miss you. Have a wonderful Christmas!" She pressed a gaily wrapped package into my hands and gave me a hug and a push. "Hurry now, catch that plane!"

Except for the long lines of people waiting at the ticket counters, the Denver Airport seemed much the same. I caught a bus to a downtown hotel, made some phone calls, and caught the next bus to Pueblo.

When I arrived in Pueblo, I took a cab directly to the beauty shop where Mickie was working. I didn't call because I wanted to surprise her. When I opened the door, the familiar smell of wave solution and lotions, the sound of hair dryers, and the cadence of many conversations made me feel at home.

Just then Mickie turned and saw me. She let out a little yell and running over, hugged me. "Oh great! You did get here in time for Christmas! Will Eddie and Mom be glad to see you!" Her voice sort of trailed off and a guarded look crossed her face.

"Could you take me out to the ranch when you finish up here?" I asked.

"Sure." Mickie headed toward the back of the shop. I hurried after her.

"All right, Mickie. Why do I have a feeling that something's wrong?" I had a lump in the pit of my stomach and I didn't like the look on her face. It reminded me of when we were kids and she'd done something she didn't want anyone to find out about.

"Well, Mom isn't at the ranch. She's at the Colvin place. Now, don't blame me. There's no way I could have stopped her!"

"No, I can't blame you. Her letters have been so vague. I just knew something wasn't right. How about Eddie? Is he going to school? He has been staying with you and going to school, hasn't he?" I could feel anger welling up and I struggled to keep calm.

"No. Mom said it wouldn't be any problem, that they could go to Rye School. But then there was a big storm in October and the kids missed a couple of weeks of school. They just didn't go back." She had a defeated tone in her voice and I couldn't help but feel sorry for her.

"How about Dyanna Sue? She's here with you, isn't she?" I asked.

"Well, no. You see, Vic got a job at the shipyards in California. He's been gone two weeks. I'm going out right after the first of the year. He says I can get on, too, and the pay is great!" A note of excitement crept into her voice.

"Well, I can't blame you," I said. "Everything is going crazy out there. But you will make good money."

"You probably don't have any warm clothes with you, do you?" Mickie asked.

"No. Do you have something I can borrow?" My clothes were all packed at the ranch.

"Sure, let's go over to the apartment. I'll get enough stuff together for a few days. At least until you decide what you are going to do." She gave a little laugh and sounded more like herself.

"Oh, I know what I'm going to do. I'm going to get Mom and the kids off that damned place if I have to burn it down!" I felt anger rise like bile in my throat.

"Take it easy, Sis. It may not be as simple as you think," Mickie warned me.

Mickie and I didn't talk much on the thirty-odd mile trip to the Colvin place. I couldn't help feeling betrayed. After all the hard work, time, and money spent to make the ranch a decent, safe place to live, Mom had moved to a broken down shambles of a shack where the kids couldn't even get to school.

When we arrived, we pushed open the door to be greeted by a barrage of hugs, kisses, and questions. Eddie wasn't saying much. As I hugged him I could feel his thin shoulders. The hump on his back had grown noticeably larger.

Mom put a pot of coffee on and hurried around getting food on the table. I watched Eddie as he sat making little circles on the worn-out linoleum with his toes, not saying anything. Wind whipped at a loose shingle on the roof and the cedar logs burning in the potbellied heating stove crackled and snapped.

Finally, all my frustration burst out in a big gush. "But Mom, you promised!" I was a little girl again, pleading.

"No," Mom answered. "I said 'we'll see' when you asked me to promise I wouldn't move up here. I have never broken a promise to you." Mom sat there, clasping and unclasping her hands.

I could feel the tears behind my eyelids. I was determined not to cry. I watched Mom's hands as she twisted them painfully. They were work-worn, rough, red, and swollen.

I thought of the ice on the small stream we crossed driving up to the house, the endless buckets of water Mom must have carried to her animals when summer was over, and she had to keep them penned.

My tears fell. I couldn't stop. I got up, went over, and put my arms around her shoulders and buried my face in her bosom. "No Mom, you never broke a promise but you're going to break my heart if you don't quit trying to do the impossible!" I looked up at her.

She nodded, as though to say, "We'll see." She pulled me even tighter to her and we rocked back and forth.

Eddie broke in then with a frog in his throat, "Okay you guys." He came over to us, "Cut it out! You're going to have us all crying."

"I brought some stuff to make fudge," Mickie cut in. "Eddie, you and Jody get it started then we'll sit down and figure out what to do."

"Sounds like a great idea." Eddie went toward the wooden shelves and reaching up with his leg, grabbed the handle of a pot, and handed it to Jody. Jody put the ingredients in the pot, and set it on the front burner of the cook stove. Eddie pulled a chair over to stand on, and every once in a while he gave the fudge a good stir with his long-handled wooden spoon until it was just right to pour into the pan. It set quickly after Mom put it on the frosty back porch.

"That fudge didn't last long," Eddie said as he handed the last piece to Dyanna.

"No it didn't, and I have to go." Mickie turned to Mom. "If you have time when you're in town tomorrow, stop by."

Mom said she would. We listened until we couldn't hear the sound of Mickie's car as it went up and over the top of the canyon wall.

"Well, let's get to bed. I want to get an early start in the morning. I've got a lot to do in town." Mom hurried about, banking the fire in the heating stove and fixing me a place to sleep.

By six the next morning everyone was up and breakfast was over. Eddie had the truck warmed up. Dyanna Sue and Jody waited inside the house, anxious to be on their way.

Mom started toward the barn. Eddie stopped her. "We'll take care of everything, Mom. Just get to town and bring back supplies. We're out of darned near everything."

Mom and the girls piled into the truck. The clang of the empty barrels in the truck bed and the noise of the engine laboring up the steep grade hung in the air. Mom carefully drove the old Dodge truck around the last curve and out of sight over the rim of the mesa.

As the sounds died away, an almost frightening silence settled over the little valley.

"Well, she made it." Eddie said. "I always worry about that last curve." The cold of the winter morning seeped through our heavy coats and I was thankful for the boots and wool socks Mickie loaned me. Eddie scraped his moccasins on the rusty piece of iron someone had nailed to the rickety porch step for a foot scraper. The ground was frozen hard under little patches of snow where the feeble sun hadn't thawed its hardness into mud. Even so, Mom insisted on trying to keep this ramshackle house scrubbed and clean.

The house was sided with gray, weathered, wide boards. Cracks between them were only partly sealed by narrow boards nailed over them, loose in places, curled away where the wind, snow, and rain of many years had seeped in to pry and clutch at them.

On the steep pitch of the roof, I could see where someone had patched the torn shingles with rounds cut off the tops of tin cans, once shiny, now rusty, and almost blending with the color of the shingles. I wondered if the roof still leaked and if it could possibly be strong enough to shed a heavy snow. The lean-to kitchen looked tacked on, like an after-thought. The half boarded-up back porch with its slab stoop seemed an even later addition. Even so, it looked old. A bare wild rosebush grew at one corner, spreading underneath the porch and sending tendrils up through the widely spaced floor boards.

"Well, Eddie," I said, "Mom moved up here in spite of everything we could do to talk her out of it, didn't she?"

"Yup. She swore she would move back to the ranch by the time school started this fall, but…" his voice trailed off, leaving unsaid how much school he had missed in his sophomore year.

"Mickie said there was a big storm in October and after that you and Jody just quit. Didn't you try to go back after that?" I asked.

"No, we had just missed too much. I knew if we stayed up here it would just be the same thing over again." He kicked the door open with his foot and we went into the warm kitchen.

"Let's have one more cup of coffee, and then you'll have to tell me what to do. I'm a little out of practice." I laughed, but it wasn't funny. "Do you think we can get Mom to move back to the ranch, Eddie? Doesn't she realize what would happen if one of you were to get hurt or get really sick and you couldn't get out of here?" I sipped at the scalding coffee.

"I don't know what she thinks anymore. Dad doesn't get home but a couple of times a year at most. It's like she's trying to prove she can do it all by herself." Eddie rose from the table.

I pulled on my coat and helped Eddie into his warm jacket. The cold air took my breath away as I stepped outside.

"We'd better chop some wood and get the animals fed." Eddie squinted his eyes and looked at the cloudbank moving in from the north then turned back toward the house. "I guess we'd better feed the hogs first." He reached up and opened the back door, turning the knob with his toes. He could kick his shoes off so fast I didn't have a chance to open the door.

He nodded toward two barrels alongside the far wall of the kitchen. "We keep those barrels in here so they won't freeze. One of them is empty. The other is full of buttermilk. Just pour half of it into the empty barrel then mix four buckets of bran and two buckets of corn into it." Eddie instructed me. Slipping out of his right shoe, he balanced on his left leg, and pushed open the door.

"All right, I can mix that. Where are you going?" I asked.

"I'll open these sacks while you're doing that. I sure hope Mom doesn't forget to get grain. We're almost out. I've been mixing corn with the mash but we need grain too."

"I hope she buys plenty of groceries. I'd sure hate to get caught way out here with nothing to eat!" I laughed.

As I dipped the creamy thick buttermilk into the empty barrel, I watched Eddie through the narrow panes of the kitchen window as he opened the feed sacks. Slipping out of his shoes, he picked up an old bone-handled knife from the porch railing. Grasping it in his toes, he cut at the twine lacing the tops of the sacks. Then he put the knife back, sat down, and pulled the twine from the sack tops. He wound it around a ball of twine. I smiled to myself as I remembered how Mom saved little pieces of string, even pieces of wire she found lying around. Eddie reached over and picked up an old coffee can and dipped bran into an empty bucket.

I stirred the bran and grain into the buttermilk. "Now, I suppose we add water to this to fill the barrel?"

"That's right, and be careful on that path down the creek bank. It's slippery!" he warned.

I got my coat and pulled on my gloves. I shivered as I walked toward the creek. Buckets of water later, my arms ached and the legs of my jeans were frozen stiff where, in my awkwardness, I'd let water splash out of the buckets. I finally had the barrel full. I thought ruefully of how long it had taken to fill the barrels and how fast they would be emptied.

I stopped by the shed where Eddie was busy shucking corn for the chickens. "Eddie, how much slop do you feed the hogs?" I asked, watching as he expertly pulled the dry husk off an ear of corn, snapping the dry end of the cob with his strong toes, throwing the husks into one pile on the floor and tossing the ear of corn onto another pile at the base of the corn sheller.

"About a bucketful to a hog, but wait 'til I get my shoes on and I'll help you," Eddie said. He pulled the cut-out ends of his socks down between his toes, held them, and slipped his feet into his moccasins.

"You won't need to help me; I can do it all right." I said.

"That's what you think! Those pigs haven't any manners at all, just wait and see!"

Mom had improvised pens from a long line of tumble-down sheds, using old pieces of lumber to build the outdoor runs. I placed one bucket on the ground and started to lean over the fence, ready to pour the slop into the trough, but Eddie stopped me.

"Wait! This old sow will knock that bucket right out of your hands. Just wait a jiffy 'til I get my board!"

I waited, not quite knowing what Eddie could do to help me but I understood when he straddled the fence and wedged his left foot in between the boards. He let his right shoe fall to the ground, "Now hand me that stick," he said, "And I'll give old Mrs. Sow a clout across her snout. When she backs up, pour the slop in her trough!"

Even so, the old sow was almost too fast for me and nearly succeeded in knocking the bucket from my hands. By the time we'd fed the fifteen sows and the old boar, the feeling of mild dislike I'd always had for hogs had changed to one of active hate. I made up my mind to talk Mom into selling the whole lot at the first opportunity. After the hogs were fed I helped Eddie finish shelling the corn.

"Is this all the corn Eddie?" I asked, as he tossed the last ear from the pile on the floor into the hopper of the sheller. I turned the handle. Golden kernels dropped with clicking sounds to the bucket on the floor.

"That's the last of it. From now on, we're going to have to buy feed for the hogs and the chickens." Eddie's voice sounded discouraged as he reached over and ran his toes through the almost full bucket of corn.

"What happened to the wheat Mom farmed on shares with Jess Dasher? She wrote me that they had a good crop."

"She did," Eddie answered. "The granary over there is full of wheat but the door's got a lock on it and a seal. I suppose we'd get sent to jail if we unlocked it and used any of it!"

"What do you mean? It's your wheat, isn't it? How can you have wheat locked in a granary and not be able to use it?"

"Sure, it's our wheat, but with this New Deal business, Mom's already sold it to the government. She used the money to pay off some of the loan she got to put in a crop and for moving the cattle up here when our pasture at the ranch dried up. The government man came out, estimated the amount of wheat and sealed the granary. So it really

151

doesn't belong to us. When we haul it to town next summer, if there's more than they figured, we get the money for that."

"God, what a temptation! A whole granary full of wheat and you have to buy feed." I pushed open the chicken house door and waited until the chickens quit their mad cackling.

"Well, you know Mom, she wouldn't touch it. Besides, if it hadn't been for Roosevelt, a lot of little farmers would have lost everything! At least he loaned us money on our cattle and bought our wheat. That's more than the banks would do! And if the bank had loaned us money, they'd probably have taken everything we put up for security by now!" Eddie kicked the empty water pan over on its side, knocking the loose straw from it with unnecessary vigor.

I could hear in Eddie's voice an echo of Mom's anger and worry at the bank's refusal to loan her money. She had faith in Roosevelt's ability to help the depression-ridden country back to prosperity.

"There's no doubt he's helped, but…"

"You're darned right he has, Hazie! And you know what?" Eddie's voice was enthusiastic, now. "If we can just hang on to the cattle for a while longer, the way prices are coming up, we'll do just fine!"

"Yes, I think you will. There's going to be a big demand for beef. Did Mom sell a lot of hogs?"

"Yeah, she sold about one hundred and ten. She made darned good money on them. I guess that's why she wants to keep those old brood sows." Doubt had crept back into his voice.

"You know Eddie, she could leave the cattle here. They would get along all right. Then she could sell the hogs."

"I suppose so, but she's so stubborn!" Eddie said, a defeated tone in his voice.

32 Snowbound

*S*tanding in the bare yard, I felt wisps of hair blowing about my face as the wind picked up. "The wind is starting to blow, Eddie. Don't you think it's getting stormier?"

"Oh, this won't amount to anything. It's clouded up like this for the last few weeks and nothing's happened." He shrugged. "The last good storm we had was that one in October."

We started toward the barn, its sagging roof a dejected silhouette against the gray sky. "C'mon," Eddie said, "Let's throw a little fodder to the cattle and then it will be about time for lunch."

"I suppose Mom gives the cows just enough feed to bring them in every day so she can count them?" I pushed back the pole gate and walked toward the far side of the corral where the feed stack loomed large within its barbed wire enclosure.

"Sure, as long as there isn't a lot of snow they can rustle plenty to eat," Eddie said. A fat snowflake plopped on his nose, then a few more, falling faster.

I opened the rickety gate to the feed stack and reached for the pitchfork leaning against the fence. I had pitched a few forkfuls when Eddie's voice stopped me.

"Maybe we'd better throw the feed in the corral, Hazel. That way the cattle will all come in and we can pen them up until we see what this snow will amount to." He grinned at me, his face ruddy under the heavy wool stocking cap pulled down over his ears.

"Yeah, it's coming down harder all the time! You're worried too, aren't you Eddie?"

"Well, if it starts to blow, they'd turn their tails to the storm and they'd be miles from here by morning. We can always turn them out if it clears up soon."

"Mom wouldn't start back in a bad storm, would she?"

"Not if it was really bad. It's thirty miles out of here. She knows better than to try to make it back in!" Eddie assured me.

"Well, let's have some lunch, maybe it will clear up!" I said. We stood out of the way as the cattle nudged one another hurrying into the corral, their furry winter coats already white with snow. We waited for the last straggler.

"That's it," Eddie said, "All thirty of them. Close the gate and let's go get warm!"

As we hurried to the house I wondered at how quiet it was. The stillness bothered me. It was so different in this mountain valley. At the ranch, I could tell when we were going to get a hard blizzard because the wind blew hard and for miles you could see it moving in.

Neither Eddie nor I enjoyed our lunch. I'd look up to catch him glancing at the window. My gaze would follow his, only to see the snow falling thicker and faster. Finally, as if he couldn't stand it another minute, Eddie scraped his chair back and got up. I followed him to the door and pushed it open. Already the snow covered everything with a blanket of white and it was hard to see the barn from where we stood.

"Looks like we're in for it!" Eddie said.

"Maybe it'll stop during the night." I ventured.

"Yeah, sure it will."

The next few hours we worked against time. I chopped wood and silently said a prayer of thanks for a razor sharp axe blade. Eddie loaded the wood into the little red wagon he had played with as a child. He fastened a rope to the tongue of the wagon, and then he would tuck the rope between his chin and shoulder and pull the wagon up beside the porch, slip out of his shoes and pitch the wood onto the back porch. Then he was back for another load.

I tried to get him to let me carry the wood to the porch, telling him that his feet were going to be frozen. He laughed. "You know I've gone barefoot all my life. My feet are used to the snow and the cold. They're a lot tougher than your hands!"

I didn't argue. I knew it would take a lot of wood to keep the fire going for any length of time. I tried not to think of all the stories I'd heard about farmers who froze to death in a blizzard as they tried to get from their house to the barn or the wood pile.

By mid-afternoon, Eddie had thrown wood as high as he could onto the porch and had stacked what wouldn't fit on the porch into an awkward pile near the stoop. I opened the barbed wire enclosure to the feed stack and tied it back out of the way. The cattle would have plenty to eat and could get into the barn for shelter. We filled extra pans with water for the chickens and gave them the last of the corn. I gave Belle, our old mare, an extra feeding of oats and turned her into the corral with the cattle.

"Well, that's about all we can do, I guess." Eddie said as we came around the corner of the barn.

"Don't you think I should give the hogs another feeding?" I asked.

"No, they can miss a couple of meals if they have to and they can eat snow for water. We'd better get to the house while we can still find it!"

I'd been so busy I hadn't noticed that the wind was blowing a lot harder. Now it tugged at us. Snowflakes had a sting to them as they bit into our cheeks. For the first time, I felt real fear grip my gut as I looked toward the house and saw only an indistinct blur floating away from us. When we finally reached the porch, I brushed the snow off Eddie's shoulders and we stomped the snow from our feet. I knew he was as relieved as I was to reach the shelter of the house.

"Well, I guess we'll sit this one out!" I said, as I poked more wood into the stove and hung our coats on the nails behind the door.

"Well, we can always play cards!" Eddie grinned back at me as I pushed the coffeepot to the front of the stove and waited for it to get hot.

Our hopes that the storm would stop during the night were in vain. It was Saturday when the snow started and it didn't stop until early Tuesday morning.

We awakened to a muffled quiet, intensified because our ears had become almost accustomed to the fury of the wind that at times threatened to blow the roof off the house. As soon as we were dressed, we hurried to the door and opened it to a strange world.

Snow had blanketed all the landmarks. Then the wind changed it all again. The jagged country looked as though frosted by the extravagant hand of a master baker who swirled his icing into gigantic dips and whirls, camouflaging familiar things and low spots of the landscape in drifts of fluffy white frosting.

"Well," Eddie said as he squinted against the blinding whiteness of sun on snow, "It's a sure cinch no one can get into this place! We'd better try to get out!"

"But Eddie," I just couldn't see how we were going to break through those huge drifts. "how are we going to accomplish that?"

"We have to. The cattle are all right but there's just enough feed for the chickens and the hogs for one meal and that won't seem like much to them after all this time. Not to mention that there isn't anything for us." Eddie said all this in a flat voice that made it seem all the worse.

I thought of the little dab of flour in the bottom of the sack and wished for the groceries Mom planned to bring. Eddie's voice jolted me out of my thoughts.

"Well, let's get at it. It's going to take Belle a long time to plow through those drifts—if she can!"

We gave the stock the last of the feed. I got out the old Army saddle. It was split down the middle. The leather along the stirrups was stiff and curled upward with age. I felt sore just contemplating the eight-mile ride to the main highway where there was a little country store and our only hope of help.

"My God, Eddie, is this the only saddle we've got?"

"Yeah, Jody rides bareback and uses a halter for a bridle. Belle pretty much does what Jody wants her to do."

"Well, here's a bridle but it's not much better." I threw it to the floor. It didn't even bend.

Eddie sat on an old box and pulled the bridle toward him. He grasped the reins between his toes, looked up at me and said, "Here, pull on this rein and see if it's going to break there where that weak spot is. I'd rather fix it now than have it break on us out there!"

I gave the rein a good, hard pull. It broke. "The whole thing is rotten. How are we going to fix it?" I threw the broken rein to the floor of the shed. "This harness must have been hanging here for years, too.

Just feel how brittle it is." I dragged the harness over and dropped it in a heap of resisting leather angles at Eddie's feet.

"Yeah, it was here when we moved up this spring," Eddie said. "We've never used it."

We tried to find one good strap in the tangled mess, stiff as only leather can be when it hasn't been oiled and taken care of properly.

"Here, I think this one will do. Unsnap it if you can break that rust on the snap. We'll probably have to soak it in kerosene to get it loosened up."

"I can't budge it Eddie. And we can't soak it. Remember, we're out of coal oil too!" I rubbed my hands against my thighs, then slapped them together, trying to get some warmth into my stiff fingers.

"Darn, how could I forget that?! We had to go to bed when it got dark—couldn't even play cards." He grinned ruefully.

I remembered the strange feeling I had when Eddie and I drained the few remaining drops of oil out of the four lamps into one. Then we'd struggled to tip the big kerosene can to get a few last dribbles from its rusty interior. How disappointed we'd been when there still wasn't enough oil to keep the wick wet. Eddie blamed himself for letting Mom forget the oil can and I tried to tell him that it didn't matter. Then we watched the last feeble flame sputter from the wick and start to blacken the lamp's chimney as it went out. That left us with only the glow from the isinglass eyes in the heating stove to light the room. All at once, the wind seemed to howl like a banshee. The loose shingles on the roof flapped madly. I'd been acutely conscious of the cold as it encroached on the heat of the pot-bellied stove.

"Well, I guess we'll have to cut this strap, Hazel. We can gouge a hole in it and tie it on with a piece of baling wire. Give me your pocket knife." Eddie held up his foot.

"I can do it, Eddie. Why don't you see if you can find a little piece of wire." I placed the strap on a box and carefully rotated the end of the blade in a circle. Slowly, I made a hole large enough to thread a piece of wire through. Finally we had the bridle repaired. One rein hung loose and pliable, the other looked stiff and awkward.

"I hope old Belle knows this trip is necessary. She doesn't look like she wants to go anywhere," Eddie said jokingly.

Belle stood on the south side of the barn, little puffs of steam rising from her wet flanks where the sun shone on her. I walked over and, using a piece of old blanket, gave her a good rub down.

"Well, I fed her the last of the oats and bran. She's got a full stomach and that's more than I can say for us." I picked up the bridle and walked toward the old mare, hiding the bridle behind me.

Eddie followed, sidling up on Belle's other side so she wouldn't get any ideas about not letting us catch her. I put my arm around her neck, then gently fastened the best rein, holding it firmly until I could get the bit between her jaws and the bridle over her head.

Belle clenched her teeth, laid her ears back against her head, stomped the snow and shook her head, saying "No!" as emphatically as she could in horse language.

"Come on, Hazel! Don't let her bluff you! Grab her ears, bring her head down and slip it to her! She knows you feel sorry for her." Eddie said, teasing me. Then he came up and rubbed his face against the soft place under Belle's ear, talking to her softly.   "C'mon Belle, old girl! Let Hazie put your bridle on. We've got to get out of here. We've got to find out what happened to Mom and Jody and Dyanna and get some feed to the rest of the animals."

Belle lowered her head as if she understood and nickered softly at Eddie as I fastened the bridle and led her toward the shed. Eddie went on into the shed, slipped out of his shoe and started shaking out a frayed, dusty saddle blanket. He handed it to me. I fitted it over Belle's back then swung the saddle up and settled it in place.

"We're going to need a piece of rope, Eddie. I'm going to tie that short-handled shovel on someplace, just in case we get stuck in a snowdrift."

"I saw a piece of rope here somewhere," Eddie said, poking through the litter on the floor. "Here it is," he called. He picked up the length of rope and tossed it to me.

I tied the last knot around the shovel and tugged at the saddle horn to see whether the saddle was tight. Belle sometimes tricked us when we tightened the cinch by blowing her belly out and making it big. Then, after we got in the saddle, she'd let her breath out and the saddle would turn. But it was tight. She wasn't in a frivolous mood this morning either.

158

"We'd better make one last stop at that outdoor privy," Eddie said. "We sure won't want to have to get unbundled any more than necessary after we get started."

I helped Eddie, then he waited for me.

"I sure wish we had some sunglasses. This glare on the snow is murder." Eddie said.

"You ride in the saddle, Eddie. I can ride behind you and reach around you so if we slip, I can hold you on. Okay?"

I helped Eddie, then swung up myself. Belle stepped out gingerly, but when she came to the first drift, she shook her head and snorted, sending snow flying as she lunged through it. Eddie and I lifted our feet above the snow and I squeezed him around the middle, communicating my thankfulness that the old mare wasn't daunted.

The wind had blown the ground bare in places, leaving a thin skin of ice. In other places, the snow was piled into huge drifts. We could skirt some of the deepest drifts while we were still in the valley where we knew how the fields were laid out. I didn't like to think of the narrow road winding up along the canyon wall.

At the first gate I had to use the shovel before I could budge it. I almost wished it was made of barbed wire instead of smooth weathered poles. It creaked and groaned as I swung it open just far enough for Belle to walk through. She turned and nudged at me as I closed it behind us. I patted her neck then tied the shovel back alongside the saddle and clambered back to my seat behind Eddie. I settled in and reached around him to grab the reins.

"I hope that darned creek isn't drifted full. It's hard enough to find the road when there's just a little snow over it," Eddie said as we started up again.

"If I have to," I answered, "I can walk across first then lead Belle after I find a safe place to cross. We sure can't risk her breaking a leg." I quit talking. The cold air made my teeth ache.

At the creek we found the snow drifted even worse than we imagined. Ordinarily, there was a cut bank about four feet high on the side we were on. The narrow road gouged out of the bank at an angle, crossed the stream, and went up the gentler slope on the other side. Now, the snow was piled smooth to about the middle of the stream where a whim of the wind had cut it off sharply leaving the far bank almost bare, showing us where the road came out.

I remembered how thrilled Mom had been that spring when she brought me to look at this wonderful place she'd found for the cattle. I looked at the huge barn with its sagging roof, and the sorry house. I thought of how, even now, ranchers built better houses for their animals than for their families. I wondered how long it had been since a family lived in this forlorn place before Mom found it.

"The grass is just wonderful," she said. "It hasn't been pastured in years. And look at that old orchard. It isn't much, but the apples would make good hog food!"

I had looked across at the gnarled trunks of the apple and cherry trees, their imperfections and lack of care hidden by clouds of soft, pinkish-white blossoms. "I know, Mom." I'd said, "But that orchard hasn't been pruned or sprayed for God knows how many years!"

"Well, I could prune it out some, and think of the free hog food. Look at those acorn thickets all along the creek bottom! No better hog food in the world than acorns!"

"I suppose you're going to start raising hogs and just let them run loose?" I remember saying, a little sarcastically.

"Well, it sure is a pretty place. You'll have to admit that."

"Yeah, in the springtime with all the trees in bloom, it's pretty, Mom. Just promise me you won't even think of moving up here. It would be fine pasture for the cows but that's it!" I was emphatic.

"We'll see," she said, and that was it for the moment.

So here we are, I thought, *Eddie and I trying to get out.* God only knew where Mom, Jody, and Dyanna might be. I hoped they had stayed in town with Mickie, or at the ranch.

Now I said, "Well, here goes, Eddie," and I slid off Belle's back to the ground. I dropped the reins, knowing Belle would stay right there until I came back. I started forward, but within a few steps, I felt nothing underfoot and dropped, foundering in snow up to my waist.

"Come back, Hazel, and try it a little to your right. There's an old cow trail beside the road on this side. I think if you can find it, the snow won't be quite so deep!" Eddie called. He knew the country better than I…he also had the advantage of being able to see better from his perch atop old Belle.

After three tries, I found a way through where the boulders didn't slide under my feet and where the snow wasn't too deep for Belle. Going back, I picked up the reins. "Eddie, can you stay on if Belle starts to fall?" I asked.

"I think so. I'll take my feet out of the stirrups and if I have to jump off, it won't hurt me. The snow's nice and soft!" He laughed but I noticed that when he took his feet out of the stirrups he held Belle around the middle as tightly as he could with his long legs.

"Come on, Belle! Take it easy now!" Belle picked her way carefully, testing each step before she put her weight on her feet, slowly plowing forward, her belly dragging the snow.

We reached the far side and I got up behind the saddle again. Dampness from the snow I'd waded through started to seep through my layers of clothes.

"You know, Hazel, if we can just hug the wall of the canyon I don't think we'll have any trouble. The road's cut out of the side and there aren't any ditches there for Belle to stumble into." Eddie said.

"If I have to shovel a path right up to the top of the rim rock, I'm not about to take a chance on getting anywhere close to the edge and sliding off," I said. "Maybe the snow has drifted away from the wall! Let's hope so!" I said a little prayer that it would be so.

There were only a couple of places where I had to shovel a wider path next to the wall. The snow had drifted away from the overhang in places, leaving a narrow aisle with vertical drifts higher than our heads. In places the ground was bare and we made up for the time we had to shovel.

"Well, how long did it take?" Eddie asked when we came out on top.

Pushing back my sodden coat sleeve, I looked at my watch. "My God, it's eleven o'clock! It's taken almost four hours! That should be the worst of it though, shouldn't it Eddie?" I asked for reassurance.

"It better be! Much more of that and you and Belle will both be worn out! Doesn't look like the snow's very deep for a ways here. I think I'll get off and walk. Get warmed up!"

Eddie lifted his leg up over the saddle and jumped to the ground. Then he started stomping up and down to force some warmth into his cramped legs.

We stood on the rim of the canyon and looked back at the tortured trail we had furrowed up the narrow road. But we didn't talk about it.

Maybe some day we'd be able to make a joke about it, telling tall tales of how we'd fought our way, inch by inch, up and out of the little valley. Just now we were too conscious of the long way still ahead of us.

I was sweating from the unaccustomed exertion of climbing and digging, and now a feeling of clamminess was replacing the warmth inside my clothing. I picked up the reins. "Come on, Belle. We'll walk and give you a chance to get your breath!"

We forged ahead quietly to save our energy. Up here on top of the plateau, the dark green of the pine trees at the edge of the canyon was the only thing breaking the monotony of snow on snow. There were no fences here, so when we came to a drift, we simply walked around it. I knew that when we came to the next gate, the narrow country road would be fenced on either side from then on. I hoped against hope that a farmer would have been along before us, breaking some kind of a trail through the snow.

Finally, we came to the gate, but the only things marring the smooth surface of the snow were the tiny tracks of birds. Sometimes we saw the tracks of a jackrabbit where he'd ventured forth after the long storm in search of food.

The road stretched ahead of us, almost bare in places, but in other places it was drifted full, the tips of the fence posts on either side just barely visible. We walked when we could, not only to keep warm, but also to keep from getting any sorer than we were already. When we came to drifts Belle could navigate, we climbed on her back and let her plow through. Sometimes I had to shovel.

Each time Belle conquered a new obstacle we'd pat her, telling her in extravagant words how wonderful she was. She'd quiver her ears back and forth and plod on, her step a little lighter for a short time with her own importance.

"How much farther is it now, Eddie?" I asked at almost two o'clock. The wind was starting to blow and some of the brilliance of the sun had faded.

"We've come about five miles, I reckon. It's three miles to the gate from our place and we've come about two since then, I guess. We've got a good three miles to go yet."

"The way we've been skirting drifts, I'll bet we've actually covered a lot more than that!" I said. "Well, if we're lucky, we ought to make it by dark."

Eddie gave a shout as we neared the next ranch. "Man, we are lucky! The old Dutchman's been out with his snow plow from here on!"

Sure enough, we could see where he'd taken off toward the main highway. Snow was piled high on either side of the road where his snow drag had plowed a smooth path through the drifts. Even old Belle pricked up her ears and her feet. Eddie and I climbed on for the last time. I gave Belle a little nudge in the flanks with my heels and she pranced a bit, almost forgetting her age and the double burden she was carrying. I gave Eddie a big hug and started singing, "We've two more miles to go, we've two more miles to go!" Eddie joined in, turning in the saddle toward me, a wide grin racking his snow burned face.

Just as dusk fell, we turned onto the main highway. The little country store already had its gas lamp lit and in the window. Eddie and I gave glad cries as we recognized Mom's truck parked near the single gas pump. I gave Belle a kick in the flanks, but she was past hurrying. I tied her to the hitching rail. Eddie jumped off and streaked into the store, forgetting his cramped legs as he hurried to see Mom. My joints creaked and I knew I'd be taking my next few meals off the mantle. I climbed the worn steps to the store more slowly than Eddie had. As I closed the heavy door behind me, I felt warmth reaching out to me from the pot-bellied stove, red around its middle. The smell of kerosene, cheese, and gingersnaps blended with that of the hay and feed stacked in the back room. The odor of manure from farmers' boots when they came in, and the smells of wet wool and sweat didn't do a thing to stop the hunger pangs that started the saliva rushing to my mouth.

Mom stood there holding Eddie tight, Jody at his other side and both asking questions. Dyanna came over to me and I lifted her to the counter, hugging her. Then I hugged Mom and Jody. I grinned as I realized Eddie was driving home a point or two in his own quiet way.

"I don't care, Mom! We're moving back to the ranch just as soon as Mr. DeVore can open up the road and get his truck in to move our stuff!" Eddie looked over at "The Dutchman," as everyone called Mr. DeVore, and Mr. DeVore nodded in approval.

"Your mother here, she's been trying to get me to go out there tonight just to see if you were alright. Now, I'll take feed to the stock on the sled, tomorrow. Then in two, three days, I'll move everything out for you! Maybe it's a good thing this storm happened. It made your mama see that it's no place for a woman and kids all alone!"

The Dutchman reached up and pulled at his ear lobe, his bright blue eyes quizzical in his red face, wondering if he'd said too much. He added, "I'll take your horse around back, feed her and give her a good rubdown." He hurried out. My heart filled with gratitude.

Mom nodded absently as if she were trying to sort things out. Then she smiled at me over Eddie's head and gave her head a little shake, the way she did when her mind was made up.

"Yes, you're right, all of you! I've had my lesson. I'll never take a chance like this again. If anything had happened to you and Eddie…!" As usual she was thinking of us, not thinking of how hard it had been for her on the God-forsaken place or what could have happened if she had been badly hurt at some time and Jody, Eddie, and Dyanna had had to get out for help.

Thank God, I thought. Everything is all right. I wouldn't have to use any of the devious plans I'd been trying to think up to get her back to the ranch where she belonged.

Old John Simon, the store owner, spoke up. "How much feed you gonna need, Mis' Higgins? I'd just as well be loadin' it on the sled for ye. Ye'll be goin' back to the ranch to stay the night, I reckon, but we'll sled the feed in tomorrow and get the road cleared for you." He'd been standing there behind his counter, taking in every word and probably figured he'd just as well be doing what he'd have to do anyway while we gabbed. His little crossroads store was a sort of clearing house for all the gossip around the countryside and he didn't miss a thing.

Mom told him what she needed while he got his cap, gloves, and a heavy old coat that muffled him from head to toe.

Eddie and I looked at each other, and then I spoke up. "Say, Mr. Simon, before you go out to start loading up, do you think you could loan us your coffee pot, sell us some coffee and a little cheese and crackers?" Just mentioning food made my stomach start to turn flip-flops.

"Yeah, and a quart of milk and some of those coconut cookies over there in the jar." Eddie said, and then added, "You know, you can sure get tired of eggs and flapjacks—and they ran out a day ago."

33 *A Late Christmas and Racing Cars*

Within days, Mom hired someone to truck the hogs and ten of the cows to his sale lot in Pueblo. He would sell them at the next auction. She arranged for everything else to be moved back to the ranch. When it was done, I noticed that Mom seemed to be glad to be back in her own home.

Dad came down from Monarch in time for Christmas and said he could stay a couple of weeks. This was great news, as it had been almost two years since he had been able to be at home for any length of time.

I had missed Eddie's birthday. Tomorrow was Christmas. There just wasn't time to prepare dinner, put up the tree, and do the necessary things to make a happy Christmas.

"Why don't we just combine Eddie's birthday, Christmas, and New Year and celebrate all of it on New Year's Day?" Mom suggested.

"That would be great! Then Dad can help us cut the tree and you and Hazel can make all the good things to eat!" Eddie was enthusiastic.

Mom's brother Ray, his wife Emma, and their son Kenny had been staying at the ranch while Mom was at the Colvin place. They planned to move to Lime as soon as the holidays were over.

Dad, Eddie, Jody, Dyanna, and Kenny went to cut the Christmas tree. Mom and I found the boxes that held all the decorations from past years and I drove to Pueblo and bought what we needed for everything else. Jody soon had Dyanna and Kenny stringing cranberries and popping corn to be strung.

Mom and I made apple pies and mincemeat pies. Then we baked a squash to be cut into small pieces and baked with brown sugar glaze. Mom marinated a big venison roast and set it aside to be baked in the morning.

Everything we could do had been done. We looked at each other with a big sigh of accomplishment. Mom poured coffee and we sat at the old oak table and were silent for a while.

"If you're going to stay in Pueblo, Eddie can stay with you and go to school. I don't want to make excuses for myself, but I want you to know I am sorry for trying to stay at the Colvin place. Eddie missed a year of school and it didn't turn out at all as I thought it would." Mom wiped away a tear.

"I know, Mom." I answered. "I would have been better off staying in Pueblo and running my shop, too. In the long run, I would have been way ahead of the game."

"From now on we'll just work together." she said. Then with a little laugh like a burden had been lifted from her shoulders, she gave me a big hug.

New Year's morning was a new beginning for all of us. We stood before the tree with its gay trimmings and little gifts piled up under it and held hands. Dad said a blessing for all of us, and then the kids started tearing into their presents.

Kenny got a Tinker Toy set from all of us. Dyanna got a beautiful doll with long blonde hair. Eddie gave Kenny some small racing cars and told him he would help him learn how to race them at the track in Pueblo. I thought Eddie would have as much fun with them as Kenny.

Dad made a table from sawhorses with long boards laid across. Mom unearthed her linen tablecloth. When the table was set, it looked very festive. Mickie and Vic brought a big salad. Although we missed Bill and Bud, we knew they'd spent a good Christmas with their grandparents.

As soon as dinner was over, Eddie got out his little cars and sat down on the floor with Kenny. He had a box with magnetic weights, miniature tools, and everything he needed in it to get the cars fixed just right. He had Dad bring in a long board and propped it up on a chair, wiggling it about until it was just right. Then he and Kenny gave their cars a test run.

"Now this is what you have to do." Eddie picked up one of the cars with his toes, holding it firmly between the big toe and the smaller toes of his right foot. Turning it over, he pointed with his left big toe at the small space beside the axle of the little car. Then he picked up a tiny magnet with the toes of his left foot and carefully placed it in the spot beside the axle.

"Now watch," he told Kenny, "See how that little weight holds the car steady on a straight line? We have to check them all out and put the magnets where they need to be placed." Kenny watched wide eyed as Eddie showed him these tricks. Soon they had the cars fixed up and they started racing them.

"Are you going to race them at the track at the Fairgrounds?" I asked Eddie.

"Yeah, you'll have to come and watch. It's going to be next Saturday and Sunday, okay?"

"Sure, I'll come Sunday," I said. "I'll bring Mom and the kids."

At the Colorado State Fair Grounds Agricultural Building, we made quite a contingent to root for Eddie and Kenny. I could tell Eddie was nervous as he gave their names and got his entry slip. The racing track was plywood with a slope and a curve that banked to the left. It looked fairly tricky and I could see the contestants eyeing it carefully. It was set up about two and a half feet off the floor to give the smaller kids room to set up their cars. Eddie could just reach up with his foot to position his cars. The track would accommodate eight cars at a time. Kenny and Eddie had been chosen to run in the first slot.

I watched nervously as Eddie reached into his shoebox to get out his favorite car, a red and white replica of a 1937 convertible. He had taken off both shoes and I could see some of the kids glancing sideways at him as he placed his car on the track, standing on one leg to do so.

The referee gave instructions, and then rang a bell for the first race. Eddie and Kenny stood back and watched their cars go.

All the contestants were yelling at their cars in hopes of making them go faster. All too soon it was over, Eddie came in fourth, and

Kenny was next to last. Kenny gave a crestfallen little shrug and Eddie told him, "Don't worry Kenny, one of these days we'll both win!"

I didn't get to all the races but I did go to the fourth race. It had become quite an event and the place was packed. I could tell Eddie and Kenny were nervous and I was caught up in the excitement of the crowd.

The starting line was arranged so that there was a space between each car. The contestants stood back. The starter tripped the wire that held them. They took off. Eddie's and Kenny's cars were in the lead. Suddenly, Kenny's car shot in front of Eddie's red and white convertible and Kenny was the winner.

Kenny grabbed Eddie around the neck so hard he almost upset him. Then Jody, Dyanna, and Mom had their turns. Kenny was red as a beet and shaking so hard he didn't reach up to accept the blue ribbon he got for winning.

Two weeks later, Eddie got a win. We were all there to cheer for him, and when he accepted his blue ribbon, everyone let out a big yell.

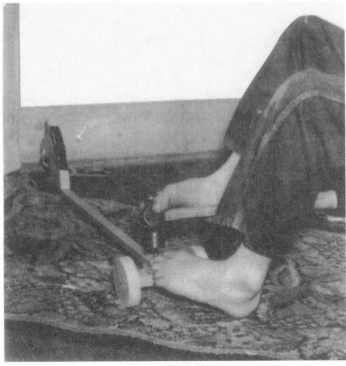

Very Talented Feet

I think Eddie's mind was racing, too, because he asked me, "What would you think if I started helping kids who are racing in the Soap Box Derby with their cars?"

"Well, you know a lot about engines, carburetors, and all that," I answered. "I think it would be a real challenge."

"Do you think you or Mom could take me to the races? I think most of the kids would bring their cars out there to work on them."

"I think between all of us we'd find a way to get you where you need to go. Gosh Eddie, that sounds exciting!"

"Well, I just wanted to see what you would say. I've got a couple of boys ready to go," he said.

"Great! I think you will get a kick out of it and maybe one day you can have your own car!"

"Yeah, I'm going to start saving my money so I can get a car and fix it up!"

34 Charlie Owen Killed

The phone shrilled. I dried my hands as I hurried to answer it.

"Hazel, this is Ione. I have some terrible news. Charlie was killed when his plane crashed in that terrible storm last night!"

Ione Owen started to cry uncontrollably. I waited a moment then said, "Mom, Eddie, and I will come up, Ione. Is there someone with you, now?"

"Oh, I wish you would. Yes, Grace Bonner is here and Deke. Remember him? He partnered with Babe sometimes." She seemed a little calmer. I remembered that "Babe" was her pet name for Charlie.

"I'll go out to the ranch right away and we'll get started. How is the weather up there? It's fine here, the storm was mostly to the north of us." I'd heard how bad it had been through Wyoming and Nebraska and couldn't imagine Charlie starting out in that kind of weather.

I tried to think of an easy way to tell Eddie. He idolized Charlie. I remembered when Charlie would ride Eddie on his shoulders and let him steer his Cadillac. When Eddie got a little older, Charlie would let him drive. He even let Eddie fly his plane on one of our trips to Denver. Charlie and Ione had kept in touch after the highway by our house was finished. If it were at all possible, they spent Christmas and Thanksgiving with our family.

When Eddie saw my face, he knew something was wrong.

"Okay Sis, what happened?" As I closed the door, he snuggled his face against my shoulder.

"Eddie, Charlie crashed his plane last night in that storm in Wyoming. Ione called and wants us to come up right away." He cried then and I held him tight.

We stood there for a while trying to comfort each other. Mom came into the room and she realized immediately that something terrible had happened. I told her what little I knew and asked how soon she could be ready to leave. I knew she could probably get Ad Bray to take care of her rabbits, chickens and pets until we got back.

Eddie and I drove up to the Bray ranch and made the arrangements.

"Mickie said to bring Dyanna and Jody to stay with her until we get back. I think she misses Vic." I told Mom.

"I guess it's hard to find a place to live near the shipyards." Mom told me. "Vic's been out there three weeks. Got a job right away. He told Mickie she could go to work the day after she got there, if she wanted to." Mom sounded proud that they would be working in the shipyards.

Eddie sat with me in front, and as we sped along he talked about Charlie and Ione and how much they meant to him. We remembered how Ione told us that she had been a school teacher in the wild country of Wyoming, with nothing but prairies, wheat fields, and coyotes howling at the moon. She only had five pupils and it was her first school. Charlie was one of her pupils, only three years younger than Ione.

His family owned thousands of acres of land. They ran Herefords and farmed wheat. Charlie didn't like farming. After he persuaded Ione to marry him, they got into the road-building business. She kept the books and could run a crew as good as any man. They had been partners in marriage and in business for about thirty years. They were very successful in both.

Then along came all the trouble in Europe, and Charlie found himself over-extended in business loans and the banks unwilling to bail him out. They were being forced to put their money into the war effort even before war had been declared.

Ione told us this that night. It was as if she wanted to tell us about the good times and the bad times. She knew we would understand. When she told us that she was going to have to sell the house and all the equipment to satisfy debts they owed, she simply said, "Babe would want it that way. He never welched on a debt. And, we've had the good years."

We understood. That had always been a policy with my parents. You paid what you owed. If there was any left over, great!

Charlie's funeral was simple, as his life had been. There were farmers in their best blue jeans and cowboy shirts, and cattle ranchers in five hundred-dollar Western suits and soft white Stetsons. They seemed to come from everywhere.

Later, we sat around the fireplace in the family room. I listened as Ione and Mom talked about their husbands. Ione was laughing sadly at some of the things she remembered Charlie doing. "Oh, that Babe!" she'd exclaim, then go on to something else.

Some reminiscences brought tears while others brought a sad smile. Ione turned to Eddie, "Eddie, you know Babe didn't plan this. He wanted to do a lot of things for you but that isn't going to be possible. I've picked out some of the things I know he would want you to have. And I want you to have this check. I hope down the way a bit it can help you get started in some kind of a business where you can take care of yourself."

She had tears in her eyes as she tucked the check into Eddie's shirt pocket. She hugged him and gave him a big kiss on the cheek. "When I get settled in Casper I want you all to come and visit. That would make me very happy." She kept her arm close around him.

"I will Ione, and I hope you come to see us too. It sure isn't going to be the same..." Eddie had to turn away.

35 A New Home, Gas Iron, and Bad Scare

$\mathcal{A}$fter weeks of looking in Pueblo for a house to rent, Eddie and I found a little house we could buy. Five hundred down and take over payments. After looking at it for the third time, we decided it would be better than renting. We were excited.

"A good scrubbing and a little paint will make it cozy," I said. "Do you think Mom will like it?"

"Sure she will. I'll plant a garden. That soil in the backyard looks good." I was happy to see him interested in something. He'd been so down since Charlie's death that I was worried about him. He didn't seem to be interested in going back to school or anything else.

Eddie did wonders with things that needed fixing at the house. One day I watched as he wrestled with some windows that wouldn't open. He pulled a chair over to a window, carefully tapping along the frame with his hammer and chisel.

Then he stood up on the chair and, balancing on one leg, he grabbed the pull at the bottom of the window between his big toe and the rest of his toes and gave a big push upward. He finally got it open enough to get the chisel under the window and soon had it open.

"I think once I get these windows loose, I'm going to take them out and sand all that paint and gook off them. There must be a dozen coats on them." He moved toward the next window.

"Eddie, are we going to have to buy a new grate for the heating stove?" I asked. He had already fixed the grate in the cook stove as we needed to use it even in the hot weather.

"Yeah, it'll have to be replaced but we don't need to worry about it yet. I'm going to start looking around. I may find a good heating stove that won't need to be fixed." He always had an eye out for bargains and like Mom and me, he knew a good antique when he was lucky enough to stumble on one.

"Gosh Hazie," Eddie said one day. "This summer is flying by." He waved his foot toward his garden, "Look at how that garden has grown! Lloyd told me his Mom would let us have some space in her freezer. I'm giving him half the veggies for helping me put in the garden and I'm going to freeze some corn and some string beans for sure. We'll surprise everyone by having corn on the cob for Thanksgiving!"

"That's great! Mom got a letter from Dad yesterday and he is going to be able to come home for a week or more. Maybe he can bring Helen with him for a couple of days." I knew Eddie and Helen were still writing to each other.

Eddie didn't say anything. He went over to a row of beets and reached over to weed. He grasped a weed between his big toe and the rest of the toes on his right foot. He pulled it up, shook the soil from its roots, and tossed it onto a pile of weeds near the fence. He slowly walked down the row, pulling weeds as he went. When he came back to the head of the next row where I was standing, he gave his shoulder a little shrug and said, "I don't know whether she wants to see me or not. She sounds like she is keeping busy and going to a lot of dances and other stuff."

"Well Eddie, it isn't like you're going steady. She probably does have a lot of friends there. Just ask her if she'd like to come for Thanksgiving. Sometimes it's more fun to be best friends." I looked at him, but he was off somewhere that I couldn't reach.

"That would suit me just fine," he said. "That's why I like Helen so much, I think. We'd go with her brother looking for old mines, go wading in some of those little streams, doing all kinds of goofy things. I'd just like someone I could talk to that didn't treat me like I was different."

"Why don't you write her and just tell her we'd all like to see her?"

"Yeah, I can do that." He sounded just a bit more upbeat. By now Eddie had pulled a whole stack of weeds. When Eddie and I got out of the car at the ranch, Mom walked over from where she had been working in her garden.

"Mom," Eddie said, "Is it too late to plant a couple of hills of watermelons?"

"I think it is a little late, Son. But if you don't mind experimenting, I'll give you some of my plants that already have a good start. You will have to keep them covered for about a week, that should do it." She gave a little chuckle and I knew she was thinking of how good it was to see him interested.

Mom agonized over the crops she was farming on the shares with Jess Dasher and Ad Bray. There had been a couple of good spring snows and the winter wheat was doing fine. But the hot, dry weather was taking its toll on the milo maize she and Ad planned on for rough forage. The cattle were still in the mountains and Jess said they were fine. Mom was in no hurry to bring them back to a dry pasture. She prayed for rain and even little Dyanna would look at the heavens and say a prayer.

Just before Mom's fifty-fourth birthday in August, the mailman delivered a heavy package. Eddie and I were just leaving for Pueblo when he arrived and we waited to see what Dad had sent.

When she had torn through all the layers of paper, she found a heavy cardboard box with a picture of an iron on it.

Eddie couldn't restrain himself. "Mom, it's a gasoline iron! It uses high test gas and you pump it up like you do the Coleman lamp!"

It was made of shiny metal and blue enamel. Mom lifted it and you could almost tell she was thinking how much lighter it was than her old fashioned flat irons. No matter how hot it was in summer, bright and early every Tuesday morning Mom fired up the cook stove and put her six irons on to heat. She usually had a couple of bushel baskets of clothes all starched, dampened, and waiting for her. She ironed everything from sheets to overalls. If it had been possible, I'm sure she would have had Dad send his heavy work clothes from Monarch for her to iron.

"Well I'll be—I will have to get used to this iron. Sonny, when you come out tomorrow, bring me a gallon of high test gas. We'll see how this contraption works." She hummed a little tune as she carefully put the iron back in its box.

Eddie and I were in the yard one morning when we heard Mom scream. We ran to the house to find Mom trying to force Dyanna's mouth open. I could smell gasoline. Mom lifted an ashen face to me. "She drank some high test gas."

I immediately stretched Dyanna out on the table and started giving her mouth-to-mouth breathing. It wasn't working. Her jaws were clenched and there was no way to get air into her lungs. By now, she was turning a pale bluish tinge. I knew we had to do something fast or she would die.

"Mom, hold her up by her heels and let me see if I can get my fingers into her throat and open her airways." Mom held her up and I pushed my fingers into her throat. For a second, all I felt was a clenched tightness, and then a sputter and a gasp. I opened my fingers wider. I knew I had to be hurting her but I also knew she mustn't clench her teeth again and close her throat. Then I felt her trying to get a breath.

I yelled to Eddie, "Get the car started. She's trying to breathe and I can give her mouth-to-mouth breaths in the car. Drive to the emergency room. Mom and I will hold Dyanna in the back seat."

Eddie drove right up to the emergency room, opened the car door for us, then rushed up to the desk and told them what was wrong. They soon had Dyanna on oxygen, taking very harsh breaths and getting some pink back in her cheeks.

The doctor came over and with a big smile said, "You can quit worrying. You saved her life and she's going to be fine. She'll have a sore throat and we want to keep her overnight to be sure she doesn't have any gas left in her lungs. Luckily, she didn't seem to swallow very much."

36 Fishing with Granddad

The mail brought a card from Aunt Clara. Granddad had been living with her for about a month. It said: "Ethel, please come up and get Dad. He wants to live with you, Clara." Abrupt and to the point.

The next day, we drove Granddad to the ranch. Dyanna snuggled up to him all the way home. I could hear Granddad telling her a wild story about Indians. The minute we got home she took great pains to see that he had a glass of water. Then she went to the garden and picked him a bouquet of yellow roses. When she put them in an old cracked vase on the little table beside his chair, he reached for her with trembling hands and drew her to him. "Thank you, they're my favorite flower." His voice shook and a tear spilled onto his shirtfront.

Dyanna and Granddad quickly became pals and conspirators. She would fix him snacks, bring a cool pan of water to wash his face and hands, and brush his few strands of hair.

Lady, Granddad's shepherd dog, seemed almost as old as Granddad. She sat beside his chair, her head on his lap, and when he moved, she adjusted herself to his position. When he rocked his chair, she rocked along with him. Dyanna would stand beside the chair and gently assist in the rocking.

One day near the end of summer, we loaded Granddad's rocking chair in the trunk along with fishing poles, a picnic lunch, and some pillows to put behind his back. He was like a little kid, first saying to let him stay home, and then when he knew he was going, he just gave a quivery smile and let us pack him in.

It was only about ten miles to the lake. I always held my breath when I came up over the little rise above the lake and looked down at it. There were a lot of willow trees making a fringe of shade and shadows on the water. Beavers had been busy in a few places and you could see them swimming, branches clutched firmly in their teeth, toward the home they were building. As we parked and started to unload, although we were quite a ways from them, they gave the water quick slaps with their broad tails and disappeared.

We chose a spot where there was a little beach with a few rocks big enough to sit on. The willows were tall enough here to give us shade. Mom and I placed Granddad's rocker in the shade, got him out of the car, and tucked him in with pillows behind his bony back. Lady, his dog, waited, and then took her position beside his chair, put her head on his lap and waited for him to give her some petting.

Dyanna found flowers and began to build sandcastles at Granddad's feet.

I watched Eddie deftly thread the line through the eyes of the poles and pick out the hooks he wanted to use. "Is this hook about the right size, Hazie?" He held up a No. 8 Snell.

"Yeah, that should do it."

He grasped the hook between his big toe and the next one. With the toes of his other foot holding the line steady, he placed the hook through the loop at the end of the line. He spilled a couple of worms out of the coffee can, chose one, and threaded it on the hook. "Hey, your poles are ready. Let's catch a fish."

Eddie grasped his pole in his right foot. Balancing on his left leg, he gave a big swing and threw his line way out into the lake. He picked out a rock and sat patiently to wait for a fish to bite.

I walked quite a ways past Eddie to an area where the water looked deeper. I wanted to try to catch a bass. There were bass, catfish, perch, crappies, and sunfish in this lake and you never knew what else you might catch.

Out of the corner of my eye I saw Eddie give his pole a quick jerk. All of a sudden the water far out churned. A fish jumped high in the air. Eddie sat back on his rock and started to maneuver his pole, first lowering it and reeling in then raising it, trying to tire his catch.

"I think you caught a whopper, Eddie." Mom put her pole down and moved closer to Eddie. "Do you need any help, Son?"

"No," Eddie answered breathlessly. "I'm going to land this one myself." And he kept working. Soon we could see the outline of the fish in the water. A deep slash of red down its side glinted in the sun. "Man, it's a rainbow! And look how big it is!" Eddie started backing up so he could bring his fish in on the shore. We didn't have a net.

I moved in closer so I could help, but this was Eddie's fight. Soon he had the fish close to shore and he lifted its head to tire it just a bit more before trying to bring it in.

"Okay, here goes. I'm going to try to get it on shore. If you have to jump on it, please do. Don't let it get away." He was out of breath and I could see his leg trembling as he steadied himself to make the final effort.

He held the pole with his right foot, reeled in with his left, holding the reel handle between his toes. He kept the line tight but would lower the pole once in a while to reel in more line, gradually tiring the fish enough to handle it. When he finally had the fish close to shore he stood up, balancing on his left leg and using the rock to steady himself.

He brought the pole in a slow arc and when the fish was less than a foot from the water's edge, he gave a hefty tug and, wham, flopped the trout about three feet up on shore. He dropped his pole and pounced on the trout. Faster than my eyes could follow, he had the big toe of his right foot in the trout's gill and his left foot firmly pushing the fish into the sand.

He waited until I brought the stringer and opened a link, then, very carefully, he pushed the metal prong into the fish's gill and out through its mouth and used his toes to fasten the line. Only then did he take his left foot off the trout.

"I've got to sit down." And he practically collapsed on his rock. "Mom, we'll have to measure that one and weigh him. I'll bet he's close to two pounds. For a while there he felt like he weighed fifty!" Eddie was still shaking but he had a grin from ear to ear. We all crowded around him and his fish. Then Mom took it over so Granddad could see it close up.

Granddad reached out and touched the red streak along the side of the rainbow. "Be proud of that one, Sonny. He'd make a dozen of those little 'uns you used to catch."

37 World War II is Declared

"Eddie, did you write to Helen about coming down with Dad for Thanksgiving?" I was sorting clothes to take to the laundry.

"Yeah, she said that she could."

"You don't sound too excited, what else did she say?"

"She just said something about not being surprised if Dad didn't get any time off for Thanksgiving. She said the company wasn't giving any vacations."

The last time Dad wrote he sounded worried that we were going to get into an all-out war. I hoped we wouldn't, but the way Hitler was riding roughshod over all the countries in Europe, I didn't see how we could stay out much longer.

"How do you feel about starting back to school, Eddie?" In the fall, he would go back to school at Centennial. I knew he wasn't happy about taking his sophomore year over.

"I guess I'm just not excited about school any more, Hazie. I can remember when I wanted to be a lawyer and had big dreams about going to college and all that. Now, well, I just can't see me doing all the reading that would be necessary to become an attorney. Then it wouldn't be over. I'd have to read up on every case and I just couldn't do it." He gave me a sad little smile.

"You mean because of your back?" We didn't often talk about it.

"Yeah, well I guess you could say it was my back, but actually I've gotten used to that damned hump that keeps getting bigger. Sure it hurts, it hurts all the time, but I guess the hardest thing is how people look at me. It's like I'm a freak or something!" His voice rose. A note of despair overrode the anger. How do you build up armor around your feelings, strong enough to keep the hurt out?

"You know Eddie, I can't walk in your shoes and knowing the way most people are, I don't think I would want to. But you have to think of all the people you have helped just by being you. Think of the little kids you have met and talked with who have had cerebral palsy, for instance. They can't walk, or if they can, it is with great effort. Speaking and writing is hard, if not impossible. Remember the kids you helped when you were racing your little cars? They will never forget how much you helped them."

"I guess you're right. You're sure right when you say I'm better off than a lot of people. I guess I've just got a good case of the blues and feeling sorry for myself." He smiled at me like the sun breaking through the clouds.

"Maybe that's what you're supposed to do, Eddie. Just help those who need help. You never can tell, it could be someone who seems to have everything but somehow they've got a hole in their heart and imagine they are really bad off."

I could remember some of the chronic complainers I'd met. No one could help them. They existed to feed off their imaginary shortcomings.

"I know you're probably right, Hazie. Come on—let's find us a real problem to solve." He gave me a lopsided grin. "You know, come to think of it, how would you like to be in Dad's shoes?" He cocked his head to one side and raised an eyebrow. "I wouldn't like it. When I think of him, sixty-six years old and battling those six-foot drifts during the winter, it's just hard to imagine. I keep hoping the company will say he can't work any more. But I don't think that will happen as long as this war scare is as bad as it is." Eddie was solemn. I felt a little chill at the tone of his voice.

"Well, we'll have a good Thanksgiving and pray for the best." I gave Eddie a big hug.

Once again we decided to have Eddie's birthday, Thanksgiving, and Christmas all together at Thanksgiving. It would be a time to say goodbye to Mickie before she left for California and for everyone to see Granddad.

The holiday was a great success. Eddie's corn on the cob and watermelons had all of us asking for seconds. Mom made squash pies and everyone said they were just as good as pumpkin pies.

I couldn't help feeling that we were just a little bit too gay. No one mentioned the war until someone said to Mom. "Well Ethel, you won't have to worry about Eddie having to go to war." Mom didn't say anything, just shook her head.

Eddie, Mom, and I were playing cards on a cold winter evening when all of a sudden the program on our little Zenith radio broke into whatever was playing.

"Japan Bombs Pearl Harbor!"

Mom started to cry. Eddie went to her and said, "Mom, we knew we were bound to get in this war. We just didn't know it would be like this." She folded him in her arms.

We stayed up all night listening to replays of the bombing, the terrible noise, and confusion, wishing there was some way we could help.

War was declared on Japan. Everyone blamed everyone else. Headlines said that Cordell Hull and Roosevelt made the error of thinking Japan was bluffing. They under-estimated Japan and refused Japan any face-saving concessions.

I could still hear Dad say, "Just wait! If they aren't careful we're going to be caught with our pants down!" And that is exactly what happened.

It was chaos! Overnight, those who were against war at any price found themselves doing everything they could to help win.

Pueblo, Colorado became the site of the Pueblo Army Depot where weaponry, arms, munitions and, some said, poison gas was stored. Pueblo became a beehive of activity. The steel mill was operating on a twenty-four-hour-a-day basis. People who hadn't worked for years were called back.

Eddie was repeating his sophomore year and I was running the beauty shop. We lived close enough to school that he could come home at noon and we'd eat lunch together.

Mom usually came in on Saturday. She still sold eggs to her customers and an occasional chicken and quite a few rabbits. Eddie would go back with her for the weekend. At times he would say, "I wish I didn't have to go to school. I'd a heck of a lot rather be out at the ranch with Mom and the kids."

One weekend, as soon as Mom left he said, "Hazel, Mom's working too hard. She won't admit it but she isn't a spring chicken anymore. Jody won't help unless she absolutely has to and Dyanna helps all she can." He pushed his half-empty coffee cup to the middle of the table.

"Yeah, I've been worried about her too. Granddad is a lot of care but I'm just glad he's with us. Dyanna adores him and helps a lot."

Eddie shifted in his chair. "You know all the cattle are still on the Colvin place. Jess Dasher is taking good care of them. There are about fifty chickens and that number could be cut to about five. That many would furnish us with all the eggs we need. And the rabbits, what do you think? There are about twenty, aren't there?"

"Yeah, that's about right." I answered.

"I'd hate to do it, but we could do without the milk she gets from Daisy. In fact, I doubt if she'd give Daisy up for anything."

"Do you think we could talk her into giving up her pets? I know she'll tell us how much money she makes on all of these animals." I thought to myself, *Yeah, right, when Hell freezes over. That's when she might give up her animals.*

"Hazie, do you think she would let us hire someone to work at the ranch? I know this kid, he's about sixteen. He's dropped out of school because he just can't learn. He got to the eighth grade and quit."

"I think she might. Especially if she thought we were going to try to talk her into selling about everything."

"He's nice looking, always neat and clean with dark red hair. He has green eyes and he's skinny now, but I think when he gets older he'll look like his Dad."

"What do you think about taking him out to the ranch with us this weekend?" I didn't want to get my hopes up but I thought this might work.

"That would give Mom a chance to meet him and, hopefully, like him, before we talked to either of them about his working there." Eddie sounded as if a load had been lifted from his shoulders.

As we drove toward the ranch, Red Barnes couldn't keep his curiosity to himself. He kept Eddie busy with a barrage of questions. "What kind of animals are there? Does your Mom have a dog?" I wondered what he'd think when he met Rowser.

I needn't have worried. Rowser found a kindred spirit. They were friends from the moment they met. Mom couldn't believe her eyes when she saw the big dog turn his sad brown eyes up and move a little closer for Red to pet him.

Eddie and I watched as Mom talked to Red and when he asked to see the animals, she went to great pains to show him everything.

"I think they are going to get along fine. What do you think, Hazie?" Eddie was watching Mom and Red as they walked up the path from the rabbit pens. "It looks like Mom is ready to baby him." he added.

"Let's not say anything now, Eddie. We can talk to Red on the way back to town and when Mom comes in, we'll ask her what she thinks of Red."

If they liked one another, it could be a perfect solution.

38 Mom Scares Us and Meet Mr. Morey Bernstein

*S*pring of 1942 was cold and raw. The wind blew incessantly and ice formed on the cedar tree branches until they broke under the weight. Even with Red's help, Mom wouldn't stay out of the weather and take care of herself. Eddie argued with her and I threatened to sell all her animals if she didn't let Red take care of them. He was capable and did a good job, but as she said, she "just had to give him a hand."

Red called me at the shop on a Thursday afternoon and just the tone of his voice sent chills down my back. "You've got to come out! Right away!" I could hear a tremble as he said, "Your Mom is sick. Real sick."

"I'll be right out, Red. Just ask her to go to bed and stay there until I can get there."

I called Dr. Crozier. He agreed to ride out with me as he was getting older and had quit driving into the country. He asked what was wrong. I made a wild guess. I thought it was probably pneumonia.

Mom seemed tiny in the bed. Her cheeks were flushed a bright red and she barely croaked when she tried to sit up and say hello. She just shook her head, feebly, and let Dr. Crozier examine her.

He straightened up and turned to me. "Your mother is very sick. She should be in the hospital but I hesitate to move her. Will you be able to stay with her and give her the care she needs?"

"Yes. Just leave me the medication I will need and instructions and I can do it." I knew Mom would be happier at home and I just hoped I could do what would have to be done. ·

I called Eddie. He wanted to come. I called the shop and had them cancel my appointments for the next week and asked Virginia to bring Eddie out to the ranch. I gave her a list of groceries, and as I thought of Mom and her home remedies, I added a large box of mustard to it.

The next week was touch and go. If Eddie wasn't at Mom's side, Red or Dyanna was. Even Jody pitched in. It seemed we were all working so hard to make her get well that Mom cooperated with us.

She gave me a weak smile when I brought in the first of many mustard plasters. I knew it was her favorite remedy for croup, pleurisy, and just a plain bad cold. Dr. Crozier sort of shook his head when he came out and saw the mustard plasters but said, "I'm a bit old fashioned myself and I've seen my share of people get well when all they had were mustard plasters slapped on them."

On the sixth day, Mom's fever broke. She was drenched with sweat but she wore a big smile. "I'm going to get well. Those mustard plasters did it." She put her hand on Eddie's knee.

He leaned over and gave her a big smooch. "Sure, you're going to get well. It won't be long before you'll be out there chasing chickens around the yard."

"Yes, I've been thinking..." and her voice trailed off and she fell into a sound sleep. When I called Dr. Crozier, he was pleased. "That's what we've been waiting for. She'll be all right now. Just give her hot chicken soup and when she gets hungry, plenty of good home cooking."

That evening, after all the chores were done and Jody and Dyanna had gone to bed, Eddie, Red, and I sat around the table and made plans. "Eddie, what would you think about driving back and forth to school until Mom gets back on her feet? I could drive us in, go to the shop, do a few appointments and we could come back out when school lets out."

"I don't know why that wouldn't work, Hazie. Red could look after things until we got home and he could call you if anything went wrong." Eddie got up and walked around the table then looked down at Red. "Would that be okay with you, Red?"

"Yeah, I could handle it. You can trust me." Red added this last with a proud little smile.

After I had put Eddie's PJs on him I said, "I'm going to make a list of things for Jody and Dyanna and Red to do while we're gone during the day. I think it will help all of them so they won't lock horns."

I handed the list to Red the next morning and told Jody and Dyanna that they were supposed to follow Red's directions. Red beamed at being given this little bit of authority. I knew he wouldn't abuse it

Mom was getting stronger and bossier by the end of the fourth week. Spring was in the air and bluebirds were flitting everywhere. Mom was in the yard poking at the mulch she had heaped over her flower beds.

"Eddie, come here!" she called. "I want you to see these tulips. And my daffodils!" Her voice sounded strong and happy. Eddie went over and with his toes started helping Mom uncover her plants.

"Can you believe all this?" Eddie waved his foot in a big circle, taking in the yard around the house, the garage, the barn on the hill and the long building near the well. "I'll bet no one would ever believe that once there wasn't a tree or a flower anywhere near this house."

Mom just smiled a proud smile as she said, "I can remember every tree and every plant that is growing around here. I remember when Art planted those four elms in the front yard. They were so tiny that I wondered if they would live. Look at them now! Way above the roof top and still growing."

"Yeah, Mom, and you know what I like? Those wild plum and choke cherry thickets beside the road to the garage. Remember the day we got those roots at Granddad's old place by the ice house?" Eddie had a far-away look on his face.

"What I remember most is how much fun we had when we found something new to plant," Mom said. "I guess sometimes we forget how darned lucky we've been." I knew she was just itching to get down on her knees and dig in the soil.

That night I told Red to keep an eye on her and gently but firmly talk her into giving him the shovel or the hoe and let him do the digging.

Eddie and I were back in town and I thought all was well. The phone shrilled one evening: "Hazel, this is Mom. The generator broke

down and the pump at the lower well isn't working. Could you and Eddie come out? I don't know what to do."

"Sure, Mom. We'll be right out. Eddie just finished his homework. Do you need any groceries or anything?"

"Yes, bring me a pound of coffee. With your Dad not here we don't drink as much, but Granddad sure likes his morning coffee."

When we arrived at the ranch, Mom turned to Eddie. I suddenly understood that Eddie was the one she relied on, not me, and not Dad. When had this happened? I now realized that for quite awhile we had been asking for and taking Eddie's advice about a lot of things.

"I think we should buy a windmill and put it on the upper well," Eddie said. "We've got a practically new pump there and the storage cistern Dad built is adequate for everything we'll ever need. Who carries windmills in Pueblo?"

Mom responded, "I'll call the man we bought our pump and well casing from. If he doesn't have them, he will know who does."

"We can't call now, Mom," I said. "Why don't I call in the morning?"

"Do you have enough water to get by on for now?" Eddie asked.

"Yes, luckily the storage tank is about half full. That will do for about a week at the most," Mom answered.

"Well, that should do it. We'll call you in the morning."

When I called the pump man, he told me he didn't carry windmills. "Try Bernstein Brothers Pipe and Machinery," he said.

I was waiting when Eddie came home from school. He shrugged out of the strap of his book satchel, went to the kitchen and reached for a cup on the counter top. Grasping the handle between his big toe and the other toes of his right foot, he placed it under the faucet. Letting go of the cup, he deftly turned the cold water faucet and filled his cup. He then stood against the sink and drank thirstily and then said, "There's no point in calling, let's just go down and see what they have. Give me a quick trip to the bathroom, Hazie, and I'm ready to go."

Our bathroom on West Street was an old-fashioned affair. The oak water compartment lined with copper was fastened to the wall. It was flushed by pulling a chain that hung down beside it. A claw footed tub stood along one side of the room and the lavatory was screwed to the opposite wall. There wasn't a light switch. A piece of cord trailed down from the bare bulb in the ceiling. We talked of remodeling but decided we would look for another house on the south side of town so Eddie could graduate from Central High.

I thought of all these things as I lifted the seat on the toilet, unzipped Eddie's pants, held his penis while he went, put it back in his pants, and zipped them up for him. I pulled the chain and listened as the water noisily filled the tank. We were out the door and on our way before the water stopped running.

Bernstein Brothers was located on South Mechanic Street in Pueblo. A two-story brick building that looked ancient was flanked on one side by railroad tracks and on the other by a chain-link fenced yard. I couldn't help but notice a vicious looking dog and immediately the phrase 'meaner than a junk yard dog' flashed through my mind.

As we entered the building, I was struck by a hodge-podge of things: bath tubs and plumbing supplies, bins with pipe fittings, copper pipe, a roll of barbed wire, a stock tank, chain hoists. How do they keep track of all this stuff, I wondered.

A dapper young man came down the stairs from what I presumed were offices. He almost collided with a tall fellow in jeans who came from the back of the building.

"That's all right, Slim. I'll take care of it. It isn't often a pretty girl walks into Bernstein Brothers." He came toward us with his hand outstretched to Eddie. He flushed beet red when Eddie held his foot up for a handshake. He awkwardly shook Eddie's foot then said, "You'll have to pardon me, I just didn't realize..." he floundered, then continued, "I meant it when I said, 'not many pretty girls come in.' Now what can I help you with?"

Then realizing he hadn't introduced himself, he said, "I'm Morey Bernstein. My dad, Sam, and my Uncle Abe own this business. My grandfather started it in the 1800s. Now, can we start over?"

Eddie let out a chuckle and I laughed, "Sure, let's start over. As long as we are doing introductions, I'm Hazel Higgins and this is my brother, Eddie. We want to buy a windmill."

"I'm glad to meet you. And I hope you'll forgive me my blunders."

"Of course we will. Now, what about that windmill?" I asked.

"Sure, we carry windmills, but we are out right now. I have a shipment due in next week. What size windmill do you want?" he asked.

Eddie spoke up, "We have a well six hundred and ninety feet deep. We had a submersible pump installed about two years ago. We have a storage tank, partly underground and covered, that holds probably ten thousand gallons of water. We don't have electricity out there and have been using a generator."

I added, "The generator was old and it finally quit working."

"Sounds to me like you need a generator to tide you over until we can get a windmill installed," he said, with a question in his voice.

"Yes, if we could rent a generator that would help." I said.

"Let me talk to Slim. He's in charge of ranch supply and he may know if we have a generator." He hurried to the back.

Eddie looked at me. "Haven't you got enough trouble? He's flirting with you, you know." His voice was flat.

"Yeah, I know. It feels sort of good for a change. I could stand having a nice young man to take me out once in a while." I returned Eddie's 'I'll-take-care-of-you' glare.

Morey came back. "We do have a generator and you can use it until we get a windmill in for you. Where do you live?"

Eddie started giving him directions and I could see that Morey was listening, but all the while he was sneaking looks at me.

"We live sixteen miles south, right on the main highway to Trinidad and New Mexico. You can't miss it. There's a little filling station beside the road called 'Prairie Junction.'"

"Let's see." Morey sounded like he was talking to himself. "Today is Friday. I'll bring Slim with me and we can install that generator for you, tomorrow. Would that be all right?"

"Why yes, that would be fantastic. I can't wait to tell Mom. She's about worried herself sick about not having any water." I gave Morey a big smile and watched as the brown flecks in his green eyes changed color. I found myself very curious about this young man.

"There's one catch to my delivering the generator on a Saturday." Morey said.

"What's that?" I asked, thinking he might take back his offer.

"I would like you to come back into town and have dinner with me. Do you think you would like to do that?"

I thought for a minute then, "Yes, I think I would like that very much."

Eddie didn't say much as we drove to the ranch. And I was deep in my own thoughts.

39 *Eddie takes Morey for a Ride*

*H*ey, Hazie," Eddie called from the yard. "I think your boyfriend is here with the generator he promised you."

"Stop teasing me. Just because he asked me to go to dinner doesn't make him my boyfriend!" I knew he would never shut up. Just like Dad, he couldn't help teasing if he had a chance.

"Hi there," I greeted Morey as I nervously pushed my shirt more snugly into my jeans.

"I brought Slim with me to help set up this generator." Morey introduced Slim then said to Eddie, "Why don't you ride up with Slim, Eddie, and I'll get Hazel to bring me up.

"Come on into the house, Morey. I want you to meet my Mom." I held the door open for him.

As I introduced them, Morey piled on the charm. "Well, Mrs. Higgins…"

Mom interrupted him, saying, "Please, call me Ethel."

"Okay Ethel. I was going to say I can see where Hazel gets her good looks." He gave her a big smile.

"Oh, go on with you." Mom sort of blushed but I could see that she was impressed. "Thank you so much for loaning us a generator. It will be good to have water on hand again."

"No problem, Ethel. And as soon as we can get a windmill up for you, your worries will be over."

"Come on, Morey." I urged him. "I know they're waiting for us." I turned to Mom, "We'll be back in a little while."

As we walked toward our old Willys, I thought, he's used to giving orders. I wondered if anyone ever crossed him.

He held the door open for me and we got into the car. As we drove up the hill to the well site, we made small talk. He was curious about everything.

A wild rabbit scuttled under a tree cactus and I asked Morey, "Do you like to hunt?"

"I don't know. I never have. I don't think I could kill anything. Probably couldn't hit it anyway." The sun caught shades of red in his light brown hair and I noticed that it fell in a close-cropped wave at the nape of his neck. "Why? Do you hunt?" he asked me.

"Not really. We kill a deer when we need it for food. We hunt rabbits mostly to keep their population down so they don't eat our entire garden." Just then another rabbit ran out in front of us.

"I don't know much about rabbits but wasn't that rabbit black and white?" Morey had a puzzled look on his face.

I had to laugh at the look on his face. "You'll have to get Eddie to tell you the great rabbit story some day. Just ask him."

Eddie and Slim were waiting for us. They had the broken generator out and the replacement was on the ground beside the well house.

"If you don't have any use for this old generator, we can take it back with us. It can go in the scrap iron pile." Morey motioned toward the old piece of equipment.

"Sure, it's no good to us anymore." Eddie waved toward it with his foot.

They set the generator and just before they took the cap off the well casing, Eddie said, "Watch this!"

I knew what was coming as I handed Eddie my cigarette lighter. Eddie reached down and with the toes of his left foot gave the cap a final twirl; he gave the lighter a flick with the big toe of his right foot. A flare of flame leapt into the air and Eddie laughed as Slim and Morey quickly stood back. It burned brightly for about two minutes, then flickered out.

"Well, I'll be damned! Why don't you cap that and use the gas for heat and…" Morey's voice trailed off.

Eddie grinned. "Don't think we haven't thought of it. We had it tested and there isn't enough gas to sustain use over a period of time. Mom still thinks there is oil here if we'd drill deep enough. But who knows?"

Once they had the generator going and water in production again I said, "I don't know how to thank you for all this work and the loan of the generator. It's like having a prayer answered."

"It's nothing. We're just glad we could do it, and it won't be long until your windmill is in." Then, as an afterthought, Morey said, "Don't you have another well somewhere? I thought Eddie said you pumped water by hand from another well."

Eddie answered, "We have a well below the road. It has a hand pump on it."

"Why don't you put a windmill on it too?" Morey asked.

"I guess we figured it would cost enough to get a windmill on this upper well." Eddie stood there, not saying any more.

"Well, when we get this order in, we'll have to see if there might be one that could be used on your lower well." Morey said. "Slim, why don't you take the truck and go on into town? I'll get Hazel to bring me in later." He turned to me. "Would that be okay with you, Hazel?"

"Why yes, I guess so. Sure, that would be fine." I felt like I was making a fool of myself. Why couldn't I have just said 'yes' without stuttering and stammering around?

After we had said goodbye to Slim and thanked him for his help, Morey said to Eddie, "Now Eddie, I want you to show me how you drive a car. I can't believe what I've been hearing. Would you do that for me?"

"Sure, where do you want to go?" Eddie asked.

"I don't care. Come on, Hazel. I just can't wait to see how Eddie handles a car."

"Let me tell Mom so she won't worry," I called over my shoulder as I went into the house.

"Watch your step," Mom said, "That young man has a look in his eye."

Morey watched intently as Eddie kicked off his loafers and shoved them under the edge of the seat.

With his right foot, Eddie picked up the ignition key. He put the key in the switch and turned it on. At the same time he fed the engine some gas with his left toe on the gas pedal.

As soon as the engine was running smoothly, he settled down on the canvas-covered cushions Mom had made for him. This enabled him to be at the right height to see out of the windshield. When we had last seen Dr. Norman he had told us, "If Eddie's back hadn't grown crooked, he'd be six foot tall by now." That didn't make us feel any better.

Morey continued to watch intently as Eddie placed his left heel on the clutch. He then stretched his toes toward the gas pedal. To shift gears, he would engage the clutch with his left heel, reach down with his right foot, and grasp the stick shift between his big toe with the rest of the toes curled tightly around it. He would shift into the gear needed at the time. He gave the engine the gas needed by depressing the gas pedal with the toes of his left foot. He used his left foot on the brake pedal when necessary.

To stop, he shifted down, then into neutral. With his toes on the gas pedal he would keep his heel on the brake until it was time to get going. He knew exactly how much gas to give the engine to keep it going. He didn't grind the gears when he shifted. When he wanted to park, he shifted down and into neutral. He would then turn the engine off before putting the engine into low gear. He turned to Morey, "It's easier for me to put the engine in low gear when I park. It's not going to go anywhere and I don't have to pull the hand brake."

Eddie did all this effortlessly. Morey watched every move Eddie made, cutting in once in a while with a "Well, I'll be damned!"

We went up the hill past the well and the hog pens. I knew Eddie was headed for the bluffs overlooking the St. Charles River. The country was rolling, with cedar trees and pinon pine nestled in clumps on some of the hills.

We came to a fence. Eddie shifted down and stopped at the gate. "Do you want to get that gate, Morey?"

"Sure, I'll get it." Morey climbed out of the car, went to the gate and stared for a while at the loops of wire holding the gate tight and upright. The gate was made of four strands of barbed wire with a short post in the middle. Morey figured out what he had to do and got the gate open. He pulled it out of the way so Eddie could drive through.

Eddie turned to me with a big grin on his face. "What do you want to bet he fastens the gate so he's on the wrong side?"

Sure enough, that's exactly what he did. When Morey realized what he had done he quickly did it over and came to the car. "You knew I'd do that, didn't you, Eddie?"

"Yeah, I sorta figured you would." We all had a good laugh.

"Eddie, you've made a believer out of me," Morey said. "Now, when anyone tells me that you can drive a car, I can tell them I watched you do it with my own eyes."

Eddie stopped near the edge of the canyon. We walked to the edge where we could see the river shimmering in the sun. A series of rocky ledges dropped down to the valley below.

"Look," Eddie exclaimed, "To the left, just beyond that stand of cedars. See that big buck just coming out of the trees?" Picking their way along behind him came his harem of does. The buck would lift his head and look around, then resume grazing on his way to the river for a drink.

"Let's just watch them for a while. We're in no hurry, are we?" Morey's voice had a little quiver in it.

Eddie and I exchanged looks. In seconds, we realized Morey had probably never seen a deer in the wild, let alone a whole herd of them.

"We've got plenty of time," Eddie answered. "Let's find a comfortable rock and watch them until the sun goes down."

I looked over at Morey. "Maybe we'll have a great sunset, too. There are just enough clouds for it to be outstanding." We found a ledge but before sitting down, I found a stick and poked under and around it. I saw Morey looking at me and wasn't surprised when he asked me what I was doing.

Eddie answered. "She's making sure we don't sit down on a rattlesnake. That would sure ruin our sunset, wouldn't it?"

"You mean there are rattlesnakes around here?" Morey started to get up.

"Yeah, we watch for them all the time. That old story about them warning you before they strike is a lot of hooey. You surprise them or get too close, they'll strike and rattle later." Eddie explained.

Morey handed me his cigarette pack and held a lighter for me. We sat there in a silent world. Soon our ears became attuned to the evening and we heard the call of a meadow lark and the soft whir of wings as quail came close and then noticed us. We could imagine the sound of the deer as they fanned out after their drink of water.

As if a curtain had been rung up, the sun started setting. The clouds bounced off rays of red and rust colors, finally setting in a haze of orange and gold.

Morey looked at Eddie and then at me, "I think I just had the most wonderful experience of my life." He waved his arm at the whole outdoors. "How can you beat this?"

40 A Beautiful Old Home

*M*om and I were busy preparing vegetables to can when Eddie and our cousin Bob drove into the yard.

Mom gave Eddie a hug and protested weakly as Bob swept her off her feet and swung her around. "Go on now, Bob! You're going to break all my bones!"

Bob chuckled and set her down. I always marveled at this cousin of ours. At twenty-two, Bob Hastings was six foot two and weighed over two hundred pounds. He had a shock of unruly reddish blonde hair, narrow blue eyes, freckles across the bridge of his nose, and a chuckle that turned into a belly laugh at the least provocation.

"So, Eddie, what have you two been up to?" Mom asked.

"Oh Mom, you should have been with us. We've been building roads for the Forest Service. You know, fire roads and logging roads. And we saw a bear and her half-grown cubs, a herd of elk and lots of deer." He stopped, out of breath.

"And I suppose you rode on all that big equipment?" I couldn't help asking.

"Yeah, and Bob let me drive once in a while!" Eddie had a proud note in his voice until he saw the worried look on Mom's face.

"Now Aunt Ethel, you don't go gettin' upset with us!" Then Bob hastened to add, "Eddie was just as safe as if he was right here beside you."

"Well I suppose so," she said then, "Well, why don't you get some of that dirt washed off and I'll rustle up something to eat."

After Bob had left, I said, "I think I might have found a house on the south side. My friend Wilma told me about it when she learned I was looking for something. She lived in the house next door all her life. It seems the house is owned by a doctor. He is quite old and he finally went back to St. Louis where he still has some relatives."

"When can we look at it?" Eddie asked.

"Tomorrow is Sunday. How about tomorrow afternoon? Would that be okay with you, Mom?" Jody and Dyanna were standing there with questions on their faces. "Yeah, you can go. After all, you'll be living there too, I guess." Mom and I had already decided Jody and Dyanna could stay with me and go to school. Jody would be a freshman and Dyanna would be in first grade.

Sunday we didn't go to church, but I knew Mom was up at sun-up, walking around her garden and saying her prayers. Breakfast was special as we each in turn said a little prayer before we started eating. Mom and I made biscuits, ham, ham gravy, and if anyone wanted an egg, there were always plenty. Red looked around at all of us when we had finished and were sipping the last of our coffee. "I want all of you to know I'm happy." He didn't say any more, just scraped his chair back and went out into the yard.

Mom said simply, "I hope you all know what an effort it was for him to say that. I'm proud of all of you for making him feel at home."

That afternoon, with mixed feelings of anticipation, we headed for Pueblo. I drove, with Dyanna and Eddie beside me. Jody and Mom held down the back seat. When we got into Pueblo, I headed straight for Central High School. Just seeing my old school brought back a lot of memories. We went on down Broadway and Mom exclaimed, "There's George McCarthy's Funeral Home. And across the street, that beautiful old church."

I turned the corner. "Yes Mom, and there is the vicarage, an alley, and here we are!"

I parked in front of a big old house with a wide porch across the front, a balcony off the second floor and a partial third story.

"Why, Hazel," Eddie said as he opened the door and jumped out. "This house is huge and it sure looks like it needs some work done on it."

"Well, let me get the key from Wilma and we'll go in and see." I went next door to pick up the key. When I came back with the key I had to round everyone up. Mom and Eddie were in the back yard. They had found a big garage that was entered from the alley.

"Hazie," Eddie exclaimed, "There's room for two cars in this garage and there's even a grease pit on the one side. It wouldn't take much to put a come-along on that beam up there and you'd have a perfect setup for fixing cars."

In fact, it already had a beam on either side of the roof. The trusses were such that weight bearing beams were lined up over where cars would be parked below.

Mom was poking around some flower beds and she pointed at a clump in the corner. "That's a snowball bush and along the back there is a solid hedge of lilacs, and these are peonies. This yard had to be just beautiful at one time. It wouldn't take much to get it back in shape."

"Yeah Mom," and I kidded her, "You're just the one to do it too, aren't you?"

She laughed, "Well I guess so. It would be fun!"

"Well come on, everyone. Let's go see what it's like on the inside." I couldn't help feeling excited.

Wilma told me that Dr. Storz's father built the house in the 1800's. Dr. Storz had stayed in the house and raised two sons who were now also doctors back East. His wife passed on four years ago. After her death, Doc, as everyone called him, sort of gave up. He decided to go back to St. Louis where he still had relatives. One day he had locked up the house, gave the key to Wilma, and left. She hadn't heard from him and didn't know what he wanted to do with the house. She told me I could write him if I was interested.

"I sure hope you buy it," she said. "I would like to have neighbors there."

The stairs of the porch were sturdy and didn't creak. The floor boards were all in very good condition as was the roof of the porch.

Eddie waved his foot toward the ceiling. "Look, there are hooks for a porch swing!"

Mom stood back from the door as I put the key in the ornate brass key shield. "This door is solid oak and just look at the window glass. Beveled, frosted, and etched in a forest design. Why Hazel, this door is priceless!"

"Hurry up, Hazie, open the door!" This request came from Jody who usually didn't show too much enthusiasm.

The door swung open easily and we all stood in awe. A carved oak stairway curved up to the floor above from an entry as big as one of our bedrooms. To the left, a wide hall went to the back of the house. I could glimpse rooms off the hallway.

"Hey Hazie, look at this!" Eddie called to me, "There are two sliding doors between this big room and the next room." Then with an "Abracadabra" he reached up to a panel, gave it a push and an oak door slid smoothly across the opening while Mom gave the door on the opposite side a shove.

I started laughing. I couldn't help it. Here we were, some of us in one room, some in the other. These two rooms together were probably 20 x 40 feet. The back room had a fireplace with pink marble tile facing and a long mantel of the same marble.

"That front room must have been the parlor and this back room, the living room" Mom mused. By now she had pushed the doors back into their slots. "I'll bet when they wanted to give a party they just opened this up and had lots of room."

The dining room opened off the room with the fireplace. Beyond was the kitchen. It was small and belonged in the dark ages.

Eddie and Mom both started talking at once. "I can just see you changing this kitchen and dining room around," Eddie said.

"And look," Mom opened a door. "There is another stairway that meets the front stairway on the landing."

"Yeah, well I don't know what I'd do with it, but something."

"C'mon, let's go upstairs and see what kind of mysteries are up there." Eddie let out a howl, hoping to scare Jody and Dyanna but it didn't work. They were two steps ahead of him.

Four large, airy bedrooms with big closets and a huge bathroom made up the second floor. The two front bedrooms opened onto the balcony over the front porch. There was a large storage room with built-in drawers and a door that led to the room upstairs.

"I don't care what that room up there looks like. It is going to be my room!" Jody ran ahead up the stairs.

"Yeah, and we'll call it 'Tojo's Castle'." Eddie teased her but she just made a face at him.

"Jody, it looks like some young man from long, long ago used this room as his castle. Look at those pin-ups!" I pointed to a lady in a bathing suit that came to her knees. She wore a bonnet, as well.

"I don't care. Look at this closet and this window seat! I just love it." Jody perched on the window seat, daring anyone to displace her.

We went downstairs, giving everything a last look.

"Oh, by the way," Eddie said. "I looked at the basement and the furnace. It looks okay but it's old. There's a coal bin and they had a washing machine down there. Can you believe that?"

"Well, what do you think? Should I try to buy it?"

"I don't think you can afford it, Hazel. It's a big house," Mom ventured.

"Why don't you make a crazy offer and see what happens." Eddie was serious. "All the doctor can do is turn you down. Remember what Dad always told us?"

"What did he tell us? He told us so many things!"

"'You never know how far a frog will jump until you poke it.'" Eddie was very solemn.

"Okay. We'll see what happens. If he takes an offer, I'd like to get moved in before school starts." We talked about the house all the way back to the ranch.

41 A House and Furniture Too

"Well, did you make an offer?" Eddie asked me the next weekend.

Before I could answer, Mom said, "I saw Ira Rambo this morning, and he said you talked to him about a loan. He told me he would be glad to loan you the money to buy the house."

"Wait a minute. You and Eddie are way ahead of me. Yes, I did make an offer. Dr. Storz called me last night and accepted it."

"What did you offer on it, Hazie?" Eddie was fidgeting from one foot to the other.

"You're not going to believe this." I paused, looking from Mom to Eddie. "I offered $2,300.00 cash and he didn't hesitate, counter-offer or anything else. He said he called me because he knew I would like to get in before school starts."

Mom's "I can't believe it," mingled with Eddie's, "Wow! When can we start to move?!"

"And listen to this. He told me he had some old furniture in storage that he had no use for. We can have it. I'm to call him today and he will arrange for us to take it out of Andrews' Storage."

"What do you think Hazie?" Eddie asked.

"I have a feeling from talking with Dr. Storz that he is happy that we're buying the house and that we are welcome to the stuff in storage. He just doesn't want to be bothered with any of it, anymore." I looked from Mom to Eddie.

"I think you're right Hazel. I know if I were old and had enough money to get along on, I wouldn't want to be worried about something so far away that I couldn't take care of it." Mom was usually right.

"Gosh Hazie, if it's anything like the house, you might get some neat antiques. Why don't you call him, now?" Eddie said.

"Okay I will. I told him I had to talk to you and Mom, so he's expecting my call." I picked up the phone and asked the operator to put my call through to St. Louis. I heard Dr. Storz's wispy voice on the line. I told him how happy Eddie and Mom were and that I would have a cashier's check in the mail today. He assured me that he would have his lawyer do all the paperwork. He said he would call Andrews' Storage and tell them to give me the key, and that we could move anything we wanted out of storage. I thanked him and told him how much we all appreciated what he was doing for us.

Andrews' Storage was in a three-story brick building that shared railroad siding with several other buildings. We climbed the stairs to the loading dock and entered the small office.

"We've come to look at the things Dr. Storz has in storage and to make arrangements to move them. Could you show us please?"

"Sure, no problem. There's quite a lot of it. You'll need a truck and a couple of guys." The warehouse man talked as we walked into the dimly lit interior of the first floor.

"Here you are," he told us and unlocked a large, heavy wire enclosure.

Mom turned to me. "We won't be able to get much of an idea of what's here until we take it out. It's piled on top of each other and a lot of it is wrapped." She sounded disappointed.

Eddie turned to the warehouse man. "Would next Saturday be okay? We'll try to be here about eight in the morning."

"Yeah, I open up at eight, so no problem." He handed me the key.

In a few more days we had the deed to the house, a note from Dr. Storz's attorney in St. Louis and a letter from Dr. Storz telling us how happy he was that the house would have a family in it. It made us feel great about the whole deal.

Red Barnes's dad brought his truck and one of the fellows who worked for him. We were at the warehouse a little before eight.

As we walked up the steps to the dock, Mom said, "I feel like Pandora just before she opened the box." We all laughed and it helped ease the tension we felt about exploring the remnants left by the family who had lived in the big old house.

Sam, the warehouse man, went back with us and I could see the surprise on his face when Eddie took off his shoe and kicked the key to the lock out of his shoe onto the floor. Then he picked it up, and with the toes of his right foot, turned the key in the lock and swung the door open. "Open Sesame!" he said and grinned.

There was a wide aisle down the center of the building and Mom asked if we could take everything out of the wire enclosure and put it in the middle of the aisle. That way we could sort out which pieces would go first into the truck.

"Oh, Lordy me! Look at this sofa. My Grandfather Aus had one almost exactly like it!" Mom was piling small boxes out of the way. Soon the truck was heaped and tied.

Eddie went with Dave Barnes and his helper to unload. Mom and I followed in the car that was also loaded. By three o'clock everything was out of storage and piled in the two big rooms of the house.

"How about lunch at Gus's? I know you all must be starved!" No one waited for an answer. We all piled in and headed for the best Italian food and beer in Pueblo.

Gus waved us to a big table at the back of the room and stood there kidding with Dave and Eddie. He knew Eddie from the time Eddie was a little boy and Dad and his friends from Lime would come in for a brew.

Dave asked whether there was anything else he could do to help.

"Not now Dave," I said, "But later, I would like you to take a look at that kitchen and see what can be done with it. You don't know how much we appreciate your help."

I handed Dave a twenty dollar bill but he wouldn't take it. "I don't want any pay for what I did today. You'll need your money to get the house fixed up. Besides, I couldn't begin to pay for what you've done for my boy. I never thought I'd see him as self-reliant as he is now." He shook hands with Mom and me, and gave Eddie a hug.

Dave went on his way. Eddie, Mom, Red, and I went back to the house on Pitkin. We couldn't wait to see what could be under all those wrappings.

Mom, never one to throw anything away, said, "Just throw all the stuff this furniture is wrapped in over in the corner. I'll go through it later. It looks like some of the wrappings are sheets."

With the exception of a few 'oh's' and 'ah's,' and 'look at this,' we worked silently. Now we took inventory. Mom was the expert because her grandfather, Aus, had many lovely pieces of furniture, and her father too, had many antiques, all lost when his home burned down.

There were two full-size bedsteads with springs; two, three-quarter beds with springs; six dressers and one dressing table, all oak and beautifully carved. There was a dining room table, eight chairs, an oak icebox, a really old couch, and two chairs.

Eddie had a tool box open before him. "Hazie, look at this. A whole set of woodworking tools. I wish I could learn to use them!" He turned to another box and started to look through it.

"Hazel," Mom couldn't keep the excitement out of her voice. "Here are dishes, silverware, and linens. Poor Dr. Storz, he must have had someone pack everything and put it in storage. Almost like that was the easiest way for him to part with the things he'd lived with all his life."

"Yeah," I answered. "I just hope he has someone there who loves him."

I had to buy mattresses for the beds but we settled in quickly. The big old house seemed to welcome us. Jody took the room on the third floor. Dyanna had a three-quarter bed in my room and Eddie had the room next to ours. I closed the sliding partitions between the two big rooms downstairs and put the old furniture in the back room with the fireplace. Eventually I would find the time and the money to re-upholster it, but for now it had to do. Actually, I liked it. It gave the house a special air.

Red's father said he would remodel the kitchen, but I needed to wait until I knew how much it was going to cost to run the house and take care of the kids.

42 *Granddad Dies*

O ne evening, Eddie asked, "Hazie, will you stop by the driver's license office tomorrow and get one of their instruction books on taking the license test?"

"Sure, you're planning on taking the test after your birthday?"

"Yeah, I know I can pass but that doesn't keep me from having the jitters." He looked so serious I had to laugh.

"It's not funny, darn it. I know I can do it, but man am I nervous!" He gave me a rueful little grin.

"Well your birthday is on the 3rd of December. Let's just hope it doesn't snow a foot deep!" I laughed.

We were finally getting settled into a routine. Jody and Dyanna reveled in the big claw-footed bathtub. It was certainly different from Saturday night baths in the washtub at the ranch.

Eddie and I said our prayers that all this would last.

When I came up the walk one evening after work, Eddie greeted me at the door. I couldn't read the expression on his face. "What's gone wrong, Eddie? You look like the roof fell in."

"Well, in a way I guess it has. When you left this morning, you told the furnace guys to make their inspection and close the back door after them when they left."

"Yes, I remember. Did they call and tell you what we needed to do to fix the grate?" I asked as I walked on toward the back of the house.

"They closed the door after them. But you won't believe what they did! They called and said they wanted to talk to you. When they wouldn't talk to me and insisted on talking to you, well as soon as they hung up I went to the basement." His voice trailed off.

"And...?" I asked.

"Hazie, they tore that furnace completely apart. They just left it all over the basement floor!" Eddie was as upset as I had ever seen him. His face was flushed red and he couldn't quit walking in tight little circles as he talked to me.

"I guess I'd better take a look."

I followed Eddie down the stairs to the basement. I felt a cool draft and realized the coal chute door was open. The furnace had its own space in a room adjacent to the coal room. As I looked around, my hands started to shake and then my knees. Rage welled up inside me and I had trouble in controlling my voice.

"Why, in the name of God, did they tear the damned furnace apart and just leave it all over the floor?" I looked at Eddie as if he could give me an answer.

"I don't know, Hazie. The only thing I can think of is that this could be their way of forcing you to buy a new furnace. They'll just say this one has too much wrong with it to fix."

The despair in his voice only made me angrier. "Well Eddie, they picked on the wrong person! I'm calling a lawyer and they'll damned well put that furnace back together or I'll make them eat it!"

We went to the kitchen and I started to make supper. "I think I'll call Morey. He should know someone who might take a case like this. What do you think, Eddie?"

"I think it's a good idea. See what he says."

When I told Morey briefly what had happened, he said to call Al Johnson. "Tell him I recommended him. He'll do a good job for you. Let me know what happens."

I called Johnson from the shop the next morning before I called the furnace people. His advice was, "Just take it cool. Take someone with you who will verify what they tell you—someone who is not close to you. If they try to sell you a new furnace, get their prices and terms of payment on paper. Then we'll see what we can do."

I asked Red Barnes's mother, Ellie, if she could go with me and told her why. When we asked to talk to the manager he was very pleasant. I told him I couldn't understand why they had taken the furnace apart.

He said, "There was so much damage and leakage, we didn't want to risk your starting it up and inhaling a lot of smoke. That is very dangerous, you know."

"Well, what alternative do I have? I can't afford a new furnace. I just don't have the money for that, right now." I hoped I looked as broke as I felt at the moment.

"You don't have to worry about that. It would cost about five hundred dollars and you could pay for it over three years. Surely you could afford that, couldn't you?" I thought there was a sly tone to his voice.

"I don't know. Why don't you make up a payment schedule showing the interest and all that and I will take it to my lender. He might give me part of the money."

"Of course. I'll have my secretary make up an amortization table for you." He was very sure of himself.

Armed with this and with Ellie Barnes at my side, we went to Al Johnson's office.

He looked over the paperwork, nodded his head thoughtfully, turned to us, and said, "What do you want out of this Hazel?"

"I would be happy to have the furnace put back together and the grate replaced. I think that is all that is needed to make it work." I thought to myself, *I just want it fixed, before winter*. I couldn't imagine anything worse than that big house without heat.

"I'll have a little talk with Mr. Ogilvie tomorrow. I may even call their main office before I talk to him. Don't be surprised at what we may accomplish." He seemed pleased with himself. As an afterthought he added, "You did tell me that your brother Eddie had started the furnace up last week and that the only thing he could see wrong was the lower grate on one side needed replacing?"

"Yes, that's right. Red and my Mother were there. Eddie wanted to show them how the furnace worked and check the pipes for leaks. There weren't any leaks."

"Good. I'll be calling you. It may take a week but I don't expect it to take any longer."

Just two weeks later when I came home, Eddie and Al Johnson met me at the door. They both had big smiles on their faces and Eddie was fairly hopping from one foot to the other in excitement.

"Okay Eddie, you tell her."

"Hazie, Al did it! We are going to get a brand new furnace and it isn't going to cost a darned penny! What do you think of that?"

"Yes, Hazel, that's right. I think Mr. Ogilvie decided it would be cheaper to give you a new furnace than to go to court and fight charges of intimidation and false misrepresentation, among other things. He's a very smart man." Al laughed and Eddie laughed with him. I just stood there letting it all soak in.

"When are they going to put the new furnace in?" I asked, still thinking Al had made a mistake.

"They are going to start at eight in the morning. It should be in and running by the time you get home from work." He looked as happy as I felt.

"Yeah Hazie, and I'm going to stay home from school and be sure they do it right! Is that okay with you?"

"It sure is, Eddie." Then I told Al, "You really did a good job for us, Al. I'll tell Morey he sure knew who to recommend!" After we said good-bye to Al, I turned to Eddie and gave him a big hug.

Mom usually came in on Saturday to deliver eggs, rabbits, and chickens to her customers. She always brought a chicken, a rabbit, and a dozen eggs for us. It helped a lot on my grocery bill. This particular Saturday, Eddie called me at the shop. "Did Mom say anything about not coming in today?"

"No, hasn't she come in, yet?" I asked, trying to keep the fear out of my voice. I was sure Red would have called if anything was wrong, but not to hear anything from Mom or Red...

By four o'clock I was beside myself when the phone rang. The little quaver in Mom's voice didn't reassure my worry.

"Your Granddad passed away about two hours ago. He's been real sick all day and I just didn't want to leave his side. I've got him all cleaned up now and dressed. I called the funeral home and they will be out soon. I just have to wait for them." Mom's voice was flat, like she was reciting something.

"Mom, I'll come right out. Why didn't you call sooner?" I knew this was a foolish question but I asked it anyway.

"Just come on out. I'll ride back in with you." She hung up.

A flood of memories washed over me. When I was a little girl I stayed with Granddad a lot during the summer. I wanted to be a Red Cross nurse, Granddad was my patient. I made a headband out of paper and painted a red cross on it. I would wash his face, trim his eyebrows, and bandage him up.

I'd ride in the old spring wagon with him to haul water from the river when the well went dry. He'd reach over and catch me as I slid along the slippery seat. I could hear the clank of the barrels in the back and the horses, Old Jim and Nell, slurping water as Granddad filled the barrels.

I remembered finding Indian beads in the ant hills and his helping me fill little jars with them, riding with him to the upper field where he would unhitch the team and then hitch them up to the mower. I would sit under a cedar tree and wave to him as he made a turn in the field. I recalled the smell of the alfalfa when it was cut, being scared out of my wits when a big tarantula came crawling toward me. He heard my scream and stopped the team and came to me, just picked up the tarantula and told me it wouldn't hurt me.

I also recalled Eddie fishing and Granddad digging worms with his dog Lady, just a puppy then, always with him, and now grown old. What would happen to her now?

I had been so busy I hadn't done a lot of little things I could have done for him. Dyanna would be heartbroken. Granddad had been her buddy. She never tired of picking bouquets for him, writing him little notes, and seeing that he had a fresh glass of water by his side.

All the way to the ranch I told myself that I would spend more time with Mom and the kids. Red and Mom came back to town with me. We followed the hearse and it was like a preview of the funeral. I told Mom, "You and Red will stay with us tonight. Then you will be here in the morning and I will go with you to make arrangements." She just nodded, but I knew she didn't want to be at the ranch that night.

All the old-timers, Mom and Dad's friends, and lots of people I couldn't remember came to Granddad's funeral. He would have been surprised to see so many people. However, Mom wasn't surprised and she said, when I commented about so many people, "Don't worry Hazel. He sees all this. He had the gift of sight, just as I do sometimes." And for her it was as if he hadn't gone.

43 Eddie Plans for the Future

*I*t snowed the week before Eddie was to take his driver's test but the sun had come out and the streets were dry. Eddie couldn't stand still as I slipped his jacket around his shoulders and gave it a tug to make it fit more comfortably over the hump on his back.

You didn't make an appointment to take a driver's test; you just went and waited your turn. When Eddie and I walked in, there were three people in the line ahead of us, two men, and an older woman who turned around and stared at Eddie. Soon it was Eddie's turn.

"I'd like to take the driver's license test," Eddie said in a clear voice.

"Just a minute sir." The young man behind the counter said in a nervous voice. He left his post and made his way through a door to the back.

By now there were two people in line behind us. In a few minutes the young man who had told us to wait returned. He followed a short, stocky fellow of middle age with heavy horn rimmed glasses and wearing a beard that didn't cover some nasty acne scars.

"Well," he barked at Eddie in a deep raspy voice, "I understand you want to take your driver's license test."

"Yes sir," Eddie answered politely.

"Well, I don't want to disappoint you but we don't give driver's licenses to obviously handicapped people who can't handle a vehicle!"

"But sir," Eddie said, "I can handle a vehicle. In fact, I can drive a truck and big machinery. I have been doing this for the last three years on our farm south of Pueblo."

"Well young man, you may drive anywhere you want to on your family farm, but if I hear of you driving, or if any of my patrolmen pick you up for endangering the highways or the streets of Pueblo, I'll personally see to it that you are prosecuted to the fullest extent of the law!"

By the time Booker Gunn (I read his name tag) got through with this long-winded speech, the line in back of us had grown to about ten people.

Eddie flushed deep red. He stammered a little then in a loud clear voice, he said, "You can't hold this job forever, Mr. Gunn, and I'll be back every year until you are out. I will get my driver's license!" He started to turn away but I couldn't keep my mouth shut.

"You may have been given authority, Mr. Gunn, but there is something you weren't given. A brain and a heart!" I turned on my heel and followed Eddie to the door.

Someone in the line started to clap and soon all the people in line were clapping, and then they all walked out. I have an idea they came back another time, but probably figured Mr. Gunn wouldn't look kindly on giving them a license that day.

Eddie was furious and so was I. I just drove around for a while then we headed for the ranch. I knew Mom would be just as disappointed as we were. There was no way I could know how deeply Eddie was hurt. He had counted so on getting his license, then to be denied even taking the test. It wasn't fair.

The war ground on and Eddie couldn't stay glum when so many terrible things were happening. Morey couldn't join the war because he'd broken his neck while in high school. Eddie couldn't go of course, but he helped our cousin Bob Hastings on weekends. Bob was building roads and doing excavation work at the new Army Depot east of Pueblo. This was vital to the war effort and Eddie felt he was helping in a small way. Plus, he was driving a dump truck and doing very well. None of us mentioned Booker Gunn and no one stopped Eddie from driving. The highway patrolmen looked the other way and Eddie drove back and forth to Pueblo on a regular basis.

"If they stop me, do you think Al Johnson would take Booker Gunn on?" Eddie asked Morey one day.

"Sure he would. I think he would feel proud to defend you on that one. From what I hear, Gunn isn't very well liked around town. His high and mighty airs have earned him a bad reputation for unfairness."

Morey heard a lot from people who came into Bernstein Brothers for one thing or another.

Dad wrote that he would get two days off for Christmas. He hadn't been home for so long and we all missed him.

Eddie said, "Let's get everything done so when Dad gets here we can just sit and visit!"

Mom answered, "That would be great Son, but who's going to cook and wash dishes?"

Jody spoke up. "Mom, Dyanna and I will wash dishes, set the table, and do all that stuff. If you and Hazie cook, we can do the rest." I couldn't believe my ears. My little sister was growing up after all. Always before, she had been the one who found all kinds of excuses to get out of doing things. Now, well, I was happy for her, and us.

Morey and Eddie became very good friends. Morey never ceased to wonder how Eddie knew all the things he knew. Morey would ask questions about machinery, crops, pumps, and all kinds of things. Eddie always knew the answers. Morey had a degree in business, but he was woefully lacking in just good old common sense. Eddie joked with him about not knowing that corn grew on a stalk and had ears. Eddie would go fishing with Morey and me at Hayden Lake and when Eddie baited his own hooks, caught a fish, brought it in, and took the hook out, Morey just marveled at it all. He soon became used to all this and then he would tackle Eddie on more complex issues.

One sunny afternoon we were sitting on the bank fishing when Morey asked Eddie, "What are you going to do when you graduate from high school?"

"Well, I guess I'll do something I love to do, like sell cars." Eddie answered.

"And how do you think you will get started in that business?" Morey always had to have a plan.

Eddie didn't hesitate. "Well Morey, I know how to fix a car up. I know what makes them tick, so I figure I'll buy some real junkers, fix

215

them so they'll run, hire someone to give them a cheap paint job and sell them."

"And where will you find these cars?" Morey prodded.

"I've got my eye on some right now. Taxi cabs. I can buy them for a hundred apiece and I figure I can make two hundred clear."

"Well, it won't be long until you graduate. What are you going to use for a workshop?"

"My Dad left me the perfect place. Have you ever looked at the garage at the ranch, Morey?" Eddie asked.

"Why no, I don't believe I have. You'll have to show me when we get back." Morey looked interested.

As soon as we got to the ranch, Morey and Eddie headed for the garage. I followed.

"Okay Morey, see these two beams running long-ways along the roof? Notice the come-alongs hanging from them? Then see that work bench along the side of the garage and the come-along on the beam above it?" Eddie was pointing with his foot.

"Yes, sure, but how is that going to help you fix up those old wrecks you're telling me about?" Morey scratched at his ear lobe.

"Watch." Eddie said, as he reached over and grabbed the chain attached to the come-along over the workbench between the toes of his left foot. With his right foot, he attached the hook at the end of the chain to the wire around a bale of hay used for rabbit nests. With ease, he coaxed the chain along, lifted the bale of straw to the workbench, and placed it just where he wanted it. He then said, "I can do that with an engine, a transmission, or whatever. I can maneuver it anywhere I need to so that I can get to it to work on. It doesn't matter how heavy it is, or how awkward. The come-along does the work." Eddie gave Morey a grin.

"Looks like you've got it all figured out."

"Yeah Morey, and see how Dad built this garage? Out of powder boxes! Each one is a storage place for parts. In fact, Dad has all kinds of parts I can use. Also, see the blacksmith forge there, and that metal barrel set on bricks? That burns waste oil so you don't freeze your buns off in winter. Pretty cozy, isn't it?" Eddie had pride in his voice.

Rural Electric Association (REA) power lines finally came to our part of Colorado. At long last we had electricity to run a refrigerator and do all kinds of things. It was about time, too.

Just the week before, our propane refrigerator quit working. Eddie couldn't figure out what was wrong with it until he had Red move it out from the wall so he could get at the fan that was housed at the bottom of the unit.

"Mom, come here," he called. "Look what that precious little Chip-Chip did to this refrigerator."

Mom hurried in. "Oh that little pest. He has used the insulation around the fan housing to build himself a nest. Would you look at that?" She went to find Chip-Chip, named thus because when he got excited that was exactly how he sounded. He was a common gray rock squirrel Mom had rescued from one of the cats when he was just a baby. He had the run of the house and was a delightful pet. He sat on the treadle of the sewing machine when Mom sewed and sometimes sat by the wheel and tried to catch it as it went around. He slept at Mom's feet and sometimes nibbled at her toes, waking her. We all loved him. It would take more than building a nest in the refrigerator to have us throw him out of the house.

Now that we had electricity to run a thermostat, Eddie decided to put a propane furnace in the basement. The basement wasn't big enough, so he decided to get our cousin, Curtis Higgins, and Red to help him enlarge it.

The first day they worked on it all day long and made very little headway. They used picks on the hard soil but it just didn't help much. On Sunday, I could see that they were pretty discouraged. Mom and I walked to the upper field and were just coming down the hill when we heard a loud "kaboom." Little clouds of dust rose up around the house.

"That Eddie and his monkey-diddling around! He's going to get us all killed!" Mom started running to the house. When she reached the corner, Eddie, Red, and Curtis came running out the back door. She grabbed Eddie, yelling at him and crying at the same time. "You used some of that dynamite your Dad had stored away, didn't you? Are you all right?" She was feeling him and sort of crying at the same time.

Red and Curtis came up behind Eddie, covered with dirt but all in one piece. They weren't saying much.

"Mom, it was just too hard to dig. We would have been forever. I just used two sticks. Just enough to soften it up a bit." he explained.

"We're lucky the house is still standing! Adobe houses aren't made to stand dynamite blasts under them. Oh, Eddie…Well, I guess as long as you're all alright." She gave him a pat and told them to go get cleaned up. "And no more dynamite, do you hear me?"

"Yes Mom." Eddie answered. I could tell he was glad to be off the hook.

44 The Great Rabbit Story

*O*ne afternoon Morey came out to the ranch. He went out to the garage where Eddie was working on an old car. "Hey Eddie," he called. "I brought a friend to go rabbit hunting. I brought enough hamburgers for everyone too. Do you think you could take us as soon as it gets dark?"

"Sure, did you tell him he has to sit on the fender?" Eddie asked.

"I sure did, and he's rarin' to go!" Morey answered. He introduced his friend Pete and asked if he could take Pete up and show him the well and the hogs and the rabbits. I gathered Pete was about as much of a greenhorn as Morey had been when he first started coming to the ranch.

Just as it started to get dark, Mom called: "You'd better come in and eat these hamburgers. I've got them all ready, and a few extras to go with them." Sure enough, she had some of her wonderful chili sauce and a bowl of coleslaw ready.

As soon as we had finished eating Eddie said, "Well, let's go! The great American rabbit hunt is about to begin."

Morey told Pete how to sit on the fender, hold his .22 rifle at the ready, and at the same time, keep from falling off into a cactus bush. He warned Pete that when Eddie chased a rabbit, it could get a little rough.

I kept my opinions to myself. Rabbit hunting had become so much fun for Morey, Eddie, and whoever Morey could find brave enough to try it. Sometimes I went along but mostly I stayed home and listened to their tall tales when they came back.

"Come on Hazel, go with us. I like to hear you yell when you think Eddie is getting too wild," Morey teased me. He had his .22 and Pete, rather awkwardly, held a brand new gun.

"Okay guys, are you ready? You don't need to get on the fenders until I go through the gate to the upper pasture." Eddie got in the car and I could see Pete watching with the same wide-eyed fascination that had gripped Morey when he first saw Eddie drive a car. Morey had probably built up quite a story.

It was a balmy night. The moon wasn't quite full and the tree cactus made weird shapes on the prairie. Cedar trees clumped together made impenetrable fortresses. A few pinon pine were scattered here and there. There were small gullies in this area but no big arroyos. Eddie knew where every rock was located and though he appeared to drive recklessly, he knew exactly where he was going.

All of a sudden a big white rabbit streaked across our path. Eddie caught it in the headlights and kept on its tail. He drove at what seemed to be breakneck speed across the rutty prairie.

Morey yelled at Pete: "Wait for a good shot. Eddie will slow down a little when it's right."

I heard Pete yell. A shot rang out. He missed. Morey shot. The rabbit just jumped up in the air and fell over dead. Morey and Pete jumped down as soon as Eddie backed up so he could shine the light on the rabbit. I noticed Pete was squeamish about picking up the dead rabbit, but Morey had no such qualms. He put the rabbit in a gunny sack and threw him in the trunk.

"Okay Eddie, let's go!" he yelled, as he and Pete climbed back on their precarious perches.

I heard Pete say to Morey, "Hell, man! They didn't teach you this at Wharton, did they?"

"No, and there was a lot more they didn't teach me either!" Morey answered.

Eddie and I were about as excited as Pete and Morey. Every time they got a rabbit we gave a big cheer. Pete only slid off the fender once but didn't hurt himself. Morey was getting to be an expert at hanging on and doing some pretty fancy shooting at the same time.

By the end of the evening, they had six rabbits between them—two black and whites, two gray, one big tan, and a sort of calico. As they dumped them out of the sack Pete said, "I've never heard of different colored wild rabbits before. Are they peculiar to this region?"

Morey started laughing, "Eddie, I think now is the time. You've been promising to tell me the 'great rabbit story' for almost three years now. Tonight is the night."

"Fine guys," I said, "But let's go in the house, I'll put on a pot of coffee. How does that sound?"

"Sounds great!" Morey and Pete chorused.

I got the coffee on and Mom brought out an apple pie she had baked that morning. We sat around the old oak table.

"Well," Eddie began, "This all happened about four or five years ago. Dad was out of work for a couple of months. There wasn't much money to do anything with and I think he just got bored. We were used to him digging around the hillsides. He usually said he was looking for mineral samples so we didn't pay much attention.

Dad with Taffy.

"I moseyed up to that flat place on top of the hill one day and just stood there watching for a while. He didn't notice me. He had a roll of fine mesh chicken wire, a fifty-foot steel tape, a shovel, and some powder boxes. The boxes were sort of placed at random around the hill there. About then, Dad looked up and saw me standing there."

"'Hey, Son. You want to help? Grab that tape and help me measure this.' He motioned to a ditch he had dug in a square, probably a hundred feet in each direction. I took the tape and went to what I thought was a corner until I noticed that he had a piece of welding rod in that corner.

"'Okay,' he says, 'We'll measure a hundred feet, and then I'll square it.' Dad was always a stickler for perfection. So we squared the corners of a hundred foot pen and then I helped him set the chicken wire in the trench and held it while he piled dirt against it. It was about five feet wide so about three and a half feet stuck out of the ground.

"When he was sure all this was to his satisfaction he said, 'Now I'll show you what I'm doing with these dynamite boxes.' He had holes dug deep enough so that when the boxes were placed in the holes he could cover them with about a foot of soil. Then he made a little runway to where he had cut an opening in each box. When we had all of the boxes placed he brought up straw and filled the boxes. He fastened water cans and feed cans to the fence at intervals and filled them with water and feed. 'Okay, now I want you and your Mom to decide which rabbits you are going to give me. I want a buck and ten does.'

"I thought, 'He's pretty sure of himself. How does he know Mom or I will give him any of our precious rabbits?' But we did.

"Well, all of this went along fine for about six months. Then one day Mom came roaring down the hill. 'Art, dammit, you and your monkey-diddlin' schemes! There are rabbits all over the damned prairie. Wild rabbits are digging under the fence and taking up with our tame rabbits. It's the worst mix up I've ever seen. I tried to catch some of them and I tell you there are baby rabbits all over the prairie! All different colors and sizes.' Mom was beside herself.

"So actually, that's the story. The rabbits liked it fine in the wild. They multiplied and now, and probably forevermore, you will see many-colored rabbits in this area."

Morey and Pete laughed until their sides hurt. "Eddie," Morey said, "That rabbit story was worth waiting three years to hear."

45 *Eddie's Graduation Party*

$\mathcal{I}$ drove Dad to the house on Pitkin. I could hear the happiness in his voice.

"Looks like everybody and his cat is here! Where did they all come from?"

"It's Eddie's graduation party, Dad. We wanted to surprise you!"

"Well, I knew he was graduating but I didn't know he was going to have a big party."

In the entry hall a little knot of people stood talking. As soon as they saw Dad there were hugs, slaps on the back and "why you old son-of-a-gun! Looks like those snow drifts are good for you!" Tony and Frank each had an arm around his neck and Lucy and Emma took their turns of planting kisses on his red cheeks.

"Can you believe all this? I didn't know that boy of mine knew so many people! Looks like half the people in Pueblo are here!" While Dad was looking around someone would come up and grab him and they would start yelling at each other above the noise. He couldn't get over all the little kids dodging the grownups and the good looking young people mixed in with the old timers.

"Let's get out of here and find a place to sit." Emma said.

"I think I saw some chairs in that room." They moved toward the living room. Dad moved toward the fireplace. He looked up and saw Eddie's picture in his cap and gown and under it in a small gold frame, his driver's license. Dad reached up, took the driver's license down and just stared at it. No one said a word. Finally he set it back in place, wiped at his eyes with his hand and said, "That's my son. He doesn't give up!"

Mom came in and wrapped Dad in her arms. They stood for a moment, then backed off and looked at each other. "You're getting fat, Art. I'm going to have to put you on a diet." She gave a hearty laugh.

"Oh no you don't. Not with all that good food I know you've got cooked up!" He turned to Emma and Lucy. "And I'll bet you brought some of your goodies, too?"

"We sure did. We made extra, especially for you and Eddie!" They were both talking at once. It brought back memories of butchering, deer hunting, so many things we had all shared. And always, the wonderful food.

Dad asked, "Hey Tony, Frank, did you bring a jug of that homemade wine? I could stand a little glass, just for old time's sake."

"We sure did Art. Ethel put it in the kitchen. Let's go find it!" They went toward the kitchen talking and laughing. It was as if time had turned back.

They were lifting their glasses in a toast when Eddie, Helen, and her brother walked into the room.

"I see you found each other. I wanted it to be a surprise. That's why I didn't tell you Helen was coming down with me." Dad gave Eddie a bear hug and Eddie nuzzled his head under Dad's chin.

"It was a surprise, all right. We were going to surprise you with my party but you pulled a fast one on me, too!" Eddie's happy laugh just started everyone laughing.

"Well Son, you'll never know how proud I am of you and all you've accomplished. And when you have time, I want to know how you outfoxed Booker Gunn and got your driver's license." Dad had a twinkle in his eye.

"It's no secret, Dad. I just went to Fremont County and they not only gave me my license, the officer who gave me my test asked me why I hadn't come there before. They were just great to me!"

Midnight came and went and there were still people making the most of Eddie's party. The big room at the front of the house was still empty of furniture and one of Eddie's friends brought a phonograph and a whole stack of records. Soon, the room was filled with dancers. Little kids were dancing with their dads. Tony and Emma were adding some fancy old country steps and Dyanna was dancing with Red. Out of the corner of my eye I watched Helen and Eddie. She held him close. They were talking, laughing, and not missing a beat.

Mom and Dad were dancing, his arms holding her tight. Then Tony and Emma, Frank and Lucy and some of the other old timers from Lime broke into the music with, "It's Three O'Clock In the Morning." And it was. Dad and Mom kept on dancing and I knew they were remembering the dances at Lime that ended with this song. It was four o'clock by the time everyone had said goodbye.

46 *Eddie Goes Into Business*

ddie was anxious to show me a location he had found on East Fourth Street. The only building was about 10 by 12 feet with a small overhang across the front. It was mostly just a vacant lot with no garage, storage, or anything of the kind.

"I don't know Eddie. What are you going to do for storage or a place to work on them?" I asked dubiously.

The Start of "Eddie's Used Cars"

"Oh Hazie. This is just temporary. I'll only have two or three cars to start. And I'm going to fix them up at the ranch and then have them painted. I hope before long I can afford to get a lot with a garage and a good building on it." He didn't seem to share my fears.

"So, have you found any cars yet?"

"Yeah, I'm taking them to the ranch tomorrow. I found a Ford sedan, a Plymouth 2-door, and a Dodge sedan. They look rough, but they actually run pretty good. I found a guy who will straighten out the dents and paint them for fifty bucks apiece. I won't know until I drive them what mechanical work I will have to do."

"I can tell you can't wait to get started. I can help you with some ads and you'll need a sign. What are you going to call your lot?"

"I'm going to call it 'Eddie's Used Cars'. Lloyd Cox is going to paint a big sign for me and we'll hang it across the front of the building above the overhang so it could be seen from Fourth Street. I think in two weeks I can be open!" Eddie's excitement was catching.

Eddie worked hard at getting his three cars ready and when they were painted and brought to the lot, they looked great, but lonely. Who ever heard of a car lot with only three cars?

"Eddie," I asked, "Why don't you ask around and see if anyone you know will let you sell their car on consignment? I'll ask some of the people I know and maybe we can get a few lined up for your grand opening." We still had a week and I was determined that somehow he would have at least a few more cars on his lot.

I enlisted Morey's help and we were pleasantly surprised when we found that quite a few people had a car, or knew of someone who had a car, they wanted to sell but just hadn't bothered.

Eddie asked them to set a high and low figure on what they would take and told them he would do his best to get what they wanted. He decided to charge five percent of what the car brought and everyone felt this was fair. These cars would be sold "as is" and it would be the buyer's responsibility to fix them if they needed work done.

By the time opening day arrived, the lot had an air of festivity. Lloyd's sign, in big black letters edged with red on a white background could be seen a block away. Mom had baked oatmeal cookies and had several jugs of cider on hand. I had a guest book ready, and Eddie was so nervous I was afraid he would blow away with the breeze.

There were two dozen cars lined up across the front of the lot. They were as clean as used cars could be and actually looked very impressive.

It was barely eight in the morning, and Eddie was busy writing up his first sale. He sat hunched over his makeshift desk on the floor with an incredulous buyer watching every move he made when, with a final flourish, Eddie reached up with the title between the big toe and other toes of his right foot. "Well Gus, here's your title. If anything goes wrong, please come in and we'll take care of it!" With a big smile, he handed Gus the keys to the Plymouth 2-door.

Gus gave Eddie a big pat on the back then sort of stood back as he realized he had touched Eddie's hump. "Eddie, I'll send all my friends. I know you'll treat them right!" He did just that and Gus had a lot of friends. They made their way to Eddie's Used Cars and sent their friends as well.

Before the week was up, Eddie sold twelve cars. He hadn't made a lot of money but he'd made enough to tell Bob Hastings, "Let's go to the auction in Denver. If I could buy a few more and not have to do much work on them, I think I'll be in business."

Bob laughed his big belly laugh and looked over at me. "Listen to him. He doesn't realize it, but he's already in business!"

Trips to the Denver auction became a weekly thing. Usually held on a Sunday, people from all over Colorado and neighboring states attended. Eddie would take his friend Jackie Mitchell, our cousins Bob and Curtis, and me when I could get away. It was hard work. We'd leave before sunup, drive to Denver, grab a quick breakfast, and be on the auction grounds by seven.

Eddie and Bob were the experts. They would range all over the lot lifting hoods, taking the keys from under a floor mat or over the visor, starting them up, revving the engine, looking for trouble. Cars started moving through the line, sometimes a double line, by nine in the morning. Eddie and Bob had a good idea of which cars they wanted to bid on. If the bids were too high, they waited.

Sometimes cars Eddie wanted to bid on hadn't run through by seven in the evening. "Let's wait," he'd say. "I've got a hunch a deal fell through for that dealer. If they run it through again I'll bet I can steal it." Many times he would. Then we'd start home, each of us driving a car. At this point, he couldn't afford any more than what we could drive back.

We'd found a barbecue place that served the best ribs I ever tasted. Tired, dirty from checking out cars, and hungry, we'd head for the restaurant, sit down, and relax. I enjoyed all their tall tales. It was "Did you see that red and white job? It went at least a hundred over value!"

Then they'd get down to the cars Eddie bought. Bob would say, "You ought to make an easy three hundred on that one, Eddie, and not have to do a damned thing to it."

"I hope not." Eddie would reply.

Eddie brought back a Pontiac Station Wagon that he worried he'd paid too much for. With winter coming on, he was afraid he'd have to 'eat' it. Bob told him not to worry, that he had bought it right and couldn't go wrong.

One day a Cadillac sedan pulled up to the lot and a very strange looking man got out. As Eddie told it, "He had enough gold chains around his neck to weigh him down, an open shirt, black leather boots, and a car full of people."

"What kind of people?" I asked, fascinated.

"Little kids, an old grandmother, a couple of young women, a young man, all of them dressed crazy, and dirty. The guy who owned the car was handsome. I couldn't tell how old he was. He could have been fifty or seventy, sort of ageless. He had a scar down one side of his face and a wicked gleam in his eyes. He just sort of sauntered over and asked me, 'What do you want for that station wagon?'"

Eddie named a high price and wasn't surprised when the fellow countered with, "I'll give you a thousand and that Cadillac as a trade-in. What do you say?"

"I don't know," Eddie said. "I'd have to give it a drive."

"Sure." The man waved a hand at the car, not saying a word, but everyone piled out and swarmed into the office. Eddie knew he had to test drive the Cadillac. He didn't like leaving his office with this motley bunch but he had no choice.

He said, "Would you like to go with me? That way you can answer any questions I might have."

"Yeah, I'll go with you." The fellow then said a few words to his family in some language foreign to Eddie. They all immediately sat down on the floor or lounged around the front of the building and made themselves at home.

The only sign that Eddie saw the man make as Eddie got in to drive was a slight raise of one eyebrow. It made the scar on his cheek lift too, and gave him an evil look. Eddie said he felt a chill go up his back. When they got back to the office, Eddie turned to the man. "Well, I've got to tell you, your car drives out good but it will take some work to get it cleaned up so I can sell it."

"Yeah, I know. I'll give you the Cadillac and twelve hundred but you'll have to trust me for five hundred of it. Will you do that?"

The fellow sounded sincere and Eddie realized that he didn't know a thing about him. "Tell you what," Eddie said. "Why don't you fill out this loan form for me and I'll see what I can do."

"I'll fill out your form for you, but it won't mean a lot. Either you trust me, or you don't. See, we're Gypsies. We don't really live anywhere. Right now our main place is near Greeley and we'll be there for another week or so, then we go south." He reached for the form and started filling it out.

Eddie looked it over when the man finished it. "So your name is Bruno Hadiz, right?"

"Yeah, that's right, and this is my mother, Catherine, my grandson, Albert and his wife, Sofia. All these kids are my great grandchildren. Now you know this part of my family." Somehow Eddie felt honored that Bruno had taken the trouble to introduce everyone.

"Oh, what the hell," Eddie said, "I guess I can trust you. Can you send me twenty five dollars a month until the five hundred is paid?"

"Yeah, I can do that." Bruno turned to his grandson "Clear the car out and put everything in that station wagon. Hurry up, now!" In minutes, it seemed, the Cadillac was empty. Belongings were then stashed in the Pontiac and everyone piled in.

Bruno reached into his baggy trousers and pulled out a roll of bills. He peeled off seven hundred in one-hundred dollar bills and handed them to Eddie with a bright smile. "Until we meet again, eh, Eddie?"

"Yeah Bruno, until we meet again." Eddie watched with a rueful grin on his face, turned to me and said, "If we ever meet again!"

47 Eddie Gets A Deer

*E*ddie had been going to the ranch as often as he could to help Mom with making the building on the hill into an apartment. Dad had plowed up the yard and made terraces across the low area in front. Mom decided she wanted to plant trees and said the terraces would hold run-off when it rained. Dad dug post holes for a fence around the yard and had made a nice cement walkway in front of the apartment and down to the where the gate would be.

Eddie installed baseboards in the entire apartment and had just about finished painting them. I made drapes for the windows and slip-covers for some old chairs. It all looked great.

Dad had gone all out to install water lines and hydrants where he thought they would be needed. The building that Charlie Owens used as a storage building was even with the front corner of the house and about fifty feet down from it. Dad decided this building could be used as a garage and he was busy fixing it up.

I was just ready to put supper on the table when Eddie came home. "Would you like to drive to the ranch with me when supper's over?" he asked.

"Sure, Morey may stop by after working late, but we'll be home by then and I'd like to see how Dad is holding up with all the jobs Mom's saved up for him."

"I want to talk to Red and see if he would like to work at the car lot a couple of days a week. We need a lot boy and that would give him something else to learn."

"That would be good for him. With Dad home, Mom really doesn't need him that much."

Dad, Mom and Red were just finishing a game of 500 when we got there. Red was thrilled at the prospect of a different kind of job and thought it would be fun living with us on Pitkin.

Dad asked Eddie how he would like to come out before dawn in the morning and go deer hunting. "I saw this herd of deer as they came up from the river where we could get a good shot at them. Close enough that if we got a buck we could load it in the pick-up."

"Would you like to go, Hazie?" Eddie asked me.

"Sure, I'll call Morey and tell him I'll see him tomorrow night. We've been out late almost every night this week. I need a change." I laughed but I was serious. Morey worked late and sometimes he didn't pick me up until eleven o'clock. I felt like I was meeting myself in circles.

"Better watch him, Hazie." Eddie quipped. "Since he gave you that ring he thinks he owns you!" I knew he was serious.

I glanced down at the ring and thought ruefully *it's gorgeous but what am I letting myself in for?*

Dad, Red, and I piled into the pick-up and Eddie drove. We were bundled up because it was still very cold early in the morning. Dawn was just starting to break through the clouds as Eddie parked in a clump of cedars very close to the rim rock that edged the mesa above the St. Charles River. Red and I took the rifles out of the back of the truck and Dad gingerly stepped down to the ground. His age was beginning to tell on him but he wouldn't let on. We loaded the guns but didn't slip shells into the firing chambers. We still had a short walk ahead of us.

We tried to make as little noise as possible. Suddenly the sun started to rise above the horizon behind us. A fierce golden ball, it grew larger and larger. The warmth felt good.

Dad silently pointed to the spot where he had seen the small herd of deer yesterday while he was cutting cedar fence posts. We were de-termined to get us a buckskin. I knew Eddie and Red had been practicing with the rifle, but I had never seen Eddie shoot.

Dad pointed again to a large clump of cedar trees. In the valley below, the St. Charles River ran through hay fields. This was where the deer fed and got their morning drink of water. It was anyone's guess as to exactly where they would come out, but Dad had seen them on a certain point, so that is where we decided to wait.

When we got to the grove we snuggled close against the gnarled roots of a squatting cedar tree. Its limbs twisted around like the fingers of an old woman's hand, clutching at its very existence. Scanning the arroyo that started at the top of the rim rock, our eyes searched it as it grew deeper and twisted and wound its way toward the river. Other small arroyos merged with it along the way, leaving a series of small curved hills rising from the floor of the valley to the rocky straight-up-and-down of the ridge where we waited. The deer could choose any of these small valleys to reach the high plateau. Knowing this, it was our plan to see which way they headed and be ready when they got within shooting range.

Along the side of one of these small hills, a herd of horses grazed. The leader of the band, a beautiful, clean-limbed palomino stallion threw his head into the air and sniffed. Then he reached down, wrenched a tuft of grama grass from its roots, and with the bunch of grass still in his mouth, threw up his head again, and at the same time he pawed the earth with his hoof. His harem of mares looked at him then went on about their business of eating all the grass they could before the wind forced them to gallop to the shelter of the trees.

Suddenly I felt Eddie stiffen beside me. "Look," he whispered softly, "Just beyond the horses. They'll be coming right to us!"

The wind was blowing my hair across my face. I quickly tucked it under my cap and pulled the brim down over my eyes.

"Let's get over to that other clump of cedars. I think it will give us a better view of them as they approach." I whispered.

We moved slowly to the other group of cedars and Dad motioned to where two bare roots twisted out and up. "Get yourself settled, Son, where we can rest this rifle just the way you want it. We've got plenty of time and I want you to get your first buckskin!" Dad's voice was quivery with excitement.

"No Dad, let Red or Hazel shoot. I don't really want to shoot a deer!"

Eddie sat down just back of the roots that came to his waist. At Dad's insistence he took the rifle from Dad with both feet and grasped the stock with the toes of his left foot and the barrel with the toes of his right foot. He took his time as he wiggled himself snugly between the roots. When he was comfortable he told Dad, "Now Dad, rest the gun so that my left shoulder is against the stock and so I can brace myself against the bottom of the tree."

Dad pushed the gun into the position Eddie wanted, and then watched as Eddie snuggled his shoulder more solidly against the butt of the rifle. When he checked out how well he could maneuver in this tight space, he reached up with his right foot and pretended to pull the trigger with the big toe on his right foot.

"That ought to do it," he whispered, "See Dad, I've got a little leverage to move from side to side."

"Can you move your head up and down enough, if you have to, Son?" Dad asked quietly.

"Yeah, see, I can do it this way." and Eddie nodded his head upward, keeping in line with the sights on the end of the barrel.

"All right. Now, get your guns ready to aim then shoot when I give the signal." Dad gazed narrowly at the deer as they came slowly toward us.

The wind was blowing our scent away from them and they fed slowly, once in a while lifting their heads to gaze around. The buck led his band right to us and I thought, *This is just too easy. They have no idea of the danger they are walking into.*

The guns were loaded and ready. Eddie peered down the barrel. His big toe was ready on the trigger. His left foot held the barrel steady. He didn't seem to be excited.

Not so Red. I could see the muscles twitching in his cheeks and couldn't help but feel sorry for him.

The deer were within good range now and I was getting nervous as Dad let them get even closer before he gave the signal.

Softly, Dad said, "Aim...Fire!"

Eddie sat more tightly and pulled the trigger. Even so, the jolt knocked him away from his seating. Red just kept firing.

Eddie said quietly, "I got him Dad. He just jumped in the air and fell. See, he isn't moving!"

"Yep Son, you did it! I knew you could!" Dad and I were more excited than Eddie. Red was completely out of control. He had put his gun down and was dancing around Eddie yelling, "You got your first deer Eddie!" He gave Eddie a big hug.

"Well," Dad broke into all this revelry. "Now comes the work part of deer hunting. Red, did you put the come-along and that long rope in the back of the truck?" Red nodded.

"Eddie, let's drive over to the rim rock and see how close we can get to where the buck fell. We may have to carry him to where our rope will reach. It shouldn't be too long a haul." Dad was an old hand at this. We did as he asked.

Eddie drove and Dad rode with him. Red and I walked. Red just couldn't forget the way Eddie had shot the deer. "Why Hazel, I was shakin' so bad I couldn't have hit the broad side of a barn! It's a good thing Eddie had a place to prop that rifle or we wouldn't be bringing a buck back! And a three pointer, too. Your Mom will be happy!"

From the rim rock, we walked the short distance to where the buck fell. "That was a clean shot, Son." Dad said. He pulled the buck around so its body was downhill. Dad then grasped the horns. Holding the head up, he made a clean cut across the throat with his hunting knife. Eddie and I turned our heads as the bright red blood gushed out, leaving stains on the grass and rocks.

Dad told Red to fasten the rope around the horns, and then I walked the rope to where Eddie was waiting with the come-along winch.

I watched as Eddie deftly used the toes of his left foot to hold the eye of the rope steady as he inserted the buckle of the come-along into the opening with the toes of his right foot. He snapped the buckle shut and started the come-along to clicking as it pulled its load up the hill.

The come-along was fastened to the axle of the truck so we didn't have to worry about its coming unfastened. We all turned our attention to guiding the carcass around rocks and cactus. We didn't want to bruise the meat, and we sure didn't want to contend with cactus thorns when we had to unload the buck. It took all of us to get the buck in the truck. We loaded the rope and the come-along in the truck bed. Red and I decided to ride in the back. On the way here we had all crowded in the front seat with me on Dad's lap. It had warmed up now, so riding in back was fine.

Mom waited at the kitchen door as we drove up. She walked out to the truck and took a look at the buck then turned to Eddie. "Well Son," she said, "How does it feel to get your first buck?"

Eddie was silent for a moment. Then with a wry little smile he looked at Dad and said, "I know you wanted me to get that buck Dad. But I don't want to ever shoot another deer. When I saw you cut his throat and the blood gushed out, something happened to me." Eddie hesitated then went on. "I could see that buck, so proud, as he led his does up to the rim rock. This was their home. Now he won't be there to protect them." Eddie started to walk away then he turned to Dad. "I'm sorry Dad."

"That's all right Son." Dad said. "I guess I just thought you would get a kick out of it." Dad walked over and gave Eddie a big hug.

48 Introduced to Hypnosis

"*I* saw Morey's brother downtown." Eddie told me. "He said the cabin he and his friends are building in Rye is almost finished."

"That's good news. They've been working on it for a couple of years. I asked Bob if I could do anything a while back, and he told me to wait until it was finished, then if I wanted to, I could help with furniture and things like that."

"Yeah. He told me he wanted to talk to Dad sometime about drilling a well but there wasn't any hurry. Probably wants to wait until next summer." Eddie shuffled his feet and I wondered what else he wanted to tell me.

"All right, Eddie, what's on your mind? You'd just as well quit fidgeting and tell me."

"Bob asked me when I thought you and Morey were going to get married. How the heck do I know, Hazie?" he blurted.

"I guess you told him the right thing, Eddie. I don't know either. We've had the license for over a month. I guess you could say we're in no hurry."

"What do you think Hazie?" Eddie, never one to interfere in my business, wanted some kind of an answer.

"We called the Rabbi a couple of weeks ago and he politely told Morey he didn't perform mixed marriages. Of course, as Morey said later, 'If I'd had a million bucks behind me he wouldn't have cared if you were pea green or yellow.' If I'd been a Jewish girl he couldn't have refused."

"So, now what?" Eddie asked. He wasn't going to let me off the hook.

"You know Eddie, Morey's family has never accepted me. His Dad asked Morey, 'Why do you want to marry this girl, except that you love her?' We've had a few good laughs over that one."

"I hope you care enough for him to not let all that crap get in the way. I don't know whether I could do it." Eddie mused.

"It won't be long now. I think we've both had enough. Morey said last night that we could get along fine without their blessing. I don't like to do it that way but we probably will." I didn't want to think about it. I was almost tired enough of all the in-fighting that I was ready to sell my shop and move to San Francisco.

"The apartment looks nice, Mom. You and Hazie have done a great job with the drapes and the slip covers." Eddie looked around the house at the ranch that we'd fitted out to rent.

"I may have a renter. Cab Arthur and his wife came by Sunday morning and a couple in their church have been looking for a place in the country. The husband works for the Highway Department and she likes to garden." Mom seemed happy about finding someone so soon.

"That would be great. I thought you were going to have a time getting it rented but it looks like I was wrong."

The next time Eddie came back from the ranch he told me he had met the Reeds and they seemed to be okay. He said, "Mom is busy with her garden and Mom and Mary Reed had already planted flower beds at the little house."

I had just finished my last customer about a week later when the phone rang. Before I could get the receiver to my ear, I could hear Mom yelling at Dad. "Mom, what do you want, what is wrong?" I asked.

"I'll tell you what's wrong! You get that brother of yours out here just as soon as you can. How could you do this to me?"

"What on earth is the matter, Mom?"

"I'll tell you what the matter is! I've got about twenty cars, some travel trailers, trucks, and I don't know what all else in the field below the road. And this mean-looking Gypsy with a scar across his cheek says Eddie told him he could camp there!" She was quiet for a moment, "Just get Eddie out here!"

She banged down the receiver. *Oh my,* I thought, *Eddie and I are in for it.* I went to get Eddie.

We weren't out of the car before Mom lit into us. Eddie let her blow steam for a while. He stood, making little swirls in the dust with his toe. I didn't say a word. I figured when she got through with him, she would start on me.

Finally, Eddie heard enough. "Mom," he said quietly, "Do you remember when Hazie and I came back from Greeley where we visited with the Gypsies at their camp?"

"Yes, but..." Mom started.

Eddie cut her off and again, without raising his voice, he said, "I told Bruno Hadiz, the Gypsy leader, that they could park down below the road if they ever needed a spot in this part of the country. In return, he said he would buy cars from me when he needed them."

Mom just snorted, but she was listening.

"So, what do you think? I know he will buy several cars and whatever else he needs from me. That can add up to a lot of money real fast. So, what do you say, Mom?" He waited for her to give him an answer.

"I suppose if that's the case, it would be all right. We're not using that ground right now, but..." she hesitated.

"Mom, Bruno promised me that he would leave your chickens alone. How about it? Let's go down and talk to him." Eddie moved a little closer. Mom reached out and gave him a big hug. Eddie snuggled his chin under her neck and I had to laugh out loud. He knew he could talk her out of being mad.

When Eddie drove up with Mom and me, Bruno came over to meet us. Eddie introduced him to Mom and he took her hand in his. He held it for a moment then said, "Mrs. Higgins, I hope we can become good friends. I will do my best to see that your land is taken care of and left in better shape than when we came."

Mom, almost at a loss as to how to treat this polite and sincere man, answered, "I'll be glad to be your friend. If Eddie says you're okay, then I'm sure you will be."

Bruno then turned to me. "While we're here, you and Eddie, and your mother and father will have to spend an evening with us. We have many talented people in our tribe. I'm sure the singing and dancing would be a pleasure for you to watch."

Mom melted at the words "singing and dancing." She missed her friends at Lime and their nightly singing, and playing violins and accordions.

"Oh, I would like that very much. Perhaps we can get our old country friends from Lime, where we used to live, to join in."

We all talked a while then Eddie said he needed to get back to town. Everyone said goodbye. On the way to the house, Mom said, "You know Eddie, I think it's going to be fun having the Gypsies living there for the summer. I'll sell him some chickens. I don't think he will bother stealing from me."

"Yeah Mom. By the end of summer you'll be dancing a Gypsy fandango. Just wait and see!" Eddie couldn't help kidding Mom a little.

"I saw Morey at the post office today. What's all this about going to Virginia Beach and Duke University next week?" Eddie wanted to know.

"Oh Eddie, I don't know what to tell you. Ever since that night last winter when Ty Williams hypnotized me, Morey has been a little bit crazy!" I answered him.

"He isn't taking all that seriously, is he?" Eddie said, with a puzzled look on his face.

"Yes, he definitely is. He's read everything he can find on the subject of hypnosis, has talked with Ty innumerable times and at this point, he's ready to go to the ends of the earth to track down some of the things he's read about." I was interested myself, but not to the extent that Morey was.

I remembered back to the night in February, a cold, wind-howling blizzard of a night. Morey called to say he would be late for our date. He had just talked with a friend's brother-in-law who was stranded at the Pueblo airport. He was flying his own plane from Denver to California, when he got caught in this storm that had matured so rapidly into a blizzard. He was grounded.

When Morey and Ty arrived, I noted that Ty was taller than Morey, tanned and athletic looking, with a shock of unruly light brown hair and gray eyes. A neat package of a man, I thought to myself. When he spoke, it was with an easy informality. Eddie came in and I introduced them. Ty said, "Morey has been telling me all about you. I'm going to have to spend more time in Pueblo and get to know you." He sounded sincere.

I asked Morey if Chuck Blatnik and his date, Earla Mae would be coming over. He said they would. "Let's have a drink while we wait. What do you drink Ty?" I looked over at him.

"Some Scotch on the rocks, if you have it," he answered.

"Can do. Eddie, I know what you want, a hot toddy, right? Morey, is vodka and water okay?" I waited until they all answered. Sometimes Morey threw me a curve and wanted something else.

As I fixed drinks, I listened to their conversation. Morey always wanted to know everything about someone he had just met.

"So Ty, why were you flying to California?" he asked.

"Well, to make a long story short, my wife Ginger passed away two weeks ago. I finally wound up all the little details and decided to get away from it all. I have a place on the Baja where I can go when I need to sort things out. Actually, that is where I'll be." He gave all of us a sort of lop-sided grin.

Morey hadn't finished. "And what do you do to keep yourself occupied?"

"You'll probably think this strange, but I am learning more about hypnosis as it applies to pain," Ty answered seriously.

"Hypnosis. That's just a lot of stage stuff where they get someone up there and make a fool out of them." Morey, always a skeptic, seemed sure of himself.

"That's what I thought too, but I heard from a friend who had taken a course in hypnosis at Cornell that it could be used to alleviate pain."

"That's hard to believe. Understand, I'm not calling you a liar, I just don't believe it." Morey wasn't one to back down.

"Well, Morey, all I can say is that I studied hypnosis and as my wife couldn't take pain killers, I tried it on her. It worked. I could hypnotize her, give her the suggestion to sleep for say, four hours and she would do so. It was like a reprieve for both of us." Ty was very serious.

"Well, maybe so but I'd have to see it to believe it." Morey wasn't about to back down.

Chuck and Earla Mae arrived on a blast of cold air and I hurried to shut the door after them. I had hardly introduced them and made them comfortable when Morey started in. "Ty here is a hypnotist. Can you believe that?" he jibed.

I could see that Ty, for all his good manners, didn't like the tone Morey was taking.

"Tell you what, Morey, if any of you will be my subject, I'll prove to you that hypnosis isn't a fake. Would that make a believer out of you?" Ty asked, a bit of an edge to his voice.

No one spoke up. I thought of Mom and her belief in hypnosis, and my chemistry teacher, Mr. Tedmond, and all he had told us about extrasensory perception.

"Ty, I'll be your subject. I don't know whether I'll be a good subject or not. I've always been interested in these things." I wanted to be hypnotized, not just for my own knowledge, but to wipe that smirk off Morey's face.

"I thought you were going to fix some of your great scrambled eggs for us. How about it?" Morey tried to back down.

"I can do that later, I'm in the mood now." I said, and then to Ty, "What do you want me to do?"

"Find a place to sit that is comfortable for you." He motioned to a chair in the living room that had a footstool in front of it.

"Yes, I like that chair." I proceeded to make myself comfortable.

Ty turned to Morey, Chuck, Eddie, and Earla Mae. "You can come in and out of the room but I would appreciate it if you would be quiet and not talk. This shouldn't take too long." He seemed very assured of himself.

Ty sat on the footstool in front of me and said, "Lean back against the chair, get comfortable and listen to my voice." He took a chain from around his neck, took a signet ring from his finger, and threaded it on the chain. He fastened the clasp and said, "I'm going to swing this chain and ring back and forth in front of your eyes. I will give you instructions as we go along. I won't say or do anything that will be harmful to you. I want you to relax and listen to my voice." He was very calm and assured.

I listened and heard an ever further-away sounding voice. The last thing I remember him saying was "Now close your eyes and go deeply asleep."

What I remembered next was Morey laughing. "Well, you sure looked like you were in a trance. How do you feel now?"

"I feel great, like I'd been on a nice long vacation with plenty of rest." I stretched and couldn't hold back a yawn.

"How about those scrambled eggs?" Morey was always hungry and by now everyone else was starved, too.

I went to the kitchen and quickly got a nice snack together. Earla Mae helped me set the table and Eddie seemed to be hovering at my elbow.

"What is it, Eddie? Have I forgotten something?" I asked.

"No, I was just wondering if you feel okay. Do you?" He seemed worried.

"Sure, I feel great. Why shouldn't I?" I countered.

"Yeah, well I just wondered. That was sure an interesting experiment."

I had placed Eddie's stool next to his chair. I put his plate on the stool with his fork at the side. We all sat down and I saw Ty glance at Eddie as he lifted his fork that he held between the toes of his right foot, to his lips. Ty caught me watching him and gave me a big smile, almost like a fellow conspirator.

Everyone was about halfway though the ham and eggs when Morey said to me, "What in the hell do you think you are doing?"

I just looked up at him and said, "What does it look like I'm doing? I'm taking off my left shoe and my stocking. Anything wrong with that?" It seemed completely natural to me.

Morey kept staring. Finally he said, "Well, I'll be damned! I wouldn't believe it if I didn't see it with my own eyes!"

Everyone else seemed to be equally amazed. They all started talking at once. Did I remember Ty asking me to do this? What did he tell you to do? And on and on.

I assured them that I didn't remember Ty giving me instructions to do anything, only to go fast asleep and listen to his voice.

Morey wasn't ready to give up. "I'll bet you can't hypnotize her again. Now she knows you made a fool out of her. She won't do something crazy a second time!"

"How about it Hazel? Will you give it another try?" Ty asked me.

"Sure, why not? I feel fine about your hypnotizing me again. I haven't felt so relaxed in ages." I cleared the dishes off the table, went to the living room, and sat down in the chair.

Ty went through the same routine. Again, the last thing I remembered was, "Now close your eyes and go deeply asleep."

After Ty awakened me, we all sat around talking. Morey asked if this was real, why weren't doctors using it to help people. Ty assured him that there were doctors using hypnosis. He would mail Morey a list he had compiled when he returned to Denver. We must have talked for about thirty minutes when I excused myself. "I've got to take a shower."

Morey said, "Why not take it in the morning before you go to work?"

I insisted, "No, I'm going to take it now." I headed for the upstairs bathroom. I was oblivious to the fact that everyone was following me.

This is what they told me happened. I got into the shower, clothes and all, turned the water on full blast, and stood there, going through the motions of taking a shower. I stepped out, grabbed a towel, and proceeded to dry myself. At this point, Ty said, "At the count of three, you will awaken. You will feel great and will not remember any of this. One, two, three…!"

I came out of it, bewildered and half angry when I realized that I was standing there dripping wet in all my clothes with an audience crowded around.

"This was a bit drastic, don't you think?" I looked straight at Ty.

"Blame Morey, he insisted on you doing this. Said if you did, he would be convinced." Ty turned to Morey, "Are you convinced now, Morey?"

"Hell yes! She wouldn't do this even if she'd had too much to drink! I'm going to look into this hypnosis thing. I'll see to it that the world knows about it!" He had a gleam in his eye and I thought, *Oh my! What will he do now?*

Finally, Chuck and Earla Mae said they had to get home. Ty and Morey left. The wind had died down and it had quit snowing.

Eddie turned to me with a wry little grin. "Hazie, you made a believer out of Morey, and me too. What do you think Morey will do about it?"

49 Meet Mr. and Mrs. Morey Bernstein

*E*ddie was waiting for me when I closed the shop Saturday afternoon.

"Hey Sis, what are you going to be doing Sunday afternoon, about four o'clock? There's going to be a big auction in Amarillo on Monday. I was thinking I'd go down Sunday. Leave about four, which would get us in there about three in the morning." He paused.

"Sure, I can take off a couple of days. Who else is going?" I asked.

"Bob Hastings for sure. He has his eye on some big machinery at an equipment auction. He wouldn't be coming back with us if he bought something. He would probably start home early." Bob was always on the lookout for big loaders and trucks. We never knew what he might buy.

"And who else?" I asked.

"Bill Mitchell said he could go." Eddie answered. "I have to be here in the morning. I want to get some bookwork done so I'll be ready to head for Amarillo. Bill can go with me to the ranch tomorrow afternoon. You'll want to take your car so you can come back to town when you want to. Bob will meet us at the ranch." Eddie seemed to have it all figured out.

As I was getting Eddie ready for bed that night, he said, "I wish Mom wouldn't worry so much about me. She acts like I'm still a little kid!"

"You might just as well get used to it Eddie. She treats me the same way. I just try to keep to myself anything she might think dangerous. It doesn't always work but it helps. I know she doesn't understand or like the way Morey's family treats me, but…" I didn't know how to continue and didn't want to get Eddie upset.

"Well Hazie, I guess none of us like it, but as long as you and Morey are together, I'll forget about his family. It doesn't seem to bother him too much." Eddie laughed and the tension disappeared.

"You're right Eddie. And Bob and I…," I thought of Morey's brother. "We're such good friends. He makes up for everyone else."

"Well, I'll see you in the morning." Eddie crawled into bed, reached up with his foot and flipped off the switch on his bed lamp. I knew he'd be asleep in just a few minutes.

Morey and I had been going together for a few years. It had been a stormy courtship. We were both so busy with our own businesses there wasn't much time for anything else. I had my house and Eddie, and Jody and Dyanna during the school year. We were both so preoccupied that neither of us chided the other for not spending more time together. So now, as I dressed to go out with Morey, it didn't bother me that it was almost eleven o'clock at night. When most couples would be getting home from a date, we were just going out. I was usually home by two in the morning.

I was surprised when Morey and Bob Bernstein came to my house the next morning about ten thirty. Usually, Morey would spend a quiet Sunday morning at "Ulcers, Incorporated" as he called their business. He liked it when the phones weren't ringing off the hook and the place wasn't full of customers. He would say, "This is the only time I can think straight around here."

"I talked to Walt Chrisman. You know him, he's a Justice of the Peace, and he said he would marry us." Morey said with an air of accomplishment.

"Yeah," Bob added, "He just asked Morey if Dad would give him any trouble." Bob had a grin from ear to ear.

I could picture Sam Bernstein, arms flailing in the breeze, screaming and yelling at Walt. And I could see Walt just standing there, a smile on his face, waiting until Sam ran out of steam. The only way anyone could handle Sam and his histrionics was to ignore him. I had been doing this for six years now, and it worked.

"So what time are we supposed to be wherever we're supposed to be?" I asked.

"Eleven o'clock, at Walt's house. He said his wife could be a witness if we needed her," Morey said.

"Okay, give me a few minutes to get ready."

Just then Eddie walked in. Bob asked him, "Eddie come with us. Your sister and Morey are going to tie the knot. You and I can be the witnesses."

Eddie didn't hesitate. "Why sure, I guess you've been thinking about this for a long time. I shouldn't be surprised."

Mr. And Mrs. Morey Bernstein

It was on August 1, 1947, after a very short exchange of vows and signing our names, that we left Walt's house as Mr. and Mrs. Morey Charles Bernstein. As we walked down the walk from Walt's house, Bob said, "I'd like to treat you all to lunch. Let's go to the Town House. I may even have some champagne! And of course, you will all join me!" Bob was having more fun than any of us.

Bob did order champagne and by the time lunch was over, we were all in a festive mood.

As we came out of the Town House, Morey turned to me, gave me a big hug and a kiss and said, "Well, I'm going to work. I'll see you later." And he was gone.

Bob said, "Lucky I've got my car here. Where do you and Eddie want to go?"

"Just take us by Kirtley's," Eddie said, "My car is there, and I'll take Hazel home in a little bit."

Bob put his arm around me and said, "Cheer up Sister." Then he added, "Where are you going?"

"I'm going to the ranch for now. Later I'm going to Amarillo with Eddie to the car auction. I'll be home Monday or Tuesday."

"Have fun," my brother-in-law said, and he gave me a big smooch.

The miles rolled by as we sped toward Amarillo. Endless cactus-dotted prairies, an occasional jack rabbit bounding along was about all there was to break the monotony. I half listened to the chatter of the men as they told their tall tales, laughed, and joked to make the time go faster. We stopped at a diner about eight and had dinner. We all got to laughing as Bob Hastings joked with the cute waitress. It was a welcome break.

It was the middle of the night, pitch black and windy when we came into Amarillo. There are two kinds of weather in Amarillo, windy and windier. It never let up.

"How about the Longhorn?" Eddie asked. It was practically next door to the auction and we could walk back and forth to it. A pair of Texas longhorns graced the top of the sign, neon lights making a path through the darkness. It had a good little bar and cafe. The night before the auction and the night following, they were open all night. They were busy when we got there but still had a few rooms left. None of us bothered to do much more than take off our jackets, stretch out, and get some rest. Seven o'clock was going to come mighty early.

Light sifted in through the Venetian blinds. Bob and Bill were half across the bed, legs and arms in awkward positions. I wondered how they could sleep twisted up like that. Bob was snoring and Bill had his head under his pillow. That must have been his way of escaping the noise.

I poked Eddie. "Come on Eddie. Let's get you ready to go. Then I'll get ready. Then we can wake up our roommates." I dug into the backpack I'd packed, bringing out toothbrushes and all the rest of the things we needed.

When we were about ready to leave the room, Eddie went over and tickled the bottom of Bob's foot, jumping quickly out of the way as Bob gave a big kick.

"Come on, get up lazy bones," he yelled in Bob's ear. "We'll meet you in the restaurant.

"The mention of food will get him going faster than anything!" Eddie grinned at me as we went out the door.

"I swear, I've got sand in my teeth. Doesn't this damned wind ever stop?" I gritted my teeth. It was worse than ever this morning.

"Well Hazie, as soon as we get some food under our belts, we'll check out a few cars. If we're lucky, maybe we can start back early. I don't like the way those clouds are piling up. Usually the wind dies down some during the night." He had a worried frown.

"Yeah, it seems to be getting stronger, if anything."

"I'm going to head over to the equipment auction, it's just a couple of blocks from here." Bob said after we'd finished breakfast. He started out the door.

Eddie grabbed at his pants leg. "Hold on there, Cuz." he said. "I'll drive you over. Then give me a call when you're through and let me know if you found something. If you don't, I can come get you."

"Oh, okay, I guess that would be all right." Bob seemed relieved.

We piled into the car and went with Eddie. I was surprised to see so many cars at the equipment auction. There were license plates from states all over the country. There was a bustle at the door as people stood in line to get registered.

"I'll get out here Eddie," Bob said. "I'm going to take a look around before I register. If there's nothing I want, there's no use wasting my time here. I'll give you a call. See you." And he was gone, his head tall above the crowd.

Eddie drove back to the motel and parked. "It's only a block, let's walk. Is there anything we want out of our rooms now?"

"We can always come back if we need anything." I was just as anxious as Eddie to see what might be available.

Bill, his lanky legs long in his jeans, told Eddie, "I think I'll go out and start looking. See you out there."

I waited in line with Eddie to get registered and get a number. I was getting excited. It was a quarter to eight and already there was a crowd waiting to register. The two auctioneers were bantering on their loudspeakers, typical Texans, with a drawl a mile long, a cigarette burning down in their fingers, broad-brimmed Stetsons pushed back on their foreheads. The backs of their shirts were already sweat-stained. It was hot.

They aimed some of their jokes at people in the crowd. Everyone knew everyone. Eddie grinned as Jake, the tall auctioneer, yelled at him, "Hey Higgins, I've got a 'red and white, and all right' tied up back there with your name on it," then he waved at Eddie.

Eddie gave his broad smile and waved a foot in Jake's direction. "You better have some good ones Jake. I'm a rarin' to go!"

Eddie had been coming to the auction in Amarillo for a little over two years. It hadn't taken long for him to win the respect of the auctioneers, owners, and car dealers from around the country. If he didn't find as many cars as he wanted to buy, he would loan a tow bar or two, to another dealer. They always brought it back and returned the favor when they could. Eddie knew the shysters. There always had to be a few, and he avoided dealing with them, just as everyone else did. He'd say, "I hope I never need anything so bad I have to lie for it."

As soon as he got his number we went over to the huge, eight-foot-chain-link-fenced yard. Just twenty years old, Eddie looked older and he acted older. Although he had a sunny disposition and always had a big smile for everyone, anyone watching Eddie would never know that down underneath there was a sadness, a place where he went when he wanted to be alone, when he didn't want anyone to touch him or get close.

This was a lucky day for picking cars. In a little over two hours Eddie had picked out the cars he wanted to bid on, plus several more that looked good. A steady stream of cars had been moving through the line and most of them had a "sold" sign on the windshield when they were driven back to the lot.

Eddie nudged me with his shoulder. "See what's happening Sis? No one likes the looks of this storm. Everyone is buying and getting out of here."

Buyers were busy fastening tow bars and getting the cars they had bought out of the lot and ready to go.

The sales building had wood shutters that could be lowered and raised according to the weather. The wind was howling from the west so these shutters were closed. Even so, the air was full of dust. Combined with the smell of exhaust fumes, hamburgers cooking, and sweat, it was almost overpowering.

The auctioneer, Jake, was half standing, half sitting on a tall stool on the raised stage in the front of the sales barn. He was all business, keeping up a steady stream of auctioneers' jargon as each car came through. I always marveled at how adept he was at twisting words and phrases into a rhythm with the facts about a car somehow clear-cut in the midst of it all. No matter how hard the bleacher-like benches above the sales ring were, auctions were fun.

The other auctioneer stood carelessly beside the first one. He noticed every flick of a finger, the raising of a hat brim just a hair, and the lifting of a number. The buyers who just made a signal were well known to the auctioneers. Sometimes a buyer called out his raise.

The bidding continued until there weren't any more raises. A clerk hovering at the door of the auction would take that particular bid sheet to the office where the clerks did all the paperwork.

"I'm going to get a cup of coffee and a doughnut. What can I get for you guys?" I looked from Eddie to Bill. I reached over and wiped at Eddie's eyes. They were red and watery from the dust. I knew if they felt like mine, anything would help.

"Sure Sis, my breakfast disappeared a long time ago. Why don't you go with her Bill? Help carry that stuff back." Eddie settled himself where he had a good view of the cars and the auctioneer.

There was a line at the take out counter of the little restaurant. My stomach was growling. It had been quite a while since breakfast.

When we got back to where Eddie was waiting I spread one of the napkins on the bench beside Eddie and put his hamburger where he could reach it. He reached over and grasped the burger between the toes of his right foot and started eating. I lifted his coffee cup to his mouth and he took a big drink.

"Man, is that good. I didn't realize I was so hungry."

I poked Eddie in the ribs as a red and white Chevy two-door came through the back door. "Is that the one Jake was kidding you about?" I asked.

"Yeah, that's it. I'm going to let some of the rest of them bid on it first, then if it looks like I can get it at a decent price, I'll start bidding." Eddie's signal to the caller was a wave of his foot.

I waited nervously as the bids went up to six hundred. Just when it looked like the bidding was over, Eddie gave a wave of his foot and yelled, "Seven hundred!" Sure enough, the other bidders were through.

"Will you make any money on that one Eddie?" I asked him.

"Sure, I'll make at least three hundred, maybe more."

Bob had stopped by earlier to have Eddie come out and look at the dump truck he bought. "Heck Eddie, I can use this for a year or two, then sell it and make money on the deal." Bob left the auction about ten o'clock. As he got into the truck he turned to Eddie. "You know, Cuz, if this wind gets any worse, if I were you I'd stay right there in that motel room. It's one thing driving a hunk like this dump truck, wind doesn't bother it much, but hauling cars, forget it!" He was very sober as he said this and I could see that Eddie was listening.

So now as I watched Eddie and Bill hook up the tow bars, I could see Eddie anxiously look at the sky and then at the debris and weeds piling up against the fence.

"What do you think Hazie? It sure doesn't get any better, does it?" he asked, a worried frown between his eyes as he squinted against the wind and the dust. The windblown sand in the air cut into our skin. There wasn't any way to keep away from it.

"Well Eddie, I can see us crawling along and maybe having to hole up somewhere along the road and as you know, there sure aren't many places to stop between here and Raton. If you want my vote, I'd stay here." I didn't want to be stuck anywhere between Amarillo and Raton.

"In that case, we should call home so they wouldn't worry. It's only five o'clock. I could go over to the auction and maybe get some real buys."

On our way back to the sales ring we stopped by the motel office and told the desk clerk we were staying another night.

"I don't blame you," the clerk said. "I haven't seen the wind this bad since last year when that tornado leveled the little town of Channing, or I should say the outskirts of the town. It was pretty bad."

Eddie said, "Well, I sure hope that doesn't happen again. This wind is bad enough." Eddie started to leave the motel but pulled his head right back in again, "I'm not going to get my gizzard full of sand again, let's go get something to eat."

"I'm with you Eddie." Bill tried to brush Eddie's hair out of his eyes. "I'm sure glad you brought the car, even if it does have a tag-a-long hitched on behind."

We went next door to the motel and had a good Mexican dinner. Several of the buyers from the auction were there. Most of them were staying somewhere in Amarillo until the wind died down.

"Well, guess we aren't the only ones that storm has buffaloed!" Eddie started talking with some of the fellows and we didn't get back to the motel until about eight.

"I don't know about you or Bill, Hazie, but I'm going to try to get some sleep. If you're awake and the wind blows itself out, wake me up."

I got Eddie ready for bed then took my turn in the bathroom. When I came out, both Eddie and Bill were sound asleep. Eddie had left enough room for me and soon I joined them.

I awakened about five the next morning. I quietly opened the door and felt a gentle breeze. I took a shower, brushed my teeth, combed my hair, and put on some lipstick. I was dressed by the time Eddie and Bill stirred.

"Come on Eddie. I'll get you in the shower. Too bad we didn't bring a change of clothes, but we're in one piece and not in a ditch somewhere."

We decided to eat breakfast along the way. Our little cavalcade made its way through the rolling hills covered with mesquite and cactus. I was thankful the wind wasn't blowing.

I remembered one trip when I'd been driving a Ford pickup and pulling a Plymouth coupe. The wind attacked every time I came out of a cut. I looked in my rear view mirror and it was all I could do to brake slowly. The coupe was flying through the air, all four wheels off the pavement.

Later we could all laugh at some of the near escapes we'd had towing cars from the auctions. One time, on a trip back from the Denver auction, we left six cars in snow banks in the Monument Hill area. Another time we could hear a hail storm ahead of us. We made it with four of the cars to a spot under an overpass. The car we couldn't make room for was a total loss.

Once in a great while someone would say to me, "Aren't you afraid to let Eddie drive?" It would be almost all I could do to not say something smart back, but usually I just said, "If I were to be in a tight spot and could choose a driver, it would be Eddie."

50 *Eddie Buys the Bartley House*

*Y*ou're going to think I've lost my mind but wait until you hear what I've done!" Eddie was excited. "I bought the old Bartley house on Claremont." He was grinning like the cat that ate the canary.

"But, how? Where did you get the money?" Bartley's owned the grocery store on the corner of Northern and Berkeley where we bought a lot of our groceries. Robert had been badly burned when his plane was shot down in the war. His brother, Gordon, was an attorney. The family home had been a beautiful big frame home on the corner of Claremont and Windsor. It had beautiful leaded glass window accents and fine carved woodwork on the doors. Now the entire home was in need of repair and I just couldn't imagine Eddie buying it.

"Well I guess I'll have to tell you. Robert Bartley has been after me to sell him that yellow Pontiac I drive. The other day he made me a proposition. He said his folks already moved into an apartment house that they owned. He, his brother, and his sister are all married. The house was empty and he said, 'Eddie, come with me. I want to show you the house.'

"So I went with him to take a look. I still didn't have a clue as to what he wanted. Sis, you'll have to see the inside of that house. Oak woodwork all the way through and lots of room. Two big baths, and it looks like everything is in good shape. It even has a third floor where they had a small ballroom. Hardwood floors everywhere. The basement is finished for a laundry room, food storage and a maid's room." He was out of breath.

"So, okay Eddie. Now just what is the deal? How did you get your mitts on this house and is it a done deal?" Robert had to know that Eddie didn't have a lot of money.

"After I looked at everything, including a double car garage in the back, Robert locked the door and said, 'Let's go over to my office. Gordon and I just moved too, into a bigger office on Northern.'"

"And…" I waited.

"Robert just sat back in his chair and said, 'Eddie, I'll take that yellow Pontiac you drive as a down payment on the house, make the sale price so reasonable you can't turn it down, and the payments can be whatever you can pay a month at six percent interest.' Then he just grinned from ear to ear.

"Hazie, my mind was racing about a hundred miles an hour! I just sat there like a fish out of water. I finally got my breath enough to tell Robert, 'I think you've got a deal. Go over all that again for me.' And he did. I had heard right the first time."

"So I suppose you worked out all the details right there and then, and now you own a big house on Claremont!" I didn't know how I felt. It was the first time Eddie had ever made a decision this big without talking it over with Mom and me, or Dad if he was home. My baby brother wasn't my baby brother any more. I didn't know whether to be sad or glad.

"C'mon Sis," Eddie said. "Come with me to the ranch to tell Mom and Dad."

Mom knew the house. She had delivered squabs right to the house for Mrs. Bartley.

"Son, I can't believe that you bought that house. When can we go look at it?" Mom's voice had an excited ring.

"How about in the morning, early, before Morey gets up?" I said. I turned to Eddie. "That way I can go too." I was as curious as Mom to see the house.

Bright and early the next morning we descended on the Bartley house. Mom and Dad didn't say much, but I could tell they were impressed. Dad looked the furnace over and said, "You won't have to worry about this furnace. It is good for enough BTU's to heat a house bigger than this.

"That's great, Dad. Now check the water lines and water heater for me. I will have to put in a larger water heater, or I may put individual heaters in some of the apartments. What do you think?" After all, Dad had worked on some of the biggest projects imaginable. A little domestic heat and water system should be right up his alley.

"Eddie, this is a lovely house," Mom said. "It seems a shame to cut it up into apartments, but I'm sure if you do, you shouldn't have any trouble keeping them rented. It's only a block from the streetcar line. That will be a big help."

"Yeah Mom. I want to make it into three studio apartments upstairs. I think young working couples would like that, or maybe older couples or singles that don't want to bother with a big house."

"You know we'll help you all we can. I'll get started on the yard. It used to be lovely but I can see it hasn't been cared for in a long time." Mom was ready to start digging.

Dad said, "I saw a few spots in the basement where you need to check on dampness. You can plaster over the spots but it's better to find out what is causing them. I think some of it may be caused by leaky gutters. We'll be sure all the water is kept away from the foundation."

"Well" Eddie said. "I guess that does it. You don't think I'm crazy then?"

"No," everyone chorused.

"I think it's one of the best buys you'll ever make," Mom said. "Gives you a nest and income at the same time." She laughed and gave him a hug.

Eddie dropped me off and took Mom and Dad to their car. I could hear them talking and I was glad they liked what Eddie had done.

I was helping Al Bensik, Manager of Bernstein Brothers plumbing department, build a "spec" house on Logan Street. A couple from the Chicago area, who had recently moved to Pueblo, had just opened an interior design business and I decided to give them an open hand with the little house on Logan and asked Morey what he thought. "Sure, go ahead," then he added, "Just don't bother me with the details."

This gave me time to work out what I wanted to do with the yard. I enlisted a man who had helped me on some other things and in two weeks the yard was finished. In another three weeks, the inside of the house was finished and Morey and I moved in.

For me, life settled into an easy pattern. Morey still liked to work late when the phone was silent and customers weren't everywhere, waiting to be waited on. He would come home for dinner about six, and then disappear until around eleven. I got into a habit of doing what housework I had to do while he was working late. That way, I had the whole day free. Morey didn't care where I went or what I did, as long as I was home for dinner or ready to go out if we had to entertain. Many times he brought salesmen home with him for dinner. They were usually interesting and we got to be good friends.

I spent my days helping Eddie get his house on Claremont in shape. Eddie's idea of three apartments upstairs and two down proved to be just fine. I drew up plans for the whole house and asked him to take a look at them and tell me what he thought and what changes I should make.

Eddie looked at the plans carefully. "I like the way you brought the stairway up the outside of the house. In fact, I think I know where there is a stairway we can buy that will just fit that space!" He had that note of excitement in his voice that meant he was on the scent of a good buy.

I thought, *Great, maybe there will be some other stuff we can use.*

"You know, they're still tearing down that old Sacred Heart Orphanage building just a few blocks from here. I went by the first day they started on it, but I haven't been back since. Let's go take a look." He was rarin' to go.

"What do you think, Sis? We have four sets of stairways to choose from. We'll have to cut any of them down. The ceilings in this old building must be a good ten feet high." We had already spent an hour looking at all kinds of lumber, locks, windows, and just about anything you'd need to build with.

"Yeah Eddie, and that doesn't count probably eight or more stair-cases upstairs and down to the basement levels." I was thinking about the four foot wide stair that we saw at the back of the building. "All I've seen so far are made of very good lumber. The stair rail to that one is great. How much are you going to offer?"

Eddie thought for a minute. "We'll have to have it hauled and I would like to be able to wait until we are ready to set it up. Then the guys who haul it can use their equipment to help set it. So, I think ten dollars should do it." He seemed sure of himself.

"Do you really think they will take that for it? Sure doesn't sound like much to me." I was already planning an entry door for it.

"Let's figure as close as we can to what else we are going to need. I think we can buy most of it here."

"Eddie, I'll bet this orphanage and the Bartley house were built about the same time. Did you notice the door hinges and brass key plates? Let's see if we can find a door to go on that outside stairway and some window latches and hinges. If we widen the back porch like I designed it, we could get all the windows and everything to match."

"That's a great idea. Let's go home and figure out exactly what we'll need. I've been thinking of using that garage on the back for a place to store lumber. If we know what we need, we can get it all delivered at the same time. They're going to have to use a big truck and hoist, so they might just as well have a load."

When we finished going over the plans we had a list of doors, win-dows, stairways, hardware, siding and even some wainscoting we could use. Eddie rechecked and added several items. When he finished, he looked up at me with a weary sigh of satisfaction.

"I think I'll offer two hundred fifty dollars for what I have listed."

"If you can get it all for that I'm going to get you a license for steal-ing." I couldn't help laughing, but he did. Plus, they threw in some old-fashioned transom doors and hardware they said would just get de-molished. It was a good thing we had the garage to store stuff in. When we got through, it was full.

Eddie hired Lou Barneycastle to do the major work on the house. Barney, as he was called, was a tall thin fellow. A shock of dark hair with a white streak fell across his forehead. He had an inquisitive ex-pression and sad brown eyes. He seemed to hurry about everything he did. About the only time I didn't see him in a hurry was when he was sizing up a job. He would stand back, look at the plans, sit on a saw-horse or whatever was handy, and take his time. When he got through looking and figuring, you could bet he would get the job done right.

He only worked at carpentry during the winter. During the summer he owned the Dairy Queen on Northern. It was always clean, the help was polite, and it made good money for him. His wife, Etta, worked at the telephone office and had been on the same job for years.

Barney told Eddie, "I think I can do a good job for you. I understand what you want, and if I don't, I'll ask." He and Eddie seemed to hit it off from the start.

Eddie enjoyed doing the things he could and Barney let him. Eddie did the wiring he could reach. When it came time to lay tile in the kitchens and bathrooms, Eddie did it. There were all kinds of things he enjoyed doing but he didn't take time away from his car sales. After all, that was where he made his money.

When Barney needed help, Eddie suggested Red Barnes's dad. Red was still helping Eddie at the car lot and made a great lot boy. He was learning about mechanics and was proud of the things he could do.

Morey and I had dinner at the ranch on Thanksgiving.

His mother and father had dinner at the world famous Broadmoor Hotel in Colorado Springs. His mom said, "We don't have any children at home. Why should I cook dinner?"

Mom, Jody, and I made all our favorite dishes. The day was nippy so Dad made a fire in the heating stove and the crackle of cedar logs and the incense of the cedar smoke tickled our noses. Frank and Lucy came. So did Tony and Emma and their son, Johnny. It just wouldn't have been Thanksgiving without them. Johnny, by now, was an accomplished pianist. He had his own orchestra and played all around the area. After everyone was properly full, Dad passed glasses of red wine for a toast.

When it came Morey's turn to make a toast, he just said, "To all the great cooks and the good wine and all the wonderful people. I'm very full and very happy!" That pretty well expressed what we all thought.

We coaxed Johnny to play a lot of our old favorites and spent a couple of hours singing and remembering. I saw a tear in Mom's eye as she glanced around at everyone dear to her.

On December third, Eddie was 22 years old. He said we shouldn't, but we gave him a birthday party. The house was full. People drifted in and out all day. If they had all come at once we would have had to rent Boseker's Hall again. Mom made two big cakes. Red's mom brought a cake and so did Jessie Boseker. It was after midnight before everyone left. I looked at Eddie and he grinned back. "Gosh Sis, I didn't know I knew so many people. How did you keep them from all coming at once?"

"That wasn't too hard. Folks who would only stay a little while or who would get tired, we told to come early. There are always people who want to get home early, so we asked them to come next. The ones who like to stay late came late and stayed late."

"I suppose you asked all my rowdy friends to come last, right?" Eddie looked pleased.

"Well, you notice who came early and stayed late? Tony, Emma and Johnny, Frank, Lucy, and the Bosekers; none of them wanted to miss a minute."

"Christmas will be a letdown after this, Hazie. What are you and Morey going to do for the holidays?" Eddie asked.

"I'm not sure. He's been on the phone with Hugh Lynn Cayce and Dr. Rhine at Duke University. I know he would like to spend some time at the Cayce Research Center in Norfolk, Virginia, so it won't surprise me if we spend a week or so there and go on to meet with Dr. Rhine." I tried to make light of Morey's increasing interest in the paranormal, but I knew he was more interested than even he wanted to admit. And so was I.

Eddie mused aloud, "Morey's so hard-headed about business. I just can't see him getting so interested in hypnosis and all that sort of thing."

"I don't worry about him taking all these new things lightly, Eddie. He's up to his neck in research." Morey was cautious. I knew he wouldn't get in over his head.

51 *Trip to Virginia Beach and Beyond*

hen Morey and I returned to Pueblo, the first thing I did was call Eddie. His voice sounded so good. When I asked him when he could come over he just said, "Give me ten minutes." How nice it was to live in a small town.

"So what did you do? Did you meet a lot of interesting people?" Eddie was full of questions.

"It was like we were on a merry-go-round! We went to Virginia Beach first. Hugh Lynn Cayce met us at the airport. We had lunch, and then Hugh Lynn took us to the Research Center." There was so much to tell Eddie, I hardly knew where to begin. "I hope you read the book about Hugh's father, Edgar, that I left you. Did you?"

"Yes. Some of it was hard to believe, but at least I know a little bit about the man. What was the Center like?"

"It's a large, rather old-fashioned building with a large research library, very well kept up. There are people on hand to help you find categories that may be of interest to you. We spent five full days just going through records. I found the Life readings fascinating. Morey has a list of people he wants to interview who could talk to him first hand. There was a Mr. and Mrs. Kahn who went to Cayce not long after they were married some thirty years ago. Mr. Kahn's mother had been ailing. The doctors hadn't found anything wrong.

"Cayce told them she needed to be operated on for a small cancer just starting in her lower colon. Their doctor in New York said that he didn't detect anything wrong and refused to operate. They took her to meet Cayce personally and he repeated what he'd said earlier. The Kahns insisted that the doctor operate.

"The operation was performed and sure enough, the cancer was there. It was removed and the mother lived to be a healthy old woman." I paused.

"Did he tell the Kahns anything else?" Eddie asked.

"Yes, they went back to Cayce not only to thank him, but to ask for readings for themselves. Like all of Cayce's readings, it was very carefully recorded. 'Mr. Kahn, you will get into the bowling business and be very successful. You will have two sons. They will be doctors. One son will be a psychiatrist, and the other a doctor of medicine. You will live long and happy lives.' Morey and I were fascinated, and as you know, we did go to New York before coming home."

"So, did you meet the Kahns?" Eddie was almost sitting on the edge of his chair.

"Yep. Morey told them we had spent a week with Hugh Lynn Cayce and asked if we could talk with them.

"They invited us to their home, and not only told us about how true Cayce's readings for them had been, but arranged for their sons to drop by so we could meet them."

"Boy that must have been a thrill. Hazie, we've got to tell Mom about this. You know she sees things and they always turn out to be true. Lots of times no one will believe her. It's only once in a while with her, but I think it would make her feel better." Eddie was excited and I knew Morey would have a staunch ally in him. I told Eddie about Dr. Rhine and his wife, Louisa who had written a book about ESP in cats. There were so many things. I knew we would be talking about them for some time to come.

I asked Eddie how the apartments were coming along. He was happy with the work Barney was doing and we set a time the next day to go look. Then I told Eddie, "You know, I want to sell the house on Pitkin and the shop in Trinidad. I have an offer for the shop here in Pueblo. It seems a banker from Nebraska is going to buy that corner on Eighth and Main and build a several story bank building."

"That's great. You sure don't need any of that, anymore. It will give you time to travel with Morey."

52 House on Claremont

e parked in front of the house on Claremont early the next morning. Barney's pick-up was there and I recognized Dave Barnes's pick-up as well.

"Let's go on upstairs, that's where all the action is now." Eddie kicked open the door at the bottom of the stairs.

"This is the stairway we bought, isn't it? It is beautiful and so strong." I noticed that Barney had tacked plywood on the stairs to protect them. Not many workers would bother. As I walked through the unfinished apartments, I could see what made Barney so special. The apartments were taking shape and he was way ahead of where I thought he would be.

"They must have been putting in some long hours Eddie. I can't believe how much they've done."

"I know, and they haven't been working ten-hour days either. Barney knows what he is doing. He's fast, and Dave seems to anticipate what Barney wants before he asks. I've never seen such a team."

Just then Barney and Dave broke for a cup of coffee. I congratulated them on the great progress they were making. "If you keep this up, you will be about finished by spring."

I was kidding but Barney was serious when he answered, "Hazel, I think by the end of April I will have done the work I need to do. Dave can finish up with help from you and Eddie. Eddie can lay the tile. You wanted to do the painting. You said you knew someone to do the paper-hanging. You should be finished by the middle of summer."

Eddie waved a foot toward the bathrooms. "I don't know how you and Dave have done it, Barney. It seems like every time I come by, you surprise me with something else finished." Eddie was proud as he could be and couldn't keep his voice even.

"I guess you're not having any trouble following my plans?" I asked. "Looks like it is pretty much the way I pictured it."

"The only thing we've changed is beneath the stairway to the second floor," Barney said. "Those stairs are so heavy and well made that we decided to use them as the ceiling and wall of the small bedroom downstairs. This gave us four extra feet and a small closet under the short end of it."

"That sounds great. Some little kid will love that room." I couldn't wait to see it.

The two-bedroom apartments at the front of the house already looked beautiful, and that small bedroom was now a fairly large room, thanks to the extra four feet. We went outside and around to the back. What had been the back porch was now a kitchen and dining room. Barney had used another of the stairways from the orphanage to make a good-looking and safe stair to the basement.

It all looked better than I ever imagined. Eddie was going to have a first class investment. "Eddie, let's go to Patti's Restaurant and get some breakfast. I know Mom gave you something to eat, but I'm starved. And I want to talk to you."

"Sure, I've got a few things to talk to you about too." Eddie gave me a devilish little grin. I wondered what he had been up to now.

Eddie ordered coffee and a doughnut and I had scrambled eggs and toast. Eddie gave me that look, like "guess what I know?"

"All right, Eddie, out with it. I don't know what you've got up your sleeve but it must be good."

"Well, you did notice at my birthday party that Jody wasn't all set to run away to town and meet someone, didn't you?" he asked.

"No, not really. I was so busy and she was unusually helpful. I guess I just wasn't paying attention, so what?"

"She was glad to stay at home and help for a change. She's married Hazie. I promised her I wouldn't tell Mom until she did, but she didn't say anything about telling you." He waited for my reaction.

"I don't believe it. Why she hasn't even been going steady, or has she?" I knew I had been busy with my own affairs, but I usually paid more attention than this.

"Well, believe it Sis. I don't know exactly when. November I think. I've met Charles Youngblood. He seems to be a nice fellow, very good looking, quiet. He's from east Texas. In fact, that's where he is now. His family lives there."

"What does he do for a living?" I hoped she hadn't just married some attractive guy who was a good dancer.

"You don't have to worry. He's about thirty years old and is a purchasing agent for Sterns, Rogers and Company. He's checking out his next job in Guaymas, Oklahoma, a big power plant." Eddie said all this with a note of pride in his voice. I could tell Charles Youngblood had made quite an impression on my brother.

"Sounds like you think he's okay."

"Yeah, I think so. He's pretty quiet, but then I just met him for a little while. Jody acted like she was crazy about him."

"I hope it works for her." I changed the subject. There'd be time enough to worry about Jody later. "All right now, let me tell you about what I want to do. When I get the shops and the house on Pitkin sold, I want to put the money in a savings account that we can draw on if we need to. I want it in your name, Mom's name, and my name. We will use it for projects that we want to do. It may be tomorrow or next year. Anyway, it will be there. I would like to use some of it to paint the outside of Claremont and furnish the upstairs apartments. What do you think?"

"Why do you want to do that? It's your money. I don't think Mom will do it!"

"I don't think you understand, Eddie. I'll try to explain, and then perhaps we can both convince Mom." I realized he didn't have any idea of the complications my life could take.

"Well Hazie, draw me a picture."

I smiled. That's what he used to say when he was a little kid and I explained things to him by drawing pictures. "I think you realize that Morey's family isn't happy with his marriage to me. Sure, they pay it lip service now, but that doesn't alter the fact that I may never be "family," which is okay with me as long as Morey and I get along." I could see the skeptical look in Eddie's eyes.

"Lots of people don't get along with their in-laws," he said.

266

"That's right, but I know my shortcomings. I could never sit home, put three meals on the table, play bridge all afternoon, and visit with neighbors. That's not me. Morey knows it. We've talked about it."

"So he understands, so what's the problem?" Eddie asked bluntly.

"Morey has an uncle who would, and will, do anything to cause trouble. I know that in the future you and I, and especially Mom, will find things we want to do. So I want to have things in such a way that he can't do too much to do us in."

"Well, sure. I can see that." Eddie said.

"So what would be wrong with having our own bank account with my maiden name so we won't have to ask anyone for money?"

"I would feel better if I had money to put into it Hazie, and I know Mom will feel that way."

"Whoa there Eddie! Who gave you a couple of thousand when you needed it for your car lot and for other things? Mom did. Who loaned me some money when I started my first beauty shop? Mom did. Stop and think!" I could remember quite a few times and a few thousand dollars when it was all added up.

"Well, I hadn't thought of that. I guess you could say some of it was pay-back, right?" He asked.

"Sure, and if along the way we want to add more to it, great. We may find a need for it. So now tell me what you think?" I asked.

"I guess it just might be the best brainstorm you ever had. For one thing, it will force us to keep better track of everything." Eddie sounded enthused now. We'd tell Mom when we saw her the next time and I knew Dad would go along with it. He had a good business sense.

I found time during the day and in the evenings while Morey worked, to do a lot of painting. Eddie and I tiled the bathrooms. Eddie had a system down pat for working with tile or floor coverings. He used a protractor to measure difficult corners and other tricky dimension stuff. He would grasp the protractor between his toes, take the measurement of an angle, and write it down on graph paper. When he traced it onto the tile, the cut was always perfect.

Barney had used wainscoting on the upstairs bathrooms. Eddie decided to keep the old-fashioned look wherever possible. He enameled the wainscoting a soft delft blue and used a matching wallpaper on the upper walls. The effect was lovely. He also used wainscoting on the lower walls of the stairwell. He installed high windows on the upper and lower landings. Fluorescent tubing recessed in the ceiling could be left on all the time.

It was time to buy furniture for the upstairs apartments. Eddie decided to buy from a wholesale company in Denver using his business license. He used neutral colors in the draperies, upholstery material, and carpeting. When he saw some good-looking throw pillows, he bought several for each apartment to add color.

Eddie was all business when it came to renting the apartments. He insisted on referrals and checked them. He asked for, and got, a security deposit, and the first and last months' rent on a six-month lease.

I kidded him. "How come you're so tough?"

He answered thoughtfully, "I don't want to be messing around hunting people down. I want to know who I'm renting to. I don't want any little kids because I don't have a fenced yard. I only want one or two people in the apartments upstairs, preferably older people. So yes Sis, I guess I'm being tough. I just hope I don't have to get tough later."

One day Morey came by just as Eddie was finishing renting an apartment. He looked around then slapped Eddie on the back. "Eddie, I didn't have any idea you had a house this big that you were working with. I just knew you were buying a helluva lot of plumbing supplies and other stuff. I suppose it's too late to give me the grand tour?" Morey asked, eager to see what Eddie had accomplished.

"I think we can do that. Some of the folks are home and I have keys to the rest of the units, come on. We can start in the back apartment downstairs." Eddie motioned for Morey to follow. I tagged along. I wasn't going to miss this for the world.

The back apartment had a kitchen, dining room, living room, and a nice large bedroom and bath. The people who rented it both worked for the telephone company. They had filled the place with lovely furniture. Eddie had told me he expected they would be there a long time.

Morey noticed that Eddie had all the utility meters installed on the large front porch. They had an attractive cover that was locked.

"Hey Eddie, that's a good idea," Morey said. "After all, the only person who needs to get to them is the meter reader. Could save a lot of trouble. And I see you've done the mailboxes the same way. Keeps people from stealing mail."

The front apartment was my favorite. We had finished the hardwood floors all through the rooms. Leaded glass sparkled above the large windows in the dining and living areas. The front door of heavy carved oak was a showpiece in itself. The two bedrooms were spacious, bright, and airy. Eddie had gone overboard on fixtures for the bathroom, using all old-fashioned replicas. It was breathtaking and looked a lot more expensive than it had cost.

Morey just looked. Finally he said, "My mother would like this!"

Upstairs, Morey commented on the fluorescent tubing in the stairwell. "That will save you a ton of money, Eddie."

The folks in the upstairs apartments were all at work, so we had a quick look through. They all looked neat, clean, and well kept. I noticed the renters had added bright and individual touches. They all looked lived-in and inviting.

We went back to the front yard. Morey took in every detail of the painting and the landscaping. Mom had done a great job on the yard.

Finally he said, "Eddie, I'm impressed. I don't know when I've seen a better detailed and finished job. I can't see a single thing to find fault with. Don't get me wrong, I wasn't looking for something to fault you about. I guess it's just that I didn't expect such a big job. You've done a helluva job!"

When Morey left I gave Eddie a big hug. "That was high praise, Eddie!"

"I know Hazie. I'm glad he liked it."

53 Flagstone Sells House

*E*ddie came around to the back yard where I was working in my garden. "I should have known I would catch you here. You're as bad as Mom when it comes to yard work."

"I just like the feel of the earth in my fingers. I can think better when I'm digging in the dirt." I laughed.

"Hazie, remember those lots I bought over near the park on Collins?"

"Sure, I remember them. Backed right up against the Bessemer ditch, weren't they?"

"What do you think of building a spec house on them?" Eddie asked.

"Why, I think it might be a good idea, how big a house?" I could see a neat little house on those lots.

"I'm thinking three bedrooms, kitchen and dining room, two baths and a living room, nothing fancy." I had the feeling he already knew what he wanted.

"I could draw up some plans for you and we could figure it all out."

"I want to find out if there is a ground water problem there from the ditch. I notice that trees grow pretty fast." Eddie was making squiggles in the dirt. "When you have time, draw up some house plans. Something different, okay?" And he took off for the car lot.

That evening I got out my graph paper and started drawing plans. By midnight, when Morey came home, I had three sketches that I liked.

"What's all this?" Morey asked as he picked up the plans and started looking at them.

"Eddie asked me to draw up a house plan for him. He has three lots on Collins and is thinking about building a spec house on them," I explained.

"And I suppose you are going in with him and furnishing the money for the project, is that the idea?" he asked. There was no warmth in his voice.

I was startled by his tone. "I don't know what you're saying, Morey. Eddie has his own money for the project. He's just asking me to draw plans. We did so well on the apartment house that he wants to do some more building." I was glad I hadn't told Morey about our piggy bank fund.

Morey stood back from the table and sort of slid the plans across the polished surface. He said, his voice cold, "I'd think you'd have enough to do, being my wife and taking care of our home." It was half question, half statement.

I thought for a moment before I answered. "What time is it now, Morey, just about midnight?"

"Yes, why do you ask?"

"I just wanted to do a quick review of your day. You left the house about ten this morning. You didn't want breakfast, just a glass of orange juice. Then you went to your Mom's at noon and had a good lunch, right?" I asked. When he didn't answer, I went on, "You came home to dinner about five thirty, six o'clock."

"Yeah, that's right, get on with it." he answered.

"And now you're home. Usually if you want to go out, this is when we go out. Never mind that I have been up since seven because I'm an early riser. I get my housework done and I'm finished by ten at the latest."

"So what's new about that?" he asked. I don't think he had a clue as to how I spent my day.

"You know I don't play bridge with your Mom and her friends, because you agreed I didn't have to. I don't go to the club and jack around water skiing and all that stuff."

A faint glimmer of interest came into his voice. "So what the hell do you do? What are you trying to tell me?"

"I usually go to the ranch and help Mom, or work with the colt I have out there, training her. Sometimes I take the kids fishing or help Eddie with the apartments."

"So you keep busy. What's new about that?" he asked.

"All I'm trying to say is that I have time to help Eddie with a building project if he wants me to." I hoped he would give me his blessing. I couldn't have been more wrong.

"So great, you can do all that but," and his voice was cold as ice, "I don't want you putting any money into any schemes your brother cooks up and I don't want you helping him build any houses or anything else!"

"Just as you say, Morey. I wouldn't want to do anything to upset you." I said this quietly, which should have told him I was furious.

The next day I took the plans down to the car lot for Eddie to look at. He liked one in particular and we decided to refine it and have blueprints made. When this was done we took the plans to a lumber yard and had them estimate the materials needed. We checked this against materials we had on hand and what was still available at the orphanage building.

We stopped at Patti's Restaurant for lunch. "So what do you think, Eddie? It's late August, Barney's about ready to close the Dairy Queen for the summer. Shall we talk to him?"

"Let's talk to Mom and Dad first. I've talked to them a little but I'd like to see just what they think." We drove out to the ranch.

Eddie showed them the plans and explained what we wanted to do. Mom was enthusiastic but Dad said, "Son, I don't want you to bite off more than you can chew. You're sure you have enough money to do this job and not get caught short?"

"Dad, we've figured every angle. Using the lots as a basis for a construction loan, with what we have in the bank, and with what I earn, we've got a surplus, if anything."

"That's good to hear. You never know when something can go wrong."

"I know Dad, I don't want to take any chances either." Eddie was sure of himself.

In the next week, Eddie and I talked to Barney, Dave Barnes, and the plumber and rechecked our supply pile. Barney was glad to have a job for part of the winter and he liked the plan.

When we asked him what he thought of using flagstone for the dining room and kitchen area he just said, "If you know where you can buy flagstone reasonable, I think it would be great. It would sure help sell the house."

Dave had an idea for the fireplace that we wanted to build across one wall of the living room. "I know where there are some sandstone blocks. They were used as the first paving stones in the streets of Pueblo. They were thrown in a dump over the side of a bluff. I know exactly where they are, if you want to take a look." Of course Eddie and I couldn't wait to see this find.

We met Dave about noon the next day at a street below what had been the dump site. Dave had already uncovered several of the blocks. I could feel a flutter when I saw the stones, roughly twelve by sixteen by eighteen inches, some smaller, some larger. All were a bright pink-ish-red, close-grained sandstone. Very heavy, I found, when I reached down and lifted one. "These are beautiful stones; do you think there would be enough of them to do a fireplace wall?" I asked Dave.

"Easily," he answered, "There are thousands in there. It's just a matter of digging them out and hauling them off."

Eddie spoke up. "I can get someone to haul them. This is a real find. Who do we have to see to get permission to take them?"

"No one," Dave answered. "Over the years a few people have taken a few of them but mostly they have been here, hidden from view."

So Eddie talked to Bob Hastings and what might have been a long, hard job turned into a two-day loading, hauling, and dumping chore.

Eddie had Bob dump them on the far side of the lot where the fireplace would be built. He said there was no point in carrying them any farther than necessary. Then he had Bob dump several loads on the vacant lots next to our house on Logan. He asked me if Morey would mind.

"He won't even notice them," I assured him.

We wanted to get all the materials we needed stockpiled and in place while the weather was nice. Plumbing materials would be bought from Bernstein's. If Morey said anything, we could always get them from another plumbing supply. We bought what lumber and materials we needed. By the middle of September, we were ready to start.

Mom and Dad came in, Barney and Dave were on hand, and we took pictures of everyone. Mom even took a picture of the vacant lots with only the pile of rocks on them.

The only thing we didn't have was flagstone. We heard of a quarry near Lyons, Colorado, about two hundred miles from Pueblo. Eddie borrowed a big dump truck from Bob Hastings. Early on a bright fall day, Eddie and I took off for Lyons.

We arrived at the quarry about noon. There wasn't a soul in sight so we found a little restaurant for lunch. Lyons turned out to be one of those friendly little towns where everyone knew everyone's business. The waitress, a cute blonde, couldn't keep her eyes off Eddie. Instead of being embarrassed, he started joking with her. By the time we had eaten lunch he knew all about her.

She told us the quarry owner would probably be late, he usually was. We went back to the quarry anyway, and he was there. He loaded us up and asked how far we were going. When Eddie said "Pueblo," he commented, "You'll never make it tonight."

"We may not make it," Eddie said, "But I don't want to stay here all night. It may be late when we get home but at least we'll be home."

We took a different route home. We topped a hill and a beautiful valley stretched below. I was busy looking at the scenery when Eddie said, "Hold your hat Sis, and say your prayers." I looked up just in time to see a sign that said "Bridge, 5 Ton Limit." We had well over five tons on the truck. By the time I said a prayer we were over the bridge. Eddie heaved a sigh of relief and went a little faster. We sang songs and joked all the way home.

By Christmas time the house on Collins was almost finished. The work went smoothly, without delays. Eddie stood in the driveway to the garage just looking, and then he said, "You know Hazie, I think it's more fun to build houses than it is to sell cars. What do you think?"

"It probably is. I know I would rather build and design houses. But Eddie, you've got to remember, you've been extremely lucky to have Barney and Dave available to do the work for you. You and I have done some of the work ourselves. Also, you've been fortunate in finding a source of materials from that old orphanage. Most builders don't do that."

"Yeah, you're sure right about that. If I had to hire every lick of work done, buy materials from scratch, and worry about workers, it would be a different ball game. I think I've been really lucky. I know all the things Mom and Dad have done. And you Hazie, well, I couldn't have done it without you." He looked at the yard, raked smooth and ready for grass as soon as the weather was warm enough. Mom did the yards with Dad's help. It was all a joint effort.

"Are you going to wait until spring to sell it, or start advertising right away?"

"Funny you should ask. A man called me this morning at the car lot. Said he had been watching the house go up. He wanted to know when he and his wife could look at it." Eddie sounded doubtful.

"What makes you sound so sad, Eddie? He might just be the one." I was kind of excited.

"He wants to look at it this evening. Do you want to be here to see what they're like?"

"Sure, it's going to be interesting to find out what kind of people watch a house being built. Maybe they've fallen in love with it."

"C'mon Sis, I'll call them right now, get it over with." Eddie started for his car. "Just as well leave your car here, we'll be coming right back."

"Yes, well, it is almost six, maybe they can come over right away. Morey said he would be working late tonight..."

Eddie called the man, Ted Brown. I had never heard the name. We went back to the house, unlocked the door, and waited impatiently.

When they arrived, Ted introduced his wife, Beth. Eddie introduced me.

"We've been here about a month," Ted told Eddie. "Transferred here from Pittsburgh, Pennsylvania. Decided to look around before we bought. First Sunday we were here we happened to drive down this street, and you and your sister were here working on the house. We wanted to barge in then and there, but decided to wait."

Beth chimed in, she was a bird-chirrupy little redhead, "We figured anyone who would come out on Sunday to work on a house had to love what they were doing so we just decided to wait and see."

"Well as you can see, the yard isn't finished," Eddie said. "It's too cold yet for that but everything else is finished." He opened the door and waved a foot at the view of the living room from the entryway.

"We could hardly wait to see what you did with the stone and flag-stone. Ted, just look at that fireplace wall, and the floors. They match, don't they?"

"Yes Beth, they sure do. Both red sandstone. What a find!" Ted was as excited as his wife.

Eddie asked Ted what his work was.

"I'll be working for the CF&I in the mining department. They have their own ore and water sources and I will be doing that sort of thing."

"That's really a coincidence," I said, "My father just retired from the CF&I a few years ago. He was in the mining department for almost sixty years. You two might have a lot to talk about."

Ted and Beth looked and talked. They couldn't find anything they didn't like, but the stone work was what really sold them. I smiled when Beth turned to Ted and said, "If we can buy this house you will never have a reason to tell me you wanted a house with some interesting stone in it, will you?"

"No, Hon, I guess not. It's about right for us." Ted turned to Eddie. "Now Eddie," (we were all on a first name basis by then), "Just how much will this house set me back?"

I was glad Eddie and I had decided on a high and low figure for the house. Knowing Eddie and his experience as a salesman, it didn't surprise me when he added a couple of thousand to the price.

Ted didn't blink. "That sounds about right to me. If this house were available where we came from, it would cost considerably more, if we could even find one like it."

Ted turned to his wife, "What do you say, Beth, do you like it? You'll be living in it a long time."

"I could be happy here the rest of my life. I just hope they don't transfer you again." She wrapped her arm around his waist and looked up at him.

"I'll have to go to the car lot and get my contracts. Do you want to drive down there? We can sit down and get the paperwork out of the way. Or if you'd rather, we could meet at my attorney's office any time tomorrow. That would probably be better. That way he could have the loose ends in place and you wouldn't have to be doing things twice."

They decided to meet at Robert Bartley's office at six the following evening. After they left, Eddie and I looked at one another. "Let's go to Patti's and celebrate Eddie. No one can tell me that fate doesn't happen, what do you think?"

"It sure does. They've been watching us build that house, almost like it was meant to be theirs from the start."

54 Walkie-Talkies and ESP and Ted & Beth Brown's New Home

"Morey asked me if I could rig up some kind of a system to send signals from one spot to another. What do you know about it?" Eddie tossed his hair out of his face.

"You know what, Eddie? The first thing I'm going to do is give you a haircut. It drives me wacky to watch you try to keep your hair out of your face." His hair was very thick and unruly.

"Okay, get out the scissors and whack away. I'll tell you how I think I can set up a signal system." Eddie moved toward the family room. "Remember those walkie-talkies Charlie and Ione gave me one Christmas? I think they could be modified so that signals could be sent, not only from room-to-room but from a considerable distance." Eddie waved his foot in the air for emphasis. "When do you think Morey will be home tonight? I can show him what I had in mind."

"He'll be home about six. Why don't you stay in and have dinner with us?" Eddie often had dinner with us when he had night appointments and didn't want to drive out to the ranch.

I cut his hair in a sort of flat-top like all the fellows were wearing. I asked him how he liked it and he said, "Great, now I won't have it hanging over my eyes."

Dinner was on the table when Morey came in.

"Hi Morey," Eddie greeted him. "I think I've got a signal system worked out for you. If you don't have to go back to work tonight we can set it up and test it."

"Yes, sure I can stay. I didn't think you could have it worked out so soon. That's great. Now I can start doing some real testing." Morey's voice had an eager note.

When dinner was over, Eddie asked Morey to help him bring in the walkie-talkies and other assorted paraphernalia.

"What can I do to help?" I asked.

"Here Hazie," Eddie directed, "Take this bunch of wires into the guest bedroom. Morey and I will be in the dining room." Then he turned to Morey. "You're sure that is where you will want the people being tested to sit?"

"Yes. We can use the dining room table as a sending point and have our paperwork there. There's a small table at my parent's house that I'll bring over. We can set it up in the bedroom. For the time being, we can use the nightstand, okay?"

"That ought to work. Now," and Eddie held one of the walkie-talkies between the toes of his right foot, "I think I have this wired right. Go into the bedroom, Hazel, and see if you and Morey can have a conversation on these gadgets."

I went into the bedroom, sat on the edge of the bed, picked up the earphones and placed them comfortably over my ears.

"Can you hear me?" Morey's voice came to me clear and loud.

"Yes. What shall I do now?" I asked.

"Just hang in there. I want to try something." Morey told me. "Do you have a pencil and paper handy? I am going to look at one of Dr. Rhine's test cards. I want you to shut your eyes and see if you can tell me what I am seeing."

I said, "Okay," and waited for him to tell me when to start concentrating.

"Now," he said. I closed my eyes and started to concentrate. In a short time I heard him say, "What did you see?"

"All I saw were poles with, like basketball hoops on them."

"Could you tell if there was a particular figure?" he asked.

"Not really. If anything, it would be a circle. That is what the basketball hoops could be." I thought for sure I hadn't seen anything important but Morey was jubilant.

"I was holding the card with a circle on it! I don't know how else you could interpret the basketball hoops."

"Whew," I said. "I thought I had scored nothing. Are you going to have to interpret everything that is sent and received?"

"I think that is a big part of it." Morey turned to Eddie. "I think these will work just fine. We'll get our cards together and get set up. Then I'll ask a few people over and we'll give it a real workout. Why don't you stay in tomorrow night and we'll see how this does? Then if there are any bugs in it, we can fix it."

"Sure, I can do that. It will be interesting for me to watch a real ESP test!" Eddie was enthusiastic.

The next evening Morey was as nervous as a horse at the starting gate waiting for Jim and Terri Plastino, Bill Thomson and his wife, Ruth, and Bill Morey to arrive.

I had several pencils, a notebook to keep notes in, and a big pitcher of ice water. Morey said nix to drinks, but when it was all over I could serve coffee and snacks. I sat at the dining room table shuffling a deck of forty cards. Only five symbols were represented: a circle, square, wavy line, triangle, and straight line. Morey decided to use a sender and receiver. Only the sender would know what sign had been sent. With forty cards, he planned a series of tests, each consisting of a run through the deck.

He started with Bill Thomson sending to Jim Plastino. When the test was completed, I matched the calls with the actual sign sent. Jim scored sixty percent. Morey thought this was very good. After doing three runs with different partners, Morey called it a night.

Taking all the scores together, a dismal twelve percent emerged. Morey tried to explain that overall, the scores hadn't been too bad. Jim Plastino and Bill Thomson had the high score for the evening.

I made coffee. We sat around for another hour thinking of ways to do the tests to perhaps get better scores. By midnight, everyone left and I asked Eddie to stay.

"If you are as tired as I am, I know you won't want to drive to the ranch." He didn't give me any argument.

Eddie and I were up early the next morning. Eddie asked me when I thought Morey would want to do more testing.

"Morey hasn't said anything to me yet, but I think he is going to want to go to New York and back to Duke to talk with Dr. Rhine." I told Eddie. "You know Morey, he'll let me know the day before. It's good that I know him so well. I just keep everything ready so I can go on a minute's notice."

"I guess I'd better get to work," Eddie said. "Selling cars seems sort of tame after building houses. Maybe some day I can do more of it. I'm going to keep my eyes open for good deals. As long as I can get Barney and Dave to work with me and you to do the plans, I don't see where we can go wrong." Eddie looked at me with a quizzical look, like, "Are you with me?"

"We'll both keep our eyes open, Eddie."

"Call me when you know something, okay?" Eddie asked.

Morey and I arrived at the Minnequa Country Club late one night and were immediately bombarded with questions about hypnosis, I should say, Morey was bombarded. He was his usual self, with outgoing personality, plus now he was selling something. Sometime during the evening, he invited a bunch of people home for a nightcap.

When it was time to leave the Club, I noticed that Beth and Ted Brown and some of their friends were in the group. They hadn't noticed me so I didn't say anything until they got to the house. When they came in I just said, "So, you've met my husband. How do you like your house by now?"

Morey walked up just then. "When did you see their house? They're new in town."

"Oh Morey," Beth said in her chirrupy voice, "Your wife and her brother Eddie built our house. If you haven't seen it you must come over. Have them bring you."

Ted added, "We have the most unique and beautiful house in all of Pueblo. Just what we wanted if we could have designed it ourselves." He helped himself to a drink, and some crackers and dip.

"Are you going to be around tomorrow?" Morey asked, "I'll have Hazel drive me by." And he turned his attention to someone else.

Tomorrow was going to be an interesting day, I thought. The evening ended as usual, with someone begging Morey to hypnotize them and Morey, after a little hesitating, complying. This particular evening, Morey's third subject turned out to be a hypnotist's dream. Her name was Virginia Tighe. Her husband was a salesman for one of the car agencies. Ginny was a petite brunette who was always the life of the party. After she had been awakened from a deep trance, she wouldn't believe it had really happened.

When the last lingering guest had left I surveyed the mess and started to clean up. I didn't want to look at it in the morning.

"Did you see what a subject Ginny was? Who would believe she would go into a deep trance? I think I may have someone I can really work with." Morey couldn't keep the elation out of his voice.

"Yeah, I think you're right. She didn't falter once when you asked her questions." His enthusiasm was catching.

But he changed the subject, catching me off guard. "Now, what in the hell is this all about a house you and your brother Eddie built and sold to the Browns?"

I hesitated, wondering how much to tell him, and decided to tell him as little as possible. Maybe seeing the house would help. "I drew up the plans and Eddie had the same people who built the apartment house build it. I had very little to do with it."

"Well, tomorrow we'll look at it, but I'd be willing to bet you did a hell of a lot more than draw plans. Where the hell did you learn how to draw up house plans anyway?"

"I've had a lot of experience. It's always been a hobby with me. In my last lifetime I must have been an architect." I laughed, hoping he would laugh with me, but he just went to bed.

I was pleased to see that the Browns had put in a lawn, trees, shrubs, and flowers. I could see Ted working at a bench in the garage. He hurried out to meet us.

"So this is it?" Morey looked around.

"Yes, and look at that red sandstone sparkle in the sun." Ted walked over to the stone and ran a hand over it lovingly. "I'm in the mining department at the CF&I and I happen to love rocks. I hope you won't think I'm a bit dotty."

"I never paid much attention to rocks. I guess I just take them for granted." Morey didn't sound enthused.

But Ted was expansive. "Eddie told me these stones were the first paving stones ever used in Pueblo. They were dug up from an area around East Third and Grand and thrown in a dump near the library."

"Hell, Third and Grand is where our big warehouse is located. They must have come out of the street that goes right by it. Well, I'll be damned!"

"Wait until you see the fireplace. It is a work of art!" Ted opened the heavy oak door, one of those from the orphanage. The fireplace formed one wall of the living room. Flagstone had been used for a raised hearth that was sitting height and extended across the wall. Ted pointed out his collection of Navajo vases and other artifacts ranged along the extended hearth. Then he took Morey's arm and led him into the kitchen-dining room area.

Beth was busy at the sink and said, "Hi, I'm just fixing some snacks. I hope you're hungry. How do you like our house?"

"What I've seen so far is awesome! I'll have to admit, I'm surprised." Morey didn't elaborate.

Ted wasn't through showing off. "Look at the flagstone in the floors of the dining room and kitchen. It matches the flagstone on the hearth. Where could you find a house that has all this; three bedrooms, two baths, a two car garage with a workbench? If I could have designed a house, I couldn't have done as well." Ted then took Morey on a tour of the bedrooms and the baths.

Morey was impressed. He couldn't help it. I loved the house before it was lived in, but now, with the loving eye for detail and the beautiful furniture, I had to admit it was lovely.

Morey sat in a big comfy chair in front of the fire and said, "Hell, it wouldn't be hard to get used to this. Quite a house you've got here."

"Don't tell me Morey, tell your wife and her brother! I've never met a man as talented as Eddie. He could build for me any time."

Beth came in with a tray of snacks. Morey pitched in. He and Ted had a lot to talk about and I found myself liking Beth a lot. She showed me the newly planted flowers in her garden. I promised to get her some cuttings from Mom's garden at the ranch.

Morey promised we would come back to visit. He dropped me off at home and went on to his office.

I called Eddie. He picked me up and on our way out to the ranch, I told him about our visit to the Browns.

"What did Morey have to say about the house?"

"He hasn't said anything to me, yet. He told the Browns it was great. I think he's trying to think up something to say. I don't know whether it is going to be good or bad. And, you know what? I don't care."

55 *Enter Jane Russell*

*M*orey and I had just returned from a hurried trip to Duke University. We went on to New York and crammed a week of meetings into three days. Morey was considering a move to New York. I thought about that as I drove to the ranch the next morning. I knew Eddie would be just as lost as I would be if I moved to New York. I shook my shoulders hoping that would get rid of the cold feeling I had. Mom must have sensed my unrest because when she gave me a big hug she said softly, "Stop your worrying, everything's going to be all right."

Mom, Dad, Eddie, and I talked the day away. Mom finally said, "Call Morey and see if he won't come out for supper. I haven't seen him in ages. Just tell him I miss seeing my favorite son-in-law."

When he said he accepted, Mom told Eddie, "Son, go catch me a nice fat rooster. We're going to have fried chicken. I know that's one of Morey's favorites."

When Morey arrived, I noticed that he looked at the apartment we made out of the building on the hill with new eyes. I think he realized that Eddie had done a lot of the work.

"Well Morey, what's this I hear about you wanting to move to New York?" Mom asked.

He was immediately on the defensive and I thought, *Oh, oh, I'll bet his folks asked him the same thing.*

"Come on now, Ethel Melinda. I don't think we'll be going anywhere for quite a while yet. Eventually, maybe." He just laughed it off.

"I hope not. You could stay in New York for a little while and just visit." She looked at Morey as if expecting an explanation but she didn't get one.

Dinner was delicious and after complimenting Mom, Morey said, "Well, I've got to go back to town." He turned to me, "Don't be too long, I want to talk to you."

"Sure Morey, I'll be in shortly."

I drove back to town wondering what Morey wanted to talk about. He didn't keep me waiting.

"I think from now on we'll hold our experiments into hypnosis at my folks' house. This house is just too small and I want to keep testing."

"Have you told your Mom about this idea?" I asked. Morey squirmed a little.

"Oh, she'll go along with it, why shouldn't she?"

"Morey, think a little, why does your Mom keep her white upholstered furniture covered with plastic wraps? Why don't you and Bob use the living room and the formal dining room?"

"I guess she doesn't want anyone messing it up, but we wouldn't destroy anything."

"I'm sure you wouldn't, but you can't be responsible for your guests. Let me show you something." I got up and walked over to one of our occasional chairs.

"So what's with the chair?" His voice was a little surly.

I showed him an ugly burn on the side of the cushion. "This is what!" Then I pointed out spots where I had scrubbed in vain to remove any hint of a spilled drink.

"Well, we could just tell everyone to be careful." Morey tried to laugh it off.

"You know it wouldn't work, Morey. The last thing you want is a half-loaded, after-the-dance crowd who, in one breath, are admonished to be careful, and in the next breath told to relax so they can drift into a deep trance."

If he couldn't see the impossibility of using the Bernstein house for his tests, he would just have to find out for himself.

Morey thought for a while and then said, "Well, what do you want me to do, rent some place?"

"No, I think you should get Barney to build you a house on the lot next door. After all, one of Pueblo's richest men doesn't have to live in a two-bedroom tract house. I like this little house Morey, but it is terribly inadequate for what you need."

"Yes, and if I do that, the God-damned house will tie me to Pueblo! You sure won't want to sell and give up your nice new house!"

"I've watched how you've tried to get Abe and Sam to sell out and retire. They may never agree, but Morey, if you want to take Ben Graham's class in New York and continue to work with hypnosis and ESP, you've got to do it." I tried to make him understand I was on his side.

"You mean you would leave your family and a new house if I wanted to live in New York?" He looked at me as if I were telling a fat lie.

"Yes. Yes, and you know I would. Give me the go-ahead and we can have a house to move into within four months."

A few days later, I was surprised when he told me he had talked with Tink Snapp. Tink was head loan officer at Minnequa Bank, and had been instrumental in getting Morey to consider being on their Board of Directors. Tink had seen the Browns' house and told Morey to go ahead, that if we needed to sell, we would have no problem.

When I told Eddie, he let out a whoop you could hear clear to the mountains.

"I hate to admit it, Hazie, but I was getting so bored I couldn't stand myself or anyone else. I love cars, but it can sure be a dull existence. When will you have the plans ready?"

"I thought I'd work on them tonight and tomorrow. If you can, why don't you stay in tonight? We'll work out all the bugs and not have to backtrack."

"Yeah, I can do that, and then tomorrow I can see Barney. I'll try to get him to hire someone to take his place at the Dairy Queen for the summer." Eddie was already lining up his work force.

"Hazie, I met the most interesting fellow today," Eddie said one day. "Dave Batt is Project Manager for Hoffman Homes, that new addition west of Lake Minnequa. They are building new homes with the living rooms facing the back yard. I guess Minnequa Bank is handling all the paper for the company and Tink told him he should take a look at the house on Collins."

"What did he think of it?" I couldn't imagine anyone not liking the house and the fact that the front room wasn't a goldfish bowl.

"He liked it a lot. He said his company would be doing much the same thing, but wouldn't include fireplaces in their plans. He asked me to bring you to their house. He thought you and his wife would have a lot in common." Eddie had a big grin. I could tell he liked Dave. "He said he would talk to Morey. I guess whenever he pins Morey down, we'll go to dinner."

The next week Morey looked up from the Wall Street Journal and said, "We're invited to dinner with Dave and Betty Batt on Wednesday. Is that okay with you?"

"Sure, Eddie told me he had talked with Dave. They sound like an interesting couple."

On Wednesday night Eddie rode over to the Batt's with us. We were welcomed with an icy Margarita, Mexican chips, and guacamole dip. Morey told Betty what a good job she had done in decorating their house.

"Well Morey, I've had a lot of help. One of our foremen is Jane Russell's brother. When she's not busy making movies, she's great at this sort of thing. I've worked with her a lot on some of our Open Houses at new projects." Betty ran her fingers through dark hair that fell almost to her waist. Her features were almost perfect. I wasn't surprised to learn that she met Dave at one of his home promotions. She was a model.

"You know," she said, "One of those swim suit models who stands beside a lovely chair and tells people about the great features of a particular home."

Betty turned to Eddie. "Eddie, what do you do beside build houses?" She loaded a chip with dip and held it to his mouth.

He took a big bite, and then said, "I sell used cars. Our lot is on North Santa Fe."

"How did you ever get into car sales?"

"I've been in love with cars forever, I think. Then Hazel bought an old house and we remodeled it. I guess that led to my second love."

I could tell Betty was impressed by the thoughtful way she looked at Eddie. "What are you doing next weekend?"

"Nothing I can't get out of." Eddie grinned, "What did you have in mind?"

"Jane is coming in Thursday night late. We're going to get three houses ready for 'Open House' on Saturday and Sunday. The furniture was delivered today so the fellows have been getting it placed.

"Dave has made three screens to be used as dividers between the living room/dining room area. Jane wants to tie-dye the burlap for them. Then they have to be stretched on the rods of the screens while they are wet.

"Draperies for the rest of the rooms have to be measured and made, too," Betty added.

"Well Betty, I can measure. Hazel can cut. Turn her loose with a sewing machine and they'll be ready in no time." Eddie was excited.

"Jane will probably put you to work doing something. We've been so lucky to have her help. Dave didn't realize when he hired Jack that Jane was his sister. We've all become great friends."

"I've had a crush on Jane Russell ever since I first saw her in a movie," Eddie said. "To actually meet her, well, I hope I don't forget how to talk."

Betty told us that Jane would get in about seven and go directly to the houses, so we got there about eight-thirty. When we walked in, I could almost hear Eddie's heart thump. We made our way through cartons, shipping boxes, and all kinds of stuff. It should have been a mess, but there was order to the chaos.

We barely got through the boxes when Betty rushed up to grab Eddie by the shirttail. With her arm around him, she said, "Eddie, this is Jane Russell. This is the Eddie I've been telling you about, Jane." Jane walked toward us.

"I'm glad to meet you," Eddie said. Then throwing all caution to the wind he said, "Oh heck, I'm thrilled to death to meet you!"

Jane gave Eddie a big hug and his face turned as red as the blouse she wore. "Well, I'm glad to meet you, too. Betty told me so much about you that I feel I already know you and your sister." Jane kept her arm around Eddie's shoulder as we walked into the kitchen.

I marveled at this woman's beauty. Physical beauty, yes, but she had a deeper, more spiritual quality. I wasn't surprised when Betty later told me Jane was deeply religious, and that she and her brothers went regularly to a Pentecostal Church.

"We're just about to decide what to do first to get these models ready for Saturday." Betty looked around at the mess of boxes, materials, and what-not on the floor and counters.

"We could get the draperies for the living room measured, cut, and sewn," Jane said. "Where are the screens to go between the living room and dining area? I could get those finished and tie-dye them.

"Once we get the draperies finished and up, that will be the hardest and most time-consuming stuff we have to do." Jane sounded as if she had done all this before.

"Eddie, how good are you at measuring?" Jane lifted a bolt of burlap to the table.

"I can do that, only I will need it on the floor so I can get to it more easily." Jane lifted the burlap and placed it close to Eddie's toes.

"Can you cut it too, Eddie?" she asked.

"Yeah, but it's easier for me to use a razor knife. I measure the fabric, and then I usually place the material on a one-by-twelve and tack it down. Using my yardstick to cut against, I cut it. Depending on the material, sometimes I can cut several layers at once."

"That makes sense, Eddie. I'll have the fellows get a one by twelve, a razor knife, yardstick, and some tacks. We'll be making draperies for the sliding glass doors, the clerestory windows in the living room and panels for the screens." She started gathering up odds and ends and clearing a spot for Eddie to work.

"I've got the measurements for everything right here in this notebook, Eddie," Betty said. She folded the notebook open and went over the figures with Eddie.

"Hazel, help me take these cartons out of the way," Betty said. "These are the Mexican tin masks and other artifacts Jane picked up in Los Angeles. Just wait and see how great they are!" Betty's enthusiasm filled the room.

It was midnight before we called it a day. Two sets of draperies were sewn. The screens had their colorful, tie-dyed burlap panels stretched on the rods and placed against a wall to dry. Betty's hands were sore from stretching material on the screens, and my back felt like it didn't belong to me. Eddie found a comfortable chair and stretched out.

Dave came into the kitchen with Morey in tow.

"It's time to quit." Dave called. "I don't pay overtime. Morey, I'd like you to meet Jane Russell. You've met her brother, Jack. He's the fellow who picks up most of our orders at your yard." I could see Morey's eyes widen.

"Well, I'll be damned! And I don't even have to go to Hollywood to meet you." Morey poured on the charm.

I turned to our new friends. "I know you're all tired. How would you like to come by the house for a nightcap and some solid snacks?"

When we got to the house, Betty served drinks. I cooked up a huge platter of scrambled eggs with ham, lots of buttered toast, and some of Mom's peach preserves. Jane and Jack, Betty and Dave, Morey, Eddie and I made short work of the food.

When everyone had gone, Morey turned to me, "I couldn't believe my eyes. That was really Jane Russell. Why she's just like everyone else."

I laughed. "What made you think she would be different?"

"Open House" for Hoffman Homes was a great success. Eddie and I dropped by late Sunday afternoon and there were still people going through the houses.

When Betty saw us she asked, "Eddie, could you drive Jane to the airport? Her plane leaves in about forty-five minutes and I hate to leave with so many people still wanting to see the house."

"Sure, I'd be glad to." Eddie turned to Jane. "Are you sure you want to ride with me?"

"I'd be honored, Eddie." Jane gave a funny little curtsy then reached over and gave Eddie a big hug. Eddie turned red as a beet. "I'm ready whenever you are, Jane."

Jane grabbed an overnight bag that didn't look big enough to hold a toothbrush and makeup. Eddie reached up, grasped the door handle with the toes of his right foot and opened the door. He stood back and waited for Jane to get settled. Betty and I watched as they drove off.

Betty looked at me and said, "I don't know whether Eddie feels more honored in getting to drive Jane to the airport, or if Jane is feeling honored by having Eddie drive her."

"Yeah, well I guess they will both have some tall tales to tell."

56 Little Tractors and Twisted Cedar Lamps

One day Morey came home early and said, "Pack a few things, we're going to Philadelphia for a couple of weeks."

"What on earth is in Philadelphia that would keep us there for two weeks?"

"Abe bought out a tractor plant that was going under, and he wants me to figure out how we can sell about a thousand tractors." Morey sounded like this might be fun, but I had my doubts.

"Is Abe there now?"

"Yeah, he's been there a couple of weeks. He rented a house and we can stay there. I guess Ernie and little Jack Rifkin are already there."

I had a feeling of chagrin when I thought of sharing a house, even for a very short time, with Abe and his buddies.

"When do you want to leave?" I wasn't surprised when he said we would leave the day after tomorrow.

"Do you think you can leave all this building and whatever else you do?" Morey asked.

"Of course. Eddie knows exactly what needs to be done. He can oversee the job."

When we got back to Pueblo, the first thing I did was call Eddie. He bombarded me with questions about our trip and the tractors. I told him they were pretty much like other tractors, only smaller. There would be a shipment in next week. Then he could see for himself.

On Sunday, Morey and I went to the ranch. Eddie cornered Morey, wanting to know all about the little tractors.

"We'll be getting about five hundred of them here," Morey told him. "It's going to be up to me to get them sold. The rest, we're going to sell overseas. In fact, we've already sold a hundred to Costa Rica."

Eddie looked thoughtful. "It sounds like they would be ideal for someone who has small acreage or for small jobs on large ranches. You could always use them on jobs where you couldn't use big equipment."

"Yeah, that would be a great market. I'll just have to figure out a way to reach it." Morey sounded weary.

"Have you ever thought of putting one on a trailer and taking it to farm sales? They're a lot like auto auctions. It would give the buyer a chance to see how it works." Eddie said.

"That's a hell of an idea Eddie, but who would bother to do it? I can't spare any of my help."

I looked over at Eddie. *Why the little fox,* I thought. *He wants to take that tractor to the farm sales.* Then my heart gave a thump against my ribs. *And Guess Who he is planning to take with him?* I waited. Morey didn't have a clue.

Sure enough, before the day was over, Eddie and Morey had a pickup and trailer all ready to go. Morey would have a thousand handbills printed. He would find out exactly where there were going to be sales from Denver on up into Nebraska. He would mail out flyers alerting farmers in the area and also put an ad in the newspapers close to the town where the sales were to be held.

Eddie and Morey sounded like two small boys with a new toy. I had to admit I was getting a little excited too.

Three weeks later, we were ready to start out. It had taken a while to advertise, call, and do everything necessary. We had a fairly new pickup and the trailer was one the Bernsteins used to haul just about everything. The pickup was black, the trailer bright yellow and the little tractor was red.

Mom and Dad came in to see us off. When they saw the outfit we would be hauling, Mom gave a big laugh. "One thing for sure, a body would have to be blind not to see you coming." Dad just chuckled quietly and wished us luck.

We were gone three weeks and worked nine sales. What we didn't anticipate was that every time we stopped to fill up for gas, have something to eat, or stay the night, we drew crowds. We handed out flyers, gave our sales pitch, and more often than not got a promise of some kind. I took down so many names and addresses, I had a notebook full. We made four sales, which wasn't bad.

Several orders came in to Bernsteins as a result of our trip and we made the name of Bernstein Brothers known in areas where it had never been heard.

Later, Morey asked me how Eddie did.

"Morey, you would have had to be there. We would pull into the sales area. The first thing Eddie did was get the trailer positioned just where he wanted it. Then he got out of the truck, looked at everyone and said, 'Hi, how are you all, today?' Then he undid the chains holding the tractor to the trailer. By now he had a crowd around him, watching his every move. He hammed it up a little, but he did go slowly enough for people to see what he was doing. I would catch a look of disbelief on some old farmer's face as Eddie picked up the chain with his right foot. Then he'd shake the key out of his moccasin and unlock the lock with the toes of his left foot. I helped him get the loading ramp in place, and then he crawled up on the tractor seat.

"By now the word had gotten around that a fellow without arms is going to demonstrate this tractor. Thank God, Eddie was used to it. He backed the tractor off the trailer, parked it so everyone could get a good look at it, then started answering questions."

"And none of this bothered him?" Morey asked.

"Not a bit. After all, this is what he has been doing most of his life, and the people were all super nice."

"Well, I'm glad it went so well. We're getting inquiries every day. I want to give Eddie one of the little tractors. I'm sure he could use it and it would be easier for him to operate than that big old machine he has now."

"Morey, he'll be tickled pink. He fell in love with that tractor. He'll find plenty for it to do."

"Don't tell him. I'll just have Slim run it out sometime this week. Just let me know what he says."

I didn't need to tell Morey what Eddie said because just as soon as he saw the tractor, he called Morey and thanked him. "And if you need any ditches dug, just let me know," he kidded.

Our new house was almost finished. Barney had outdone himself. Everything was just as I had wanted it. I started getting it furnished and hoped to be finished by Thanksgiving.

I gave the couple who had decorated our small house the go-ahead to do this one. When Morey finally took the time to look at it, he was amazed at what had been accomplished.

I wasn't surprised when he asked Eddie if he could install a two-way signal system like he had done in the other house. Eddie got to work on it and before long, Morey was knee-deep in experiments again.

During the winter Eddie and I had made some lamps out of twisted cedar. One day Dave and Betty Batt stopped by while I was sanding one of them, preparing to give it a coat of wax. When Dave saw the lamp he asked me where I had bought it

"Oh, I didn't buy it. Eddie and I made two of them last winter just to see how they would turn out. We thought if we made any more we would sand-blast them to get a more natural look. The color of the cedar is so beautiful we want it to shine through."

"You don't know what you have there, Hazel. I would love to have some to put in our model homes. Put a 'for sale' sign and a price on them and I'll bet you could sell a lot of them." Betty was excited.

"This is just a hobby sort of thing," I said. Also, the cedar is so darned hard to saw it took us forever to get just a few to work with."

"Do you know where there is more twisted wood like this?" Dave asked.

"There is an unending supply back of the ranch. You can pick and choose whatever you want. It was just so hard to cut that Eddie and I sort of gave up." I remembered how Eddie and I would take turns and still be worn out.

"Why don't we take a weekend and see what we can do," Dave said. "I've got chain saws and I'll bet we can get enough cedar to make several lamps."

"Sure, I'll tell Eddie. I know he'll want to do it.'" So we planned for the next Sunday.

We decided to take the truck and my car. That way, we could take a blanket and lunch fixings. Dave and Betty hadn't met my family and I was happy when Betty just went over to Mom and gave her a big hug. Mom hugged her back and then we were all talking at once with Betty telling Mom how much her mother would love the ranch and how she raised race horses and followed the racing circuit. Mom was fascinated. So was I.

"I'll show you my race horse," I told Betty. "Her name is Queenie. A lady in Pueblo used to race her but then they both got old. Hannah, her owner, asked me if I wanted her. She just wanted a place where Queenie could roam and be happy. So that is how I acquired a race horse. She's gentle as a lamb and still looks great, despite her eighteen years."

"Too bad she's so old. I'll bet she could have a beautiful colt." Betty patted her sleek black coat.

As we walked back to the house, Dave and Betty asked Eddie all kinds of questions: How deep is your well? How many rabbits do you have? Do you mind driving back and forth, and so on.

Dave confided that he had been raised in a big town and although he knew the lumber business, that was the extent of his knowledge of the country.

We filled our water jugs and put big hunks of ice in them. Mom promised to have a snack for us when we returned from our twisted cedar hunting trip.

Eddie drove the truck and Betty rode beside him. Dave and I sat on a bale of hay in the truck bed. As we started the little climb to the high plateau above the river where the cedars were thick, Dave marveled at the view of the Sangre de Christos to the south and Huerfano Butte closer to us. He asked about lakes, water, and all kinds of things. It was fun to talk to someone so curious about what was second nature to me.

Eddie stopped near the edge of the rim rock where the trees were thick and even more gnarled because of the wind coming up from the valley. He laughed when Dave said, "My God, Eddie. There is enough twisted cedar here to make hundreds of lamps. I can see a dozen pieces from where I am standing.

"Yeah, I guess so," Eddie answered. "Hazie and I tried to picture how a piece would look standing on a table. Then we would try to cut so that, hopefully, we'd only have to make that one main cut and it would stand properly."

Eddie and Dave walked over to a particularly twisted tree. It looked like it had grown up fighting a battle with the elements and whatever

Eddie, Rusty, and one of our twisted cedar lamps.

else got in its way. Eddie crawled over one twisted limb and with his foot, made an imaginary line where he thought it should be cut.

"Yeah Eddie, I see what you mean. You will actually be able to get maybe two or three lamps from this one cutting. You can take it home and do the other cuts there, right?"

"That's the ticket, Dave, and as long as we have a couple of sharp chain saws, we should be able to get enough material to keep us busy for quite a while."

I wondered how Dave would feel when he found out how tough these cedars were.

Betty and I found good pieces for the fellows to cut.

After Dave had cut several of the cedars, Eddie said, "Let me do that one, Dave, I can sit on this log and brace my back against the one behind me. I can get a good lick in just where we want to cut."

He proceeded to get himself settled and braced. Then he held out his left foot. Dave passed him the saw. Eddie got a good grip on it. Then, with his big toe and the toe next to it, he turned it on. Holding the saw with both feet, he could move his big toe to the gas feed easily. It took about three changes of position of the saw as he made his cut. Eddie leaned back and placed the saw on the ground.

Dave stood as if he had been hit in the head. "I can't believe how you handled that saw Eddie. Those trees are the toughest thing I've ever tried to cut. I know how hard it is to just hold the damned saw steady."

"Yeah, they're tough all right, but using the chain saw is a heck of a lot easier than using a regular saw. It took Hazie and me forever until we finally decided to use a chain saw."

Betty pointed to our next tree. Dave and Eddie discussed just where to make the cut.

"Let me do this one, Eddie," I said. "That will save you and Dave for the tough ones."

I cut through and took in deep breaths of the wonderful smell of fresh sawn cedar. Then I picked up the piece and threw it into the truck. "What do you think, Eddie? Most of these cuts will make two, maybe three lamp bases. Let's just look around and see if we can find a really unique piece."

"Great, we can take a little walk and enjoy all this." Eddie waved his foot at the vista before us.

We had a drink of water and set off. We walked to the edge of the rim rock and stood, taking in the small herd of cattle near the river, a covey of quail hiding under a cedar tree, and a handsome palomino stallion with his harem. Betty let out a little gasp when she saw the stallion. "I wish my Mom could see him. He is so wild and free."

"We've watched him before. He doesn't let anything get close to his mares. In the spring we come here just to see how many new colts are in his family." Eddie said.

"Look at this tree!" Betty was excited at her find. "Do you think it would be possible to get anything this large?"

The tree had grown along the ground then arched itself upward with a twist that turned into a complete circle of gnarled wood. Then it twisted and turned the other way before it shot up to a tree limb with growth on it. We looked and pondered how this could be cut.

Finally Eddie said, "What do you think of this? Cut it off where it first comes out of the ground. There are three pieces there that go on to make that huge gnarl in the middle. Then go on up and cut it where it starts to get leaves." He laughed at himself, "Or whatever you call them, then when we get it home we can take it to a saw mill and get them to cut right through the middle of the gnarl."

"That sounds great, Eddie. That way you could have two lamps." Betty said.

"Or better yet," Eddie said, "How about a table, glass topping the middle portion of the gnarl, then a lamp that would sit exactly on the cut of the other part of the gnarl?"

Dave marveled. "It would look like the tree just grew right through the glass of the table top. My God, what a piece of art that would make Eddie! I don't see why we can't cut it where it comes out of the ground. I think we should have something to brace the weight of it, though. It could twist a saw right out of your hands."

"I'll get the truck." Eddie said. He and Dave took off. Betty and I sat down on the tree limb and waited. Betty looked a little frazzled.

She said thoughtfully, "I don't know how the cleaners shrunk my pants. I never noticed them being so tight before." She took a deep breath and pulled in her stomach.

"Yeah, they do that sometimes. You just have to watch them" I answered, thinking Betty was so thin, the least bit of weight gain would show.

Eddie parked the truck alongside the tree. He and Dave fastened a chain around the tree so that when it was cut, the chain would hold it in position. This done, Dave started sawing. It didn't take long. A sharp pull and the part of the tree that we wanted hung free on the chain. It took all four of us to load it.

"Well, that's enough for today. Let's go see what Mom has cooked up for us."

Dave and I sat framed in a halo of branches as the truck rumbled along the rutted path.

Mom came out to meet us and exclaimed over our load of limbs. "Your Dad would say you had a fair load of firewood, and he would say this wood is too twisted for fence posts." She laughed and shooed us into the cool of the house.

I talked to Mom while everyone washed up, and then I took Eddie into the bathroom and washed his face. "I think we really got a good bunch of wood this time, don't you?" he asked.

"We sure did. I think Dave and Betty want to help with the lamps too, don't you?"

"Yeah, Dave was telling me he likes to do that kind of stuff."

When we came out, I could smell coffee. Hot as it was, it smelled like heaven. Mom had little ham sandwiches on fresh-baked bread, salad, and apple cobbler. Dave ate with relish and asked for more.

We left our wood at the ranch and vowed to come back soon and get it all cut to the right sizes. I would call Mr. Viola in Penrose and ask him if he could cut the big gnarl in two for us.

It had been a great day.

57 Crazy Frank

*E*ddie had just moved into a new location with a larger lot, and with him came a partner, Vic Barlish, my brother-in-law.

Across the roof of their new building, the sign read "Western Car Sales" in big block letters, black on white with shades of yellow worked in on the letters.

"How do you like it?" Eddie asked.

"I think it's great! You can see it way down the block." I liked the way the letters stood out.

We went into the office. Vic had refinished an old desk of Eddie's and bought a good swivel office chair. A pad of sales slips lay on the desk and on the wall above the desk hung a cork board. On it were Eddie's and Vic's sales licenses, the license for the "Western Car Sales" business and written in longhand "Special of the Week," a 1950 Chevy sedan.

"You can see Vic's been busy." Eddie reached up and pulled the pad of sales slips toward the edge of the desk. Sitting in the office chair, he deftly flipped pages.

"Darned good. He hasn't had the office open two weeks, and he's sold eight cars and a pickup. If we can each average two or three cars a week, I'll be happy."

Using his left foot, Eddie crooked his big toe around the pull and opened the desk's bottom drawer. He reached in and brought out his sales pad, pen, and Blue Book. He reached under the chair and pulled out a large calendar pad that he put in front of him on the floor. He put the sales pad on it and showed me how he'd write out an offer.

"I guess you've thought of about everything, haven't you?" I asked.

"Not really. If we ever have to hire a couple of salesmen we've actually thought of using the front part of the garage for office space. We could partition it into three spaces and soundproof the partition between the offices and the workshop. We'll just have to wait and see how busy it gets." Eddie sounded enthusiastic.

We walked out to look at the garage. One end of the garage/workshop had a grease pit and air lift to put cars up so you could get underneath them. At the far end, their mechanic had his tools laid out on the workbench. He also had a large tool chest that opened into several tiers. About half way down was a door marked "restroom." If they did partition the work area, the bathroom could be entered from the garage or office space. I was impressed.

"What do you think, Hazie?"

"Eddie, I think you've got one heck of a good location. I don't see how you can go wrong."

Mom's friends, the Ancels, bought a small farm in Rocky Ford and planned to move before Christmas. "They are all excited. I wish Dad and I were." Mom told me.

"You'll lose your card-playing partners, won't you?" I joked. I knew she would miss them a lot.

"They told me they would come up often, but I doubt it. There will be so much to do; they'll just never make it."

"Well, Mom, now might be a good time for you to sell the ranch."

"No. I'm not going to sell. There are a lot of things I want to do."

"I sure wish you'd think about it, Mom." I knew it wouldn't do me a bit of good to argue with her.

"Did you see Eddie's new location? He seems a little happier with the new lot and all, don't you think?" Mom asked.

"I hope so. I just wish he'd talk to me but he just clams up. What do you think is bothering him, Mom?"

"I think he just sees all his friends getting married or going steady and he feels left out. He won't go out of his way to try to find a girl to go with."

I realized Mom was probably right. "Well, Mom, I don't know how to cheer him up. I just wish he could find someone to go with." I didn't want to keep talking about it. I knew Mom was worried enough already.

"Eddie has been working evenings and some weekends on the cedar lamps. He's finished three. They are beautiful." Mom went to Eddie's room and brought out the lamps.

"Oh Mom, these are spectacular! I want Dave and Betty Batt to see them." I hadn't realized how different each lamp was going to be when we first started working on them.

A few days later, Eddie brought the lamps to Pueblo. Betty and Dave asked us to come to dinner and bring the lamps. When Dave heard our car, he came out and helped us in with the lamps.

I brought the shades separately and we tried them to see which was best on which lamp. The shades were made of a rough-textured material. They were in an ecru color which was quite effective with the reddish tones of the cedar.

Betty wanted to get them all finished the day before yesterday. Dave was more practical. "I've got a machine that I use to sandblast timbers now and then. Why don't we use that to sandblast the rest of the cut pieces? That will take a lot of the work out of finishing them. If you want to bring the rest, I'll get them all sandblasted. Then Eddie, we can get together and decide where to saw the wood into lamp material."

"That would be great Dave. This new lot is keeping Vic and me plenty busy." Eddie turned to Betty and me. "Maybe you girls can put them together and wire them. Do you think you could?"

"Sure we could Eddie, and when we get them together, let's take a few of them to that shop in Colorado Springs." Betty was excited. After an excellent dinner, Betty laughed and asked me, "Remember when we were cutting the cedar trees and I thought my pants had shrunk?"

"Yeah, I remember. I was worried about you. You looked a little woozy."

"Well, it was for a good reason. I'm pregnant!" Betty gave a little trill of a laugh.

"Oh Betty, I'm so happy for you! I'll bet Dave is thrilled to pieces, isn't he?"

"Oh, yes. I called my Mom. He called his Mom and Dad and everyone we know from Boston to Los Angeles."

Betty took me into the spare room. She pointed to the walls. "I couldn't resist making this room like a circus. I'm still working on a crib spread and curtains." She waved her hand at the sewing machine on a table surrounded by material.

"Did you do all these animals and that mobile? I knew you were an artist but this is more than good." I walked closer to examine the little elephants, donkeys, zebras, and other animals painted as a border around the room.

"I hope it's a little boy. If it's a girl she will just have to learn to love animals." Betty laughed.

"Dave is learning how to get his work finished during the day instead of bringing it home with him." Betty's voice, when she spoke of Dave, took on a tone that told me how much she cared for him.

"Are you and Dave going to Phoenix for Christmas?" I asked.

"No, he is letting most of his key help off for Christmas, so we will take time off around New Year's."

"Why don't you plan on spending Christmas with us at the ranch? I would like to have us all together."

With Dave and Betty's help, we had the lamps finished before Christmas. A photographer took pictures of the lamps and I made a brochure about them. We took several to a shop and they sold out. They wanted more, but we had to say no for the time being.

A few days before Christmas, Dad, Eddie, Red, and Dyanna went after the tree. As they went toward the truck, I thought back to the times when the kids were little, their short, chubby legs barely able to slog through the deep snow. Dad was young then, too. He carried the axe over his shoulder and broke a trail for the little ones. When they came back, Dad would set up the tree while the kids got out their paper chains, popcorn strung on cords and homemade ornaments. Mom saved every one of the chains and ornaments down through the years. To us, they were more precious than any store-bought trinket could have been.

It didn't seem right that there were no little kids making paper rings. Jody and Charles wrote that they would be going to Texas. Vic said his and Mickie's little boy would be spending Christmas with Mickie. I would have been surprised if she showed up.

I helped Mom get a ham, rutabagas, and beets from the cellar. Dyanna carried up jelly and canned peaches. There were apples for apple pie, and Mom had made mince meat. I got hungry just looking at everything.

Morey was going to work part of Christmas day and I said, "Fine, just be there for dinner." He promised to make it.

We asked Tony, Emma, Johnny and his girlfriend, Frank and Lucy, Clint and Jessie Boseker, and Jay and Jessie Ancel. Mom and Dad were now living in the small house on the hill, but Mom set up a big table in the living/dining room and three small tables in the bedroom.

Dad and his Lime buddies sat in a far corner with their bottle of red wine and told their tales of times gone by. I knew that in times to come, it would be increasingly rare to get us all together.

When the day was over, Jay and Jessie stayed for a last game of cards with Mom and Dad.

Eddie looked over at Morey and me and said, "Just look at them. I think they are getting more fun out of everything than we are. I hope I can be as cheerful when I'm that old."

I stopped by the car lot to see how things were going. Vic was behind the desk working on the books and Eddie was nowhere in sight. "Where's Eddie?" I asked as I sat down.

"He left a few minutes ago. Eddie spent a while with some guy here on the lot, then the guy wanted to drive the car, or I should say he wanted Eddie to drive him around in it. Seems he didn't have his driver's license with him." I didn't like the tone of Vic's voice.

"What are you worried about, Vic? Does that happen very often, not having a license, I mean?"

"Not really. Usually if someone's looking to buy a car, they've got a license so they can drive it."

We both jumped when the phone rang.

"What do you want me to do, Eddie?" Vic said. "Hazel's here. I'll get her to drive out there. Meanwhile, I'll call the police and State Hospital. Stay put." Vic hung up and immediately dialed the police. I listened anxiously.

"I have a salesman showing a car. He thinks the fellow he is showing it to has escaped from the State Hospital. The salesman is in the restaurant at Eden Interchange. He told the fellow he had to fill up with gas and went in and called me. He said to hurry, he can't keep the guy there forever." Vic rubbed the sweat that had gathered on his forehead. He hung up and turned to me. "I don't know what good it will do for you to go out there. I guess you could talk to Eddie and just hold up the deal until the police arrive." I could tell Vic was worried.

"Sure, I'll go," I said. "I guess Eddie pulled the keys or the fellow might be gone by now."

Eden Truck Stop was about three miles north of Pueblo. I pulled up at the side of the restaurant, went in, said hello to Eddie and ordered a cup of coffee.

"How does your customer like the car? Do you think he'll buy it?" I asked.

Eddie laughed a little. "Oh, he'll buy it all right. In fact, I think he's going to have a little help right about now," he said as we watched a police car pull up beside the gas pump. Eddie got up from the stool where he had been sitting and started toward the door.

I stayed a little behind him and watched. The policemen got out of their car. One went to one side of Eddie's car. The other cop took the opposite door. When the first cop opened the door, the escapee got out, protesting feebly.

About the same time, a car from the Colorado State Hospital arrived and one of the attendants walked up to the escapee. "Well, Frank," he asked, "What did you think you were going to do? What made you think you could get away with trying to steal a car?"

"I wasn't trying to steal a car. I just wanted to take a ride." That was his story.

Eddie's story was a bit different. He told the police and the State Hospital attendants that the fellow, Frank, walked into his sales office and asked to see a car. He had been wandering about the lot for a few minutes and Eddie was just getting his shoes on to go see what he wanted.

Frank seemed fine while Eddie drove him around until Eddie asked how he wanted to finance the car.

When the potential customer hemmed and hawed and didn't seem to have the slightest idea about financing, Eddie got suspicious. Then, Eddie said, the fellow wanted to drive.

"When he asked me to stop the car and get out so he could drive, I just knew he had escaped from the State Hospital. I told him I had to put gas in the car and usually gassed up at the Eden Truck Stop where I had a charge account.

"Frank started to protest a bit, saying he didn't want to drive far. I just drove to the truck stop and pulled up to the tank. I slipped the key out of the ignition, put it in my shoe and went into the station. You know the rest."

"Weren't you afraid Eddie?" I asked.

"You're damned right I was afraid. He had me at his mercy. The only thing I could do was to get to a phone." Eddie continued, "I was lucky."

We drove on down to the lot and Eddie told Vic the story. Vic's only comment was, "You used your head on that one Eddie. You never know what kind of people you'll have to deal with."

58 From Gas Station to Restaurant and Eddie's Shell

"Hazie! Am I glad to see you. I had a call from Bob Bernstein. He wants me to pick him up a car at the auction. He thought he would like a Plymouth Fury, if I could find one." Eddie had a smile from ear to ear.

"Did he tell you how much you could spend? What if you can't find a Fury?"

"I know a lot of the dealers. I don't have to buy it at the auction. I'm not looking to make money on the deal, so I can find something that will be okay," Eddie explained.

"I hadn't thought of that. I guess I just thought you always went through the auction. Will he come back to pick it up? I hope so because I want to ask him some questions about his cabin. He sort of turned me loose, but there are a few things I'm not sure about." I had finished making draperies for the windows and I wanted to show him some of the ideas I had for the sun porch.

"From what he said, he plans on coming back for a short time. He sounded real good." Eddie answered. Then he changed the subject. "I think Mom finally found a renter for the big house. A man and his wife, his father and sister were out the other day. I haven't met them, but Mom thinks they will be okay. It seems they want to put a little barbecue restaurant in the old station."

"Would there be room enough in the station? I know Dad ran some water lines to it. They would have to go to some expense to get it going."

"From what Mom told me, they want to do an open grill and use apple wood to barbecue. They would serve just hamburgers and chicken, cold drinks, and coffee. I guess they asked Mom if they could set up some tables back of the station under the big trees."

"Well, I can see why Mom would be enthusiastic about a deal like that. She's all for someone doing something different." I could just see it, and it had a good chance of doing well. There was more traffic on the highway all the time.

"We're going to have to hire another salesman. How would you like to do some plans for half of the garage in the back?" Eddie knew I was a sucker for doing plans.

"Sure, when do you want to get started?" I asked.

"Like day before yesterday." Eddie grinned at me.

"Do you want to make space for two salesmen and maybe a small conference room? You have plenty of room and sometimes an extra space like that comes in handy." I could already imagine it.

"Yeah, that would be good, and a decent bathroom. I'm amazed at how many lady customers we are getting. I kid Vic, telling him they've got their eye on him." Eddie laughed.

Vic wasn't handsome, but he had a good build, steady gray eyes, and a shock of unruly brown hair. He was polite, with good manners. Actually, for a fellow probably almost forty, he was a pretty sexy guy.

Bob Bernstein told Eddie that the car Eddie had found for him was just what he wanted. He was very happy with it. I needed to know just what I could do at the cabin and I wanted Bob's go-ahead. We drove up to the cabin one afternoon.

"Since the other guys are out of the cabin deal," Bob said, "It's pretty much up to me. I have to deal with Abe and my Dad, but I can handle that. You said something about window covers for the sunroom? That's a good name for it. With windows around three sides, the view is great but the sun beats in."

"There won't be any trouble if I use Bernstein Brothers' store license, will there?" I asked.

"No, that would be okay. What did you have in mind?" Bob looked at me like I could grab rabbits out of a hat.

"How does this sound? Pueblo Tent and Awning has some light-weight striped canvas. I could buy a bolt of it and make roll-up shades. It would be heavy enough to keep out the sun and could be rolled out of the way so you could see the view."

"That sounds great. It would sort of go with the log cabin effect, right?"

"Yeah. And another thing Bob, we need some kind of walk from the back door to where the steps go up to the deck in front. In fact, it would be nice if below the deck we made a place where you could sit."

"What did you have in mind?" Bob walked over and looked at the area I was talking about.

"What do you think of getting the saw mill to take one of those huge pine trees and cutting it into four-inch thick rounds. We could mix up some creosote and linseed oil and dip them and lay them just like you would tile."

"Boy that would look great! I can just see it all finished."

"We've trimmed a lot of the lower branches off the big Ponderosa Pines so we can get a great view," I pointed out. "Red and a helper did that. There's still about two days work to get the rest of that darned oak brush dug out. We can bring the little tractor up for that."

"How about the well, Hazie? It just doesn't seem to have enough water. The well driller in Rye said we ought to drill a well in the bottom of the arroyo. That's where our neighbor dug his well and it never goes dry." I knew Bob was thinking of all the times we'd pumped the well dry, waited until it filled up again, and then had the darned mess of priming it.

"It should be done. Dad could help with the drilling. After all, that's what he did for years and it would save quite a bit." I told Bob.

"I'll talk to the well driller while I'm here," Bob said. "I can't expect Eddie to take time off to do all this." Bob knew how much time Eddie, Red, and I had spent working around the cabin. For me it was a labor of love. I could bring my dog during the week and enjoy doing whatever I could.

"That should about do it, Bob. Are you going to be able to spend a little time before you go back to California?" I wanted him to stay for a week or two at least.

"Yeah, I want to spend this weekend and next, and then I have to go back. I'm working at the Palo Alto Times and I really enjoy it." Bob told me.

"Morey wants to come up this weekend. Who else should we ask?" I asked Bob.

"I don't know whether Marietta will be in town or not but I'll let you know so you can plan on what to cook. How about I go to Frank's Market and pick up some steaks?"

"That would be great, and then I can get everything else ready. Sounds like fun!" Bob was always so thoughtful and never let me down.

That weekend, Eddie left the car lot about noon and brought the little tractor up so we could pull oak brush the next day. There was a crowd visiting. Everyone wanted to drive it or have Eddie give them a ride. It turned out to be a fun evening. Bob broiled steaks to perfection. We sat up into the wee hours of the night, catching up on everything, almost as if we would never have another evening like this one.

Mom rented the big house and the station to George and Helen Otte. His father, George also, and their daughter would be coming from Nebraska in about a month. I asked Eddie what he thought of them.

"They seem nice enough," Eddie said. "I think George has a brother who is some kind of a boss at a local packing company. That is why George and Helen came here." Eddie didn't seem too enthused. In fact, he didn't seem happy at all.

"What's the matter? You sound like you lost your last friend."

"Oh, I just can't seem to get interested in anything, seems like."

"Why Eddie, the car lot is doing great and you know a lot of people. You can't say you don't keep busy."

"Hazie, you probably know me better than anyone else does, but you don't really know me. Most people see me as a cripple. It's obvious that I don't have arms. That just crosses me off as someone who could fit into society and do the same things others do." Eddie looked me in the eye as if he wanted me to contradict him.

"There are times when I want to be the same as other people; to be able to fall in love and lead a normal life."

"Maybe you just need to let yourself. Just go for it." I said.

"Oh, sure. Then I realize that although I may feel the same as others, I can't be like them, so I just hold back and crawl into the shell I've made for myself."

He said this last with such an air of dejection that I didn't know what to say. "But Eddie, think of all the things you do. All the people you know."

"Maybe so, but you know who I'd like to be? The average Joe, the guy who carries a lunch pail, has a mortgage, and comes home to a wife and a couple of kids." He paused, then, "He's the guy I envy."

"But Eddie…"

"No! Try to understand. Business-wise I get along fine. It's a challenge and I can do what I have to do to compete. But with girls, and that's what it boils down to, I just can't make it."

I couldn't read his expression. I tried to think of something, anything to say.

"I know. I'm better off not tempting myself," he said with a cold finality.

59 Introduced to Dr. Abt, John Seeley, Kessler Institute, and IBM

"*I*'ve been talking with Ben Graham and I definitely want to take his course at Columbia University on Under-Valued Securities next year. I want you to get your affairs in order and be ready to move to New York in 1952." Morey waited for me to protest. I think he was surprised when I didn't.

"I think that would be great Morey. Maybe we can go before the first of that year to find an apartment." I didn't want him to feel that I would hold him back.

"I'm glad you feel that way." Morey had been doing more with hypnosis. Ginny Tighe was still his best subject and he continued to work with her.

For now, we were off to New York for a brief visit. It was a hot, muggy day and I wasn't looking forward to New York weather. Morey brought a briefcase full of reading material. I picked up a Life magazine at the newsstand. As we settled into our airplane seats, he reached over, took my magazine and said, "Let me skim through that and I'll give it right back to you."

I was lost in my own thoughts. I kept hearing the last conversation I'd had with Eddie. "*But with girls...I can't make it! I'm better off not tempting myself.*"

As far as I knew, there had only been three girls Eddie had cared about, Lily, Helen, and Susie. I suppose Susie didn't count because she was his cousin. Now most of his sidekicks were married or going steady. I knew Eddie felt very alone.

Morey interrupted my reverie, showing me the *Life* magazine open to an article, "Man Without Arms To Demonstrate Electric Arm."

"Look that over and see what you think. We'll get in touch with them when we get to New York and maybe this can help Eddie."

"Wouldn't that be wonderful Morey?" I said as I started to read. A Dr. Abt, in conjunction with IBM, had been working for some time on an electric arm. Kessler Institute for Rehabilitation was part of the team. As I read, my excitement grew. I couldn't wait to talk to John Seeley, the "man without arms."

Morey had appointments with Ben Graham and Henry Belk. I called IBM and asked for John Seeley. I was given an extension number then they connected me.

"This is John Seeley, how can I help you?" The voice was firm and confident.

I answered, "We read the article in Life and I would like to set up an appointment with you. You see, my brother Eddie was born without arms. My husband and I are interested because the electric arm might help him."

"I would like very much to meet with you. Could you ar-

THE JERSEY JOURNAL, (100,000 Copies Daily)
THURSDAY, APRIL 14, 1955

CONQUERS HANDICAP—John B. Seeley, double amputee, at work in the Fine Arts Department of International Business Machines where he does bookkeeping, photography and research. Seeley will speak today at a meeting of the Hoboken Kiwanis Club on 'Employ the Handicapped.'

John Seeley

range to come to our office here in the IBM Building? I am here every afternoon, or morning if you would prefer. Just give me a call so I can be sure that Dr. Abt will be available to answer any questions you might have."

With Morey's agreement, we were set to go the next afternoon. I could hardly contain myself. What if!? There were so many "what ifs?"

We were directed to a huge workroom on a lower floor of the IBM Building. It housed the electric arm project as well as the art department.

As John Seeley approached, Morey held out his hand, but drew back when John said, "You'll have to excuse me. I can't shake hands today. My arm is on the workbench." He gave us a warm smile. I was impressed. John Seeley was about thirty years old, built like a wrestler. He was very handsome, with deep-set, shadowed blue eyes. I instantly liked this young man.

We walked to the back through an area that contained many projects in progress. Men were everywhere, on ladders, perched on high trapeze-like affairs. Along the way, John stopped and called out: "Tom Douglas, I would like you to meet some people from Colorado."

John told Tom Douglas that my brother had been born without arms. I realized that Tom Douglas was his first name. His last name was Jones.

Tom Douglas was the most charming man I had ever met. He raised my hand to his lips, and with Old World charm, told me how glad he was to meet me. He was a polished, not too tall, handsome man. I learned later that he was head of the art department for IBM and was quite famous in his own right for various art projects.

Finally we came to another workshop area. There on a table was John's arm. I couldn't believe all the pieces. Tiny springs, wires, electrical devices – things too numerous to comprehend.

"This is Morey Bernstein and his wife, Hazel," John introduced us to Dr. Abt, a short, dark, roly-poly man. "Hazel's brother, Eddie, was born without arms. They hope that an electric arm might be of help to him."

"We are still working to get the kinks out of this arm," Dr. Abt said. "I think we are finally at a point where we might be able to fit it to different people. You have to understand, every person who has lost an arm in one way or another, presents a different set of problems."

Yes, I can see why that would be so," I said. "My brother was born with no stubs at all. It is as if they were taken right off at the joint. I should imagine it would be easier to make arms to fit someone who had something there."

"That is true, however, we are in hopes that we will be able to make an arm usable for almost everyone," Dr. Abt replied.

"Does your brother use his feet to do anything?" John asked.

"You would have to see what Eddie can do, to believe it," Morey answered. "He uses a typewriter, drives a car, doesn't matter if it is automatic or standard shift, drives big equipment, loaders, dump trucks, back hoes, feeds himself, uses an electric saw. Eddie does all these things and more."

"Life magazine sort of jumped the gun on us," John said. "It will be this fall before we are ready to demonstrate our electrical arm. We have reserved a time with UCLA in September and we are working frantically to get ready by then. At that time, when a definite date is set, we'll meet with companies from this country and Europe." John was very serious.

"Would it be possible for your brother to attend this conference?" Dr. Abt inquired.

"How long will the conference last?"

"Probably a week," Abt replied. "We would pay his expenses. I believe that many times, someone who has lost arms after having them fails to try to use their feet. Perhaps seeing what Eddie can do, would be encouraging. Of course, we also want to see if the electric arm would help Eddie."

During our short stay in New York, I spent most of my time at the workshop of Dr. Abt and John Seeley. I was fascinated with their work and they were helpful in answering my questions. John did volunteer work at Kessler Institute for Rehabilitation in New Jersey. He asked if I would like to go with him and spend the day.

I accepted. I was amazed at the work being done there. Dr. Kessler was a tall, excitable man who wore his lab coat with an aura of authority. Red hair and freckles gave him a sort of little-boy look that was quickly dispelled. He lectured for two hours in the morning, not only to his staff, but to people who were there for rehab, and visitors who wanted to know more about his work. He talked about causes of birth defects. He said that no one knew exactly what caused most cases, but he discussed drug causes, accidents, and other reasons.

I talked to him afterward and he opened a new avenue of thought for me. He said that in various regions of the country where there were known (and sometimes unknown) mineral deposits, uranium for instance, there were more birth defects. He asked me if there were ore deposits where we lived. I didn't know.

John had told Dr. Kessler about Eddie and Kessler said he was looking forward to meeting him.

The evening before we left New York, Morey and I had dinner with Ben Graham. I would finally meet the man that Morey felt was his personal guru.

We met Ben at Peter's Back Yard, our favorite restaurant in Greenwich Village. When Morey said, "This is my wife, Hazel," Ben took my hand and just held it.

"My fourth wife was a Hazel," he told us. I was fascinated by Ben. He had twinkly brown eyes, a great tan, and looked like he probably played tennis every day. He reminded me of a mischievous little boy. He had an easy laugh and kept up a lively conversation.

Morey wanted to talk about the stock market. After many tries, Ben reached over and covered my hand with his. "When I have the company of a lovely lady Morey, I don't talk business. That is for boardrooms and, in my case, lecture halls. You'll get enough of business in my classroom."

Morey sat there like a fish with its mouth open, at a loss for words.

Ben looked at me. "You'll have to teach this boy to take his time in life. It can't be hurried."

I grinned. "I'll try, but it won't be easy."

Too soon, dinner was over. The next day, we caught a flight home to Colorado.

The first thing I did when I got home was go to the ranch to see Eddie, Mom and Dad. After big hugs, I asked, "So what has been happening since I've been gone?"

"Not much, Hazie," Eddie said. "George and his wife have been working on the station. They are just about ready to open. We'll walk down after while and take a look." He sounded pleased with what was happening.

"When will George's dad and sister be here?"

"They are supposed to be in on Friday," Mom answered. "I'm anxious to see what they are like. George and Helen seem nice enough, so I expect they will be okay."

Dad chimed in then, "I think they mean business. George has hauled in several truckloads of apple wood. I let him pile it up on the other side of the garage."

"Just the thought of an apple wood barbecued burger makes my mouth water. I'll bet they will have people driving out from town. It isn't that far." I had a hunch this would be a huge success.

"We have most of the work done on the changes to our garage, Hazie. It's going to work out great. And we've been busy enough to hire another salesman. Just part time until we get the space out there finished, but he has been busy." Eddie seemed a little more like his old self.

Mom introduced me to George and Helen Otte.

"We've heard so much about you," Helen said, "We feel we know you already." She gave me a broad smile.

She was tiny, with a shock of curly black hair and blue eyes. George was tall and light haired. He had a sort of stern look that disappeared when he smiled. They made a handsome couple and seemed happy about how things were going.

Helen showed us what they had done. "We decided to do nothing but barbecued hamburgers and chicken. We'll serve it wrapped in a heavy napkin and give them extra napkins. We'll have two or three long picnic tables with benches out there under the trees."

"I think it's a great idea. That way, you don't have dishes to wash and you won't have a bunch of extra food that can go bad. Also, they'll smell that apple wood smoke way down the road."

"We're going to check it out tonight. We want all of you to come down and have a burger or some chicken with us, okay?" Helen asked.

"Sounds great to me, how about you guys?" I turned to Mom and Eddie.

"Sure, I'm hungry already," Eddie agreed.

George had used the small space in ingenious ways. A long, narrow barbecue grill extended from the building. It was on rollers and could be pulled back under the overhang when they locked up. Beside it, he made a shelf where the burgers and chicken could be picked up. Just behind this space he installed a long ice tray for containers of mustard, mayo, ketchup and homemade salsa.

When I asked about the chili sauce, Helen laughed and said, "It's an old German recipe. It's hot, but most people come back for more.

From the sample we had that night I was sure their endeavor would be a success.

"You want me to go with you to buy a jacket? Are you sure? Give me twenty minutes and I'll meet you on the main floor by the elevators. See you!" I hung up the phone and thought, now what?

As I drove down the tree-shaded streets of Pueblo I thought about what Eddie said before I went to New York. What was it about girls? That he was better off not tempting himself? That was it. I couldn't remember when Eddie had wanted me to go with him to buy clothes. A new jacket! Why, he hadn't shown the slightest interest in clothes for years. He was perfectly content to let Mom or me pick out what he could wear. Usually, he was so busy at the car lot, or at the ranch, or helping me that he didn't bother to dress up in the good clothes he had. So what happened? It had to be a girl.

I pushed open the heavy plate glass doors of Pueblo's only department store and made my way to the elevators. Eddie stood waiting, a little to one side. His light brown hair was messed a bit by the wind. His blue eyes looked bluer in his sun-tanned face because his lashes and brows were so dark. He shifted self-consciously from one foot to the other. A big grin cracked his face and crinkled around his eyes when he saw me.

I grinned back at him. "Come over here where we can talk for a minute. Now tell me," I shooed a salesgirl away, "Why all this interest in clothes?"

"Well," Eddie hesitated, then blurted all at once: "I've got a date, George's sister Betty. We're going out tonight." Eddie laughed at his own jumbled account.

I had never seen him so bubbly. "When did you meet her? Is she going to stay and help George and Helen with the barbecue?"

"She got here a few days after you got back from New York. She was so easy to talk to. Every night I'd go down and hang around while she worked. She didn't seem to mind."

"She must be something to put that look on your face."

"Well, I finally thought, I'm going to ask her for a date. If she turns me down, at least I'll know, but she didn't. She seemed to be real happy that I asked her."

"I can't wait to meet her. Anyone who can put that spark in your eyes has to be special." I was sincere. I just hoped she wouldn't hurt him.

"How can I tell you what she looks like? Well, she's tall and skinny like you, with blonde hair, but lighter than yours, and her eyes are blue, real dark blue. She's pretty. At least I think so."

"Yes, she sounds pretty, although you wouldn't win any prizes for description." I laughed.

"Well, this morning before I came to town we got to talking. I asked her if she liked the mountains. She said she'd only seen the mountains from a distance, like from the ranch. I guess they just have low sand hills in Nebraska where she came from. I'm still wondering if she wanted to go with me because I told her I'd show her the mountains, and she wants to see what a mountain looks like up close."

"So, you've got a date! Well come on, let's go find a jacket and whatever else that will match." We left our private little corner and took the elevator to the fourth floor, Men's Wear department. Turning slightly I looked at our fellow passengers. Five women I thought, and I don't know one of them although we'd lived in Pueblo all our lives. Abruptly, I became aware of the woman at Eddie's right. She was staring. Oh, oh, I thought, she's going to start asking questions.

"Were you in an accident, honey?" The woman put her face close to Eddie's. I looked away, hoping she'd shut up.

"No ma'am." Eddie answered quietly.

I had heard him say it the same way many times, quiet like, with a tinge of "please don't ask me any questions" in his voice. Why doesn't she just shut up? I thought.

"Well, you did break your arms, didn't you?" Fat face was openly curious now.

"No ma'am." Eddie answered, again.

I felt the deep-down stifling mad feeling I always experienced when people started asking Eddie questions. What must he feel? He never acts mad. When children ask him he always answers and is really sweet with them, but when people like this fat, ignorant slob question him, he always clams up. He draws into his shell and says as little as possible. I waited. I knew old fat face wouldn't stop now.

"Well, young man, what did happen to your arms, then?" She was loud and demanding.

"I don't have any arms ma'am. I was born this way." Eddie quietly told her.

I could hear the uneasy shuffle of many feet on the elevator floor. The fat face flushed red. She showed her embarrassment and turned away, but she couldn't get out of the elevator. Neither could Eddie, but he was used to it. He had been living with it for twenty-five years.

When the elevator reached the fourth floor, the fat woman pushed her way through and got off first, waddling down the aisle. We waited, hanging back to be the last ones out. The door slid shut behind us.

As we walked toward the racks of men's clothing, Eddie and I exchanged glances. Then, he straightened his shoulders and some of the excitement came back into his eyes.

"Let's look at some things in gray," he said, "Betty mentioned that she likes gray."

A salesman came up to us, his handkerchief folded just right in his pocket, his shoes shined to perfection. He said to Eddie, "Well, what can we do for you today, feller?"

I wanted to tell him to get lost and let us look for ourselves.

"I would like to look at a sports jacket. Something in gray if you have it," Eddie said, his voice shy.

The sound of metal hangers sliding against the metal rack was a tinny grating noise filling the small second of silence as the salesman flicked his eyes uncertainly at this customer without arms. "What kind of a jacket do you usually wear sir?" There was a helpless note in his voice.

"I usually wear Pendleton wool shirts, but I'm thinking of something a bit heavier. I see something about in the middle of the rack there that might do." Eddie slipped out of the loafer on his right foot and walked quickly to the jacket he had spied. "This one," he said, and reached up, and with his toes, lifted the jacket, hanger and all, from the rack. He held it toward the salesman.

The salesman took the jacket and said, "It looks like it might be about the right size." Then he stood there, not quite knowing what to do.

"I like this Eddie, the material is beautiful." I reached over and took the jacket from the salesman, tucked the ends of the sleeves into the patch pockets, then slipped it over Eddie's shoulders.

It was hot. Eddie hadn't worn a jacket. The sleeves of his shirt were tucked neatly into the armholes. I smoothed the coat over Eddie's back, making sure it was long enough to cover the curvature of his hump. I buttoned one button and stepped back, wishing as I always did, that Eddie had a straight strong back and arms to fill the sleeves.

"It looks very nice," the salesman suddenly said, then added, "That color is especially good on you, sir."

Eddie turned to the long mirror, critically eyeing himself up and down. A slow smile spread over his face as he walked toward a chair, still self-conscious, but better now.

"I have to give it the real test now. I wouldn't want to pop any buttons should it be too tight," he said, as he sat down, then bent over slightly, reached up and forward with his right foot, as he tested to see if it was roomy enough across his back.

"You see sir, I'm a salesman too. I sell used cars. I have to wear something I'm comfortable with when I sit down to writeup my orders." He gave the salesman a big smile. That did it. From then on, both of them seemed more comfortable.

"Now what do you have in a pair of slacks, size thirty, thirty-two? I'd like them in light weight tweed, maybe with a little blue mixed in."

As Eddie and the salesman walked toward the long racks where the slacks hung in their neat rows, I wondered, as I always did, at the casual front Eddie assumed for strangers. He usually put people at their ease and I heard a sure note in the salesman's voice now as he explained the virtues of his wares.

"How do you like this pair?" Eddie asked me, as he pointed his foot toward the pants draped over the salesman's arm.

"I like them," I said. "Just enough blue to look cool."

"Yep, and let's see if they have a couple of shirts that will match." Eddie gave me a grin as though to say, "How am I doing?"

"I think those shirts are just right Eddie. They will be cool, too." I watched as Eddie felt the material between his toes.

As the salesman made out his sales slip, I reached into Eddie's pants pocket and took out his billfold. I counted out the bills and took the change. Eddie asked me to get out one of his business cards. He gave it to the salesman, "What's your name, sir?"

They exchanged names. "When I can afford a car, I'll be over," the salesman promised.

Eddie thanked him and we left.

"You know, it's funny, I always hated to try on clothes, but this has been fun. Do you think Betty will like them?"

"Of course she will, and if she knew how you hate to shop, she would like them even more." The power of a woman! I thought.

"You're coming by the ranch in the morning, aren't you?" Eddie asked as we left the store. He knew I wanted to get some more work done on the Bernstein cabin.

"Yes, I want to see if Dad and Mom want to come up Sunday. I thought maybe Dad would like to go fishing for a while at the lake."

"I know he would. He keeps his worm can full and his fishing pole ready." Eddie said.

"Eddie, Morey has to go to a meeting in Denver with his uncle over the weekend. Why don't you knock off early tomorrow if you can. Bring Betty up for dinner. Then you and Betty can go on back to the ranch and bring Dad and Mom up Sunday morning. We can all have the day together."

"Yeah, that would work. It sounds like fun!" Eddie had an excited tone to his voice.

"We'll forget about work this weekend. I think we could all use some fun."

Eddie slipped his foot out of his moccasin. With his toes, he dragged his keys out of his shoe where he always kept them. He balanced on one leg and reached up and unlocked his car. Then he opened the door and held it while I deposited his packages on the seat. He put the key in the ignition and started the car, letting it idle until we said our goodbyes.

I closed the door and waited on the sidewalk until he pulled away from the curb. I watched as he expertly got into his traffic lane and took off. I never ceased to marvel at how easy he made it all look.

I went home, made myself a tall drink and a list. I decided to call Red Barnes to see if he could go up with me to the cabin tonight. He'd been living at home and helping Eddie at the car lot part time. He liked to go to the cabin with me and enjoyed the work. Sometimes, I thought it was good for him to get away from Eddie. He depended too much on Eddie to tell him exactly what to do. I tried to make Red think for himself.

I went to the meat market and the grocery store and was ready to pick Red up by seven. We stopped by the ranch. Mom came out to meet us.

"I suppose Eddie has left already?" I asked her.

"Oh, yes, he looked so nice, all dressed up." We walked toward the house.

"Red, why don't you find Dad and help him get his fishing stuff ready," I said. "He and Mom are coming up Sunday and I thought we would go to the lake."

Red sort of hung back. I knew he wanted to hear what Mom and I were going to talk about. I waited until he was out of sight around the corner of the barn.

"So Mom, tell me what you think. This is the first time Eddie ever wanted to pick out his clothes and he wanted to be sure Betty would like them."

"Well, she's beautiful," Mom said, "And young. I'm just afraid that when she meets more people, she'll start going with someone else." Mom couldn't hide her concern.

"Oh Mom, maybe she really likes Eddie. Maybe at last he's found someone. He's got to take a chance. If he gets hurt, well at least he will have lived a little bit."

Mom stooped down and started to pull some weeds, as if that would make her fears go away.

"Mom, the reason Eddie is as strong as he is, well, it's because you and Dad would never let any of us coddle him. It's worked for him so far. Let's not let him know how we feel." I reached down and put my arm around her.

"Oh...you know I would never let him know how I feel. You'll have to admit, you're worried too."

"Of course I'm worried, how could I help but be?"

Red and Dad came around the corner then and Mom said, "Have you had supper yet? I have a bit of cornbread and pork chops left."

"Sure, I could eat a little more. You know me, Mrs. Higgins." Red never turned down Mom's cooking. Even after living with Mom and Dad off and on for the last few years, Red still called Mom "Mrs. Higgins."

While Red ate, I took some of Mom's fresh vegetables to the car. She walked out with me. I put my arm around her. "Quit worrying, Mom. It's going to be okay."

"No. He's so happy thinking of this girl and having a date. She is pretty but she doesn't know anyone here yet. As soon as she gets acquainted with more people she'll give him the gate. You'll see. This won't be any different. He'll just be hurt all over again and..." Mom stooped down and started furiously pulling weeds as if by doing so, she could pull hurt from Eddie's life.

"Come on now, Mom, don't be silly. Maybe he really found the girl for him. Let's be happy with him. If we have to pick up the pieces, well, we can do that, too." I reached down, pulling her to her feet.

"Eddie says you want us to come to the cabin on Sunday. Says we can ride up with him and Betty. Is that right?" she asked.

"Yes, I asked Eddie to bring Betty to dinner Saturday evening. That way I can get to meet her. I almost feel left out. Everyone has met her but me." I joked.

"Well, she's a worker. Works right along side her brother and seems to know what she's doing. I can't say that for many young girls now-a-days." Mom said grudgingly.

"I've got to be going, Mom. I'll see you Sunday." I yelled at Red to come on.

As we drove away I looked back. Dad had his arm around Mom as they walked toward the house.

60 Meet Betty Otte

The smell of alfalfa and Timothy hay scented the air as we entered the valley below Mount Baldy. The cabin was another three miles distant. I bypassed the little village of Rye and took the back road. Soon we were above the cabin, surrounded by tall Ponderosas. My dog was excited and gave a little yelp as a squirrel crossed our path.

Red had been unusually silent all the way. Now he said tersely, "Is Eddie coming up tomorrow?"

"Yes, I asked him and Betty, the girl he had a date with tonight, to come to dinner tomorrow night. I haven't met her yet," I said.

Red didn't say anything else and I didn't offer anything. It would be soon enough after we met Betty.

I pulled into the long circle drive in front of the cabin and came to a stop near the back porch. I just stood there for a few moments gulping in fresh mountain air. I looked at the peeled logs of the cabin as it sprawled along the south slope of the small clearing. We had trimmed the lower branches from the towering pines so we had a view to the east. I let my love for this place envelop me. Slowly I felt the tenseness ease from my body to be swallowed up by the quiet and serenity broken only by the call of a blue jay and the scampering of a squirrel in the lofty branches overhead.

All of a sudden I wanted to hurry. Hurry to put a bright shiny face on the cabin so it would welcome the girl Eddie would bring.

Red had started the pump and was busy unloading the car. I put things away and filled the ice-cube trays. I always brought an extra bag of ice just in case.

As Red carried in firewood and placed it on the hearth, I started supper. While everything was cooking, I mixed myself a tall drink and sat on the back porch, relaxing.

After dinner, Red and I sat by the fireplace for a while. I wondered and worried a little at how Red would take Eddie having a girl friend. I couldn't help but feel it would be very difficult for Red not to have Eddie to lean on. Eddie had tried his best to make Red self-reliant, but he still depended on Eddie. Maybe it would be good for Red to have to think for himself. I didn't know.

Early the next morning, I took a walk down into the valley. My dog chased chipmunks. I gathered flowers. When I returned, I filled an old vase and a broken-handled pitcher with the blossoms I had picked; daisies, Black-Eyed-Susans, and a white frothy flower that looked like the lace on a dance frock.

I put Red to work leveling the areas where we would place the rounds from the saw mill. It was quite a job, as there were fairly good-sized rocks mixed with the soil. He put those aside so we could use them to border flowerbeds.

By the time I heard Eddie's tires crunch on the gravel of the drive-way, everything was ready. The smell of a roast was in the air, a fire was crackling in the rough stone fireplace that took up one wall of the living room, and even my dog had an air of expectancy.

Tall pines cast glimmering shadows on Eddie and Betty as they walked toward me. I waited for them at the foot of the steps. She was tall, taller than Eddie, and thin, but she had all the curves in the right places. She walked with her head up, the soft lavender of her cotton dress swished against her bare legs, soft white ballerinas on her slim feet. She looks so proud, I thought.

"Hazel, I want you to meet Betty." Eddie's his voice had a note I'd never heard before.

"Hello," I said, almost breathlessly. "I'm so glad to meet you. Come on in to the fire."

She put out her hand to meet mine, shyly, but when our fingers met, I felt strength. I looked into her eyes and saw a wall of blue ice. My smile didn't do a thing to melt it.

As we walked into the living room, Red got up from where he sprawled on the floor in front of the fire. The firelight enhanced the

329

red in his hair and his cheeks were glowing. He held out his hand and grumbled a "Hi-pleased-to-meet-ya."

"Hi," Betty said. "I'm glad to meet you. Eddie has told me so much about you." She turned to me. "What a beautiful cabin. I didn't expect anything like this way up here in the mountains."

"We're very lucky. My husband's brother, Bob, and three of his friends started this cabin. They had a carpenter do a lot of the work. They added the sun room as sort of afterthought. Then Burt got married and wanted out, then Ed, then Bill. So Bernstein Brothers bought the cabin. I spend a lot of time here. Eddie, my Dad, and Red have worked their tails off, but the cabin is finally getting finished.

"Does anyone want a drink before dinner?" I asked, knowing they would all say no. This wasn't Morey's crowd, many of whom would rather drink than eat.

Eddie took Betty out to the sun room and started telling her all about the cabin.

I found myself thinking, *why this girl isn't more than seventeen, or eighteen and I think she's scared of me. Yet she seems so much older. And her eyes, why, her eyes are so reserved, almost withdrawn with a sort of hurt look behind them. Why did a girl so young and in her cool poised way, more than just pretty, have this reserved, almost cold manner?*

Then, we were in the living room all talking at once. Betty had her back to us, her hands stretched out to the fire. She turned and smiled at me and changed so completely that I was reminded of a small child who, upon meeting strangers, covers his fright with sullenness. When he finds he is among friends, he smiles and lets the whole world in.

I smiled back, a smile that started right from my toes and ended with my lips, and the ice was broken.

"What do you think of our mountains, so far?" I asked.

"Oh, I'm still breathless! We don't have mountains like these in Nebraska. All I can say is that I want to see more of them." Betty's voice had a husky quality and she looked over at Eddie as if asking him to show her more.

Eddie's look said he would be glad to show her anything. "We started a little early this afternoon," he said, "I wanted Betty to see the sunset on the valley. You know that high point on the back road, just down from the cabin? We parked there and walked over to that big rock that

Eddie showing Betty the Mountains

juts out, the one the kids call 'God's Rocking Chair'. Well, we just sat there and watched."

"It was wonderful." Betty said, her eyes far away.

We were all silent. For Eddie and me this spot was special. It had a lot of meaning, not only to us but to anyone who had ever been there. We had found several arrowheads in the vicinity.

"I'd better quit dreaming and get dinner on the table." I said, breaking the spell.

"Can I help?" Betty asked, getting up from the couch where she had been sitting beside Eddie.

"No, it's all ready. All I have to do is make the gravy and put it on the table."

I went to the kitchen and I heard Eddie telling Betty about the cabin. He told her more about who built it and about Bob, Morey's brother. I heard him say, "Just about everything is finished. There is still about a day's work grubbing out the rest of the oak brush, then

331

Hazel wants to make walks and a larger area around the back porch and at the bottom of the stairs off the sun room."

I couldn't help but listen and as I did, I thought, how modest he is. Why doesn't he tell her how he has worked up here every weekend this summer helping me? Oh, well, if she's around much, she'll find out.

Then I heard Betty ask, "Does your sister spend much time here?"

"Yes, and she has plenty of company. Sometimes she brings my sister's kids or the neighbor kids. Morey comes up on Saturday nights and usually he brings several people with him, but they leave that night or early the next morning. Hazel's friends, sometimes they stay longer," Eddie explained.

"Why, you could sleep about ten people here, couldn't you?" Betty said.

"Yes, and I've seen a lot more than that. This place really jumps sometimes," Eddie told her.

"I'll bet they have a lot of fun." Betty sounded wistful. She came into the kitchen, Eddie right behind her. "I think this cabin is just scrumptious, Hazel. Eddie has been telling me all about it. I don't blame you for wanting to stay up here all the time."

"Well, I'll have to admit, I wish I had a house in town I loved as much. Of course, it isn't just the house; it's the mountains and the quiet. Just getting away, I guess. Betty, if you want to wash up, the bathroom is just off the back hall here."

Eddie showed Betty where the bathroom was, and then came into the kitchen where I was tossing the salad. I took this opportunity to ask, "Do you want me to help you with your food?"

"No Hazie, just put my plate on that stool, cut up my meat for me and I'll eat like I always do. Betty might just as well see me do things the way I do them. If she can't take it, I'd just as well know now as later."

So much he could do, but things like eating with his toes, the personal things, were what kept him tied to his family.

"Let's eat," I called, "Come on Red. I know you're starving." I had set our four places at the end of the long table that would seat twelve. I seated Ed and Betty on the side of the table so they could watch the flames in the fireplace. I carved the pink-centered slices of roast beef.

While Betty helped herself to mashed potatoes, gravy, corn, and tiny buttered carrots, I cut Eddie's meat for him.

I noticed that Betty's eyes flicked toward Eddie as he stooped over to put food on his fork with his toes then lift the fork to his lips. As he sat up straight to chew his food, her hand, which had been holding her fork in mid-air, resumed its path to her mouth. We ate silently until the first edge of hunger had been satisfied.

"Mmmm, this tastes so good. Could I have just a little bit more of everything?" Betty asked.

As I helped her, I asked Eddie and Red, "How about it you guys? I know you're not full yet." I sliced more beef and put it on their plates. I gave Red his plate and watched as he heaped on more potatoes and gravy and corn. I cut corn off another ear for Eddie and put his plate on the stool.

Between bites, we talked about our next project. Eddie asked me if old Cradwell at the saw mill had finished cutting the rounds for us.

"Why don't you take a run up there in the morning, Eddie?" I asked. "I'll bet Betty would like to see a real old fashioned sawmill. Mr. Cradwell lives right there in a house the Cradwells have lived in for about four generations."

"Sure. Let's make that a project for next weekend. Red and I could finish leveling what needs to be leveled. If you could stop by the ranch and pick up that old washtub that's back of the garage, we could use it for the creosote and I'll see if Cradwell can deliver the rounds Saturday afternoon. We still have some oak brush to pull and clear out. I think we should get that done first." Eddie said.

We had discussed using creosote to preserve the log rounds after they were laid in the ground. I told Eddie I would pick up a couple of five gallon cans at the lumber yard.

"Maybe I could help," Betty offered. "George's barbecue won't be completely ready for a couple of weeks yet. I think it would be fun."

I looked at her, trying to imagine what she would look like in a pair of old jeans, dipping logs in smelly creosote and Eddie said, "Sure, if you want to, but I'm warning you, it won't be any fun. It will be a messy operation." Eddie looked at Betty as if she was out of her mind to want to help us with this dirty job.

It was all right, I thought, *for us to be all messed up and dirty. After all, we'd been mixed up in plenty of dirty jobs like cleaning out the barn, tearing the plaster off the walls of the apartment house when Eddie remodeled, cleaning the hen house, all kinds of things. Necessary but fun once started. Let her help. The best way in the world for people to get to know each other is to work together.*

"I think it would be great if you really want to, Betty," I said. "You could come up with Eddie. You'd sure find out what we do in our spare time. It's not all work, though. When we get through, we usually go fishing at the lake or swimming, if you like to swim." I didn't want her to think that all we did was work. I didn't want what we were doing messed up by a weak female, either.

"I'm pretty tough. I was raised with five brothers. There were seven kids in my family. If I wanted to play with my brothers, I had to keep up with them. I've worked since I was twelve." Betty just said this as a matter of fact. It was almost as if she knew what I was thinking.

"How nice, I've always liked big families. You never run out of things to do." I told her, and looked at her with new respect.

I took Eddie to the bathroom just before they left. "Hazel, there must be some way I can learn to take myself to the can! Damn it, it's about the only thing I can't do for myself. I'm going to figure out some way to do it! I'm not going to be dependent on Mom, or you, or someone in the family, to do it for the rest of my life."

"We'll find a way, Eddie," I answered. "Maybe you could have an old-fashioned button-hook fixed with a clip that you could wedge in a drawer or something to get your zipper down. That might work. As far as getting your pants off and on, you can do that. It's just getting the damned things zipped and unzipped that throws you."

"Well, I'm going to do it one way or another," he said, determination in his voice.

As we walked back to the living room where Betty waited for us, I thought, *meeting her has opened up a lot of doors for him. He doesn't want to depend on us anymore. He wants to be able to go places with this girl, do things, and he was right. It was going to be hard for both of them. Thank God, she'd been brought up with five brothers.*

Betty took his jacket off the back of the chair and placed it over his shoulders, giving it a little shake to fit it over his hump. As she buttoned it she told him how good looking it was and how much she liked the material and how nice he looked in it. All very matter-of-fact.

I stood there feeling left out, but glad to be left out. I watched Eddie as he self-consciously submitted to Betty's ministrations and listened to her compliments. I saw his ears get red and heard his voice, huskier than usual, as he tried a flippant rejoinder and I knew he loved every minute of it.

Later, I realized I had learned very little about Betty. She had a sort of subdued belligerence when she said she had worked since she was twelve and that there had been seven children in the family. Did that mean that her family had been poor and she'd hated it? Could that be why she was so proud and so willing to help? How could anyone so young understand, or be the kind of person who would want to be with someone without arms?

Eddie's car lights wavered down the mountain road. I went into the living room where Red was sprawled in front of the fireplace.

He looked up at me. With a touch of malice in his voice he said, "So that's the girl Eddie is going with?"

"Yes, Red. She seems to be a nice girl. I think it would be great if Eddie found someone to date." Red muttered something under his breath and stalked off to bed.

Why, I wondered, does a new friendship, or a new love have to break up the old? Why can't a person be like a huge pie, so that there would always be enough pieces to go around? Then no one would ever have to feel left out.

My dog scratched at the back door. I let him in. I reached down, stroking his rough coat, ordering him in a low voice to stop, as he clawed at my bare feet with his sharp toenails. He followed at my heels as I went to my room. I could hear Red snoring from the sun porch where he was already sound asleep.

As I snuggled into my bed I thought how much Eddie's friendship with Red had meant to both of them. For the first time I realized that Red, despite his splendid physique and brash manner, was almost as handicapped as Eddie. Each had found strength in the other's weaknesses.

I fell asleep, a little prayer on my lips, that Betty would understand Red as I did and try to help him too.

61 Creosote Soaked Chain Gang

*R*ed and I were up with the sun the next morning. I made breakfast while Red brought in wood for the fireplace. No matter
how hot it was during the day, evenings were always cold.

"What do you want me to do this morning, Hazel?" Red asked as he
finished his bacon and eggs.

"I guess leveling the rest of that area at the bottom of the back
steps. Then, rake out a place in the basement where we can store any
extra wood from the log rounds." I thought that would keep him busy
until lunchtime.

The sun was high in the sky when Eddie and the folks arrived.
Mom brought a big bowl of potato salad and a quart of pickled beets.
Dad had a gallon can of fish worms and his fish pole. Betty wore short
shorts that showed off her long legs and Dyanna had a bright red swim
suit on under her jeans.

After lunch, Dad said, "I think I'll take a little nap." He stretched
out on the sofa and was soon snoring.

Red went out to finish up what he had started. Eddie and Betty
took off for the sawmill. Mom looked over at me as she put some left-
overs in the fridge. "So what do you think of Betty by now?"

"I don't know, Mom. She's lovely, she wants to help, and she treats
Eddie as if she really enjoys his company. She jokes with him and doesn't
seem at all put off by the fact that he doesn't have arms," and then I
added, "She treats him just like you'd treat anyone else."

"Well, I guess time will tell. I just hope she doesn't lead him on,
then dump him." Mom said, with a sort of defeat in her voice.

"She wants to help pull the rest of the oak brush next weekend and
creosote the logs. If anything will prove her fickle, that ought to do it,"

I mused, thinking of how much work it would be.

"Well, she's a worker. I've watched her help her brother fix up the old station and she gets as much done as anyone."

Mom suddenly realized that Dyanna wasn't in the room. "Where did Dyanna get off to?"

"I imagine she's pestering Red and driving him crazy. Haven't you noticed? She's got a man-sized crush on him."

"She's fifteen. I guess I still think of her as a little girl. She's never acted like she was boy crazy. Well, I'll be..." and Mom let her voice trail off as if she were remembering.

"No, Mom, she's pretty level-headed, but I'm glad Red isn't living at the ranch anymore."

Eddie and Betty got back about three. Betty was full of the sights they had seen. "I just can't understand how they get those big trucks loaded with huge logs down those twisty steep mountain roads. Eddie tells me the logging roads are even worse. He even said he helped his cousin Bob, make some of those logging roads." Her eyes were wide with awe and admiration.

"Yes he did," Mom answered. "And I was scared all the time he was working with Bob. Bob is such a daredevil. He's had a lot of close calls." Mom didn't tell Betty about the time when Eddie and Bob, with Eddie driving, had missed a curve on Burntmill Road and ended up in Mr. Fitzpatrick's corn field.

"Let's head for the lake. It's starting to cool off a little. Maybe the fish are biting." Eddie gave Dad a poke in the ribs. "Come on, Dad, get your fishin' pole. We're gonna catch a big one," Eddie joked.

When we got to the lake, I waded out until the cool water wet the bottoms of my shorts and just stood there, casting as far out as I could.

The quiet was suddenly broken by a squeal from Betty. "I've got a big one. Eddie, come help me," she yelled, as she stood up, walking to the edge of the water where you could see the ripples the fish made as she got it closer to shore.

"Boy, I guess you do have a big one," Eddie yelled.

I got the net, which we seldom had to use, and stood ready. "Okay, you're doing fine. Just get him as close as you can and I'll try to get this net under him." In a few more nerve-wracking minutes, the fish was close enough for me to get the net under him.

Everyone gathered around to eye the catch. A catfish, probably a couple of feet long and heavy, struggled in the net.

Mom said, "Betty, you just caught my favorite fish. If you want, I'll bake it for you and we'll have your brother George and Helen up and have a real fish fry. What do you say?"

"I think that would be great. Wait 'til I show them." Betty hopped from one foot to the other, beside herself at catching such a big fish.

We'd caught crappie, a couple of bass, four trout and now this whopper. We were ready to go home. As we gathered up everything I said, "Red can go with me. I'll go lock up the cabin and he can ride into town with me later. I'll stop by the ranch and take enough crappie with me to make a feast for Morey. He loves crappie. Let me know when you want to have that fish fry and I'll be there." I took the fishing poles that belonged at the cabin. Red gathered up the chairs and other stuff.

It didn't take long to drive to the cabin and lock up. On the way to the ranch, I asked Red if he'd had a good time.

"I guess. It sure seems funny for Eddie to have a girl draped around his neck." He said this in a surly tone.

"Well, Red, I notice that you had a girl on your heels all day, what about that?" I asked.

"Oh Hazel, Dyanna's just a little kid, she doesn't mean anything." I glanced over at him. His cheeks were as red as his hair.

I stopped by the ranch just long enough to pick up the fish for Morey, and headed for Pueblo. When I dropped Red off, I asked if he wanted to work at the cabin the next weekend. "Sure, I guess so. I'll be working at the car lot all week. I'm saving up enough money to buy me a car." He said this with pride.

"Red, that's great! With all the extra work you've been doing, it won't take long." He'd come a long way from the frightened little boy who couldn't get a good grade in school and had dropped out his freshman year, to this young man who felt secure enough to want to buy his own car.

The next weekend, Red and I got to the cabin on Thursday night. I told Eddie to bring Betty, if she still wanted to come, and be there in time for breakfast on Friday. I heard his truck coming up the hill and looked out the back door. Just then, I smelled coffee and heard it hiss as it boiled over onto the stove. Damn, I thought, and cleaned up the mess.

My dog barked a welcome to Eddie and Betty as they clambered down from the high seat of the pickup.

I put bacon in the pan and broke eggs into my old yellow mixing bowl. "Mmmmm, does that bacon ever smell good," Betty said. She helped Eddie off with his jacket and turned to me, "Can I help with anything?"

"Sure, we make toast the old-fashioned way here. Just take that loaf of bread and spread it on the broiler rack. When it gets brown, turn it over. Take it out and butter it when it's ready. By then the eggs and bacon should be done. You can get some of Mom's chokecherry jelly from the fridge"

I gave the eggs a final stir and then spooned them into an old blue serving bowl. The toast was ready. I poured coffee and we sat down to eat.

"Lordy that was good, Hazie! There's nothing like getting up with the sun and coming to the mountains for breakfast. I was hungry as a horse." Eddie nuzzled against Betty. She put an arm around him and drew him close.

Betty helped me with the dishes and we had them out of the way in a few moments. I couldn't help but appreciate the lithe grace of this girl. Her blue jeans were faded from many washings. They fit so snugly she looked like she had been poured into them. Her waist was cinched tightly with an old belt that looked like a hand-me-down from one of her brothers. Her blue-checked shirt accented the blue of her eyes. This morning she had pulled her hair back tightly into a ponytail. The whole effect, from her high cheek bones and deep-set eyes, to the slightly concave hollows beneath her hip bones, was one of lovely bone structure, padded just enough to let everyone know she was a woman and not a long-legged boy.

"Red, would you get those tools out of the trunk?" Eddie called. "I had them sharpened. The axe and the grub hoe, too."

"I'll bet Red will appreciate some sharp tools," I commented, "I know he hates a dull axe." Red went toward the car, looking back as Eddie laughed.

Red ran his fingers through his shock of unruly red hair. "Yeah Eddie, if you've got any trees, or anything tough to chop down, be sure and give me a dull axe. I wouldn't know how to work with some good sharp tools."

Red was chiding Eddie and me about the first time he worked for us at the cabin. We didn't have the proper tools and wore ourselves out trying to use a dull axe and a saw that hadn't been sharpened for ages. Red kidded us about trying to gnaw the lower branches off the tall pines so we could have a view. Since then, we had acquired some good tools and a proper ladder.

Eddie and Red coaxed the stubborn little tractor into life. Betty and I put the axe, the grub hoe, and a short, sharp knife on the back of the tractor.

Eddie beckoned to Betty with his foot. "Climb up and I'll give you a ride to the bottom of the hill."

Red and I watched them as we walked down the hill. I smiled at Red, but all I got in return was a scowl.

At the bottom of the hill, Betty got off the tractor and watched Eddie maneuver it into place near the roots of the oak brush. Red pulled the chain tight around a root and stood back as Eddie gave the engine just enough gas for a steady pull.

"How on earth does Eddie manage to run that tractor?" Betty asked. "I don't see how he can back it when Red signals him, stop it just so, and then give it just enough gas to pull those darned roots."

"I can't explain it, Betty. When they get this bunch of roots pulled, why don't you ride up there with Eddie and he will show you how he does it. All I know is that he has better control over it than any of us. He seems to know just how much strain the chain will take and just how much power the tractor needs to do the job."

I ruefully remembered how Eddie tried to teach me all the fine points of driving the tractor. I goofed every time I got in a tight spot and gave it too much gas so that it hopped like a scared jackrabbit. I would have a time getting it started again and would finally give up. I told Eddie that if we were to ever get the damned oak brush pulled, he would have to drive the tractor, and let me and Red fasten the chains.

Betty and I were using the axe and knife to get at small roots and dig them out. We had quite a stack. By ten thirty I was spitting cotton. I knew Red and Eddie must be thirsty, too. "How about taking a break?"

I yelled at Eddie over the noise. "I've got a pitcher of lemonade in the fridge."

Betty walked beside Eddie and reached up with a wad of Kleenex and wiped the sweat off his face. Red and I trudged behind, not saying anything. When we got to the cool of the cabin Eddie said, "Whew, I'll bet it's a hundred and five in town today. It feels like it's that hot here."

Betty and I filled tall glasses with ice and lemonade. Betty placed Eddie's cup where he could reach it and we just sat silently, quenching our thirst and getting a short rest.

"I wish old Cradwell would show up about now. We could get those logs unloaded and sort of see what we've got." Eddie said.

"It won't take more than a couple of hours to finish up those roots, will it?" I asked.

"That's about it. It sure looks great. I didn't realize how open it would be with that brush gone. It will be better this winter too, give the sun a chance to shine through and warm things up."

Eddie got up, stretched, and gave me a nod. I went with him to the bathroom. When we came out, Betty said, "Say Eddie, do you think you could teach me to drive that tractor?" She looked at Eddie over the rim of her glass.

"Why sure, if you really want to, but it will crunch your stomach down into your shoes."

"Wait'll my brothers find out I can drive a tractor!" Betty squealed, forgetting her poise for a moment and acting her age. Then she added, almost as an afterthought, "They never would let me drive, said I was too young. I'll show 'em!"

"You'd better watch her, Eddie. Next thing she'll want to drive your car." Red's freckled face looked blank, but his green eyes were wary. Eddie would never let Red drive his blue Buick, his pride and joy.

"Oh, I guess Betty's old enough to learn to drive a car." Eddie said, and then glanced at her, almost as if he was wondering how long this added bait would keep her interested.

"Man, what's your mother going to say if you let some girl drive your car, when you won't even let her drive it?" Red seemed about to continue along this line, but something in Eddie's silent gaze suddenly shut him up, and I could see a flush creep over his already ruddy face and merge with the red of his hair. Red laughed a little uncomfortably, pushed his chair back with a loud screech, and said, "Well I guess we'd better get back to that damned oak brush."

On our way out, I reached into the hall closet and pulled out my old work gloves. I fumbled around and found two battered straw hats. "Here." I handed one to Betty. "You'd better wear this. The sun really beats down here in the mountains and there isn't any shade where we'll be working now."

She placed the hat on her head at a jaunty angle. Despite its dilapidated condition, she wore it with the air becoming a fifty-dollar creation. We walked down the slope toward our work site.

Eddie motioned to Betty with his foot, "Come on Betty, and climb up here. This tractor wasn't built for two, but you can sit on the toolbox until you get an idea of how the gears work. Then maybe we can both sit in the seat, and I'll show you how to drive this thing until you catch on." He motioned toward the toolbox, a fairly large, precarious-looking perch at the right of the high driver's seat.

Red called derisively from where he was squatting, snubbing one of the chains tight. "Better watch her, Eddie. You'll dump her off when that jumps out from under you. You'll pitch her flat on the ground."

I fastened another chain then worked my gloved fingers down through a matted layer of leaves into the soft loam. I had to bring the grub hoe to get at the gnarled root cluster before I could tighten the chain.

"Okay Eddie, we've got them fastened," I called. "Give it your best pull." Red and I stood back out of the way, and then waited as Eddie explained the fine points of handling the tractor.

"See this little cross bar here?" He pointed with the toes of his left foot to the bar between the brake and the clutch.

"Yes," Betty murmured her head close to his as they leaned down and looked at the bar. "Well, you push down on both the brake and the clutch, then slip the crossbar into place so they will stay down while you start the engine and put the gears into low range." Eddie showed her as he talked, his feet fairly flying through all the motions.

"You're going to have to slow down, Eddie. Your feet go so fast I can't see everything you do." Betty told him.

"Okay, I'll slow down. Then you start the engine." Eddie raised his right foot and with his big toe, turned the key in the ignition. When the engine started, Eddie joggled the gas feed with the toes of his left foot until it was running smoothly. "Now, you push the gears into low." And with the toes of his right foot, he showed her where low was on the shift bar. "Now, at the same time, you release the crossbar." With the toe of his left foot, he deftly released the bar, let up on the brake, and slowly released the clutch so he could get an even pull on the chain. With his left foot on the crossbar, Eddie released it, at the same time releasing the brake. Then with the heel of his left foot on the clutch and the toes of the same foot on the gas feed, he slowly released the power of the engine against the load on the chain until all the slack was taken up.

The chain tightened. The engine growled, digging the tractor's huge rear wheels into the soft earth as Eddie gave the engine more gas. All of a sudden, the stubborn roots pulled free of Mother Earth and sent cascades of soil spraying into the air. We all gave a big cheer.

Eddie had his right foot on the steering wheel, gripping the wheel between his big toe and the rest of his toes. His feet were so strong that he could hold it on course through almost anything.

"But Eddie, how can I learn all this?" Betty asked.

"I'll teach you. It isn't hard once you get on to it." I heard a sure note in Eddie's voice. He stopped the tractor and called, "It's time for lunch. I'm going to show Betty how to drive this tractor without a load on it."

Red and I watched as they dodged in and out of the trees. Betty squealed as they went around a corner too fast. Eddie was showing off, I thought, but who could blame him with such a great audience.

Then Eddie said, "All right now, you can drive it up the hill." And he changed seats with Betty.

"Climb on the back and we'll give you a ride up the hill," he called to Red and me.

"I think Red and I'll walk, Eddie. It will take you a while. I want to call Morey and get lunch on the table."

I called Morey. He wanted to stay in town. He had some exciting tests going and it would give him a chance to work on them. "I'm sick of all this business stuff and everything that goes with it," he said. "I'll be glad when we can go to New York and do what we enjoy doing."

I got lunch on the table. Eddie and Betty finally parked the tractor and came in.

"She's gonna make a good driver." Eddie told us, paying no attention to Red's silence.

"That's great. Betty, you've got a good teacher." I told them.

"Yes, well look at me. My knees are shaking. I was scared to death that I was going to hit a tree. That darned tractor is hard to steer."

But I could tell she was proud of herself.

We were putting the last of the lunch things away when we heard the sound of old Cradwell's truck laboring up the hill. Eddie and Red scraped back their chairs and went to meet him. Red hadn't said a word all through lunch, just sat with a scowl on his face.

Betty turned to me. "What gives with Red, anyway? At first he acted like he liked me. Now all at once I'm poison. What did I do to him, anyway?" She looked puzzled and defiant.

"You haven't done anything to him, Betty. It's a long story. I'll give you the low-down when we have time. All I can say for now is that the poor kid is jealous."

"Jealous, jealous of what, for Pete's sake?"

"He's jealous of you and Eddie. You see, for a long time he's had Eddie all to himself. Red didn't have any close friends. He was a slow learner who dropped out of school his freshman year. Eddie knew his father and mother and talked them into letting Red stay at the ranch and help our mother when she needed help. Later Eddie gave him a job at the car lot and taught him to drive. All of this has helped Red believe that he could do something. Now, with you here, he just feels left out and he's jealous."

"I sure don't want to hurt his feelings. He doesn't look like he'd need Eddie or anyone else, the big..." Betty stopped, not finding a word to express what Red seemed like to her.

"Don't let that strong body and wise remarks throw you. He's just a mixed-up little kid underneath. It's only in the last few months that he has been able to speak up for himself." I hoped she would understand.

As we left the cabin she said, "Well, I wish he'd quit picking on me, but if that's the way it is, I'll try not to get mad at him."

Well, that's a start, I thought.

Ed yelled out to Betty, "Come on, lazybones. Help me throw these logs off the truck."

I watched as Betty nimbly climbed up over the high truck bed. Eddie told her how to roll the log rounds out of the truck so they wouldn't crack.

Old Cradwell came and stood beside me, his seamed, leathery face showing the years he had spent in the sun of summer and the bitter cold of winter. His body was crippled by rheumatism and you could almost hear him creak as he walked. I could remember when he had come to the country dances when I was a little girl. His body had been tall and strong and he was one of the best dancers around.

Cradwell's fingers clutched at the bowl of his pipe. Between puffs he asked me about Mom and Dad and commented on the work we had done at the cabin.

"Well, I guess I'd better help them unload that wood," I said. "I'm sure glad you could bring it down today. It's just exactly what I wanted."

"You're going to have to go some to beat your brother at unloading that truck," Cradwell remarked. "He sure can handle those feet of his." He watched Eddie deftly grasp the rough bark on the edge of a heavy round with the toes of his right foot, balance it against his left leg, then with a quick flick of his foot, send it rolling easily off the back end of the truck.

"Yeah, he keeps us all on our toes." I answered as I climbed into the truck. I cleared a little place to stand, stooped, and picked up the heavy wood to place it where I could give it a roll. We were soon down to the scrap stuff and the limbs Cradwell had sawed up for us to use as firewood.

Eddie called to Cradwell and asked if he could move the truck close to the door to the basement. That way we could unload the scraps directly into the basement.

"Sure Eddie. You just show me where you want this truck and I'll put her right there for you." Old Cradwell climbed laboriously into the cab.

Eddie walked down toward the back of the cabin, stood near the door to the basement and directed Cradwell right up to it. "That's it!" Eddie held up his foot with a stop motion.

When the truck stopped, Eddie said, "If I shove this scrap over the end, can the rest of you toss it to each other and heave it clear to the back of the basement?"

"Sure Eddie," I jokingly answered. "We'll pretend we're a bucket brigade, and try to put out a fire at the far end of the basement."

Eddie stepped onto the high running board of the truck. He climbed to the solid ledge at the bottom of the truck bed using his chin and shoulder again to help him balance. First he got one leg up over the edge, then the other. The hard part was over. From a sitting position on the high edge of the truck bed, he gave a little jump and landed on the bed. He was ready to start shoving the broken chunks to us. We waited below him.

I turned to Betty, "Do you want to stand out here and throw the chunks to me inside the door? I'll throw them on to Red. He can give them the final heave ho. Okay with you, Red?"

"Yeah, sounds like a good idea, start throwin'." he said.

It didn't take long to empty the truck. Red got rid of some of his mad by giving the big chunks of wood a strong throw. He grunted with satisfaction every time they hit.

I asked Cradwell in for a cold glass of lemonade and paid him. I told him how happy we were with the rounds and invited him back to see how they would look when we finished laying them.

As his truck went over the hill and out of sight, I looked at the piles of uneven rounds. A heady scent of pine rose from them. I could imagine this mixed with the acrid odor of creosote. I wondered how long it would take the sun, wind, and weather to turn the bright yellow of the fresh cuts to a soft gray.

"You weren't joking when you said you bought the whole tree," I told Eddie. "See how twisted it is. I can see why he couldn't cut it into lumber, but it's perfect for what we want. We can make paths from the road down to the cabin, a nice area around the back porch and down to the lower level. I'll bet we even have enough to go clear to the well if we want to."

"Well, we've got all day tomorrow to get started. I brought out two five-gallon cans of creosote. If that isn't enough we can get more." Eddie sounded eager to start.

"It's almost six," I reminded him. "I'm going to Rye to buy some steaks but first, I'm going to mix myself a tall bourbon and soda. How about you guys, do you want a drink? I've got Cokes, rum, and about anything else you can think of. What can I mix for you?"

Betty spoke up, "I'll have a tall Coke with lots of ice and a little shot of rum."

"Okay, that I can do. Eddie and Red, how about you?" I waited.

"How about it Red, do you want to try a rum and Coke?" Eddie said.

"Sure, might as well." Red sounded more like his old self.

"Okay. Betty, do you want to help me?" I asked, and we started mixing drinks.

I took our drinks to the back porch, which was actually a small deck. It was large enough for a couple of chairs and, since we had cut the bottom limbs off the pine trees and got rid of the oak brush thickets, you could see the rolling plains to the east. I put some crackers and cheese on a platter, knowing it would be gone by the time I got back. We sat and relaxed, the first cool breezes of evening fanning our cheeks.

I finished my drink and called to Eddie, "Is there anything you want from the store?"

"No, we're fine, just hungry." He laughed. It was a standing joke. Eddie and Red were always hungry.

The little market in Rye had the best steaks you could buy anywhere. I selected half a dozen and a dozen ears of corn and some garden fresh tomatoes. Strawberries and a half gallon of homemade ice cream completed my purchases. I bought a small ice cream cone for my dog and held it for him to lick as we went up the hill. The kids had spoiled him rotten by letting him lick on their ice cream cones and now I bought him his own.

Eddie had the charcoal just about ready in the outdoor barbecue pit. I put water on for the corn and made a salad while Betty set the table. I took Eddie to the bathroom and gave his face a good scrubbing.

By then it was time to put the steaks on the charcoal and the corn in the kettle. It didn't take us long to demolish the food. I looked around the table and couldn't help but think we must look like a bunch of stuffed, contented cats.

Later, we had all showered and were lounging by the fireplace. Although we were all dog-tired, it wasn't late.

"Does anyone want to play some poker before we turn in?" I asked, looking toward Eddie and Betty where they sat on the couch, and at Red where he sprawled in front of the fireplace.

Eddie and Betty paused in their conversation and in the silence Red spoke up, his voice jeering, "Oh, let 'em alone, can't you see they've got personal things to talk about?"

Eddie flushed. Betty sat up straighter. I thought, *Why Red's trying to pick a fight. The poor kid, he's been lying there eating his heart out and the only way he can think of to get even is to pick a fight.*

I spoke up quickly. "How about it, are you all too tired? Would you rather just sit here for a while? Should I make some fudge?" I was running out of ideas.

"Yeah, put some fudge on, Hazie, I'll count out the poker chips and we'll play for a little while." Eddie said.

He got up, stretched, and reached for the chip holder in the middle of the round coffee table. He started to count out chips and put them in neat little piles. As he dealt the cards he said, "God, I'm tired." Then he turned to Betty, "How about you, Betty?"

"I sure am, too, and look at my hands. I think I wore some blisters on them." She held her hands out for Eddie to look at.

"Here, let me see. You probably got them pulling on all those levers this afternoon." He lifted his right foot and stretched it out to take Betty's hand.

I watched, my breath caught in my throat. I waited to see if Betty would draw back, not wanting to be touched by Eddie's feet. But Betty didn't flinch, she moved closer and held her hands, palm up, to Eddie's touch and examination. He stroked the blisters with his toes. Then he dropped his foot and said, "We'll get you some gloves before you do anything else. Gosh, your hands must be tender." Then he said to me, "Look Hazie, don't you think a couple of these blisters should be opened?"

I looked. "I sure do. I'll get a needle and sterilize it. I'm sure we have alcohol and mercurochrome in the medicine chest.

"Gee, they don't hurt that much," Betty protested. "Wait 'til we finish playing cards." Betty picked up her cards, embarrassed that a fuss had been made over her.

"Stay around here long enough and you'll get toughened up," Red said.

"Well I don't care. I'm learning to drive the tractor anyway." Betty answered him.

Eddie broke in, "Sure, and you're doing fine, too. You really started picking it up fast after you started using the gears."

I chuckled, thinking of the system Eddie and Betty finally worked out. She shifted the gears. Eddie fed the gas and handled the clutch. It was hilarious at times, but having to actually coordinate with Eddie taught her much faster than just watching.

By the time the fudge cooled we were all ready to quit playing cards. I made coffee, but after a while, even that failed to keep us from wanting to go to bed. As I carried our empty cups to the kitchen, Eddie followed me.

"Did you find everything I'll need to open those blisters for Betty? I'll open them, and then I'm going to hit the sack."

"Sure, just a minute, I've got it all together. All you need to do is sterilize the needle." I laid everything out on the coffee table where he could get at it.

I watched. Eddie carefully unscrewed the lid from the bottle of alcohol with the toes of his right foot. He poured some onto a piece of cotton and wiped the needle with it, then stuck the needle in the bottle cork. He swabbed the blisters with cotton, working gently as Betty flinched a bit. Then he gently inserted the needle flat against the flesh until it entered the blister. He squeezed. Fluid ran out leaving the blister flat. Soon he had taken care of all the blisters. He painted them with mercurochrome and sat back.

"That should do it." He looked at Betty.

"You know, Eddie, that didn't hurt a bit. I can't believe how much better it feels." She held her hands up for me to see.

"I was afraid it would hurt, but you didn't even squirm," Eddie praised her.

"Well, I guess I'll get ready for bed." Eddie stretched. He stood up and I followed him into the bathroom.

As we came out to go to Eddie's room, Betty stood waiting, a box of bobby pins in her hand. Her hair fell softly about her shoulders. She looked like a little girl wrapped in her faded blue bathrobe.

"Do you have an old glass I can put some water in?" she asked me. "If I don't pin up my hair it will be a mess tomorrow."

"Sure, I'll get you one, Betty. There are extra blankets in the closet if you get cold. It really gets cold at night here."

"I can't believe how cold it gets. In Nebraska it stays so hot all night you can hardly breathe. I'm going to love sleeping up here." Betty hugged her robe more tightly around her, filled the glass with water, and started for her room. She turned and said, "Good night everyone, see you in the morning."

Eddie called to her, "Yep, get plenty of sleep. You've got a lot more to learn about drivin' that tractor tomorrow."

Red stood wide-legged before the fireplace and just grunted something and went to the sun porch where he slept.

By the time Eddie and I got ready for bed, Red was snoring happily. *Thank God for sleep*, I thought, as I felt a surge of pity rush over me. I hoped Red would get over his jealousy and enjoy what we were doing.

I caught glimpses of the rising sun as its rays filtered through the tall pines to the east. I put a pot of coffee on, sure that the smell of it would wake Eddie and Red. Betty was already up. I could hear her puttering about in her bedroom.

Eddie came out, sleepy-eyed, carrying his pants and shirt under his chin. We went into the bathroom where I washed his face and ran a comb through his close-cropped hair. When we came out, Red was waiting.

It took Betty a bit longer to get ready for the day's work, but she wore a pair of jeans as faded and worn out as the rest of our clothes. I laughed, "We look like some escapees from a chain gang, don't we?"

As we were eating breakfast, I asked Eddie, "Do you think the market might have some ice tongs laying around? I remember they used to have an ice house before they got packaged ice delivered."

"I'll give them a call. If they do, Betty and I can go down and pick them up while you and Red get an assembly line ready." Eddie called. Sure enough, they had ice tongs and were glad to let us borrow them.

Red and I got several of the rounds laid out. We filled the tub just deep enough to cover the bottom of a round as we dipped it, and placed piles of logs at intervals down the hill. We were ready to go.

The tongs proved to be a Godsend. Red picked up a round and set it in the tub. We let the creosote soak in for just a minute. Then, with the tongs, I would take the round out and pass it to Eddie. He would get it into position and Betty would move it so there would be about two inches space between rounds

"Let's take five," I called out after a while. "I need a little rest." Eddie, Betty and Red promptly dropped what they were doing.

We sat in the shade on the back porch drinking lemonade and admired our efforts.

"When the rounds get settled in and you plant some clover around them, they are going to be beautiful," Eddie said. "I don't see any reason why they won't last a long, long time."

"I don't either. I know fence posts treated with creosote don't rot. Why should these rounds be any different? As fast as it's going, we're going to be through by noon tomorrow." I said happily.

"It's going to take an hour to get all this goop off our hands. I'm just going to throw my clothes in the garbage. They weren't much good anyway." Eddie laughed. He suggested that we use any remaining rounds to make an area around the barbecue pit, so it wouldn't be muddy.

By noon the next day we were finished. Eddie and Red cleaned out the tub as best they could and gathered everything we had to take to town. Red put the tools we wouldn't need again in the pickup. Everything else went in the basement. He locked the door and came up the walk.

I had lunch ready.

"I'm going to wash up. I don't think I could eat a bite with this smelly stuff on my hands." Red said.

"Here's a bar of Lava soap, Red." I handed it to him. "I used it on my hands and Eddie's feet. It works pretty well.

"Yeah, it even worked on my hands." Betty held her hands up.

"How are your blisters today?" I asked.

"Oh, they're practically gone. I can't believe they healed that fast."

Eddie chimed in, "Well, you had a good doctor."

"Okay all of you," I interrupted. "As soon as we finish lunch I'm going to pack up the kitchen things. Betty, could I get you to strip the beds and put the sheets and dirty towels in the trunk of my car?" It was great to have so much help.

"Darn it, Hazie, why didn't we think to bring the camera? I sure would love to have a picture of these walks and all of us in our creosote-stained rags." Eddie laughed.

"You can all come up next weekend, just for fun," I said. "I'll be sure to bring the camera."

When we got to the ranch, the first thing Betty did was tell her brother George, "I learned to drive the tractor, and you should see the walks we made out of logs!"

I hadn't realized just how excited she had been to do all that.

I looked at Eddie. I realized that he was happy too, for her, and for himself.

62 "Just a Hindrance"

$\mathcal{M}$orey and I took a brief trip to Durham, North Carolina to meet with Dr. Rhine at Duke University. From there we went to New York and met with Morey's college friend, Lenny Oestricher who showed me several apartments and before we returned to Colorado, Morey looked at two of them. He gave Lenny an idea of what he wanted and Lenny said he would find us something when we were ready.

When we met Dr. Rhine he had given Morey a book to read on our way home. We'd settled down and after Morey had read for awhile, he practically knocked me out of my seat as he shoved the book in my face. "Here read this! If he can do it, I can do it!"

I read the passage he had marked. I noted that the book had been written by Sir Dr. Alexander Cannon, an English psychiatrist, and it told how Dr. Cannon, using hypnosis, had taken his patients back to infancy, but he hadn't stopped there. He had taken them back into past lifetimes, and through these past lives, had often cured them of underlying fears that had crippled their lives today.

He grabbed the book back. "You know I can do it! Don't you?" He didn't wait for my answer; he was deep into the book again.

Oh my! I thought, *here we go again!*

When we got home, the first thing I did was call Eddie.

"Hazie, I got a call from John Seeley. He says the conference in Los Angeles regarding prosthesis devices for paraplegics is on and will start the first of next week. He would like for us to come out with all expenses paid. We've got five days to get there!"

"That doesn't give us much time…but sure I can do it, how about you?" I asked.

"Sure, I can make it!" he answered.

"That will give us plenty of time. I want to take Mom and Dad. They've never seen California and the states in between. We could visit the Grand Canyon on the way. What do you think?" I was excited just thinking about it.

"I'll tell them when I get home tonight. That will give them time to get ready. Me too!" he laughed.

So it was decided.

We had left the Grand Canyon earlier in the morning. My mind kept skipping back and forth over both what we had seen while standing on the edge, and what we had said while standing on the edge. I hoped this trip would help Eddie to clear his mind of doubts.

I thought of all this and of the day we left Pueblo to start on this trip. I looked over at Eddie as he sat on his leather seat and expertly drove along Route 66. His face didn't tell me anything, and I hesitated to start a conversation about how he felt. Right now I hoped against hope that this conference somehow would change his mind. Perhaps make him see more clearly that he could marry and have a life away from family.

"Do you want me to drive for awhile, Eddie? Looks like Mom and Dad are taking a little nap." I asked.

"No, this stretch of road is pretty boring. I'm not tired. You can drive when we get to the next town." He didn't say any more.

By mid-afternoon, we had left the desert country of Arizona behind us and were ready to cross the huge Hoover Dam with its breath-taking view of the Colorado River with Lake Mead backed up for miles behind it. We decided to stop and take a tour. Dad was especially impressed because of his work with dynamite and drilling in rock structures. Long after we had left and were on our way again, he was still talking about this marvel of dam building he had just seen.

By evening we were on the outskirts of San Bernardino, California, and Mom couldn't quit talking about all the palm trees, flowers, and lush vegetation.

"Do you think we can take some of these flowers home with us?" she asked.

Eddie responded, "Sure Mom, we'll find some way to keep them damp and I'll bet they'll grow for you!"

There were all kinds of motels and we finally saw one that looked good to all of us. We had a good dinner and didn't waste any time getting to bed and to sleep. We were up very early the next morning and on our way.

We bought a map and found the UCLA campus and then decided we would look for a rental on Malibu Beach. We drove up and down the beach having a good time comparing motels, apartments, and just about everything we saw. We finally found a place that advertised a small apartment by the day or week. That sounded great plus there was a restaurant and a deli across the street. If Eddie and I got tied up in meetings, Mom and Dad could walk across and get a bite to eat.

We looked the apartment over, and over Mom's protests, we rented it for five days. Mom's objection was that the apartment was built on pylons and although the front part of it was on solid ground, the back was over the water. It was low tide when we rented it and later that evening as the tide started to come in, Mom was sure we would all be drowned.

"Just look at those waves!" Her voice had a real note of fear in it.

"Yes Mom. And look at those kids out there on surf boards! Doesn't that look like fun? They wouldn't be out there if the tide was dangerous," I told her but she still worried.

Eddie asked, "Mom, do you and Dad want to go with us? I called John Seeley and he can spend the evening with us. I thought we'd go to the deli across the street and get stuff for dinner."

"I don't think so Son. You and Hazel go pick up John. Dad and I will go to the deli. We can cross at the light, so don't worry about us."

"Okay, and when we get back, the tide will still be out, maybe I can talk you into a walk on the beach. How about it?" I asked.

"We'll see." Mom didn't commit herself. She still didn't trust this vast ocean, although she had to admit it fascinated her.

John Seeley was waiting for us in front of the dorm. I don't think he realized that Eddie could drive a car. I was sure that I had told him, but I couldn't help but grin at his look of amazement as Eddie deftly threaded his way through the afternoon traffic.

"I walked around the exhibit rooms today Eddie," John said. "Even I, as used as I am to all this…Well, I was amazed at the work being done in the field of prosthesis. We have a company from Belgium that looks to me like they are ahead of everyone in the field."

"I didn't know there would be that much interest in the armless." Eddie ventured.

"Yeah, well there is, and about time. It still will take time to perfect a lot of the ideas but a lot of big companies are trying. Take IBM, for instance. When I started working with Dr. Abt, he was more or less on his own. The Kessler Institute was backing him, then IBM got interested." John sounded like the impact of IBM becoming interested meant a lot to him.

"In what other ways has this been important John?" I asked.

"Well, for starts, I have a full time job with them. When I'm not working with Dr. Abt on the electric arm, I am being sent by IBM to seminars all over the country to give pep talks to various groups." John tried to explain.

"Do you think you will ever be sent to Colorado?" I asked.

"Yes. In fact I have a date early next summer to speak at the Air Force Academy. Perhaps you and Eddie could come up and listen to me make a fool of myself." He gave us a self-assured grin.

"We'll sure try. I don't know whether I'll be in Colorado or New York, but if I'm close, I'll be there." I told him. I thought it would be great if Eddie would go too. He needed to realize that he could be an inspiration to a great number of people.

When we reached the apartment, Mom made John welcome. Dad in his quiet way, asked him how he liked the ocean.

"I love it and I miss it. When I was small we lived near a beach and it became part of my life." He didn't say anymore and I wondered if this place had been near where he had the train accident that had cost him his arms.

Eddie turned to Mom, "I know you probably have dinner all ready, but can it wait until we all take a walk on the beach?"

"Sure, Dad and I will trail along. I've been waiting for you to go for a walk. I guess I'm still a little bit afraid of this ocean." Mom ventured.

There was an easy flight of stairs down to the beach and we all took our time, not wanting to hurry Dad and Mom.

The wind was kicking up and made it difficult to talk so we just enjoyed the feel of the salt spray on our faces. I looked back and saw that Mom was finding seashells that she put in her pockets, every now and then holding up a special one for Dad to see.

I nudged Eddie and motioned for him to look. I thought, they won't miss us now. I knew they would spend their time beach combing, and I wondered how many shells Mom would want to take home.

The first full day at the conference was mind-boggling for me. I hadn't realized how much research was being done all over the country. We stopped by the various booths and Eddie and I were fascinated by the arm being made in Belgium. Maybe because the hand was so life-like. It was covered in a soft leather that almost matched the skin tones of the wearer and the motions he could get out of it were amazing. John helped to explain that the motions were obtained by using a foot control system and it had a lot of possibilities for the future.

"However," he told us, "If you will notice, that arm doesn't have the range of activities the IBM arm has. Wait until you see what I can do with my arm."

"Will you be doing a full scale demonstration, John?" Eddie asked.

"Yes, tomorrow I'm scheduled to do my strip tease for everyone." He joked.

"Does it make you nervous, John?" I asked, thinking how hard it would be to get up in front of all these people and do what John would do.

"No, I'm used to it. And I want anyone interested to know they can accomplish almost anything if they set their mind to it!" His voice carried conviction.

Then we were in front of the IBM booth. Dr. Kessler was talking to a young man about sixteen. We learned that Sam had lost his arms in a farm accident when he fell off a tractor and the mower blades had mangled his limbs. He had been at Kessler Institute a short time and was just learning to use his prosthesis. John introduced Sam to Eddie.

"Sam, I want you to meet Eddie. Eddie will show you many of the things he can do with his feet tomorrow. He was born without arms but he can do almost anything with his feet. I want you to start learning to use your feet right along with your electric arm."

"Sure, I'll be glad to show you all I can," and Eddie and Sam stepped aside and started a conversation.

Eddie told me after he had talked to Sam, "Gosh Sis, I didn't realize how important it has been for me to have Dad and Mom for parents, and you for my Sis!" he said in a sober tone of voice.

"Why Eddie, I think that's the nicest thing I've ever heard you say. I've got to tell Mom and Dad!" I exclaimed.

"No Hazie. I want to tell them. I think we forget things that are important until it's brought home to us!" Eddie gave me a big grin as he walked toward the next booth.

About closing time, John walked over to us with Sam and Dr. Kessler in tow. "Eddie, Dr. Kessler would like for you to drive him and Sam around a bit. He would like Sam to see what you can do with your feet!"

"Why sure. My car's in the parking lot, is there any place special you would like to go?" Eddie asked, a sly little grin on his face. Oh, oh, I thought.

"No place special. Just show us a bit of the city," Dr. Kessler said.

I sat in back with John and Sam, and wasn't surprised when Eddie took off toward Hollywood and Mulholland Drive. We had been up there before and Mom had squealed when we encountered some of the hair pin curves on our way to the top. I looked over at John and noticed a big smile on his face.

When we got to the top Eddie stopped the car, parked, and waved his foot at the panorama of Los Angeles spread below us. "Where can you find a view like this?" he chortled.

Dr. Kessler turned to all of us and said, "The view is magnificent Eddie. But the way you handle this car and your confidence is what inspires me. It will give me the steam I need for a few more years of research."

"If it's not out of our way too much, I would like to meet your parents Eddie. I'd like to tell them what a wonderful job they have done in giving you the self confidence you have!"

"Why sure. I know they would like to meet you, too." Eddie answered.

John said, "Do you think it would be too much for them to spend a day at the conference? They could see me do my thing and perhaps get some ideas from it to help you."

"I think they would be honored to have you ask them John. I know they have been wondering just how all these things work." Eddie answered.

When we got to the apartment, Mom and Dad had just returned from a shell gathering trip. When John introduced Sam and Dr. Kessler, Mom said, "I'm so happy to meet you. I think your work is so very important. We didn't have anyone like you when Eddie was born."

Dr. Kessler responded, "From what I can see of Eddie and the things he has accomplished, I wish I could have had you on my teaching team all this time."

"We tried to do our best by the boy." Dad added.

After a few minutes of talk, Dr. Kessler said he must get back, "I hope you and Mr. Higgins can come to the conference tomorrow. We'd be proud to have you as our guests."

Mom accepted the invitation with a thanks and we were on our way back to the dorms. No one said much as Eddie drove through the late afternoon traffic.

We said our goodbyes until tomorrow.

Chairs fanned out in an ever widening semi-circle in front of the small stage. Mom, Dad, Eddie, and I sat in the second row. I was excited and apprehensive at the same time as I waited for John to make his appearance. Dr. Kessler and Dr. Abt said a few preliminary words and it was time for John to show us how he used his electric arms.

John made is entrance in a pair of red and white striped boxer shorts. I felt like giving him a whistle, but resisted the impulse. He stood there for a moment, his keen blue eyes, deep set in their sockets, surveying the room. He then turned his back on the audience, and made his way a few steps to a dresser. He opened the bottom drawer with the toes of his right foot, and getting his foot under the contraption, he turned to the audience and held up his electric arms.

"I don't want to seem to be dramatic, but these wires, leather straps, springs, and all the other mechanisms you are looking at, these are my arms. An extension of my being that I have learned to depend on for many of the things I do in my daily life. It took me almost a year to conquer them and make them work for me.

"And now, I want to show you the mechanics of making them work for you or for someone you know who has lost their limbs."

There wasn't a sound as John started doing all the things he had to do to get on with his daily business. We sat, entranced for almost an hour and a half, as he went through every possible item necessary to use the artificial arms in his daily life.

By the time he had told us about the different ways to bathe, dress, and do all the necessary things, I was worn out.

He told us that it had taken a little over a year for him to become proficient at doing all this. Now, he said, he could get up, don his arms, dress himself, and be ready to go out the door in about an hour. I thought to myself *this is miraculous!* I knew some women who took that long to curl their hair and pick out what they were going to wear for the day.

When he was through with his demonstration, Eddie and I went up and asked if he would join us for lunch. We had found a little place near the campus the day before that had great roast beef and we thought he might like it.

"Sure. I'm ready for a break. What did you think of my act?" he asked.

Mom spoke up, "You know John, I don't know how you do it day after day. It seems like it would be so hard for you." She wanted to baby him, just a little, I could tell.

"I just figure I'm lucky Mom. Can I call you Mom?" he asked.

"It would be an honor. I have learned a lot from you that I think will help Eddie," she told him.

Over dinner we talked about the conference. Eddie had a meeting with Dr. Kessler and Dr. Abt scheduled for the next morning. I didn't know what the outcome of this would be, but I had an inkling that Eddie wouldn't want to be saddled with the electric arm.

John asked us what we were going to do when the conference was over.

"I think we'll go home by way of Northern California. Dad has a daughter Gracie, who lives in Clear Lake, California. He hasn't seen her for years. Also, we'll get to see the Redwood Forest, and other things we'll never get another chance to see."

Eddie and I were at the center by eight the next morning. Dr. Abt and Dr. Kessler were there waiting for us.

"Well Eddie. Do you think you want to try to be fitted for an electric arm? Or for both arms?" Dr. Abt asked this with a little smile around the corners of his mouth and a twinkle in his brown eyes.

"I don't want to seem ungrateful. I've seen some marvelous things here the last few days. But, I don't think they are for me." Eddie answered.

"I thought that would be your answer, Eddie," Dr. Kessler said, and then added, "You've shown all of us what can done with determination and perseverance. I realize that you can do more with your feet than we can offer with a prosthesis at this time."

Dr. Abt turned to me, "I understand that you will be spending some time in New York. I would appreciate it if you would drop by once in awhile. Maybe we'll get a break-through that could be of help to Eddie."

"I would like to do that. Also, after we get settled in, if there is anything I can do in the way of volunteer work, I would be happy to do it."

"I'll take you up on that, Hazel," Dr. Kessler said. "With your experience you could be very helpful."

We said our good-byes to the two good doctors and John went with us. We sat over dinner for a long time, grateful that this little restaurant wasn't busy or noisy.

"So John, what are your words of wisdom for me?" Eddie asked, half jokingly.

"Eddie, I haven't said much about my wife and kids. Lois and I have been married almost seven years. John is just six and Joey is three. The best thing that ever happened to me to make me sit up and take notice, was marriage. Before that I was drifting along. Trying one thing after another and not being serious about anything. Marriage snapped me out of all that and made me into the guy I am today." John laughed.

"It evidently worked for you!" Eddie answered him.

I had told John just a little about Eddie and Betty. But the way John said what he had said, it was a statement of his true experience.

Soon it was time to go. I felt like I was leaving a lot of good friends. John put his artificial arms about Eddie and hugged him close. "I'll see you again, I hope. Meantime, good luck with your life!" He turned to Mom and Dad, "Take good care of him." John turned and went up the steps to the dorm. He would be leaving for New York the next day.

We went back to our little apartment, took a last walk on the beach, gathered a few more shells, and got ready for our trip the next day.

I lay awake, far into the night, thinking of the 'what-might-have-beens' and wondering what kind of a difference it would have made if Eddie could have been fitted with artificial arms.

Finally, I had to agree, at least in my mind, that he was right when he had said, "Hazie, forget about it. They would just be a hindrance. No help at all!"

63 Meet Mr. and Mrs. Edward Higgins

*T*he first thing we did after we got home and gave everyone big hugs and kisses, was to find a place for Mom to set out her plants. She had kept them damp all the way home and just knew they would grow for her. She selected a spot outside where it wasn't too sunny and carefully placed them in short rows. "This way, if I need to, I can cover them during the winter,"

The Bar-B-Que Pit kept George and Helen busy and I could see that they could use Betty's help. I wanted to, but didn't ask about Betty, who had returned to Nebraska. I thought I would let Eddie do what he was going to do. I knew he missed Betty. Coming back to the ranch was in a way, harder for him than being away. I wanted to talk to him but he didn't give me an opening, so I let it ride.

Almost two weeks later, I went to the ranch and Mom met me at the car.

"Eddie called Betty last night. They talked for over an hour. She's coming back!" She was out of breath by the time she finished telling me this news.

"I'll pretend you didn't tell me, Mom. I'll let Eddie tell me himself." *If he will,* I thought.

I stayed at the ranch for supper and when Eddie walked in I could see that he was happier than I had seen him for weeks. It didn't take him long to blurt out, "Betty is coming back. She should be here to-morrow!" His voice couldn't hide his excitement.

"Oh Eddie! I'm so glad. I know how much you've been missing her." I was happy for him and anxious all at the same time.

"Yeah, I guess being away from her showed me how much I care for her. I've been a damned fool, but it won't happen again!" Eddie stood up a little straighter as he said this.

Morey had made arrangements with the manager of the apartment he had rented in New York to take care of the boxes we had sent on ahead of our arrival. Our house in Pueblo now looked bare and un-loved. I had decided to spend the next couple of days at the ranch and Morey was staying at his folks' house.

The weather was cold and blustery. Mom was agonizing over our flying in such weather. "Mom," I told her, "It won't be as bad as driving from here to Trinidad. And probably a lot safer if the roads are icy."

I helped her cut out quilt pieces from old wool scraps to make a warm quilt for Eddie and Betty.

"They won't tell anyone what their plans are, but I know they are going to get married one of these days, and I want them to have a warm quilt."

Down through the years Mom had made warm, wool quilts for all of us. She cut the pieces into random patterns and sometimes did a star pattern or a wedding ring pattern. When I looked at the pieces she had cut, I wasn't surprised to see the wedding ring pattern emerging.

"They will love this quilt, Mom. Are you going to have enough wool to finish it?" I asked.

"No, I won't have. I was going to ask you if you would like to go to town with me tomorrow and go to the Salvation Army. I could prob-ably pick up a couple of wool coats in the colors I want. Then I could get this finished."

"Sure, until the weekend I am at loose ends. I have everything packed and shipped." I really needed something to keep me busy.

I changed the subject, "Mom, you and Dad are really comfortable up here on the hill, aren't you?" I asked.

"Why yes. It is just right for the two of us and I love the way the windows face south and with the house dug into the north it is really snug."

"And all your trees have a good start. It won't be long until you will have as much shade here as down at the other house." I looked out the window and pictured the five or six foot trees spreading their shade over the house.

"I think George and Helen are going to close the Bar-B-Que Pit until summer. He has a job with his brother at the packing plant...Where is Dad? I want to tell him good-bye." There, I had said it...'Good-bye' I didn't like the sound of it, but I had to face up to the fact that we were actually going to New York to live. I knew we'd be back part of the summers but somehow it seemed so final.

I walked up the little hill behind the house where the well and the big water tank were located. Dad had the door to the pump house open and as I looked in I could see that he was putting more insulation in the walls.

"What are you doing, Dad?" I asked as I stood there in the door. "Do you think it's going to get colder?"

"Yes, I do. I think the rest of this winter is going to be bad. Really bad! So far, it's been almost like Indian summer. It's getting ready to fool us."

I reached down to give him a hand up. He had built the pump house so that about six feet of it was below ground level.

"We'll be leaving tomorrow Dad. You take care of Mom and Dyanna and keep an eye on Eddie."

Dad pulled me close to him and kept his arm around my shoulders as he said, "Don't worry about anything here. We'll get along fine. We don't have the cattle or the pigs to worry about, and the few rabbits and chickens are no trouble. Your Mom and I are snug as bugs in a rug." He gave a little chuckle.

"I know you are. And I guess I thought Eddie would always be with you, but I think he and Betty will be getting married soon." I waited to see what he would say.

"Well, he doesn't spend much time at home anymore. He comes to sleep and sometimes they are off on a trip somewhere." Dad smiled.

"He'll be okay Dad. I know Mom has her doubts, but Eddie has a right to marry and have a family just like anyone else!"

"We tried all his life to bring him up to be, and do, like anyone else. And like I told your Mom, this isn't the time to stop." Dad's voice carried conviction in it, and I was glad because I knew he would help Mom to get over the fact that Eddie would go his own way.

"Come on now. Let's go to the house and see if Dyanna is there. I know she wants to say good-bye, too."

As we walked toward the house I noticed that Dad's steps were a bit unsteady. He was getting old and there's nothing anyone can do about it.

Mom and Dyanna were fixing a bite to eat. I heard Eddie's car and in a few moments Eddie and Betty came in.

Eddie came over to me and I gave him a hug. "I suppose you are ready to take off tomorrow, aren't you?" he asked.

Finally it was time to go. After hugs all around, Mom, with tears in her voice, said, "It seems like you're going to the ends of the earth. We're going to miss you so much!"

"I know Mom. But think of it this way, it's going to be exciting and I will be just a few hours away."

As I drove down past the big house and onto the highway, I drove slowly, remembering all the things that happened at the ranch, both good and bad.

By noon the next day Morey and I were on the plane headed for New York.

We arrived in New York mid-afternoon. They had cabs lined up at the airport and we grabbed one and went to the Waldorf Astoria where we would stay for the next few days.

The next morning we went to the apartment. It was on the seventeenth floor of a light brick building. We told the elevator operator, "Seventeen" and he introduced himself, "I'm Pat and you must be Mr. and Mrs. Bernstein. I have all the boxes you sent in the storage room. I'll have them brought to the apartment right away."

"Thanks Pat. That would be great." Morey told him and gave him a tip when we got off the elevator.

We walked into a small vestibule with a coat closet. To the right I saw a bedroom and I supposed the bath was beyond that. To the left was a living room and dining area. I walked through this looking for the kitchen. "Hey, Morey! Come see this kitchen. There isn't even a stove, just a two burner gas plate. How on earth did they ever cook anything?"

"You'll think of something. I think Lenny told me that the people who own this live in Connecticut. They had this apartment for when he needed to be in town overnight and to entertain guests."

"Well, it's sure shabby. It's going to take a week to get it clean enough to live in." Already I could see that doing anything drastic would be an uphill battle.

The next day I asked Pat, our elevator man where to find some good help. With his help, I found a cleaning service and a company that shampooed carpets and furniture. By the end of the week it was as good as it was going to get.

Morey would start classes at Columbia the first of the week, and I enrolled in an English/Writing class. I intended to keep busy hoping it would help me not to miss the folks at home. I talked with Mom and Eddie at least once a week, and they kept me posted on what was going on.

One evening Eddie called. "Hazie, you can't imagine what Betty's father has done!" His voice was shaking and I couldn't tell if he was mad or hurt.

"Slow down, Eddie. Now tell me what happened! I couldn't imagine old George doing much of anything but sitting in a corner, chewing tobacco, and spitting it at a can he used as a cuspidor. "He told Betty he wasn't going to have his daughter marry a cripple and that she better go back to Nebraska to her mother and forget about me!" I had never heard Eddie so upset before.

"So what did Betty say?" What had brought this on? I wondered. "She just said she should have seen it coming. That he had always been mean and that her brothers had all left home as soon as they could. I guess he beat on them and at one time he was going to beat her with the harness rein but her brother George kept him from it." Eddie seemed a little calmer.

"Did he forbid her to see you?" I asked.

"Oh yes. Threatened her." he didn't elaborate.

"So what are you going to do?" He must have some kind of a plan, I thought.

"I talked to her brother George and he told me to just ignore him. Said their dad's done nothing but make trouble for all of them all their lives. He told me to wait until just before Easter and he would go with Betty and me to Nebraska so I could meet her mother. He seemed to think she would be able to help us. Meantime, we're going together. What can he do?"

I didn't see how he could do too much. Old George depended on George and Helen at this point for everything. He had hounded his sons to the point that none of them would stay on and help him work his farm so he had to give it up.

"Just take it easy Eddie. As long as you and Betty love each other, I don't see how he can do anything." I hoped he wouldn't let it break them up.

"I was hoping you would say something like that. I'm not going to let her go. You can count on that." His voice sounded better, and I had a hunch old George had bit off more than he could chew.

We talked awhile longer. He assured me that Mom and Dad were fine. The next evening Mom called. When I heard her voice I didn't know whether she would stick up for Betty's dad or not. I knew she had been worried that Betty might take off with someone else. I needn't have worried. The first thing she said was, "Do you know what that ornery old George told Betty?!" she started out.

And I heard the story all over again. "So what do you think Eddie should do Mom?" I waited for her answer.

"Why, I think he should tell him to go…to the devil! They'd make good company!" She was most vehement.

"Well, Mom, I'm glad you feel that way. Eddie and Betty are going to need someone to stand up for them. With her mom so far away, she needs you." I told her.

"That's what I told Eddie and Betty. I want them to be happy, and they will be if everyone leaves them alone." she added.

"Did you get the quilt finished, Mom?" I asked.

"Yes, and you should see it. It is beautiful. Betty has been helping me with the finishing touches. She wants me to teach her how to sew." Mom had a proud note in her voice.

Everything seemed to calm down. Morey and I were so busy we caught ourselves coming and going. I was caught up in the excitement of New York and took advantage of everything I could.

I hurried to answer the phone. Morey had been expecting a call from his dad and had told me to take the message. But this was Eddie. "Hi Sis! You're talking to a married man!" he laughed.

"Well, congratulations! When did all this happen?" I asked

"We took George's advice and we're here in this little town outside of Beatrice, Nebraska. We're staying with Betty's mom. You would re-

Mr. And Mrs. Edward Higgins

ally like her Hazie. I can see why she left George. She is full of fun and I just can't imagine her ever married to that old sour puss." Eddie was talking so fast the words were tumbling over each other.

"Tell me all about it! Did George stay for your wedding?"

"No, he went up with us, visited with his mom for awhile, and then took a bus back to Pueblo. He couldn't stay away from his job too long. But he wanted to tell his mom how old George had been acting."

"And you liked Betty's mom? I asked.

"I sure did. Betty looks a lot like her, but her mom is more outgoing. She laughs a lot and seems like a happy person." Then he added, "I just can't imagine her ever married to Betty's dad.

"Her mom went with us to get the license and a blood test. Then we had to wait three days so during that time, her mom helped Betty find a dress."

"So what kind of a dress did they find?" I was so glad for him that Eva had been helpful.

"Her dress was a pale yellow chiffon with a long skirt. I'm no good at describing dresses. You'll have a picture soon; then you can see." Eddie paused.

"Where did you get married?" I wondered if Betty had friends there who would come to the wedding.

"We were married by the preacher of Betty's mom's church. It was just a little church, but real pretty with stained glass windows." Eddie sounded as if he were there again.

"Did anyone else go with you?" I asked.

"No, just us. A friend of Eva's sang two beautiful songs for us and she came with us afterward."

"Where did you go afterwards?" I asked. I knew he must be getting tired of all my questions, but I couldn't shut up.

"That was about it, Sis. We stayed a couple more days and came home." Eddie still sounded excited.

"What did old George do or say when you got home?" I hoped he had the sense to wish them well.

"I guess George must have had a talk with him. He actually wished us well." I could sort of imagine this.

"So where are you going to live, Eddie" I wondered.

"The couple in the front apartment on Claremont moved, and Betty and I are living there. She has bought a couple of things and it is real nice. She says she likes it." Eddie gave a little laugh.

"How about Rusty? What does he think of all these moves?" I had given our dog, Rusty, to Eddie when we left.

"When we moved back into town, he ran away a couple of times, but he's fine now."

"Let me talk to Betty, I want to tell her how glad I am for both of you!" I waited until Betty got on the line.

"Betty, all I'm going to say now is that I'm so happy for both of you I want to cry! I know you are going to have a wonderful life together. What do you want for a wedding present?" I asked.

"Gosh Hazel. We really don't need anything, just whatever you want to give us." Betty sounded great and happy.

Eddie got back on the line, "Sis, don't go getting us a lot of stuff. Just come home and Betty will cook dinner for you and Morey." Eddie gave a big laugh.

"That sounds good. Well, I have to go. Take good care of each other and enjoy your happiness. I love you both!"

I walked out on the terrace and looked out over New York City. What will fate have in store for them? Will they meet the challenge life has handed them and make the most of it? Somehow I knew they would.

EPILOGUE

My brother Eddie died on January 31, 1984. He was 57 years old. The cause of his death was slow suffocation due to the hump in his back gradually collapsing his chest cavity so that his lungs could not expand sufficiently to take in air.

He left behind a handsome son, three beautiful daughters, and 12 wonderful grandchildren.

A FEW FAMILY PICTURES

Our Mother, Ethel Melinda
Mitchell/Higgins

Our Father, Arthur Edward
Higgins

My Brother Eddie,
Edward Ernest Higgins

Eddie's First Born Son,
Richard "Rick" Higgins

Proud Daddy with
Richard "Rick" and Kimala "Kim"

Eddie
with "Kim" a little older

Two of three beautiful daughters
Katherine Olivia "Kathi" and
Michelle Lynn "Chelli"

Son "Rick" with his wife
Deborah "Debbie" Parker

MAKING IT IN THE NEWSPAPER

There were numerous newspaper pictures and stories about Eddie through the years. The following is a sampling of a few:

1938

Who's Downhearted says Edward Higgins, 11-year-old boy, who was born without arms but is making good in life in spite of his disadvantages. He lives with his parents, Mr. and Mrs. Arthur E. Higgins, and his sister, Shirley Jo, at Prairie Junction, fifteen miles south of Pueblo. He has won a national penmanship contest, writing with his toes against thousands of boys and girls using their hands. He finished the sixth grade this year with "A" in all subjects. He operates a soda pop stand by the roadside, raises rabbits and uses a saw and hammer and can drive a car. He is shown here with his sister.

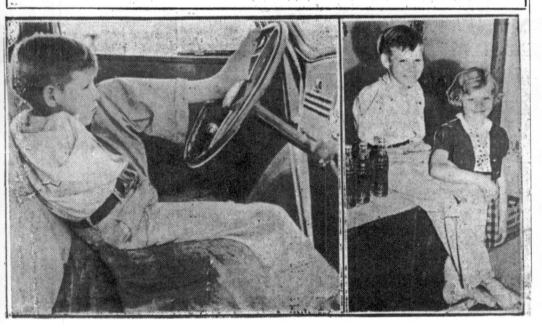

Grade School Days Will Be Over

Thursday for armless Edward Higgins, of Prairie Junction, when he will be graduated with honors from Verdi school. An "A" student, Edward is shown writing with his foot at his class room desk and on the blackboard. As a third grader, Edward won a national penmanship award. His teacher, Miss K'Niess Sewell of Pueblo, is shown in the inset, while in the group below are shown the members of the 1940 Verdi school graduating class. They are, from left to right: Karel Burk, Edward Higgins, Bobby Kurtz and Jean Bodle.

By ED ORAZEM

Edward Higgins, the boy who was born without arms, but who has not allowed his handicap to stand as a barrier in accomplishing everything within range of any other youngster of his age, is to be graduated Thursday night from the elementary school at Verdi.

Edward, 13 years old last Dec. 2, is to be graduated as the honor student of his class and will serve as valedictorian in his school's graduation exercises.

Verdi school is located about 1½ miles southeast of Pueblo and can be reached by turning off the Rye road a short distance south of the Fisher ranch. Or, it can be reached by turning to the left off the Rye road soon after passing Prairie Junction, where Edward's parents operate a service station and refreshment stand.

To become the honor student of his class Edward compiled the highest average of the group in the various studies during the school year now ending. An "A" student in every other year that he has attended school, Edward maintained that record in his "senior year," according to his teacher, Miss K'Niess, Sewell, graduate of Colorado State Teachers college at Greeley and Central high school of Pueblo.

Missing only four days of school the entire year, Edward attained his honor rating by excelling in writing, reading, arithmetic, Colorado and United States history, geography, English, spelling and art. When it is considered Edward has to write and draw with his feet, his accomplishment can only be termed remarkable, as Miss Sewell pointed out.

But, as it already has been written, this was not the first year that Edward accomplished the almost unbelievable. He won a national penmanship award as a third grader.

Reading, spelling, working arithmetic problems, English, geography, history and studies the like of

apparently it's no more difficult for him to write and draw with his feet than it is for the average person to do the same thing with his or her hands.

In his art studies, Edward sometimes is required to cut out figures with scissors, which sounds impossible. But, his teacher vows that he can use the scissors as adeptly as any pupil in the school. And, when it comes to writing, he can work with pencil or pen and paper, or chalk and blackboard. If he had to, he even could write his lessons on a typewriter.

There's little he can't do with his feet, even to pitching horseshoes, opening doors, threading needles, sewing, whittling with a knife, driving nails with a hammer, driving a car, removing caps from pop bottles.

One of the features of the graduation exercises is to be a presentation of a play, "Poison Ivy." Edward is to play the part of the policeman. Other members of the cast will be Kenneth Burk, Bobby Kurtz, Shirley Higgins, Edward's sister; Darlene Bodie, Jean Bodie, Ervin Stewart, Karel Burk and Miss Sewell.

The graduation address will be by Rev. Lawrence Carlton, pastor of Minnequa Congregational church. Bobby Kurtz will deliver the salutatory and Tommy Bodie will recite a poem. "The Student." Betty Stewart will recite "Annabelle Lou," another poem. Lon Martin will sing "South of the Border," which will be followed by poem, "The Learner," by Roland Harris; song, "Our Farewell Singing," by all the pupils; poem, "Ambitious," by Hugh Stewart; the play, song, "The Graduates," by the lower grades pupils; dialogue, "Why We Didn't Graduate," by Lon Martin, Ervin Stewart, Hugh Stewart, and

Roland Harris; reading, "Books, Why Can't You Tell," by Jean Bodie; accordion solo by Bobby Kurtz; song, "When Clouds Roll Away," by Karel Burk, Edward Higgins, Jean Bodie and Bobby Kurtz; class will by Karel Burk; class prophecy by Edward Higgins, Karel Burk, Bobby Kutrz and Jean Bodie.

The address by Rev. Mr. Carlton, valedictorion by Edward and a poem, "A Last Word," by Ervin Burk will conclude the program.

Friday, the annual school picnic will be held in City park here with both pupils and their parents and patrons of the school attending.

Edward, who aspires to become an attorney, expects to enter high school, probably in Pueblo, in the fall. His father and mother, Mr. and Mrs. Arthur E. Higgins, plan to move their home here or wherever it is decided to enroll him in high school.

January 20, 1939

PUEBLO YOUTH IS HONORED BY JOURNAL

Pueblo, Jan. 20.—Edward Higgins, 12-year-old Pueblo junior high school student who was born without arms, was named Thursday one of "ten outstanding young Americans of 1938" by Harry Miller, editor of Youth Today, a New York journal for high school students. Higgins was winner of the national award for penmanship despite his handicap.

PAGE
ditorial.
rial.
'our:

ST. LOUI

(78th Year)   ST. I

Uses Feet to Steer

—Associated Press Wirephoto.

EDWARD ERNEST HIGGINS of Pueblo, Colo., demonstrating how he drives an automobile even though he was born without arms.

ARMLESS DRIVER KEPT IT UNDER 60, HE SAYS, IS FREED

COLORADO SPRINGS, Colo., Dec. 15 (AP)—An armless motorist who says he has driven 16 years without accident was acquitted yesterday of speeding and reckless driving charges.

A justice court jury of five men and one woman deliberated 25 minutes before clearing Edward E. Higgins, 29 years old, a Pueblo (Colo.) used car dealer who drives with his feet. His wife, Betty Lou, 20-year-old mother of an infant daughter, was acquitted of aiding and abetting him.

Higgins and his wife disputed Under-sheriff Clinton H. Haugh's charge he halted their car Nov. 25 after a wild chase at speeds up to 106 miles an hour. They said they were driving under 60.

NO ARMS, HE DRIVES WITH TOES—Armless driver Edward E. Higgins drives an automatic-shift car—steering with the toes on his right foot. Higgins, a 29-year-old used-car dealer in Pueblo, Colo., says he got his driver's license in January, 1954, after a 2½-hour test with a state patrolman and Pueblo license bureau officials. Born without arms, he learned to operate farm machinery when he was 12 years old and to drive a car when he was 16. Higgins works the brake and accelerator with his left foot. He was recently charged with speeding more than 100 m.p.h., but a Colorado Springs, Colo., jury found him innocent.

378

My Brother Eddie

The most wonderful person I've ever known

by Hazel Higgins Bernstein

ON A RECENT trip which I made with my husband, I overheard two well-dressed women in a hotel lounge commiserating with each other on their misfortunes.

One of the women, it appeared, had a teen-age daughter who stammered when she got excited, and the other was heartsick because her son, who was also in his teens, hadn't grown as tall as she thought he should. Both women seemed to think nature had treated their children very shabbily, and expressed the fear that their "handicaps" would affect their psychological development and impair their happiness all through life.

As I listened to those women I felt sorry for them. Their distress was genuine. But I wished they could know my brother Eddie. If they knew Eddie, I felt, they might realize that nature hadn't treated their children so badly, after all. They might discover, moreover, that the human spirit can rise above the worst flaws of the flesh, and come to understand that even a grave handicap need not hamper a child's healthy development nor prevent him from becoming a useful, happy, and well-adjusted adult.

My brother Eddie doesn't have any arms. He was born that way. For some reason which the doctors have never understood, arms failed to develop while he was in his mother's womb. He had never even had stumps to which artificial arms might be attached.

When Eddie came into the world 26 years ago, we felt that a grim catastrophe had befallen our family. We were poor people and we thought that all his life Eddie would be

helplessly and pathetically dependent upon us—a burden both spiritually and materially. We feared that his mental and emotional growth might be warped too by his shocking physical inadequacy.

But we were wrong about all that. Thanks to courage and common sense on the part of my parents, and love and faith in God, one miracle has followed another over the years, and what appeared to be a tragedy has turned into triumph. From his earliest childhood my brother has proved to be a source of joy and satisfaction to our whole family. Far from being a burden, he has always been a help and an inspiration to the rest of us. He has supported himself for years, and is now also supporting a wife and helping to take care of our parents. He is spiritually generous, too—a giver rather than a taker in life.

In fact, my brother Eddie is the most wonderful person I've ever known, and for that reason I'm going to tell his story here. Perhaps it will help other persons suffering from real or imagined handicaps—or those who love them, like the women I overheard in the hotel lounge—to realize that no physical defect need interfere with successful fulfillment in life. . . .

I WAS a long-legged, pig-tailed girl of 12 when Eddie was born. I lived with my parents and my sister Mickey, 9, in a small mining settlement called Lime, now a ghost town, about nine miles south of Pueblo, Colo. My father was a foreman of the powder gang in a limestone quarry there, and eked out his wages by doing a bit of farming. We children had a fine time helping our parents and playing with the children of other hard-working men, of more than 40 nationalities, who also were employed at the quarry.

Both Mickey and I were old enough to understand where babies came from and were wildly excited over the prospect of having a new brother or sister. But we prayed that it might be a brother. My parents also wanted a boy, for a change, and felt sure the new baby would be a boy. In anticipation of having a son Dad put on his best white shirt and bought a jug of wine and a box of cigars to pass out to his friends.

But early on the morning of Eddie's birth, I knew something was wrong. I saw it in the face of our Aunt Jodie, who lived next door. Aunt Jodie had been helping Dr. Epler in Mom's bedroom, and when she came out she brushed past Mickey and me without saying a word. When we looked into her face we saw she was crying. Neither Mickey nor I had ever seen Aunt Jodie cry before.

Believing that my mother must

IN TELLING HERE the inspiring and almost unbelievable life story of Eddie Higgins (left), his sister, Mrs. Hazel Bernstein (right), says she hopes to bring comfort and renewed faith to all who fight to overcome handicaps
— The Editor

379

My Brother Eddie

(*Continued from page* 15)

surely be dead or dying, I rushed straight to her bedroom. Mom looked very weary, but to my unutterable relief I found she was alive and awake—and had a beautiful smile on her face. Holding her hand out to me, she told me not to cry, told me I had a baby brother, and said she was fine. Just tired. I asked her if I could see the baby and she said, "Of course. Just ask Dr. Epler."

That made me feel better, but when I went into the kitchen where Dr. Epler was talking with Dad I was again overwhelmed by that something-is-wrong feeling.

My father was a strong man and could be a hard one when necessary. But now Dad looked so helpless and broken that my heart stood still and my knees quaked as I went toward him. He looked at me with a mute, blank stare, and unrestrained tears streamed down over his clean white shirt.

"What's the matter, Dad?" I asked him. "Why are you crying? You've got your baby boy."

He drew back as I reached out to him. "Yes, I've got my boy," he said. "I always wanted a son. Now I've got one, all right, but he hasn't got any arms!"

I didn't understand. I looked toward Dr. Epler. He nodded, then said, "Come here, Hazel, and see your new brother."

Eddie was lying in a basket on the kitchen table. He had a darling, wrinkled, snub-nosed little face like other newborn babies I'd seen, but when I reached down and felt for his arms I found it was true. He didn't have any.

As I stood there looking at Eddie for the first time, he started to cry, and his thin little wail did something to Dad. He turned on Dr. Epler in an almost violent mood. "You can't take him to her!" he exclaimed. "You should have let him die when you saw how he was. She can't stand it. You can't do it, Doc!"

Dr. Epler placed his hand on Dad's shoulder and tried to quiet him. "Look at me, Mr. Higgins," he said. "Believe me when I tell you God will help your wife. He will help you in this time of trouble too, if you will let him."

Dad threw the doctor's arm from his shoulder. He cursed God. "What kind of a God is it," he demanded angrily, "that would let this happen?"

It was Aunt Jodie who finally convinced Dad that Mom would have to be told. "All right," he said; "you tell her. I'll be in shortly."

I tiptoed after Dr. Epler and Aunt Jodie when they entered Mom's room. Her eyes had been closed, but she opened them and put out her arms for her baby. Her face turned white as she looked first at Aunt Jodie and then at Dr. Epler. "Where is my baby?" she asked. "Why didn't you bring him to me? What is wrong with him?"

Dr. Epler sat down on the edge of the bed and spoke quietly to her. "Your baby was born without arms, Mrs.

Higgins," he said. "I don't know why. He is perfectly formed and absolutely normal in every other way, but he doesn't have any arms."

Mom lay there for a few moments without speaking. Then she said, "Bring my baby to me. He needs me, poor little darling."

Later, Dad came in and sat beside Mom. He stroked her arm and patted Eddie's red little forehead. "We'll have to make the best of it, old girl," he said. "That's all. I guess it will be kind of rough on the poor little feller."

Since Eddie had no arms with which to move his body, it was obvious that he would have to develop more supple leg and back muscles than other children if he ever was to sit up, stand, and walk. With this in mind, Mom gave him regular exercises on a table every morning after she had undressed him for his bath.

Holding his tiny feet with one hand, she would hoist his little behind off the table with her other hand over and over again. Then, holding him in a sitting position, she would raise one of his legs and then the other high in the air. Finally, she would lay him flat on his back and raise him gently, gradually to a sitting position. Eddie loved this routine, would coo with pleasure, and when Dad came home at night he would give him a workout, too.

After a few months these exercises started bearing fruit. Dad and Mickey and I were sitting on the front porch one evening when Mom rushed to the front door in high excitement. "Hurry," she cried; "come in quick and see what Eddie is doing!"

We all dashed inside after her, and there, lying on his back in his bassinet, Eddie was having the time of his life. Mom had placed a baby's rattle in the bassinet and he had grabbed it with his tiny toes. Now he was shaking the rattle as hard as he could and shouting with triumphant laughter.

Mom and Dad were so pleased that they laughed and cried at the same time. "Just look at that little rascal," Dad said, shaking his head in wonder; "just look at him!" Both he and Mom looked happier than they had in months.

It wasn't long after that before Eddie was holding his bottle between his feet and doing with his toes most of the things which other babies do with their fingers.

Then, when he was ten months old, he bowled us over with another feat. He inched himself to the side of his crib one day and, using it as a support, sat up all by himself. After that he insisted upon sitting up much of the time, and when we placed him on a quilt on the floor, soon became highly mobile.

He could not crawl in the way other babies do, of course. But he would sit up straight, bring his fat little knees up to his chest, and then straighten his legs. In this way he could scoot on his bottom wherever he wanted to go. Before long he was scooting all over the house, and he wore out his pants so fast that Mom had to sew extra thicknesses of cloth to the seats of them.

Eddie's learning to scoot was an im-

portant milestone in his early development, but not so important, in my opinion, as another turning point which occurred shortly afterward. This one grew out of three of the first words he ever uttered.

As she held him in her arms and loved him, Mom had fallen into the habit, unconsciously I think, of calling him her "poor abused boy." She didn't mean to make him feel sorry for himself, of course, but one day he looked at her with his sweet little smile and said "poor 'bused boy" right back at her.

Mom was upset as well as startled by his words, and when she told Dad what had happened he viewed the incident with something very much like consternation. "That's not good," he said gravely. "We can't have him saying or thinking things like that. It may be hard for all of us, but, mind you, we've got to treat him just like any other kid and not let him think he's different in any way."

Mom agreed with Dad and, at a family council, it was decided that thenceforth Eddie should not be pampered or babied or, above all, pitied by any of us. Looking back, I think that was one of the wisest decisions my parents ever made. Had they not acted as they did, Eddie might have grown up to be emotionally as well as physically handicapped. But at the time, not babying him was hard—so heartbreaking on many occasions as to seem unbearable.

This was especially true when he was learning to walk. Since he had no hands with which to cling to things or catch himself when he fell, it was much harder for him than most babies. He fell over and over again, and for a period of weeks had a permanent black-and-blue bump on his forehead. Every time he fell Mom and Mickey and I felt an almost overpowering impulse to pick him up and comfort him, but, in keeping with our resolution, we restrained ourselves.

As a result of this Spartan treatment he learned self-reliance at the same time he learned to toddle. To avoid landing on his head, he acquired a knack of rolling up in a tight ball and turning a somersault when he took a spill, and he developed a fine sense of balance. By the time he was 2 years old he was walking and running as well as any child of his age.

That was just one of the ways in which the folks taught Eddie to depend on himself at a very early age. At meals, much the easiest thing was for one of us to sit beside him and place his food in his mouth, and we did this when we had guests or were eating away from home, but Mom and Dad realized there might be many times in his life when Eddie would have no one to feed him. For this reason, they encouraged him to learn to eat with his feet.

They did this by putting him in a high chair and placing food on a low table in front of him. He made a mess of it at first, as other little children do when learning to eat with their hands, but he gradually acquired skill with a knife, fork, and spoon. As a result, he never had any fear of going hungry if there was no one around to place food in his mouth. . . .

Right from the start, my parents also insisted that Eddie learn to wash and dress himself to as great an extent as he could. He soon learned how to wiggle his way into a shirt or coat which was placed over a low chair for him, and to step into a pair of pants hung on a low hook. Buttons were a problem for him, but one which was alleviated by the advent of zippers, which Mom sewed on his clothes and he could zip or unzip with his toes. He was unable to tie or untie shoelaces, of course, but the folks coped with that situation by buying him little leather moccasins which he could slip his feet into or out of easily. He did so constantly, and gradually became so supple, well co-ordinated, and adroit with his toes that he could do most of his own dressing. By the time he was 3 he could even don his cap. He would stand on one foot and pull it on his head with his other foot.

At the same time when they were teaching him to take care of himself physically, Dad and Mom instilled into Eddie the idea that he was a responsible member of the family. He was spanked when he was naughty like any other child, although some of our neighbors thought this was terribly cruel of us, and he was given small chores to perform. He fed the chickens as soon as he could walk, by carrying them a pan of feed tucked under his chin; he helped Mom pump the treadle of our old-fashioned sewing machine when her legs got tired; and with his tiny feet he joyously helped

mix the adobe we used in building a house on a small ranch which Dad bought near Lime, after his work at the quarry became intermittent owing to the depression then gripping the nation.

At the ranch Eddie toddled after me constantly as I went about my chores of caring for the cows, pigs, and rabbits. He was generally as gay and carefree as any child could be. But one day I found him sitting in the doorway of the feed shed drawing circles in the dust with his bare toes and looking very thoughtful. Then he asked me a question I will remember as long as I live.

"Hazie," he said, "why don't I have arms like other little boys and girls?"

That was a question we knew he was sure to ask some time, but it came so suddenly that it took my breath away. I sat down beside him and silently prayed for an answer.

"Honey, God didn't give you arms like other little boys and girls," I said finally, "but I am sure God will give you many other things that will be much better." Then I hugged him to me hard and said, "Okay now, Eddie?"

My answer seemed to satisfy him. He toddled off to look at the rabbits. And he never asked the question again.

I think that was because Eddie, like all the members of our family, already had a very real faith in God and His goodness. We did not attend church often, but Mom read to us regularly from the Bible and, living in the country with nature very close to us, none of us ever questioned the existence of a benevolent Higher Power any more than we doubted that the snow would melt in the spring or

that rain eventually would come after drought.

At any rate, the adequacy of my answer to Eddie's question was demonstrated a few weeks later when, at the age of 3½, he became the brother of a baby sister, Shirley Jo. The doctors had told Mom that she need have no fear about having another baby, because her chances of bearing a perfectly normal child were just as good as those of any other woman, and when Shirley Jo arrived, complete in every detail, Eddie was simply beside himself with joy.

As soon as the baby was dressed and placed in Mom's arms, he climbed up on the edge of the bed to examine her, and when he discovered she had arms he couldn't restrain himself. "Oh, Mommy," he shouted at the top of his piping little voice, "baby sister's got arms! God gave her arms!"

Eddie was permitted to hold Shirley Jo in his lap before any of the rest of us, and he loved to take care of her. He had a little rocking chair in which he would sit, and we would place Shirley Jo in his lap, and he could manage to get one chubby leg over her to hold her. Sitting there in his little chair, he would rock her and sing to her and talk baby-talk to her by the hour.

At about this time Eddie also became fascinated by things mechanical. It started when he "helped" Dad fix an old pump at the ranch. Eddie was sadly thwarted at first because he couldn't place screws and bolts in the holes designed for them, but Dad encouraged him to keep trying, and eventually he mastered the knack of putting a screw or bolt in place with the toes of his left foot, and tightening it with a screwdriver or wrench held in his right foot. After that there was no holding him. A whole new world unfolded for him and he had a grand time tinkering with cars and motors.

But that was nothing to what was to come. A highway construction gang moved into our community and the man in charge of it, a rough but wonderfully kind person named Charlie Owen, took a great fancy to Eddie. He often took him to work with him, perched on his shoulders with his little legs around his neck, and would let him steer his car or work the controls of road-building machines with his feet. By the time my armless little brother reached school age, he had had the thrilling experience of helping to operate real cars, trucks, tractors, and even massive bulldozers.

His first day at school was a black one

for Mom. She enrolled him in the one-room rural school in our district and had a long chat with the teacher beforehand. She thus knew that nothing very terrible could happen to Eddie at school, yet she cried all day after the school bus picked him up, with his little canvas satchel, containing his lunch, slung by a strap over his shoulder. "Oh, if I could only keep him little," she wept. "Now he'll really have to take it."

But Mom's fears were unjustified. Eddie came home beaming after his first day at school. He had had a wonderful time, and he continued to have a wonderful time during all the eight years he went there. Some of our gloomier friends had shaken their heads and predicted that a child as badly handicapped as he was could never hope to get through school, unless he attended some special institution, but because we had never let Eddie pity himself or feel he was inferior to other children he got along fine.

To learn to write, he had to place his tablet on the floor under his desk instead of on it, and manipulate a pencil or pen with his toes, but he learned to write so well that he won a prize for penmanship, and he was good in his other studies, too. When he graduated from the eighth grade he was valedictorian of his class.

On the playground, Eddie adjusted to school life just as beautifully as in the classroom and participated in most of the games the other kids played. He became the marble-shooting champ of the school and even played baseball. He could not bat or throw, of course, but he was wonderful at running bases for slower boys.

Dᴜʀɪɴɢ the years he was going to grade school, Eddie also developed into a tower of strength for the rest of us. Dad was away much of the time, working at a quarry near Salida, Colo., and during his absences Eddie served as our "man of the family." He learned to ride a horse, to shoot, to round up cattle which had strayed off the place, to kill rattlesnakes, and perform many other masculine tasks which ranch life entailed.

In addition, Eddie helped to operate a small filling station which we opened on a highway which ran past our property, and augmented the family income by occasionally towing disabled vehicles to a garage in Pueblo. He had learned to drive beautifully by sitting on a cushion in the driver's seat and operating the steering wheel with one foot while he manipulated the accelerator and brake with the other. Several years passed before he was granted a driver's license, first because of his age and later because of his handicap, but the local police officers all knew how well he could drive and never challenged him.

Looking back on those years, however, I believe that Eddie helped us more by his never-failing courage and cheerfulness than in any other way. Like thousands of other families, we had a hard time just scraping by during the depression, but with Eddie's example in front of us we simply couldn't feel very sorry for ourselves. Since he never griped or

gave way to discouragement or used the words "I can't," as Dad loved to point out, the rest of us felt it would be shameful and ludicrous if we complained of our lot.

Eddie entered a large high school in Pueblo when he was 14, and again Mom had serious misgivings. So did I. The high school had an enrollment of more than 1,500 students, and for the first time he would be thrown among total strangers. When he came home in the afternoon we asked him breathlessly how he had gotten along.

"All right," he said cheerfully, "but I don't think the other kids got along so well. They were so busy watching me that they couldn't keep their minds on their work."

Then, characteristically, his thoughts turned away from himself to another student he had seen who he felt was much worse handicapped than he was—a boy who had trouble getting up and down the school stairs because his legs had been crippled by polio. "I'm thankful I haven't got legs like his," Eddie said, without considering the fact that the other boy had sound arms and hands.

Iɴ sᴘɪᴛᴇ of the embarrassing amount of attention he attracted at first, Eddie quickly adjusted to high school and made countless friends. During the first two years he lived with Mickey, who had married and moved to Pueblo, and later, when I opened a shop in the city and bought a small house, he moved in with me. Nearly every afternoon two or three of Eddie's school pals would drop in, often driving hot rods which he helped them repair, and in the evening he was forever helping some kid with his homework.

Eddie also did endless favors for me. He rigged up an electric fan draft in the basement which made my old-fashioned coal furnace keep the house as warm as toast, and he got up early every morning and prepared breakfast before I came downstairs. On weekends and during vacations he drove to the ranch and did things for Mom and Shirley Jo. I don't believe any boy with two strong arms was ever a greater asset to his family than my brother Eddie.

During his high-school period, however, Eddie went through one phase which worried us. He became acutely conscious of girls for the first time and was extremely shy in their presence. Girls had always liked him, and I knew of several who would have been glad to have dates with him, but he didn't ask them, because he felt it wouldn't be "fair" to them. For this reason, he refused invitations to join several high-school social clubs.

But my little brother eventually took that psychological hurdle in his stride just as he had so many others. He had a long talk with a Methodist minister from Texas, who was the father of a boy who also was physically handicapped, and the minister advised him to meet all life situations halfway—including girls. Eddie took his advice, and by the time he finished high school had largely overcome his sensitiveness concerning feminine sex.

How on earth can a boy like that ever earn a living?

That was a question we heard many times from tongue-clucking friends and neighbors during the years when Eddie was growing up, but it didn't turn out to be any problem, at all. During the seven years which have elapsed since he graduated from high school, he has engaged successfully in several different occupations and, without ever trading on his handicap, has done at least as well as or better than most young men of his age.

The first thing he did after getting through school was to go into the used-car business. He invested his small savings in a down payment on five sadly beat-up old taxicabs, rented a vacant lot in downtown Pueblo, and set about repairing and rebuilding the cabs. Handling both power tools and hand tools with his feet, he did all but the very heaviest work himself, sold the cabs at a nice profit, bought more beat-up cars, and within a few months was earning a larger income than many a veteran mechanic.

With cash which he accumulated from this business, Eddie then made a down payment on a large but run-down dwelling house and remodeled it into an apartment building. Again, he did most of the work himself. He put in a new heating plant, installed the new wiring required, laid asphalt block floors throughout the building, and tiled the bathrooms. He rented the apartments without difficulty, and has now almost completely paid for the building. The apartments bring him in about \$350 a month and, after all running expenses and taxes are paid, he nets \$150 a month from them.

In addition to that venture, Eddie has designed and helped build several new houses of modern design in the Pueblo area, including one for my husband and me. Using a tractor, he invariably does all of the excavating for the houses he builds, as well as the electrical work, floor-laying, and tiling. He supervises all the other construction work and, being blessed with sound business sense as well as mechanical know-how, has made a profit on every house he has built. In one instance, he sold one of his little houses for almost twice as much as we thought he could get for it.

Right now, Eddie is engaged in another profitable enterprise: He has set up a workshop at our old home ranch, where he makes highly decorative lamps out of interesting chunks of gnarled old cedar. These lamps, which fit in beautifully with the décor of modern ranch homes, are sold at retail through a smart furniture store in Colorado Springs at from \$90 to \$150 each.

Yᴇꜱ, my brother Eddie has become quite a prosperous young man, but, far more important, he is a happy one. He was married last spring to a lovely girl named Betty, who was reared on a Nebraska farm and educated in nursing, and they are very devoted to each other. They live on the ranch with my now elderly parents, who never cease marveling over what a wonderful "little rascal" Eddie is, but make frequent motor trips all over Colorado—trips on which they combine business with pleasure. They hunt for unusual growths of cedar for Eddie's lamps and, at the same time, make a hobby of seeking out places of rare mountain beauty. I doubt if anyone in the state knows more remote beauty spots than Eddie and Betty.

Speaking of this hobby of theirs, Eddie told me recently that he couldn't understand why so many people are unable to appreciate the many lovely things in the world around them. "I'd much rather have the body I have," he said, "than be perfectly normal and have a blind spot like that."

When he is working in his shop Eddie has many visitors, and most of them are young people. Teen-agers from all over the community still seek his advice on their hot-rod problems, and he helps a lot of younger kids rig up their little wagons and carts for use in soapbox derbies. He is never too busy to help them.

Now and then one of the smaller children will ask him why he doesn't have any arms and, when they do, he gives the same answer he always has. "God didn't give me any," he says very simply.

But, as I promised him when he was a child, God has given Eddie many things which a lot of other people don't have. And God will do the same thing, I am convinced, if He is only given a chance, for anyone who has a handicap great or small!

It is because I wish to make that point very emphatically, and for that reason only, that I have written this story.

THE END ★★

ABOUT THE AUTHOR

Hazel Higgins

Today, in June 2005, 90-year-old Hazel Higgins is still "one going machine." Except for her failing hearing and eyesight, she is still the pleasant, positive, passionate person I first met when I was just a little girl. She still has her intelligence, beautiful smile, and soft throaty chuckle; she also still has her guts, and determination.

Read her wonderful tribute, *My Brother Eddie*, and you will also learn a great deal about the author, my friend Hazel.

Elizabeth Anderson
(Betty Alora Thomson)

Give the Gift of

My Brother Eddie

to Your Friends and Colleagues

CHECK YOUR LEADING BOOKSTORE OR ORDER HERE

❖ ❖ ❖

☐ **YES**, I want _____ copies of *My Brother Eddie* at $19.95 each, plus $4.95 shipping per book (Colorado residents please add $1.46 sales tax per book). Canadian orders must be accompanied by a postal money order in U.S. funds. Allow 15 days for delivery.

My check or money order for $_____ is enclosed.

Name _____

Organization _____

Address _____

City/State/Zip _____

Phone_____ E-mail _____

Please make your check payable and return to:

Prairie Junction Press

P.O. Box 9281
Pueblo, CO 81008

www.AsEverEddie.com